International Relations and the Challenge of Postmodernism

Studies in International Relations
Charles W. Kegley, Jr., and Donald J. Puchala, Series Editors

International Relations and the Challenge of Postmodernism

Defending the Discipline

D. S. L. Jarvis

University of South Carolina Press

© 2000 University of South Carolina

Published in Columbia, South Carolina, by the
University of South Carolina Press

Manufactured in the United States of America

04 03 02 01 00   5 4 3 2 1

Library of Congress Cataloging-in-Publication Data

Jarvis, Darryl S. L., 1963–
  International relations and the challenge of postmodernism : defending the discipline / Darryl S.L. Jarvis.
    p. cm.
  Includes bibliographical references and index.

  ISBN 1-57003-305-6 (cloth)
  1. International relations—Philosophy. 2. Postmodernism—Political aspects. I. Title.
JZ1249 .J37 2000
327.1'01—dc21   99-6115

For Dad
John Stuart Jarvis
July 12, 1933–April 15, 1997
My Love Always

Contents

Preface	ix
Chapter One **Theory and Metatheory in International Relations:** The Third Debate and the Challenge of Postmodernism	1
Chapter Two **Contemplating the Crisis in the Crisis of Contemplation:** Identity, Perception, and Derision in International Relations	35
Chapter Three **Sentinels of Dissidence:** A Typology of Postmodern Theory	51
Chapter Four **Richard K. Ashley and the Subversion of** **International Political Theory:** The "Heroic" Phase	89
Chapter Five **Continental Drift:** Ashley and Subversive Postmodernism	118
Chapter Six **Feminist Revisions of International Relations:** Identity Politics, Postmodern(isms), and Gender	142
Chapter Seven **In Defense of Theory:** Reaffirming Reason, Rearticulating Relevance	178
Notes	205
Bibliography	239
Index	263

Preface

Of the many thousands of words written about postmodernist perspectives and international theory, of the debates and disputes between the new converts to postmodernism and the defenders of modernity, Chris Brown's recent musing is perhaps the most informative, capturing the essence of this intellectual divide in a way that would seem to make stark the contrasts between them. Of postmodernism he writes, "Those that like this sort of thing will find this the sort of thing they like—those who do not, will not."[1] And this, perhaps, has been the extent of the "Third Debate" to date, an intellectual rift interspersed with ritual denunciations and affirmations of likes and dislikes. If the Third Debate were meant to bring clarity to a discipline otherwise congested with new approaches, issues areas and perspectives, then it has surely failed. The lexicon of postmodernism, its eclectic and discursive styles, has succeeded only in making more obtuse the issues, problems, and debates afoot in the discipline. For want of clarity the Third Debate has become little more than rehearsed statements of intransigence, spoken by those who announce and celebrate its arrival and those who would forestall its colonization and spread. Beyond such declarations, however, the Third Debate exists in name only, having been neither explored in terms of its consequences, nor appraised critically in terms of its offerings and contributions.

This study attempts such an appraisal by exploring critically the motifs of postmodern theory in International Relations. It does so out of a desire to make sense of the Third Debate and render it intelligible. Indeed, for many in the discipline the Third Debate and the subterfuge of postmodern theory have become somewhat of a malediction: a cumbersome exercise in semantic obfuscation that seems to cloud still further the subject of International Relations and lose it amid a continental vernacular. If only because of its abstruse nomenclature and penchant for interdisciplinary travels, many in International Relations remain perplexed by the new interpretivism and the challenges it poses to the discipline, its intellectual boundaries, and its theory. Critical assessments of postmodern theory and the Third Debate have therefore been few. Robert Gilpin, for example, can but lament the need for an English translation to such approaches and announce that, in the absence of one, he has "no idea what it means."[2] Amid pronouncements of this new beginning and interpretive turn, among the debris of old theories and the invention of new ones, among new methodological perspectives, deconstructive strategies and postmodern theories, practitioners, theorists and students alike find themselves stumbling about with incertitude, lost in a discourse that prizes epistemological and ontological logomachy above clarity in communication.[3] This is a "great debate" like none the discipline has ever experienced before.

This book therefore aims to construct a baedeker to the Third Debate and postmodern theory in order that practitioners in the field might traverse the subterfuge of these debates and approaches and assess them critically for their utility to the study of international relations. In a sense this study might also be understood as an operating manual to the mechanics of postmodernist discourse, a means of glancing inside such theory to see its inner workings, suppositions, motivations, biases, aims, and objectives. I do so, however, not to celebrate the language deracination endemic to postmodern perspectives, but so as to bypass it and thereby make transparent the ontological and epistemological foundations on which postmodern theory is itself constructed. The originality of the study therefore lies in its attempt to expose the politics of postmodern theory in International Relations whereby certain varieties of postmodernist scholarship have been plundered and pillaged of particular motifs, imported into International Relations, and used in the pursuit of political ends. It is in this context that I also explore the unknown continent of postmodern scholarship generally, attempting to develop a series of heuristic typologies of postmodern theory in order that we might distinguish those varieties otherwise useful to International Relations from those that are not.

The rationale for this undertaking, however, is not purely pedagogical but stems from a deep-seated concern about the growing irrelevance and ethereality of theory in the discipline. The discourse of International Relations has moved to a plateau so incorporeal as to make its relevance to the actualities of international politics and the people whose lives and concerns are the real stuff of international relations extremely tenuous. Cries of crisis, disjuncture, theoretical perspectivism, and the umbrage of a "dividing discipline" would seem to be making meaningless those disciplinary boundaries that otherwise give us a sense of purpose or common project.[4] Theory in International Relations seems to be less about international politics than about metaphysical reflections of how it is that we have come to know of international relations. Arguably, the sociology of knowledge has become the defining motif of the Third Debate, causing us to lose sight of the subject we once used to study. This book is thus an attempt to regain sight of the subject of International Relations and a call to practitioners to return to theoretical endeavors that aim to explain and understand the phenomena of our subject matter.

More specifically, though, this book is also born of a suspicion of postmodernism, at least in the context of its importations into International Relations. The growing popularity of postmodernist perspectives in the discipline, the ready acceptance by many of the need to engage in deconstructive practices, the allegations of moral improprieties, and the imputation of disciplinary culpability in numerous horrors waged in the name of modernity and science reeks of a political witch hunt not before seen in the discipline. Theory, while always a powerful tool that can be used in the service of specific rationalities, seems increasingly to be a political instrument, hijacked for its destructive potential and wielded in accusatory and threatening fashion. This book is thus a defense of the edifice of theory as "one of the crowning achievements of the past several centuries," of ". . . theory as an idea," as Nicholas Onuf puts it, of "theory as an enterprise, theory as an economic statement of what we think we know about the world and ourselves," and of "theory as the grounds for judgement."[5]

Doubtless this study will prove unpopular with postmodernists. It neither compliments their work nor finds many saving graces that might recommend it to others. At the same time, though, this is a work inspired by postmodernism—albeit as a reaction against it. More accurately, it is a reaction against a particular motif evident in the majority of so-called postmodernist discourse operative in International Relations today. This should not be confused, however, with any derision toward the exercise of the Third Debate itself. Intellectual self-examinations are a necessary part of any disciplinary/intellectual endeavor and should be done periodically, although perhaps not perpetually. Rather, my concern is with a particular variety of postmodernism that, in International Relations, has come to dominate dissident scholarship to the exclusion of other postmodern perspectives. As Chapters 4, 5, and 6 will more fully elucidate, I target what I call subversive postmodernism, exemplified in the writings of Richard Ashley and Robert Walker and, more recently, in radical feminist postmodern writings for taking the discipline down an ideologically destructive road. Where the Third Debate might have proved a productive and highly valuable exercise in theoretical evaluation and intellectual renewal, its intellectual hijacking by subversive postmodernists has caused its devolution into a meaningless and divisive exercise bent on destruction. Voices otherwise involved in the process of intellectual renewal and critical self-examination (Wendt, Onuf, Lapid, Biersteker, Spegele, Cox, to name but a few) have thus tended to be drowned out by the babel of cantankerous perspectives that allege numerous improprieties and disciplinary violence.

The task of this study is thus to tackle these issues and confront the challenge posed by postmodernism and the Third Debate. The study begins with a broad introductory chapter that foreshadows the issues, debates, and problems endemic to the Third Debate: theoretical endeavor, identity politics, and the new interpretivism. In particular, I turn to an analysis of the functions of theory in International Relations in an attempt to impart some sense of what theory ought to be about, ought to look like, and what we can reasonably expect theory to do. My discussion thus attempts to offer some criteria for evaluating theories in International Relations—and postmodernism more specifically.

Chapter 2 then turns to an historical overview of the development of the discipline and its attempts at theory construction. This is an effort at demonstrating the problem of "discipline" in International Relations and of relating theory to that endeavor. However, rather than an exercise in historiography for its own sake, chapter 2 attempts to demonstrate the historical ambiguity of International Relations both as an intellectual exercise and an academic discipline. Its purpose is therefore heuristic, intending to illustrate the intellectual challenge posed in studying international politics. More than this, though, chapter 2 attempts to contextualize the current "crisis" in International Relations within a tradition of scholarship itself suffused with ongoing incertitude as to its intellectual enterprise, purpose, and parentage. I endeavor to demonstrate, for example, how the genealogical peculiarity of international relations has precipitated not only a crisis of contemplation about its epistemological basis but also its historical point of departure.[6] To this end, the chapter is divided into two main sections. The first attempts to demonstrate how much of the incertitude over disciplinary identity and theoretical parameters is a consequence of the poverty of our intellectual heritage. With few historical markers, few bequeathed works of significance, and with little historical definition as to our project, aims, and objectives, International Relations continues to vacillate over its very being. If there is an historical pedigree to International Relations, it rests, I shall argue, in the historical absence of International Relations as a discipline and as a discrete intellectual concern. In the second section, I point out the theoretical and disciplinary flux occasioned by recent importations of continental philosophy. These, I argue, have caused yet further consternation for practitioners still in the midst of defining their disciplinary project let alone engaging in epistemological and ontological debates.

Chapter 3 then turns to postmodern theory and attempts to make sense of this latest idiom by developing a series of thematic ideal types. The project is one of taxonomy and classification in order to simplify the generic postmodern into specific categories that can be dissected and analyzed. I do this via two strategies. In the first I offer two interpretive discussions of the leitmotifs of postmodern theory as popularly understood: postmodernism as deconstruction, and postmodernism as epochal change. These discussions provide a brief overview of the aims, issues, and concerns of postmodernists and illustrate the scope of the postmodernist "project" while contextualizing its intellectual parameters and location in relation to its modernist counterpart. In the second section I develop a series of heuristic typologies or, more accurately, thematic ideal types. These I employ as ordering categories that, in subsequent chapters, are used in the construction of a critical genealogical account of the way certain postmodernist theories have been expropriated, imported, and applied to the study of international relations and in the construction of international political theory.

Chapters 4 and 5 then apply these categories to an analysis of Richard Ashley and poststructuralist theory. My aim is to provide a critical overview of Ashley's intellectual ruminations amid his political ambitions by concentrating first on his formative development or "heroic" phase in chapter 4, then his subversive or deconstructive phase in chapter 5. In this respect, my approach is somewhat novel, assessing his works interrelatedly as a "project" rather than as a series of disparate writings. My argument is therefore revisionist, challenging previous unreflective observations about Ashley's writings while suggesting a new means of assessing his scholarship. In particular, I attempt to read Ashley politically, circumventing his facade of interpretivism and thereby avoiding those pitfalls that have otherwise impeded a more perspicacious understanding of Ashley's discourse.

Chapter 6 then extends the analysis to the latest subversive-deconstructive agendas inspired by debates over gender and feminist perspectives in International Relations. The work of Christine Sylvester, Cynthia Enloe, and V. Spike Peterson, among others, is addressed. However, this is not so much a critique of their work as an attempt to engage critically the postmodern motifs they employ as they attempt to "remap" and "reinvent" International Relations and make the "gender variable" the central ontological starting point for understanding international politics. Chapter 6 thus focuses on the new-found importance of "identity politics" in International Relations, and the issues, debates, and theoretical implications this approach harbors. In particular, I analyze two of the most dominant motifs evident in feminist scholarship in the discipline today, what I term *constructivist* or epistemological feminism and essentialist or standpoint feminism. Each of these perspectives is outlined and then analyzed critically from the perspective of its logical cogency, political implications, and effect on theoretical endeavor in International Relations.

Finally, chapter 7 explores the legacy of Ashley's form of postmodernism and the subfield he has inspired, briefly addressing his latest contribution to the Third Debate, or what he terms the conversational battlefield of International Relations, and how this makes problematic the intellectual contributions of many of his would-be followers and intellectual disciples. Chapter 7 also looks at the damage wrought by Ashley in terms of the false agenda in which he has embroiled International Relations. In particular, I suggest that postmodern theory in International Relations, largely because of Ashley, has evolved only one dominant motif, subversion, or deconstruction, to the detriment of its other, and perhaps more useful, thematic applications. To this end, I also address briefly the more productive avenues International Relations might pursue within the ambit of postmodern theory.

In the course of preparing this book I have incurred many debts, both professional and personal. First, to Professor Kalevi J. Holsti of the University of British Columbia, my thanks for his supervision, considered comments, and the time and effort taken to read what amounted to numerous drafts. Professors Robert Jackson and Philip Resnick, also of the University of British Columbia, were kind enough to read earlier versions of the manuscript and provided valuable feedback and suggestions. Dr. Martin Griffiths of the Flinders University of South Australia and Terry O'Callaghan of the University of South Australia have also been more than generous in reading various portions of the volume and helping me formulate ideas and arguments. I was also greatly assisted by the close readings and detailed comments furnished by Prof. Nicholas Onuf of Florida International University and Prof. Richard Mansbach of Iowa State University. Both were gracious in their comments and encouragement. Robert Crawford of the University of British Columbia, perhaps more than any other, has listened patiently to my ideas and, over the years, helped me distill and organize them in ways which have greatly benefited the organization of the book. Finally, Jim Poon has also been more than charitable in his endless, and very proficient, proofreadings of the manuscript, numerous editorial suggestions, and good nature which never faulted. To all concerned, my sincere thanks and gratitude.

By no means last, however, my greatest debts have been personal. To my mum and dad, Jean and Stuart Jarvis, and my sister Nichola, words alone cannot describe their unending love, faith, help, and support over the years. In no small measure, this book derives from the wisdom of their good counsel, their encouragement to further my education, and their support that made it possible. Thus, it is for my father who never lived to see the fruits of his love and encouragement, that I dedicate this book, comforted that he watches over me and will always be with me.

Chapter One
Theory and Metatheory in International Relations
The Third Debate and the Challenge of Postmodernism

> The specific function of science appears to me to be precisely . . . that it renders problematic the conventionally self-evident.
> —Max Weber

> Scientific explanation consists not in moving from the complex to the simple, but in the replacement of a less intelligible complexity by one which is more so.
> —Claude Levi-Strauss

> No Science deserves the name until it has acquired sufficient humility not to consider itself omnipotent, and to distinguish the analysis of what is from aspiration about what should be.
> —Edward Hallett Carr

The distinguished scholar of International Relations, Stanley Hoffmann, concluded a recent autobiographical article with the following advice for graduate students: "Avoid fads, resist the pressure to begin your career by showing your dexterity with grand theory, remember that theory is necessary only as a help to understanding, as a path to interesting questions, but that it can all too often become a hindrance or screen. Remember that much empirical research, of the sort that leads to further investigations and therefore, ultimately, to middle-range theory, does not need to start by leaning on the brittle crutches of grandiose models."[1]

Doubtless this is sound advice—and this study all the more foolish for not having taken it! Yet any student who embarks upon the study of international relations today cannot help but stumble into the quagmire of theory. The Third Debate is upon us whether welcomed or not, and the issues that resonate throughout the discipline are distinctly metatheoretical in nature. No longer can students of international politics look for neatly compartmentalized theoretical divides that dichotomize between two or three contending schools of thought. The waters have become considerably more muddied, clouded with debates over universalism, foundationalism, postmodernism, relativism, interpretivism, and issues of representation.[2] And all this, arguably, before we even get to study those things called international relations.

While Hoffmann might well be correct, these days one can neither begin nor conclude empirical research without first discussing epistemological orientations and ontological assumptions. Like a vortex, metatheory has engulfed us all and the question of "theory" which was once used as a guide to research is now the object of research. Indeed, for a discipline whose purview is ostensibly outward looking and international in scope, and at a time of ever encroaching globalization and transnationalism, International Relations has become increasingly provincial and inward looking. Rather than grapple with the numerous issues that confront peoples around the world, since the early 1980s the discipline has tended more and more toward obsessive self-examination.[3] These days the politics of famine, environmental degradation, underdevelopment, or ethnic cleansing, let alone the cartographic machinations in Eastern Europe and the reconfiguration of the geo-global political-economy, seem scarcely to concern theorists of international politics who define the urgent task of our time to be one of metaphysical reflection and epistemological investigation. Arguably, theory is no longer concerned with the study of international relations so much as the "manner in which international relations as a discipline, and international relations as a subject matter, have been constructed."[4] To be concerned with the latter is to be "on the cutting edge," where novelty has itself become "an appropriate form of scholarship."[5]

Such bouts of theoretical reappraisal are, of course, not new in International Relations. Theorists of international politics are, by nature, hermeneutical creatures, sporadically beleaguered by periods of self-doubt, theoretical incertitude, reinvention, and rearticulation. These episodes we usually celebrate as great debates—an optimistic terminology suggesting intellectual renewal, or at the very least, atonement. Indeed, International Relations has evolved a peculiar approach to theory, a general lack of interest that every now and then erupts into incessant preoccupation. Yet as John Weltman notes, even these episodes have not been all that instructive: "Methodological controversy and self-awareness have been endemic in international relations. Yet it is curious how little genuine debate this has engendered, if we understand by 'debate' an arena in which arguments are joined rather than one in which assertions are juxtaposed. One has instead a number of separate guilds, each of which proceeds on the basis of its own indigenous premises, conscious of the work of other groups only as caricature."[6] Amid this diversity in the scholarly activities of International Relations, Robert Rothstein is not alone in fearing the loss of a shared goal that might otherwise provide "a degree of unity for all these very different theoretical endeavours."[7]

Such sentiments, however, are historical echoes of the past, nostalgia for a discipline that once was. Instead, we are left today amid the rejectionists and deconstructionists, the latest bearers of "crisis," who not only question theoretical purpose and our disciplinary identity, but seek to make us nonexistent as authors and readers by reducing us to so many more textual ramblings. The shibboleths of discipline, knowledge, theory, and progress are no longer ours to enjoy but modernist fictions endemic to the "Eurocentrism of Western scholarship."[8] The Third Debate has arrived, and so it seems have new ways of thinking, doing, and being.

We should not be surprised, then, that the "prevailing view concerning the development of theory in international relations is that the field is beset by a bewildering variety of theoretical approaches, models, and concepts—that it is in as much of a state of change, chaos, and confusion as the contemporary world scene which it seeks to comprehend—and that theorizing on international relations is of only fairly recent origin."[9] What should surprise us, though, is that this assessment was written by Arend Lijphart some twenty years ago, indicating how incessant this sense of crisis has been to the normal discourse of International Relations. Fourteen years earlier, for example, Stanley Hoffmann made a similar lament, noting that, "as a discipline, international relations are not in very fine shape" and disposed to splintering parochial approaches.[10]

Calamity has become a way of life for theorists of international politics who seem accustomed to episodes of depression whenever they turn to theoretical activity. In this context, it might be more appropriate to understand the great debates not as infrequent storms that occasionally blow away debris, remove dead foliage from the trees, old moss, and dust from the branches so that we can see the forest again, but as a series of ongoing climatic changes that, bit by bit, are killing the forest altogether. This, indeed, is the intention of the more extreme proponents of the "Third Great

Debate": a leveling of the forest altogether to precipitate new growth and propagate new species.

This change in theoretical orientation has not gone uncontested. An endless Socratic conversation over the sociology of knowledge, many argue, will lead to "bottomless pits of epistemology and metaphysics."[11] Still others welcome this trend, arguing that epistemology "is one of the key remaining issues international relations has failed to examine."[12] Thomas Biersteker, for example, notes that "the vast majority of scholarship in international relations . . . proceeds without conscious reflection on its philosophical bases or premises."[13] Ostensibly, the Third Debate attempts to correct this by addressing the metatheoretical concerns of epistemology and ontology rather than "specific research programs and projects."[14] More specifically, the Third Debate is about theory: what it is, why we do it, what it is used for, who uses it, and what type of theory we should endeavor to construct. No longer is theory a benign investigative tool. According to the poststructuralists, theory is power. The facts considered, the choices presented, the remedies suggested, and the views legitimated are all considered outcomes of epistemology. Poststructuralists are therefore suspicious of, indeed hostile to, those epistemologies that, in their view, are used in the service of dominant interests, that silence certain voices while presuming to speak for others. Where Hans-Georg Gadamer, for example, could argue that theory was rendered anonymous by virtue of the objective detachment of the enterprise itself, critical theorists insist that "theory is always for someone and for some purpose."[15] Postmodernists thus contend that there can be no commensurability in theory, knowledge, or purpose. These dissipate amid a montage of differing interests, opposing views, contrasting perceptions and dissimilar cultural enclaves, and makes theory a latent tool of those who wield it.[16] The acts of theory construction, diagnosis, and prescription thus become impossible since poststructuralists equate these with the imposition of values, the silencing of minorities, and the marginalization of dissenting voices. Those engaged in certain types of theory, whether modernist, empirical, realist, or problem-solving-technical theory—in short those engaged in the disciplinary pursuits of studying international relations—are denied the efficacy of their enterprise, its objectivity, purpose, progress, and legitimacy. Rather, as poststructuralists see it, we stand today "over the ruins of the positivist project" and at the beginning of a new season of hope.[17] Again, it seems, we are witness to "yet another preface to a major project . . . yet another call to a new beginning, another meta-theoretical debate for the consumers of international relations theory."[18]

Purpose and Method in International Relations

For the outside observer it must seem extraordinary, if not bizarre, that those preoccupied with international relations still consume themselves not with their study, but with their definitional parameters and with the nature, role, and purpose of theory. What it is we do or should be doing and how we should do it are perennial ruminations that seem to haunt us with each additional great debate. Yet again it seems necessary to (re)consider theory and to rearticulate what it is we mean by the study of international relations. But definitions, as should be obvious by their continual dispute and revision, are problematic devices at best, perspicacious only to the extent that their capricious imposition atop arbitrary phenomena makes apparent an otherwise obtuse area of investigation. As Hoffmann notes, "The function of a definition is to indicate proper areas of inquiry, not to reveal the essence of the subject."[19] Indeed, the imposition of a rigid definition is counterproductive, presupposing not only the end of history but the end of theory. Definitions can only ever capture perceptions in time of processes that are constantly changing. "How," asks Hoffmann, "could one agree once and for all upon the definition of a field whose scope is in constant flux, indeed a field whose fluctuation is one of its principal characteristics?"[20]

Clearly, however, some operational definition is necessary if we are to reclaim the disciplinary integrity of International Relations from the deconstructionists of the Third Debate and delineate a disciplinary basis from which scholarship and theoretical endeavor may proceed. Accordingly, I offer the following not to distill an essence to the subject of International Relations but to indicate, like Hoffmann, "what I think we should investigate."[21]

Unlike the more extreme proponents of the Third Debate, I remain convinced of the need for constructive theory, that theory has purpose, and that this resides in the notion of "discipline." International theory and the discipline of International Relations are concerned with the study and understanding of the interactions between nation-states and various multinational and transnational actors: the reasons, rationales, and motivations that propel them, and the consequences, effects, and fallout of these interactions. This definition—cum observation—we can understand as the systemic mantel from which the numerous issues, problems, and phenomena that we deal with as theorists of international politics arise. That is, the fact of nation-states as a (now universal) form of territorial organization is the nodal point from which originates our subject matter, whether, for example, international regimes and institutions, global environmental politics, multinational corporations, international trade, security, the distribution of global wealth, international justice and human rights, or normative debates over new worlds and better forms of global governance. In all these instances, the nation-state is either causal factor, context, or mediating variable through which we experience, attempt to control, regulate, administer, or study such multifarious phenomena. Thus, a definition so ostensibly "narrow" to imply that International Relations concerns merely the study of relationships between nation-states, is, in point of fact, extremely broad, encompassing the multitude of actors, issues, phenomena, and normative concerns that necessarily accompanies these interactions. It is for this very reason that the nation-state and their relationships have so concerned theorists of international politics. As Hoffmann notes, the fact of the nation-state as the basic cartographic division of humanity presupposes not only its importance but, also, he argues, the stipulative concerns of our discipline which should focus on those "factors and . . . activities which affect the external politics and the power of the basic units into which the world is divided."[22]

There is, however, a danger of definitional hollowness here. To what extent has Hoffmann defined tautologically the study of international relations to be concerned with the study of international relations? Indeed, if this is an attempt to render more apparent precisely what it is we should be studying, then it succeeds only in demonstrating how broad and ill-defined are the discipline's concerns. We are, after all, concerned not with a single unit but numerous units, and not with a finite but an inordinate number and combination of factors and activities which can affect directly or indirectly, and in different degrees and various circumstances, the activities and power of those historically contingent basic units whose form, function, and dimension are changing constantly. If considered carefully, Hoffmann's definition is really no definition at all, but a call to perform the inauspicious task of gathering facts by cataloguing those factors and activities causally related to interunit politics.[23] There is, in effect, no problematique on which to base this fact-gathering enterprise, only a directive that we should do so. But gathering facts is not enough if, in the absence of robust and meaningful theoretical parameters, we have failed first to formulate those questions we most want answered.[24] Indeed, facts are mostly irrelevant to the study of international relations if encountered in the absence of an overarching problematique that otherwise inscribes purpose and meaning to the act of studying international relations. Empirical and middle-range theory, for example, are useful only to the extent that questions have been asked to which these epistemologies have then been directed. Thus, while I tend to agree with Hoffmann, there is really nothing to agree about since he fails to articulate a precise problematique on which to situate the discipline and scholarly activity. Without purpose, International Relations would be a vacuous activity, facile and devoid of meaning. Scholarship would be conducted, but with no aim in mind. Facts would be gathered, but for no purpose other than satisfying bibliophiles fond of reading facts. And of themselves, these facts would reveal no knowledge or understanding, but testify only to their own appearance. As Kenneth Waltz notes, "If we gather more and more data and establish more and more associations . . . we will not finally find that we know something. We will simply end up having more and more data and larger sets of correlations."[25] The point, Waltz urges, is to "get beyond the facts of observation," and look deeper toward the aetiological basis of facts if we wish an understanding and explanation of them.[26] Implicitly, Waltz is suggesting that facts are meaningless other than in the context of epistemological constructs, and that in order to approach an understanding of them, and ascribe meaning to them, it is not facts that need to be understood but the epistemological and ontological orientations that underlie their interpretation. Put another way, we need recognize that while we gather facts, we do so only in the context of reflective purpose. "Purpose," notes Carr, "whether we are conscious of it or not, is a condition of thought."[27] "We cannot study even stars or rocks or atoms . . . without being somehow determined, in our modes of systematisation, in the prominence given to one or another part of our subject, in the form of the questions we ask and attempt to answer, by direct and human interests."[28]

These interests not only give facts meaning, but, more obviously, render the study of international relations an inherently normative enterprise. International Relations came into being in response to a popular demand, a passionate desire to prevent war.[29] And this desire remains central to the study of international relations, albeit that it now exists as one among many interests that the discipline attends to. Definitions thus become sensible only to the extent that they help define, or clarify, the purpose to which we wish to devote our energies. To the extent that we are able to agree upon a common set of questions and concerns (a problematique), this is all that will ever define us amid an otherwise indefinable discipline. Stipulating, through definition, the direction of theoretical investigation in International Relations is therefore impossible. Serendipity, premised upon purposive reflection, will lead genuine intellectual exploration in no firm direction.

To talk about an operational definition, then, is really to talk about "purpose," a set of questions which informs a problematique for which we wish answers. And this is really the hub of our enterprise, one that might tentatively be defined this way: how some six billion people through the formation of culture and community, the abstraction of geographical territory and the imposition of social, political and economic space, interact, organize, regulate, govern, trade, travel, communicate, peacefully coexist, and on occasion, collide and make war.

Within this problematique there are, to be sure, contending approaches, different epistemologies and ontological disputes over what the most important actors, issues, and structures are, and the most appropriate form(s) of theory to best explain and understand these phenomena. But amid these disputes we find the essence of our enterprise, if indeed the notion of essence is warranted. After all, as Philip Windsor notes, while International Relations "literally considers the fate of the world" and is therefore "comprehensive by virtue of its preoccupation . . . it can not be unitary because of its preoccupation."[30] The bounds of our disciplinary concerns are necessarily diverse and, consequently, so are the theoretical approaches used to study them. Theory, therefore, will always be a messy, contentious, discursive, and provocative affair, eliciting the bridled passions of the profession as we collectively strive to understand. Moreover, theory in international politics will always be an endless activity if only because what we study is fluid, in the sense of being socially constructed and therefore prone to the vestiges of change. Some of our most cherished disciplinary tools of analysis like anarchy, nation-state, sovereignty, power, and the demarcation between domestic and international society, for example, are problematic concepts rather than naturally inscribed attributes of the global arena. And while such concepts are staples for theorists of International Relations, at best they represent nebulous inscriptions imposed atop a sea surface of constant movement and redefinition. While we might recognize, for example, that "statesmen act and think in terms of interest defined as power," as Hans Morgenthau did, we must also recognize as Hoffmann points out that, while this is true, it is true "only at a level of generality that is fatuous."[31] Consequently, while international theory can often be conclusive, in the sense of identifying important actors, recurrent patterns and themes and defining normative objectives, it can never be concluded. We are, in this sense, condemned to theory, not because it is the object(ive) of our study, but because it is a necessary consequence of our disciplinary pursuits.

As for the purpose of this enterprise, I hold this to be self-evident, albeit in need of rearticulation in this time of the Third Debate. Theory development and scholarship ultimately have purpose: scholarly gratification, understanding, diagnosis, and prescription. We do theory not only to know and understand and advance knowledge, but also so that we might diagnose and solve problems. As Hoffmann noted, "theory is no more than a set of tools whose usefulness is tested in their ability to solve concrete problems."[32] Yet as Edward Carr reminds us, theory is both normative and empirical, situated amid the wish to understand and the wish to change what is understood. "Political thought," he wrote, "is itself a form of political action. Political science is the science not only of what is, but of what ought to be."[33] And herein lies the complexity of theoretical endeavor in International Relations, the juxtaposed ambition of wanting to understand, to explain, to elucidate reality, while concerned with the prospects of changing that reality for a better one. Reality, in other words, has a way of intruding into our disciplinary concerns and of making apparent the purpose of International Relations as an academic pursuit.[34]

The development of theory in International Relations has thus often been prescriptive and purposive, aspiring to contribute to the avoidance of war and peaceful relations, the aversion of international crises, the mediation of disputes, the maintenance of security, the development of international resolution procedures and negotiating forums, and the establishment of institutional and legal apparatus for the peaceful administration of international politics. Frederick Dunn probably expressed it best when he wrote that, because "the questions with which IR [International Relations] deals arise primarily out of social conflicts and adjustments, its approach is in large part instrumental and normative in character."[35] International Relations, Dunn continued, "is concerned primarily with knowledge that is relevant to the control and improvement of a particular set of social conditions. Its goal is not merely knowledge for its own sake but knowledge for the purpose of molding practical events in desired directions."[36]

The Role and Functions of Theory in International Relations

While the history of theoretical endeavor in International Relations can thus be ascribed to an instrumental or purposive normative agenda, the precise role, function(s), and character of theory remain more nebulous. In International Relations, theory is rarely codified so much as the word itself invoked to connote a whole series of meanings and inferences. What it is we mean by theory and what it is we expect theory to do are questions that are rarely posed if only because they prove so difficult to answer. This is true of the social sciences and humanities generally where the word *theory* is bandied about so imprecisely as to render its meaning obtuse. It has become common parlance, for example, to interchange the word *theory* with that of perspective, approach, paradigm, method, or even opinion. Students and professors alike often predicate statements with "my theory on this matter is . . . ," when what they are actually expressing is an individual belief rather than a theory. Yet few would agree that this is what we mean when we think of theory. By theory we mean something much more reasoned and perspicacious than simply an opinion or perspective. Implicitly, each of us knows that a theory is a potent instrument comprised of reasoned argument, observation, reflection, logical associations, and perhaps prediction.[37] It represents, as Nicholas Onuf notes, "one of the crowning achievements of the West over the past several centuries," and is understood not only as an enterprise, but also as an idea and objective whose purpose is to systematize "what we think we know about the world and ourselves" in order to provide a basis for judgment.[38]

Arguably, however, in International Relations there is a relative dearth of such theory, and what theory exists is often lost amid a preponderance of ideologically informed opinions that masquerade as theoretical endeavors. One of the unfortunate characteristics of our field, as Chris Brown reluctantly admits, is the lack of a stock of theoretical knowledge such that "each writer [on international theory] is more or less obliged to re-invent the subject from scratch."[39] Yale Ferguson and Richard Mansbach tend to agree, seeing theory in International Relations a scarce creature, with each generation of graduate students reinventing the wheel as they plunder the "old theories home," often unaware of the historical lineage of the ideas they borrow.

In International Relations we seem averse to building stocks of knowledge, preferring, instead, to clean out house periodically and start anew. Under this formula, old knowledge cannot be relevant knowledge, and new knowledge is assumed to be better. The great debates have thus arrived with perennial regularity, heralding "new" frameworks and theories as we yet again spring clean the discipline, disposing of anything in danger of becoming permanent. The result is an ever-present need to (re)invent, one that often generates banal insights of previously explained phenomena but with new labels and increasingly technical jargon. For many practitioners in the discipline, such developments have spawned not greater understanding but greater confusion replete with a propensity to ignore completely, or at best make little use of, the scholarly literature in the field.[40] Novelty, rearticulation and reinvention have themselves become prized academic pursuits, often to the detriment of explanation, analysis, and the deepening of our theoretical knowledge. We have only to scan the literature on international relations to see how faddish have attempts at theory construction become. Methodologically, we have run the gamut of traditional-classical, behaviorist, and now reflectivist approaches, and theoretically an entire volume of theories has been invented: functionalism, systems theory, linkage politics, dependency theory, world system theory, complex interdependence, long cycles theory, integration theory, and regime theory, just to name a few.

Doubtless, we have come a long way since the founding of the discipline, yet in other ways we have traveled no distance at all. Brown is quite correct to suggest that each of us nearly always ends up at the beginning, if not reinventing the wheel, then at least walking in a circle. This perpetual need to know where to begin and end our project, where to place our disciplinary markers and hang our theoretical hats seems never to be answered satisfactorily. Students of economics, for example, can start with Adam Smith and *The Wealth of Nations;* sociologists with Max Weber, Emile Durkheim, and Karl Marx; political philosophers with Plato's *Republic* and Aristotle. But where do students of international relations begin and what theoretical tools do they begin with? Are we to study theories of international relations, diplomatic history, interstate rivalry or cooperation, the structure of global politics, decision making and foreign policy, trade, regimes, international law, strategic studies, international organization, international political-economy, or the nation-state-as-actor? The short and most obvious answer is yes, we are to study them all; and no, we cannot possibly study them all as individual scholars. Hence the problem with theory: a theory of what, for whom, to do what precisely, and how and why? Like Ferguson and Mansbach, I too have just reinvented the wheel, begun at the beginning, and find myself, like Brown noted, starting from scratch. And perhaps the end of our project lies in the fact that it leads us back to the beginning, to those basic ontological and epistemological questions they lead back onto themselves. This, perhaps, is the Socratic lesson. The end is in the beginning, in redefining the wheel so that it better explains what it is we are trying to do, want to accomplish, and hope to achieve. For these are not necessarily persistent and recurrent objectives. On the contrary, they change, but only at the procedural level. Systemically, at least, international relations displays remarkable continuity, most recently in terms of the nation-state, and historically in terms of the search for security among contrasting epistemic communities. The variations in theory, method, and perspective come not from these relatively continuous patterns of recurrence and repetition in our epistemic relationships, but in the procedural-methodological approaches that change depending upon context and through our seeking to explain these relationships better.

Thus, theory in International Relations must be understood in this context and its perpetual reinvention a result not only of "change and debate within the subject itself," but an effect of the "influence of new ideas within other areas of social science" as well as "the impact of developments in the real world. . . ."[41] Theory, after all, is a social construction, prone to social pressures, needs, and wishes, and has meaning only insofar as it is constructed in these contexts. This is evident enough in International Relations, a subject whose very being was born of a social-politic sickened by the First World War, alarmed at its recurrence in the Second World War, and matured under the Cold War which, as Fred Halliday points out, has "shaped its focuses at least as much as inter-paradigm disputes."[42] We perhaps forget how much theory is driven by social need, real or perceived, and how attentive we are to these demands for relevance, diagnosis, prescription, action, and solution. Nor is this wrong. I for one do not claim theory for its own sake. To read for pleasure or to delight in intertextuality is a pastime, not a pursuit, and its concerns are rightly situated among the humanities that nurtures such arts. International Relations, on the other hand, is not situated within the social sciences by pure chance; it has a social charter no matter how irresolutely it is sometimes stated or how buried it seems amid the vernacular of formal theory, rational-actor models, and the language of science and technical jargon. Indeed, it is amid this social charter—one that might be defined as the search for peace, the maintenance of order, the avoidance of war, and the establishment of community—that we can begin to put together the discipline of International Relations in all its varieties.[43]

Fred Halliday conceives of international relations as a constellation of three essential elements: "the inter-state, the transnational and the systemic." These, he notes, "allow of many specializations and varying theoretical approaches."[44] Within this ambit, the various subfields or specializations each addresses one of these constituent elements: decision making and foreign policy, for example, concern the interstate aspect of international relations; international organization, the systemic; and international political-economy, the transnational. While separated by their specialization, all these approaches are united under a common disciplinary roof—a composite rubric that is defined, albeit imprecisely, by the social charter that underlies the motivation of our scholarship. At times, of course, this is far from evident if only because the nature of specialist sequestration obscures the larger metatheoretical project all of us are engaged in. Just as preoccupation with a particular tree obscures from view the forest, so too does exclusive preoccupation with one branch of International Relations cloud from view the discipline as a whole. This, perhaps, is what makes for our perennial sense of crisis in International Relations. As we occasionally look up from our particular specialization, we see only an immense blackness and become anxious about where precisely we fit into this grander disciplinary project and how we are connected to other specializations. Cries of perspectivism, disintegration, and pluralism make us seem like so many obtuse interests competing for attention as we hurriedly go about our research agendas unsure of how, and if, they all fit together. Our disciplinary house assumes the character of a divided one as we add yet more rooms whose perspectives and concerns are rarely known to others in the house, busied as they are with their own vistas and perspectives from their own rooms.

Arguably, however, this is not a crisis in the discipline so much as a failure to codify and map the parameters of our disciplinary house, its various rooms and their particular views.[45] Ours is not a static disciplinary dwelling but a dynamic one. We add and demolish rooms, refurbish, redecorate, and remodel with ever-increasing rapidity. The architectural specifications of our home are constantly changing, and the conduits and hallways that connect the rooms are often poorly specified or simply assumed and left unexplained. Indeed, disciplinary renovations often proceed without recourse to architectural blueprints, more often prompted by empirical developments than by theoretical innovations. Theory in International Relations frequently comes after the fact: we did not observe realism; for example, we saw war, anarchy, and insecurity and developed realist theory to explain these. Similarly, atop these three constituent elements of international relations and the various specializations and approaches they harbor, theory too must be imposed to make sense of their interrelationships, to expose the conduits between them, and make apparent the connection of each approach to the broader disciplinary project.[46]

This is the function of theory in International Relations, a means of imposing conceptual linkages upon a subject matter whose very nature divaricates into numerous issue areas. The task of theory might thus be seen as the process of codification of the discipline's social charter: an awkward metatheoretic project that analyzes not only the "oughts" of international theory but also the "facts," and in doing so attempts to reconcile these two pursuits within an enterprise that undertakes empirical investigations of international realities but set amid a desire to contribute to normative objectives that aim to better these realities. Practically speaking, Halliday suggests that this involves the theorization of these three constituent elements: the nature of their interrelationship, the mutual effects of each on the others, and the effect of historical change on the dynamics of these interrelationships vis-à-vis their social, political, and economic consequences. In this way, the function of theory becomes not only the task of explaining international history, but a project of educating and forewarning about the dangers of repeating certain aspects of that history. The latter is a normative process involving ethical considerations about future worlds, and of making argument and convincing others that these future worlds should indeed be made. The functions of theory are thus twofold: (1) a desire to know, understand, and explain international phenomena, not simply for their own sake but in the context of; (2) a desire to shape, manipulate, and control certain aspects of international relations in the hope that those aspects which cause harm can be avoided. Kimberly Hutchings describes this dual aspect of our enterprise this way: "International relations is one of the areas of social science which most clearly brings home the tensions involved in the dual relations of inquirer to object of inquiry, as both scientific observer and moral judge, particularly in times of war. As social scientists, we are required to understand and explain our object, as moral beings, we are required to judge or evaluate it."[47]

This, perhaps, is what makes the study and theory of international relations fuzzy, or what Nicholas Rengger described as international relations' "irreducible fluidity and contextuality, the sense that its centre is everywhere and its circumference nowhere."[48] Imposing rigid boundaries upon so nebulous an exercise as normative discussion of future worlds or of critical reflections upon present ones (the "ought" of international theory) is obviously an inappropriate response, reminding us that those who attempt closure commit "a massive violation of Aristotle's injunction not to try to treat a subject with a degree of exactness it will not admit of."[49] The normative/moral/critical aspects of international theory must necessarily be allowed freedom to roam the corridors of idealism and critical reflection, thinking about how we think and writing about how we write. But this is not an invitation to stray from the purpose of this enterprise, an attempt to think critically about how we understand, and how, through understanding, we might realize better worlds. Normative theory too has a certain circumference, an outer limit beyond which its concerns cease to be those of International Relations. To admit as much is not to "marginalize" certain approaches as postmodernists accuse, but to recognize that some issues begin to fall outside the purview of our discipline.

The problem, of course, is how to center our discipline and decide what its purview is. This too, however, is the task of theory, one that must recognize that definition of our discipline is a constant process precisely because, contextually speaking, its concerns and issues change due to their historical contingency. Unlike other social sciences, the boundaries of our field are thematically and intellectually porous. Certainly there is a systemic mantel upon which International Relations rests, but upon this the socially constructed nature of international politics causes variation and difference that theory must take account of. This is the perennial "tension between structure and history in the study of international relations" which renders extremely complex an understanding of the reflexive ontological relationship "between the individual and society or, put differently, between action and structure."[50]

This particular axiom might be seen as the point of contention between postmodernists who favor social constructivism and realists who favor structure. More specifically, the contention here is over the nature of theory in terms of representation: does theory represent reality or, does theory in the process of representation itself, construct it? Depending upon one's disposition, ontology or epistemology is favored as the appropriate theoretical axiom on which to base knowledge. To date, neither school has bridged the gulf between these two approaches successfully.[51] Postmodernists largely ignore structure, seeing agents' free wills constituted by a series of intertexts, and argue that the basis of explanation and understanding does not lie in theory that turns to a world of ontological fact, but in the way in which interpretation, perception, and the recombination of ideas, words, and meanings come to comprise epistemological narratives and grand interpretive constructs of history. Realists, on the other hand, have tended to favor structural interpretations, sometimes forgetting the importance of agency in terms of historical change, and argue that ontology precedes epistemology. As Roger Spegele notes; "It is only on the basis of a discursive argument leading to some sort of consensus concerning what [international relations] is that we shall be able to arrive at any intelligible methodological prescriptions about how, ideally, it should be studied."[52]

The nodal points for intellectual investigation in the discipline, then, tend to divaricate from two essential positions: epistemological investigation in the case of postmodernists and ontological explanation in the case of realists. The latter, in particular, has had an important influence upon theorizing in the discipline, tending to focus upon ontology as theory rather than theory as epistemology as the postmodernists would have it. Martin Wight, for example, understood the study of international relations and the incidence of normative theory to be mutually exclusive, the former not a theoretical province since it was concerned with the base human instincts of power and survival. Power, statecraft, and diplomacy had simply to be observed, described, and recorded. If theoretical considerations were to enter the study of international relations, they were to be merely ontological ones over the appropriate units and levels of analysis.

Much theoretical debate in International Relations has therefore centered on the explication of what it is we are, or should be, studying. Description has preceded explanation. Ontological debate has constituted theoretical discourse, largely precluding epistemological considerations or issues of the sociology of knowledge.[53] Enunciating the distinct domain and practices of international politics and those entities operative within it has defined the task of theory. Realism, for example, the doctrine that understands international politics as the play of power relations between sovereign units in an anarchic system, assumes ontological description as the first order of theory: what cannot be first described cannot be explained. As David Dessler argues, ontology is prescient to explanation and is the "basis of a theory's explanatory power." Ontology defines "the concrete referents of an explanatory discourse." It "consists of the real-world structures (things, entities) and processes posited by the theory and invoked in the theory's explanations."[54] But for realists, ontology is not merely descriptive. It also has an explanatory appeal that lies in the processes of causality it establishes between "certain designated kinds of things" and the "connections or relations between them."[55] Thus, for realists, the ontological description of international politics is both means and ends: the observation of the nation-state-as-actor, the identification of anarchy and the pursuit of power as structured entities, and a description of the connections or relations between nation-states via the ontological presumption of sovereignty and contending interests in a situation of anarchy enables an explanation of the causes of war, the aims of diplomacy, the need for security. Theories, as Waltz argues, show why associations obtain:[56] "Theory is a picture, mentally formed, of a bounded realm or domain of activity. A theory is a depiction of the organization of a domain and of the connections among its parts."[57] Obviously, the crowning achievement of International Relations as ontology is Waltz's *Theory of International Politics*.

There are, of course, problems with ontologically derived forms of theory. Postmodernists naturally dismiss this conception of theory and are not entirely wrong for doing so. Realism is not above criticism, and structural-realism even more so.[58] But then again, neither is postmodernism! But this is not the point. I am not here attempting to defend realism against postmodernism or to dismiss postmodernism entirely from the purview of International Relations. Rather, what I am attempting to do is defend the institution of theory against postmodernism which, in its more virulent forms, aims at its deconstruction and obliteration. So too am I attempting to defend the ontological aspect of theory against those who would engage exclusively in epistemological debate. For there to be theory in International Relations, ontological description must be the first order of things; without first defining the domain of international politics, identifying those entities and things we wish to explain and understand, epistemological debate would be altogether pointless. Save for this, the discipline threatens to transpose itself into philosophy and not International Relations, to be condemned to perpetual metaphysical reflection but without reference to the social world we are attempting to understand. Of course, this does not exonerate us from previous mistakes. International Relations, largely because of the dominance of positivism in the discipline, has, in the past, been apt to ontological description in the absence of epistemological reflection. Practitioners in the discipline have rarely seen a need to question the epistemological basis of their scholarship as Thomas Biersteker forcefully acknowledged.[59] Yet, as he also reminds us, developing theory and generating knowledge requires judicious use of both ontological description and epistemological explanation. These are not mutually exclusive dimensions of theoretical discourse, but the elemental ingredients necessary to the construction of discourse itself. The exclusive focus upon one dimension to the detriment of the other probably explains why, according to William Kreml and Charles Kegley, "International relations research today . . . has failed to reach agreement about several fundamental issues . . . (1) the central questions to be asked, (2) the basic units of analysis (e.g., states or nonstate actors), (3) the levels of analysis at which various questions should be explored, (4) the methods by which hypotheses should be tested and unwarranted inferences prevented, (5) the criteria by which theoretical progress is to be judged, and (6) how inquiry should be organized in order to generate the knowledge that will lead to international peace, prosperity, and justice."[60]

As should be obvious, these issues contain both ontological and epistemological dimensions, reminding us that the road to theory in International Relations is both long and hard and involves examining ". . . not only what it is that we know but how it is that we know it."[61]

The Arrival of the Third Debate: Postmodernism and International Relations

As with the term *theory*, the *Third Debate* too is a catch phrase as vague as it is meaningful for those who employ it, bandied about with such imprecision so that what matters is not what the term actually means (if indeed it has any intrinsic meaning) so much as how it is employed, in what milieu, and what context. Like most concepts in International Relations, the Third Debate too is inherently malleable, displaying a capacity for housing numerous, and often very diverse, debates. In this sense, the Third Debate might be thought of as a kind of market place where those who wish to refine their theoretical tools, critique the tools of others, or simply grind axes and question the nature of being, the discipline, scholarly purpose and meaning meet to display their wares and do business. It thus represents a site of critical reexamination, dissension, methodological scrutiny, and ontological and epistemological interlocution, where the basic premises, assumptions and knowledge systems on which the discipline, theory, and understanding have been built, have been exposed to ongoing critical analyses. The history of the Third Debate has thus been exploratory, starting in some recantings with the death of a single unifying paradigm, realism, and lamented under the banner of the "dividing discipline" or the "interparadigm debate."[62] Conversely, it also has an etiological path descended from a repudiation of realism, or at least a recognition of its failure and growing inability to explain global phenomena. When Ray Maghroori and Bennett Ramberg wrote of the Third Great Debate, for example, they did so with reference to the discourse over the emergence of globalization, transnationalism, and what was seen as the declining importance of the nation-state and thus utility of the realist state-centric view of the world.[63] For Richard Mansbach and Yale Ferguson, on the other hand, the Third Debate is more appropriately understood as the outcome of Kuhnian knowledge development, representing the interstice between fact and theory. For them, it is a disciplinary expression of "significant and unanswerable anomalies" in global politics vis-à-vis our theoretical tools. The end of the Cold War and the fall of the Berlin Wall, for example, were two momentous events in global history that were completely unpredicted and unforeseen by theorists of international relations. The Third Debate is thus our Kuhnian revolution, a place of introspective self-analysis, probing reflection and "unanswerable anomalies"; a place between celebration and despair where the "quest for theory" is now understood as problematic.[64]

But if the genesis of the Third Debate can be ascribed to a dissatisfaction at the increasing gap between fact and theory, its more recent history has been spurned by methodological debate. Critical theorists like Robert Cox, for example, have attempted to infuse into the Third Debate Gramscian method as a means of more fully understanding the basis and operation of power and hegemony.[65] Indeed, the Third Debate's more recent history suggests a preoccupation with things metatheoretical. Steve Smith, for instance, sees the critique of positivism as one of its core elements. Smith's aptly titled edited book, *International Theory: Positivism and Beyond*, and the earlier offering by Claire Turenne Sjolander and Wayne Cox, *Beyond Positivism: Critical Reflections on International Relations*, both capture perfectly this concern with epistemology and method.[66] So too, Richard Ashley's *The Poverty of Neo-Realism* addresses the methodological and epistemological tendency to structuralist theory in International Relations, along with its innate proclivity for microeconomic analysis and the logic of economy. With increasing urgency, the Third Debate has compelled practitioners to reexamine not only the "ontological, epistemological, and axiological foundations of their scientific endeavors," but to begin to wander further afield and assess their "theoretical options in a postpositivist era."[67] Moving beyond positivism, or more bluntly, rejecting the methods of science as germane to the study and understanding of international politics has been one of the most obvious, and in many instances much needed, developmental avenues of the Third Debate.[68] These have appeared in numerous guises, most obviously as efforts to articulate a critical theory cum historical materialist perspective in International Relations, but also as instances of international political-economy where theorists have attempted to integrate the study of international politics into the tradition of scholarship concerned with relations of production and exchange, capitalism, the phenomena of globalization and set amid debates over the diminishing sovereignty of the nation-state.[69] In this guise, the Third Debate has been a methodological one over the most appropriate means of explaining and understanding international politics. Theorists have thus debated the relative merits of a positivist versus postpositivist approach, for example, or a structural realist, political-economy, constructivist, or critical theoretic approach. While such debates have involved considerations of epistemology and ontology to be sure, most have occurred within the epistemological confine of modernity, rationality, and the thought of the Enlightenment.[70] Critical Theory,[71] for example, while radical in the sense of seeking to restructure social and political theory, transcend positivist social science and construct new emancipatory projects, nonetheless remains committed to Enlightenment principles and the tradition of scholarship associated with the Frankfurt school.

More recently, of course, this has not been the case. Increasingly, the entire epistemological edifice that otherwise houses the discipline of International Relations, its theory and knowledge, has come under attack. Since the late 1980s, and especially in the 1990s, the Third

Debate has evolved into a more curious creature, one not necessarily concerned with practitioners reexamining the "ontological, epistemological, and axiological foundations of their *scientific endeavors*" (my emphasis) as Yosef Lapid suggested, so much as ridding such "scientific" endeavors from the discourse of International Relations entirely, indeed of ridding the discourse of notions of discipline, rationality, Enlightenment thought and its appeals to foundationalism, universalism, and metanarratives. As understood and related to us by Yosef Lapid, then, the Third Debate might be said to no longer exist, or at least that phase is now being challenged. This, after all, was a phase which, as Christine Sylvester writes, reveals Lapid's Third Debate to be no more than a "lingering of the second debate issues into the third era . . . an arena of debates-within-debates about how to proceed to find method, how to keep method at bay, how to deal with all of our bounded and/or differently configured rationalities."[72] To the contrary, the new Third Debate represents a more profound challenge than did Lapid's characterization, one whose genesis, historical lineage, and approaches are both alien and extraordinary. The Third Debate is now more properly understood not merely as a site of critical reexamination, but one of deconstruction, intertextual readings, dissident thought, and a relocation of the temporal plain of perception to include such mediums as place, space, and contextualism, not to mention gender, identity, signs, symbols, and images as ingredients in the intersubjective construction of truth, meaning, and reality. Boundaries otherwise used as means of demarcation and intellectual ordering devices are now understood as mediums of "modernist exclusion," mechanisms of "marginalization" that have "silenced" voices or, worse still, been used in the service of specific interests to plunder and pillage peoples of wealth and well being. For postmodernists, the point is a political one as Chris Brown notes: "In the twentieth century the instrumental rationality of the West has so often found itself at the service of dubious causes that it has become itself politically suspect."[73] The once-privileged status of Western thought is no more, but collapsed under the mantra of its own contradictions which, postmodernists argue, opens up new sites of thinking space and leads to dialogism. For postmodernists, this is a place where "we can learn things about ourselves by studying our history and reading our literary inheritance . . . *[but only after] we have removed the monological tendencies past readings have assigned to these genres*" (my emphasis).[74] History, in other words, is to be rewritten, or at least written from the perspective of those who have not written it before: women, people of color, gays and lesbians, indigenous peoples, and so forth.

As presently constituted, then, the Third Debate represents a site of radical rejectionism populated by postmodernists and poststructuralists who seek not to reexamine methodological approaches, but replace them and the epistemological and ontological edifice upon which they rest. The implications are profound, challenging conceptions of theory and knowledge in the discipline as traditionally constituted. In the context of disciplinary identity, for example, postmodernists place the Enlightenment project in danger by insisting that "there is nothing outside of the text."[75] Reality is reduced to an imaginary experience brought about by the consumption of signs and symbols in a kind of hyperreality constituted in the simulacra.[76] Here, there is no original experience but a circuit of signs: secondary images that reflect not reality but other images and signs. The discipline becomes a fiction imposed in time, an imagined space evolved through textual practices that condition thinking and make "real" the fiction. Learned traditions are merely the textual inscriptions of those who have been privileged enough to write: white males of largely European descent who, either wittingly or unwittingly, have replicated and legitimized the social and political order. International politics, on the other hand, are representations of these fictions evolved as practices whose "reality" is only so because so many are duplicitous, or simply duped, into replicating these practices that these become coterminous with the events and facts of international politics. Practice, thought, theory, interpretation, and knowing are all reduced to a form of perspectivism, where the vantage point from whence we stand to view the world, or to write and develop theory about it, contaminates knowledge and makes "knowing" a function of place, identity, and individual experience. These form the experiential background tapestry for readers and authors alike, which, in turn, makes interpretation of the facts of international politics, multifaceted, contradictory, and ambiguous. Reality, in other words, becomes a perspectivist phenomenon, unique to each purveyor, interpreter, author, and reader.

This linguistic turn in social and political theory is, of course, emblematic of a much broader and deeper crisis in Western thought. At its most basic it represents a crisis of confidence, if not loss of faith, in those tools which have traditionally provided the means of knowing. So too it represents an absolute rejection of those tools not simply because of their failure to provide uncontaminated knowledge, but because that knowledge is now seen itself responsible for realities it was meant to transform. Far from liberating humankind from the shackles of nature and transposing human existence to a new, higher plateau, postmodernists charge Enlightenment thought with creating those conditions that have made for greater immiseration, destitution, and dehumanization. Things are discernibly worse, they argue, not in spite of Enlightenment thought, but because of it. Likewise, rather than the discovery of truth and meaning, modernity is charged with having simply imposed another interpretation, no better than previous creeds and beliefs, while arrogantly assuming its creed to be superior to all others. And the ontological object of this creed, "Man as a sovereign being," fully in control of "his" destiny and, through the power of rationality, able to understand fully the existential realm of "his" existence, is now dismissed by postmodernists as a project in shambles and disrepute. Such thinking, they charge, has ontologically privileged mythical "Man" and placed open to "his" exploitation and abuse all of nature. Only now, in an age said to verge on a postmodern one, can we see how shallow is this creed, how vulnerable and incapable of explanation it is. Only now, as humanity faces ecological and environmental crises, increasing global inequalities, and the growing crisis of spiritual identity and purpose, can we see the impending danger, despair, and nihilism that modernist thought, theory, and practice represents. Intertextualism is thus one response to this perceived crisis, as is identity politics, relativism, perspectivism, and countless other creeds that discount the possibility of knowing, living, and liberation via science, rationality, and Enlightenment thought. The common thread that connects these creeds together is an emancipatory ethic but conceived in post-Enlightenment terms; a form of systematic skepticism to every possible interpretation except its own.[77]

In the context of International Relations, the emergence of postmodernism and its historical development can thus been seen in part as a reaction against the professions of science, indeed of the failure of scientific International Relations to deliver methods of understanding, and solutions to, the problem of war, famine, inequality, ethnic cleansing, territorial disputes, and countless other plights that afflict the human condition. Equally, however, the emergence of postmodern/poststructural epistemologies is also bound to a political project aimed at transforming these realities and the modes of conceptualization they hold responsible for them. In postmodern discourse, as with critical theory and Marxism before it, theory and practice are inextricably connected, bound to a process through which action and thought are mutually constitutive. Postmodernism is thus a proactive instrument, seen not simply as a means of theoretical discourse but as a medium of political praxis. Its emergence in International Relations has thus been simultaneous with the politicization of the discipline: a process of reappropriating an intellectual and physical space for those who charge that they have been made "invisible" or "marginalized." Such has been a familiar process throughout the social sciences, encompassing calls for greater inclusiveness, the increased representation of women, along with ethnic, sexual, and religious minorities amongst the ranks of the profession. Indeed, postmodernist discourse is as much about identity politics and the politics of visibility as it is about new mediums of intellectual investigation. For postmodern feminists, for example, the Third Debate represents a means of deconstructing the masculinist identities of a largely white-male discipline and of infusing the issue of gender into the discipline and its theories. For them, "the theory and practice of international relations have always been gendered, and . . . international economic and political institutions contain, affect and are affected by understandings of gender."[78] The "difference that gender makes," as V. Spike Peterson explains it, is that knowing is a perspectivist phenomena, where knowledge is received by each of us not as human beings but as gendered beings. The world is thus said to be shaped pervasively by "gendered meanings," so that the postmodern feminist project becomes one of "revealing systematic masculinist bias and systematically adding women."[79] For Christine Sylvester, this translates into asking "what it means to know, who may know, where knowers are located, and what the difference among them mean for the knowledges that result."[80] Contextualism belies the basis and biases of knowledge, and for poststructural feminists of this genre, textual analysis reveals hidden meaning(s) that expose the relationship of knowledge to the workings of power by making conspicuous the underlying assumptions they harbor. Consider, for example, the opening lines to her recent article, where, from "Little Red Riding Hood" she quotes the following words: "What big teeth you have. The better to eat you with." From this, Sylvester notes, "There are many texts encrusted in this simple dialogue, having to do with violence about to happen and the breakdown of security; having to do, as well, with sex, cross species relations, gender relations, cross dressing boundary practices, and aesthetics. Perfect for an era of feminist international relations."[81]

Sylvester's opening remarks reveal how disparate are postmodern approaches to theory and international politics compared to the more traditional perspectives rehearsed some pages previous. Contrast, for a moment, Martin Wight's image of theory with that of Sylvester's, who notes: "Telling tales in the ISA [International Studies Association] and reflecting on revelatory moments in one's turn towards feminist analysis can be thought of as writing theory at the cusp of IR and feminism." Similarly, Cynthia Enloe notes, "Every time a woman explains how her government is trying to control her fears, her hopes and her labor . . . theory is being made."[82] Theory, in other words, should not be thought of as a noun but as a verb. Theory is not a tool, it is something we do—we theorize. Consequently, argues Marysia Zalewski, "Theorising is a way of life, a form of life, something we all do, every day, all the time. We theorise about how to make cups of tea, about washing clothes, about using the word processor, about driving a car, about collecting water, about joking. . . . We theorise about each of these everyday activities, mostly subconsciously. This is relevant to international relations scholars," argues Zalewski, "because it means that first, we are all theorising (not just 'the theorists') and second, that the theorising that counts or matters . . . is not confined either to policy makers or to academics."[83] The institution of theory is thus transformed into a politics of situationism, "a lower than 'low politics'" that, for Sylvester, is located amid the everyday people who constitute the "real" actors of international politics, those who live amid the "households, factories, farms, remote rural areas, and international immigration posts in lesser as well as great power settings."[84] These are the "real theorizers" of international relations, but "located in a wide variety of places, not just at the reified core of what has become international politics."[85] As a practical example of such theorizing, Zalewski suggests that "in order to understand more about the Cold War," for example, "we might want to pursue Farah Godrej's analysis of the sex industry in the Philippines. Her description of a common T-shirt slogan worn by servicemen referring to the local women which reads, 'Mind Over Matter: I Don't Mind And You Don't Matter,' might be a good place to begin," Zalewski notes. "From such a starting point, which could be both that of the men who wore the T-shirts and that of the women who were the 'subject' of them," Zalewski argues that, "we can attempt to understand the construction of Filipino women's debasement and the servile and compliant sexuality, which is inextricably linked to the construction of both 'other' and militarism itself."[86] Theory becomes a narrative told by the marginalized and thus challenges a discipline said to admit "only official-decision makers, soldiers, statesmen, terrorists, kings, and the occasional 'crazed' religious group to the fold."[87] In this way, "theory" becomes the journal entries from the travels of a "U.S. academic living on a kibbutz" in Israel, the recollections of those who gather at ISA meetings and exchange narratives, or those who tell of their fears and, from their own situation, recount their struggles, histories, and stories of exclusion.[88]

To be fair, however, even Sylvester recognizes the hermeneutic logic of such a position, quoting Joan Scott who notes that "experience is at once always already an interpretation *and* in need of interpretation."[89] In what sense such approaches or discourses can be said to constitute a theoretical/explanatory treatise, or indeed to advance our understanding of international politics, is thus problematic. Narratives, irrespective of how compelling they may be or from what marginalized space they are authored, are still only personalized, impressionistic translations. Yet the point of postmodern and poststructural interpretation is not, ostensibly, to offer an alternative theoretical vignette or to impose an interpretation as "totalitarian" as modernist theory is said to be. Instead, critique, deconstruction, and making problematic the boundaries of the discipline that otherwise "exclude" or make "invisible" various minorities are its first order of business. Postmodernists are, then, perhaps best understood not in the context of what it is they want to do, but what it is they want to undo. The postmodern, as Nicholas Rengger points out, might therefore be better understood not as an -ism, but a mood, a mood of skepticism manifested as rejectionism and practiced as deconstruction and subversion.[90] Contemporary theoretical debates in International Relations have thus been witness to a voluminous array of deconstructive efforts. And most, of course, have aimed their sights on the cherished centerpiece of international theory—realism. For in the cauldron of postmodern discourse, realism has come to be seen as emblematic of everything said to be wrong with the discipline, its approaches, and research agendas. For postmodernists, realism is theory, patriarchy, the "special case," science, practice, prescription, and Enlightenment thought all in one. All have been mixed together and attacked as mutually constitutive of a modernist sensibility. This, then, might be seen as the latest version of the Third Great Debate.

Reinscribing the Role and Functions of Theory: Realism and Postmodern Discourse

If realism is both the nemesis that afflicts international relations as practice as well as the representation of that practice in theory, it is also in large measure the raison d'être for the emergence of postmodern perspectives in the discipline. Despite this, though, the responses it engenders are notable for their discursive and contradictory character, illustrative of how complex realism is as an image, theory, representation, and practice of world politics. Postmodernists are thus forced to deal with realism in ways that seem abstract, textually tortured, and at times nonsensical. There is, however, a common thread: realism, and the image of theory it represents, is now dismissed universally by postmodernists as reflecting a particular moment in the history and theory of the discipline that, for them, no longer represents the true scope, nature, and realities of international relations.[91] Indeed, postmodernists not only dismiss realist theory but think that the image of global politics it validates is synonymous with modernist thought otherwise seen as obsessed with control and technical problem-solving. Realist theory is technical theory; theory to control, manipulate, and orchestrate the events and facts of international politics. Unlike modernists who see theory as an instrument of explanation and understanding, something to be placed atop the facts and events of international politics to infer their systemic meaning and thus expose patterns of repetition or causal connections, postmodernists see theory as inculpated in these facts and events. Practitioners in the discipline are thus admonished for ignoring "the degree to which . . . theories themselves do not simply provide the means for describing, discussing and directing phenomena, but help to constitute such phenomena."[92] In other words, the image of global politics represented in realism, for example, is itself accused of being responsible for realist power politics. As Richard Ashley argues, "the modern sovereign state is never more than an effect of realist practices."[93]

Such a view changes implicitly the functions and role of theory as well as the task of the theorist in International Relations. No longer are we above the fray of international politics, cataloging the facts, researching the histories, or attempting to formulate remedies to the problems that afflict global politics. Rather it is the case that we *are* international politics, the actors who make up those practices and reproduce them in our daily rituals. As taxonomists of the discipline and its theories, for example, postmodernists argue that we give rise to realism, and as bibliophiles who gather facts produced by realism, we create traditions through the construction of social structures that conduce social action. In the social world, and perhaps even the purely physical world of the hard sciences, postmodernists see thought, thinking, and practice forming the interstitial interface between action and structure. "Physics too," they argue, "is only an interpretation and arrangement of the world . . . and *not* an explanation of the world."[94] Consequently, the task of the theorist in International Relations is not to study the phenomenon of international politics as if such were objectively given, but, as Steve Smith argues, to understand how "our rationalization of the international is itself constitutive of . . . practice." For Smith, we must recognize that the "ways in which international theory has been categorized, and the debates within it presented, fail to acknowledge the link between social practice and the constitution of social knowledge."[95] Where Locke, Hume, Comte, and Popper understood theory as a "cognitive reaction to reality" and an intellectual medium for ordering it into categories that could be analyzed and dissected for purposes of understanding, postmodernists view modernist theory as a site of imposed interpretation that belies a relationship between knowledge and power.[96] The very idea that theorists can observe passively the events of international politics as they "peer over the shoulders of statesmen" and assess objectively their deliberations, calculations, and motives is dismissed by postmodernists as fallacious to the point of being complicitous in the practices of international politics. Theory does not come after the fact, but is responsible for the facts. It thus makes no sense to speak of reality as existing "out there," since, for postmodernists, reality is constituted via the amalgam of social practices endemic to everyday life. Realism, for example, is viewed as a contingent condition derived through its repeated reconstruction, and reality in this context extends only to the practices that reproduce such entities and inscribe them in social realms. As an objective reality, realism does not exist. There is no systemic condition between nation-states that can be identified as realpolitik. Realist imagery that assumes international politics to be a necessitous realm of repetition between actors attempting to survive amid a condition of anarchy is seen by postmodernists as an historically contingent practice by virtue of its social inscription. Importantly, then, the disciplinary apparatus erected to study such realities, the theoretical apparatus developed in support of this project, and the modernist narratives that have resulted are otherwise rejected as "a fiction imposed in time, a misrepresentation of what is really present, a misrepresentation that owes its power to the fact that it is misrecognised and made to count as a horizon of truth and meaning."[97]

Under the regime of postmodernist discourse, realists have thus become both observers of international politics as well as the constitutive agents of the practices they observe. Yet as clever as realists are in making real realist practices, they are not, apparently, very clever at understanding the practices they create. "Contrary to any Realist doctrine," claims Jim George, reality cannot be grasped by realist theory since it is "detached from the everyday experience of so much of that world."[98] Realists and realist theory are thus oxymoronic entities: realism as theory cannot understand its own hermeneutic logic nor account for the practices of global politics since its understanding of these practices is mediated via a flawed epistemological proclivity for positivist-modernist theory. Yet by the very act of utilizing such epistemological entities, realists actively create the world they study (albeit unbeknownst to them) and thus are constitutive of realist international realities.

International Relations theory, specifically modernist-realist theory, is thus attacked on two fronts: the first for being out of touch and out of date with the "true" realities of contemporary international relations; and the second for being responsible for those realities it purports to be studying objectively. One might ask, however, how realism can be out of date while its practices are allegedly responsible for the contemporary configuration of global politics? Regardless, my point should be obvious: postmodernists embroil us in a strange paradox, a want to litigate realism for the structure, practices, and horrors that emerge from a world of sovereign states who practice realism, but also a desire to repudiate realism on the grounds of its congenital inability to theorize the state, account for the practices of global politics, or the new realities of transnationalism and globalization. More obtusely, postmodernists want to conduct this litigation at the level of philosophy and metatheory, indicting not realism per se, but its supposed intellectual mentors: positivism, rationality, and modernity. This is what makes the Third Great Debate so distinctive. Where the previous great debates were contributions to the discipline, to theory, to the advancement of knowledge and understanding through their efforts to delineate better avenues to scholarship, postmodernists reject this and argue, instead, that such was a disciplinary project masking practices of exclusion, oppression, and domination, and foisted under cover of modernist narratives of "progress" and "emancipation." The Third Debate has thus devolved into a battleground between defenders of the discipline and adherents to traditional conceptions of theory and those, who, under various labels and banners, challenge such conceptions, disciplinary boundaries, and projects, and suggest that the road to understanding, real emancipation, and better worlds lies in very different mediums and sites than has traditionally adorned the field.

In International Relations, as in social and political theory more generally, the functions of postmodern theory are thus defined by the political program that underlies its metatheoretical commitments. These can be seen as antagonistic to traditional images of the discipline and modes of conceptualization. So too are they antagonistic, if not diametrically opposed, to modernist conceptions of theory, insisting that theory is practice. Theoretical knowledge is thus understood in instrumental terms, reinscribing theorists from a position of relative obscurity as observer of the facts to active participant and creator of these facts. In this way, the role and functions of theory are transformed into a political instrument whose task is to expose the interests that underlie grand narratives, universal projects, and the pretension to inclusiveness. For postmodernists like Jim

George, for example, theory is an expression of dominant interests manifest as practice, such that the task of a postmodern approach must be to "re-frame the politico-ethical debate in a manner which confronts the essentialism and universalism of dominant modern realisms."[99] For George, as for other postmodernists, the canonical sin is to utter the word *we*, to presume to speak for others, to dare to generalize and thereby universalize. And the point of this project, profound or otherwise, is "to establish that the *universal*, in this context, is always a *particular* representation of a power politics formation accorded foundationalist status."[100] Restated in language plain to all, George has rediscovered the age-old realist adage that "the strong do what they have the power to do, and the weak accept what they must." History is the preserve of victors who write it, not the weak who must suffer and endure it. Realist theory thus commits the ethical sin of generalizing but in a manner that reflects specific, and not necessarily universal, interests and values. In this instance, realism is really the handmaiden of American power politics, transposing American interests onto a universal (read global) plane but whose real and substantive basis is particularistic national interest.

The startling banality of this observation, of course, is that George has rediscovered realism and how nationalism and self-interest are at work not only in international politics but also in the articulation of theory in International Relations.[101] However, this is not old-fashioned Yankee imperialism cast in terms of a spatial neocolonial dimension as with the old "new-left" of the 1960s and 1970s, but for George an imperialism of discourse and thinking practices, where certain images, modes of conceptualization, and textual practices and readings are obscured by an ethnocentric intelligentsia who define thinking space in such a way as to make invisible gender, women, patriarchy, people of color, issues of race, sexual politics, and other "marginal" discourses. It is realism as a mode of thinking, George argues, that "infiltrates in dangerous ways the policy prescriptions and strategic formats of states seeking foundational legitimation for their power politics ambitions." For postmodernists of this persuasion, then, the battle lines are not really between classes, genders, colors or sociopolitical systems so much as thought practices which predominate and make some discourses, subjects, and histories visible and others not. The postmodern project in various of its manifestations is thus to think "otherwise," and in doing so to construct alternative worlds. George, for example, makes a plea "for a more serious regime of reading/writing about questions which have no simple all encompassing answers or ultimate totalising solutions."[102] But as to what such worlds might look like, we are never told, for to do so would be to proscribe meaning and interpretation in a world that admits only to multifarious outcomes, readings, and understandings.

Despite this, though, there is in George's project a degree of self-disclosure, albeit hidden amid a pretense to disturb continually monological narratives. George, for example, defines his role as a concerned scholar/citizen of the 1990s, one who, contrary to realists, seeks to "open up closed discursive practices to the creativity and critical capacities of peoples seeking to understand and change their worlds in their own ways and through their own struggles."[103] The "ethical" basis of postmodern discourse thus resides in "a philosophical life in which the critique of what we are is at one and the same time the historical analysis of the limits that are imposed on us and an experiment with the possibilities of going beyond them."[104] This is a call not only for emancipation from modernity, but from Enlightenment thinking practices that define implicitly what exists beyond modernity. Save for such a "postmodern ethics," humankind can but celebrate a global order "circumscribed for nearly fifty years by unparalleled violence, superpower exploitation of every corner of the globe, and increasing structural inequality and human misery." But for a postmodern ethics, argues George, we are left with rationalist, pseudoscientific realist thought that has steered policy makers to choose the arms race, "proxy war fighting, support for neo-fascist thuggery, and global containment."[105] For George, realist theory, Enlightenment thought, rationality, and a modernist sensibility represent perilous thought practices whose legacy has been all too frequently felt in the death camps of Auschwitz, genocide, Hiroshima, Nagasaki, and ethnic cleansing. Where for Weber "fate decreed that the cloak should become an iron cage," so too for the likes of George it threatens to emasculate us in the name of science and rationality. Liberation thus lies in dismantling such thought practices, eradicating them from discourse, and starting afresh. For the discipline this means deconstruction, and for the stock of knowledge and theoretical tools that have served us to date, their burial. The solution to the problems of international politics thus starts with the end of International Relations.

The Battle Lines Drawn: Let the War Begin

"The study of international relations," notes William Wallace, "is not an innocent profession. It is not like the classics, or mathematics, an abstract logical training for the youthful mind. The justification for the place it has gained in the university curriculum rests upon utility, not aesthetics. The growth of the social sciences in Western universities in the past century, and their remarkable expansion over the past thirty years, has been based upon their perceived contribution to better government, in the broadest sense."[106] Since the founding of the discipline of International Relations, there has always been a volatile tension between those who would sing the "siren song of policy relevance" and those who measure good scholarship and academic purity in terms of the distance one is able to achieve from government. The latter, of course, are accused of scholasticism, often engaged in sterile, arcane, and incestuous debates written by university professors for university professors. The former, on the other hand, are derided for what Wallace calls their presentism: the penchant for designing research programs in terms of today's newspaper headlines and government funding priorities.[107] The danger in which International Relations stands, for some, is that we have gotten in bed with government, and, for others, that we no longer even know where the bedroom is. Michael McKinley, for example, warns that the "infiltration of the university by the bureaucrats-in-residence" will circumvent the creed of the university as the celebrated "employer of unconventional intellectuals whose theoretical concerns are complemented by a willingness to subject all that passes before them to a radical critique of a type not possible within the bureaucracy."[108] Perpetual critique, however, might cause the bureaucrat to stop calling altogether, leaving scholars estranged from the outside world and their work "relevant" only to the extent that it is read by other scholars and foisted upon unsuspecting pupils. Indeed, as is so often the case, to be seen "collaborating with the enemy" and dirtying one's hands in the empirical stuff of public policy, or at least engaged in theory with a modicum of relevance to the realities of international politics, is to expose oneself to allegations of anti-intellectualism and the rabid insults of the likes of McKinley, who, among other things, alleges that such conspirators are "reigning imbeciles" who have "efficient enough brains" but display an "all too limited intelligence and imagination."[109] To fall from grace and engage with the security policy discourse is thus to descend to "mediocrity," a condition that "drives out that which is superior on the basis of weight of numbers and political power and interests." The wrath of "professional," "scholarly" denunciation even extends to namecalling, when, for example, McKinley notes that the appellation that best describes such conspirators comes from ancient Athens, "iditotes, from which is derived the common English language expression 'idiot.'"[110]

Such self-imposed closure from the world of policy and a willingness to ridicule those who dare to dabble in its murky waters is indicative of postmodern perspectives that tend increasingly toward scholasticism. Wallace defines this as a condition that develops when "practitioners shift from attempts to address common questions from different perspectives to competition among different 'schools' in which each multiplies definitions and explanations, develops its own deliberately obscure terminology, and concentrates much of its efforts on attacking the methods and terminology of competing groups."[111] Much debate in International Relations is of this nature—obtuse, terminologically confusing, and antagonistic. Postmodern discourse, however, has perhaps perfected this art, developing its own intellectual idioms and nomenclature in an attempt to dismantle competing modernist schools and the theories associated with them. Calls for deconstruction, the celebration of estrangement from the mainstream, and the abandonment of intellectual precepts associated with Enlightenment thought are all uniform in their attempt to reduce to rubble International Relations and start afresh.

The battle lines are thus drawn: a discipline that attempts to develop theory and knowledge in the pursuit of better understanding and, hopefully, better policy and better worlds; or a postmodern sensibility that calls for the end of International Relations amid a regime of word games, a diaspora of previous knowledge and understanding, and the pursuit of intertextuality and interpretivism. There is, to coin a postmodern phrase, a distinct change in the "structure of feeling" in the discipline, a growing sense of uncivil war as Kalevi Holsti calls it. "The objects of attack from the new methodologies/epistemologies are not likely to concede gracefully," notes Holsti, "that 2,500 years of the study of politics based on observation, classification, and comparison—the Aristotelian legacy—should be thrown out because Nietzsche and a few other continental philosophers of despair have declared that rationalism and empiricism are the sources of all that ails the world today."[112] Nor, indeed, are postmodern adversaries likely to halt their campaign because of derision of their new intellectual luminaries. Attempts to reinvent or simply abolish International Relations thus persist. No longer is the discipline conceived in the image of exploration, observation, and investigation of the causes of things in the world, but reconceived as a project that attempts to change it. As Mark Hoffman notes, "The point of International Relations theory is not simply to alter the way we look at the world, but to alter the world. It must offer more than mere description and an account of current affairs. It must also offer us a significant choice and a critical analysis of the quality and direction of life."[113] These comments, however, neglect our disciplinary history, assuming that better government and better worlds have not before been uppermost in the minds of theorists and practitioners alike, and that, somehow, postmodernists and critical theorists have a monopoly on this virtue. More pernicious, though, is the implication that scholarship in International Relations has had nefarious purposes, whereby thoughtful reflection based on observation, prudent comparison, and resignation to a life of books, readings, teaching, and, where possible, the conveyance of professional knowledge and advice to policy makers is responsible for causing our problems rather than merely elucidating them. Traditionalists now stand accused of "totalitarianism," their work of little substance, shallow, sterile, and prone to primitivism.[114] For postmodernists the means to progress (conceived in nonteleological terms) lie in standing outside of this tradition and celebrating, instead, resistance to it, dissidence from it, and the deconstruction of it. The very purpose of scholarship, in other words, is transformed by postmodernists. Does one, as William Wallace notes (and Ralf Dahrendorf and David Martin before him), attend the London School of Economics for professional and scholarly training, or does one take up cloth at the "London School of Friars" as preacher, prophet, and Jesuit whose mission is earthy change in this life rather than salvation in the next?[115]

Reference to prior readings, of course, would show these antithetical themes to be perennial in International Relations, reflecting the epistemological dualism of our disciplinary ancestry, idealism and realism, or, as Edward Hallett Carr put it, "the inclination to ignore what was and what is in contemplation of what should be, and the inclination to deduce what should be from what was and what is."[116] Postmodern discourse might thus reflect little more than a new neoidealist sentiment in International Relations, albeit one unaware of its own intellectual pedigree.

There is, however, a distinct difference between idealists of the past and postmodernists of the present. Previous idealist thought, for example, was interspersed with constructive endeavor to erect new forms of international organization through constitutional means or the rule of law; legislative proposals were suggested to outlaw war and mandate peace; resolution procedures were suggested for the mediation of disputes; and public education was pursued as a means of forewarning populations of the horrors of war and the dangers of unrestrained nationalism. While such might have seemed fanciful in view of the political realities of the day, all were engaged in the world of policy to one degree or another, and all attempted to contribute to, and strengthen, civil society. In the haste to resistance, however, progress and achievement are now measured by one's contribution to the subversion and undermining of civil society. And, in a rather perverse rendering of political relevance, postmodernists operate from the assumption that terminological obfuscation, epistemological debate, and ontological altercation will yet save the world and make it better for all. That the "Great Epistemological Pause of the 1990s," as Holsti calls it, is bent on saving the world from positivism and that there are those among us who think that the lives of ordinary women and men will be improved because of it should be ringing alarm bells that a self-absorbed intelligentsia lost in obscure specialism no longer has much to say to the world they write so passionately about. We are, in short, in danger of becoming irrelevant and de-inventing ourselves, have become too clever with words and games, and altogether too preoccupied with things unconnected to international relations. As Stephen Chan notes, "There is a retreat into introspection, perhaps into an exemplary 'life as art' syndrome—much beloved by the interviewers and biographers of Foucault." Yet, as Chan also reminds us, the question remains, "exemplary for whom, on behalf of what?"[117] Deconstructed or not, the problems of international relations are still with us and will not go away.

Chapter Two

Contemplating the Crisis in the Crisis of Contemplation

Identity, Perception, and Derision in International Relations

> One must begin somewhere. Perhaps there is no beginning, and the search will lead in circles.
> — Nicholas Greenwood Onuf

> Philosophy forms a circle. It has a beginning, an intermediate factor (for it must somehow make a start), something unproved which is not a result. But the *terminus a quo* of philosophy is simply relative, since it must appear in another terminus as a *terminus ad quem*. Philosophy is a sequence which does not hang in the air; it is something which begins with nothing at all; on the contrary, it circles back into itself.
> — G. W. F. Hegel

Any book that purports to deal with theory or the development of ideas and modes of conceptualization must, as a matter of course, reflect on the past in order to relate how we arrived at the present and where we might go in the future. This seems straightforward enough. Disciplines have intellectual histories, a lineage of intellectual discourse that, if plotted, mapped, and narrated, lead us to the present. If done eloquently, such historiographies provide students with an invaluable source of information. We come to know our genealogical ancestry and how the complex tapestry of ideas, theories, debates, intellectual revolutions, methodologies, discoveries, and findings have come to comprise our discipline, its knowledge, and thematic concerns. As students of such histories we plod through these intellectual bequests attempting not only to understand them but through our own innovations and interpretations to contribute to them. We too become part of the history of ideas, adding to the intellectual lineage of disciplines, theory, and knowledge. This we do all the time as students of economics, history, sociology, medicine, physics, philosophy, chemistry, and countless other disciplinary specializations. There is little new in this. This is the way knowledge, understanding, and wisdom are transmitted across the generations and how, collectively, our respective deliberations and investigations either add to or transform knowledge and advance it.

For many, however, such an evolutionary scheme does not reflect the intellectual machinations of International Relations, either in terms of its disciplinary or theoretical development. Richard Mansbach and Yale Ferguson, for example, imply that International Relations is not yet matured to the level of theory. While endlessly sought after, theory, they argue, remains unrealized, an elusive quest.[1] Similarly, for James Rosenau we suffer amid attempts at pretheorizing.[2] Before him, the eminent Cambridge scholar F. H. Hinsley had reached an even more alarming conclusion, noting that the study of international politics was "still in the state in which biology was before Darwin."[3]

Writing about the history of theory in International Relations would therefore seem to be premature if not oxymoronic; how can one write on something that has not existed historically? As Martin Wight so aptly put it, "Now the difficulties begin: it is easy to recognize political theory, but not so easy to recognize international theory, and one might suspect that historically there was no such thing. There is no obvious tradition of enquiry, or body of theory and speculation, about relations between states, and about the problems of obligations that arise in the absence of government. So the attempt to answer the question, 'What is international theory?' only poses a second one, 'Where is international theory?'"[4]

Such an intellectual heritage few disciplines would envy, for unlike other disciplines, it represents no heritage at all, merely footnotes and scattered references that make international theory hard to discover.[5] There is no interconnected genealogy from which scholars can define a lineage of theory concerned with international politics. Where most social scientists are able to "build on firm ground and strong foundations because these are deeded to them by their disciplines," the theory on which the study of international politics is conducted is fabricated retroactively, reconstructed from scattered writings and references and from traditions of inquiry more concerned with history, law, and philosophy than with relations between nation-states.[6] Historically speaking, this was necessarily the case. Only with the Peace of Westphalia in 1648 did international relations as constituted in the modern European era come into existence.[7] And only since then have international relations been viewed as the consequence of the "reasons of state" rather than "the reason of nature of Grotius or the reason of humanity and religion of Erasmus."[8] Despite our readings of Thucydides and his observations of the Peloponnesian War, ours is a new discipline which lacks longevity and the deeding of concretized methodology and theory.[9] Much of what we know of international politics, diplomacy, and war has thus been "communicated less in the works of political or international theory than in historical writings." In these, as Wight so astutely observed, we can begin to trace a semblage of concerns germane to our subject matter, albeit that they often appear as disparate and marginal reflections. Indeed, it is to these same historical writings that Holsti refers when he writes of a three-centuries-long classical tradition in international thought, not an organized compendium of writings involved in theory construction, but a series of historical reflections that, over the ages, have pondered the central tenets of their times: the causes of war and the conditions of peace, security, and order.[10] This, at least, has provided a commonality of concerns from which we have pieced together our intellectual heritage. But the point remains, whether due to a "kind of recalcitrance of international politics to being theorized about," as Martin Wight insisted, or to a general disinterest in theorizing the international, political philosophy historically has tended to consider most that is important occurs within the nation-state rather than between nation-states.[11] Soliciting the "principles or theories of international politics" from the philosophical discourse of the moderns thus "requires wide reading and considerable discrimination."[12] Save for this, much of our disciplinary heritage is simply hidden or, more correctly, absent.

For better or worse, the concerns of Enlightenment philosophy preferred to focus upon the obligations between monarch, state, and citizenry, reflecting the emancipatory ferment of rationalist thought and science as it struggled against feudalism. More obviously, however, our philosophical heritage reflects the prejudice imposed by the sovereign state upon Enlightenment philosophers, who assumed "the roots of man's being [to] lie in the separate state" and that what was "right and good for him was centered there." The concern with the modern nation-state, of the obligations between it and those within it made international politics a wasteland between states.[13] Enlightenment philosophers were therefore predisposed to a "juristic . . . belief in the sovereign state as the consummation of political experience and activity" which, as Martin Wight argued, had been the quintessential essence of Western political thought since the Renaissance.[14]

Not only did this prejudice circumscribe reflection on things international, but so too did it influence what little reflection there was. The state's bounded and territorializing rationality, for example, particularly its physical embodiment but also its contractual essence of rights and obligations, gave rise to a precontractual understanding of the international sphere. Thomas Hobbes, for instance, assumed society a contractual outcome among moral agents, enforced via the authority of a common law. The international sphere, on the other hand, approached the state of nature where, in the absence of bounded authority and contractual obligations, the "... *condition of Man*" prevails, ... *a condition of Warre of every one against every one* ... "[15] Outside the bounded territorial authority of the nation-state existed nothing but anarchy and the rule of nature. It was what international politics was not, as judged by referents internal to the nation-state, that defined the so-called classical tradition of international theory exemplified in the writings of Hobbes:[16]

> I put it for a general inclination of all mankind, a perpetual and restlesse desire for Power after power, that ceaseth only in Death. And the cause of this, is not always that a man hopes for a more intensive delight, than he has already attained to; or that he cannot be content with a moderate power: but because he cannot assure the power and means to live well, which he hath present, without the acquisition of more. And from hence it is, that Kings, whose power is greatest, turn their endeavours to the assuring it at home by Lawes, or abroad by Wars.[17]

There was no community of states, only the presocial existence of independent agents who, because of the "Competition of Riches, Honour, Command, or other power" would be "enclineth to Contention, Enmity, and War."[18] If any tradition of thought can be said to have guided the study of international politics it is surely this one: the realist tradition or, more ignominiously, the men of "blood and iron and immorality."[19] Of this tradition alone can we trace a lineage of recurrent themes. In Hegel, for example, international politics was a "... maelstrom of external contingency and the inner particularity of passions, private interests and selfish ends, abilities and virtues, vices, force, and wrong. All these," he said, "swirl together, and in their vortex the ethical whole itself, the autonomy of the state, is exposed to contingency."[20] Still later do the writings of Hans Morgenthau reaffirm Hobbes's dictum that "... the state creates morality as well as law and that there is neither morality or law outside the state."[21]

As the "untidy fringe of domestic politics," international politics was easily relegated to the status of poor cousin, attracting the interests of scholars only as a residual exercise.[22] Few were disposed to reflect upon things international, a fact that Olson and Groom blame for making the "period between *Westphalia* and the defeat of Napoleon" an era "characterized neither by peace nor by any systematic theory of international relations."[23] Instead, ceded to us was a philosophical pedigree that tended to reflect "on the future of relations among states either as philosophers of history certain of the direction history would take, or as reformers convinced that there were institutions, methods, and ideas which could ensure that harmony prevailed among nations and whose triumph it was necessary to insure."[24] In such light can we understand the texts of the Abbe Saint-Pierre, later of Kant, Rousseau, and Bentham, and still later of Woodrow Wilson.[25] These were philosophers of future worlds, reformers who sought to transform international organization and thereby banish war. Admirable though such attempts were, this heritage is, regrettably, obscure, ". . . repellent and intractable in form, . . . scattered, unsystematic, and mostly inaccessible."[26] As Stanley Hoffmann noted, apart from the "the recipes of Machiavelli; the marginal comments on the state of nature by Hobbes', Locke's and Rousseau's writings, some pages of Hume; two short and tantalizing essays by Kant, compressed considerations by Hegel, and oversimplified fragments by Marx," Enlightenment thought bequeathed little to contemporary theorists of international relations.[27]

In large measure, philosophy has refused to exist outside the nation-state. By definition the nation-state has tended to represent the ethical whole, a territorial space where the trade of philosophical reflection and moral debate could be plied. Outside this ethical whole, however, was an amoral vortex, a nonspace where philosophy had no meaning and could not exist.[28] This, of course, was an extension of the Hellenic tradition. Cicero, for example, argued that the interests of the *polis* and of those under its jurisdiction were above morality; Thucydides, that the "strong do what they have the power to do and the weak accept what they have to accept"; and Thrasymachus, "that justice or right is simply what is in the interest of the stronger party."[29] Beyond the bounds of the state existed only the particularity of state interests where government was "a matter of particular wisdom, not of universal Providence."[30] In comparison to other social sciences, our inheritance displays an etiology situated more in the speculative realm of what-ought-to-be, as Hegel put it, an endless speculative project "since its actuality depends on different wills each of which is sovereign."[31] Morgenthau was inclined to agree, noting that men have generally "dealt with international politics on one of three levels, all alien to theory: history, reform, or pragmatic manipulation. . . . That is to say, they have endeavoured to detect the facts and meaning of international politics through the knowledge of the past; or they have tried to devise a pattern of international politics more in keeping with an abstract ideal than the empirical one; or they have sought to meet the day-by-day issues of international politics by trial and error."[32] Consequently, from Hobbes to Rousseau and from Kant to Bentham, there were few systematic attempts at explaining and understanding the nature of international politics. In its place, observation, and description were offered as poor substitutes for explanation, and the bestowal of a theory of human nature and the will to power was hardly a sufficient basis for the construction of theory concerned with an increasingly complex set of global phenomena.

Thus it is that international political theory, if by that we mean the systematic study of international relations, is a relatively recent development.[33] Only in the twentieth century can we begin to observe anything like a tradition of scholarship concerned with analyzing interstate relationships and developing analytical and theoretical apparatus to explain these. Yet it is not apparent that even our most recent past has served us well. While we now talk of a discipline of International Relations, for example, we often do so euphemistically. As scholars we are more likely to be found in departments of political science, history, or law. And the quest for theory, at least paradigmatic theory of the Kuhnian type, despite decades of earnest investigation, remains elusive.[34] While histories of the theories of international politics have been constructed, traditions invented, the pages of political theory and philosophy reread duly noting references to things international, to war, and to the reason of state and diplomacy, we still have no Darwin, Durkheim, Smith, no Plato nor Aristotle upon whom to build theoretical foundations with certitude.[35] Try as we may, we can never make the parable of Rousseau's Stag Hunt, or the Kantian idealism of a single human republic tailored on Dante's *imperium mundi* the foundational stuff of international political theory.[36] Save for a few disparate treatises, the poverty of our intellectual heritage makes ours the saddest of disciplines.[37]

The Deeding of Strong Foundations?

In many respects, this rather incongruous, dissymmetric ancestry prefigured recurrent problems the discipline of International Relations and its theory would experience. Martin Wight, for instance, argued that despite intellectual advances, international theory continued to be marked "not only by paucity but also by intellectual and moral poverty." The discipline it seemed was forever condemned to intellectual incertitude over its origins, role, and intellectual concerns.[38] In fact, debate over the founding of the very first chair of International Relations in 1919 reigned as late as 1935, illustrative of the lack of intellectual discipline prevalent even throughout the interwar years. Sir Alfred Zimmern, for example, then Chair of International Relations at Oxford, argued against a separate subject and instead urged a world orientation of sociology, politics, and history.[39] As to what constituted the subject matter of international studies, Zimmern advised ecumenically that "the indispensable nucleus of the subject was contained in political science, political economy, international law, geography, history, sociology and political and moral philosophy!"[40] Despite a touch of sarcasm, Zimmern's comments captured not only how tenuous were the discipline's intellectual foundations, but foreshadowed how polymorphic its subsequent development would be. Indeed, for the greater part of its history the study of international relations remained subsumed among the disciplines of history and law, where the history of international relations and the study of legal norms which attempted to order these relations obviated inquiry into their politics.[41] As a political phenomenon, foreign policy was only democratized in the twentieth century. Only then did diplomatic issues finally move "from the calculations of the few to the passions of the many." What had previously been the "sport of kings, or the preserve of cabinets—the last refuge of secrecy, the last domain of largely hereditary castes of diplomats"—became debated increasingly in the public domain and thus amenable to analysis in the academic one.[42] No longer was the phenomenon of war a discrete matter between combatants in far-off lands. The First and Second World Wars, the advent of total war and the deaths of untold millions brought foreign policy, diplomacy, and the politics of interstate relations into the homes of average citizens. International relations were thus politicized and an intellectual space made for their analysis.

It was amid such calamities that E. H. Carr and Hans Morgenthau first crafted their writings.[43] Both were responding to the travesty of events in Europe and elsewhere, and both set about the construction of theoretical models not only to explain the calamity that had befallen the world but also to instruct how to avoid its repetition. Where Carr argued the case for avoiding the excesses of either idealist or realist thought, preferring to see these two traditions as contentious but inseparable, Morgenthau displayed a tendency toward realist thought and empiricist methodologies.[44] The latter reflected not only Morgenthau's zest to reform, educate, and "erect an empirical science opposed to the utopias of the international lawyers," but also the nature of the subject matter and, not least, the country in which these formulations were most obviously attempted, the United States. International Relations is, after all, "an American Social Science" as Hoffmann so elegantly told us, "born and raised in America."[45] Yet it was born and raised not so much from intellectual deeds as from circumstance and need. The role the United States played in global affairs after 1945 and the growth of the discipline of International Relations are therefore inseparable events.[46] America's new-found superpower status and role as world policeman made ripe the conditions for the development of a policy science that would analyze, advise, and guide the United States in its dealings with foreign governments. Governmental patronage of the discipline was therefore ensured. And although it would be wrong to see the discipline of International Relations as the handmaiden of the State Department, so too would it be wrong to discount the influence that the allure of power held over scholars. Being policy relevant and having the ear of those who make the foreign policy of the United States, no matter how implicit or overt, inevitably affected the intellectual agendas and theoretical endeavors of scholars and the character of the "American" discipline. Theoretical development in International Relations was therefore drawn toward empirical analysis, reflecting the ease with which empirical theory could inform the conundrums of foreign policy, military preparedness, nuclear proliferation, and strategic planning. This, combined with the postwar reaction to the ideological excesses of fascism and communism, made empirical theory attractive in that its purported neutrality supposedly offered a means of escaping dogmatism in the pursuit of knowledge. Whatever the case, empirical theory became the foundation stone on which international political theory would be constructed. For Hoffmann this seemed only natural since ". . . the contrast between the precepts of law and the realities of politics was sufficiently greater in the international realm than in the domestic realm, to make one want to shift from the normative to the empirical."[47] On this perspective, Morgenthau easily defined the parameters of our discipline, noting that we must consider "the national interest defined in terms of power, the precarious uncertainty of the international balance of power, the weakness of international morality, the decentralized character of international law, the deceptiveness of ideologies, the inner contradictions of international organization, the democratic control of foreign policy, the requirements of diplomacy, the problem of war."[48] It was these "phenomena and problems of international politics" that Morgenthau insisted "theory must take account."[49]

From these beginnings, however, we cannot pronounce a discipline exuding theoretical certitude or, indeed, a consensus over its role, purpose, and very existence. There is, as Paul Keal notes, increasing "dispute about how international relations should be interpreted and understood."[50] Incertitude in our ways of knowing and doing international political theory, of what is to be studied and how, is ever more prevalent. And as if foretold in the story recounted above, the debate over empiricism and positivism and the nature, role, and purpose of the discipline now consumes much intellectual energy. Rather than strong foundations and the building of a robust stock of theoretical knowledge, international theory looks to be cracking at the edges, its foundations crumbling amid the onslaught of perspectivism and epistemological debate.

Wither the Foundations

The current machinations in international political theory are in marked contrast to only a few decades previous when James Rosenau, for example, could write of a science of international relations: "As a focus of study, the nation-state is no different from the atom or the single cell organism. Its patterns of behaviour, idiosyncratic traits, and internal structure are as amenable to the process of formulating and testing hypotheses as are the characteristics of the electron or the molecule."[51] Rosenau reflected no more than conventional wisdom prevalent since the founding of the discipline. Sir Alfred Zimmern, for example, had seen in political science the means to good scholarship contiguous with precision and proof. "That politics can be studied in Universities," he wrote, "in as scientific a spirit as any other subject of study, whether human or natural, is a proposition which does not admit of discussion in a University such as Oxford, which has been a home of such studies since the days of Occam in the thirteenth century."[52]

The scientific method, under the auspices of the behaviorist revolution and falsificationist techniques, would do for International Relations what they had for the natural sciences: provide certainty, foundations, and the basis on which to build cumulative knowledge. In science lay certainty and clarity, so much so that Zimmern in his inaugural lecture at Oxford in February, 1931, spoke of "a Chair for the preaching of International Relations" to correct an age exceptionally stupid in character.[53] Rigor in our scholarship coupled with the precision of science would provide the basis for analysis, diagnosis, and prescription. Much as scientists had found a cure for polio and identified the virus that caused tuberculosis, social scientists too might identify the causes of societal afflictions like poverty, delinquency, or the causes of war. Such ambition, though admirable, inspired an outpouring of premature theoretical formulation. More conspicuously, it reified science in the discipline, unleashing a "desire to calculate the incalculable" with ever more data sets and "objective" methodologies.[54]

In the end, however, science too has proved less than adequate as a panacea to the problem of war and countless other social phenomena.[55] And like so many traditions before it, not only the sanctum of science, empirical theory, and positivism, but also the metatheoretical traditions of rationalism and Enlightenment thinking are now also being challenged. The new reflectivist approaches, for example, along with deconstructivist methodologies, intertextual readings, and interpretivist scholars, all disparage the Enlightenment project and champion interdisciplinary travels and theoretical perspectivism.[56] Arguably, this has nurtured a "more complex theoretical conspectus than has previously prevailed," one increasingly aware of the economic, technological, and environmental dimensions in international politics as well as a more sophisticated theoretical discourse cognizant of its own subjective dimensions and limitations.[57] Greater theoretical complexity, however, has not been accompanied by increased theoretical clarity. Ideas and approaches have not been distilled so much as they have multiplied, leading to theoretical fragmentation if not outright confusion. International theory now resembles a complicated montage that houses a plethora of competing research agendas, academic interests, theories, methodologies, and projects under the generic rubric of International Relations, or, still more eclectically, International Studies. We seem to be a little bit of everything, but nothing in particular. Everything these days appears to be globalized: the environment, the economy, trade, investment, even such mundane things as television programs, fashion, and consumer products. We "are engaged in international studies," remarks James Rosenau, "when the world is no longer organized along international lines," but instead is transnationalized, no longer state-centered.[58]

At base, these arguments derive from what are perceived to be new realities that change systemically the "location of political [and economic] life." They represent a crisis of sovereignty where "accounts of political community formalized in the principle of state sovereignty are being rearticulated in response to profound structural transformations on a global scale."[59] Whether it be the proliferation of "international agencies and transnational organizations," the "increasingly complex political division of labor that cuts across national boundaries and blurs the dividing line between foreign policy and domestic politics," or the effects of technology, economic interdependence, and global production and markets, all these "call into question the traditional understanding of state sovereignty." What theorists might be discovering, of course, is a recognition that the European state system is contingent, fluid, and prone to change, and that absolute sovereignty was only ever a transitory phenomenon that hardly existed prior to the Renaissance and seems to be diminishing after it. Forms of political-territorial organization change, new forms emerge, where multiple sovereignties crisscross over space and loyalties to produce what Hedley Bull long ago described as a New Mediaevalism.[60] Consequently, as Joseph Camilleri observes, it is not simply the "size of political entities or even the demarcation of their boundaries" that is important any longer, but that the very meaning of boundaries and of political domain makes illusionary the notion of state sovereignty, compelling us to abandon our traditional theoretical categories and develop new ones.[61] The whole gambit of our enterprise, of what is to be studied and how, what theory should target for explanation and understanding, indeed what type of theory is appropriate has become a veritable conundrum of competing interpretations and intransigent ideological battles.[62]

This sense of rupture is perhaps best captured by Kalevi Holsti's oft-quoted statement that "in the past decade, the three-centuries-long intellectual consensus which organized philosophical speculation, guided empirical research, and provided at least hypothetical answers to the critical questions about international politics has broken down."[63] These days we can but lament the loss of commonality in our collective deliberations, a sense that our project is one and defined by a concern for the causes of war and an investigation into the conditions of peace, security, and order. Instead, pessimism, or at least anxiety, seems to color the discipline, with leading theorists pronouncing that international theory is in a state of disarray, that the discipline is divided and prone to the vestiges of parochialism.[64] Fred Halliday, for example, describes international political theory as beset by a "pervasive sense of entropy, and even of crisis."[65] For Mark Hoffman, the discipline is at a major crossroads, caught within an intellectual malaise such that there is no "longer any clear sense of what the discipline is about, what its core concepts are, what its methodology should be, what issues and central questions it should be addressing."[66] Ashley, Walker, and Campbell tend to agree, seeing previously marginalized voices and intellectual dissidents fragmenting the hitherto dominant narratives of realism.[67] The resulting metatheoretical ferment has forced international political theory into a self-imposed epistemological critique which, for James Der Derian, questions the very language, concepts, methods, and history that have governed the tradition of thought in the field. In fact, notes Der

Derian, "International Relations is facing a variety of philosophical insurgencies" with most of them questioning the discipline's existing foundations and theory, and all of them responding to the monologue of tradition by revalorizing a dialogical approach.[68] For Yosef Lapid, this confirms his "lingering suspicion that something is still radically wrong with international theory."[69] The theory question, as Lapid puts it, is again resonating throughout the discipline, marking perhaps the greatest interlocution of all the great debates the discipline has yet experienced. For Ferguson and Mansbach, however, this has made for unprecedented disarray in the theories of international relations. As they sardonically note, "Like the walls that kept people apart, those separating schools of thought are also tumbling down, but, as a result, there may today be less anarchy in world politics than in theories about it."[70]

Symptomatic of this metatheoretical flux is the "lack of an agreed core to the subject." Unlike previous theoretical debates, the Third Debate lacks a central theoretical matrix.[71] This is not a battle over levels of analysis, contending actors, or different methodological and theoretical paradigms. Rather, "current developments in international theory constitute a shift of a much greater order and magnitude" than observed in the previous four decades, one that might be characterized as the "search for thinking space," to paraphrase Foucault.[72] As George and Campbell note, this "new dissent . . . [is] concerned with the discourse of international relations, supplementing concern about the subjects of international relations with a focus on the discourse of those subjects that makes them (and not others) historically possible."[73] The classical consensus which concerned itself with developing theory to explain the conditions of war, peace, security, and order is thus supplanted. As Scott Burchill explains, "there is now an increasingly large number of theorists who recognize a second category of theory which reflects upon the very process of theorizing." For Burchill, these theorists "believe we should be just as concerned with how we approach the study of world politics as we are with explaining events, issues, and behaviour of actors in the global system."[74]

Such concerns reflect a general disquiet throughout the social sciences, a "growing sense that something is wrong with the way in which the relevant issues and options are posed" and a desire to change the "categorical structure and patterns within which we think and act."[75] For Lapid, this presupposes an excursion into an intellectual labyrinth, a protracted period of metatheoretical anxiety as students of International Relations examine critically their modes of theory construction and "consider afresh the problem of how to picture world society."[76] Questions of theory and methodology, particularly epistemological and ontological debates, have thus found a new "prominence . . . in the discipline's heartland, the United States."[77] As Higgott notes, this has reopened "the speculative nature of international relations as a discipline in which our tools of trade—concepts such as balance of power, state-as-actor, sovereignty, national interest, security and so on—are not treated as givens and asserted but seen . . . as 'essentially contested concepts' in need of continual redefinition, contextual location and explanation."[78]

Higgott, however, fails to appreciate the depth of rupture; it is not merely that structures and processes have been problematized and exposed to continual redefinition, but that those knowledge systems which informed such definitions and explanations in the first place are now themselves contested. Indeed, for Hoffman, it is not simply "reinterpretation but a reinscription of what 'theory' is all about" that is needed. Theory, its function and purpose, as well as the process of theorizing are thus now exposed to critical interrogation and reinterpretation.[79]

Consequently, international political theory is now a fundamentally contested domain, where, says Michael Banks, it is naive to discuss international relations on the basis of the facts.[80] The tradition of inquiry that answered Gabriel Almond's plea for scholarly involvement through detachment, "a passionate belief that the world . . . [could] be improved through dispassionate enquiry," is now challenged via the importation of deconstructionism and semeiology into International Relations. Where knowledge systems were once considered benign investigative tools, now they are thought to be instruments of power; specific rationalities reified into what Rorty has called privileged representations.[81] Theory construction and the discipline have lost their innocence, and theory itself, not what it purports to explain, has become the battleground. In the process, everything previous, whether accumulated facts, learned wisdoms, inculcated knowledge, traditions of inquiry, schools of thought, or various methodologies, are rendered problematic. For postmodernists, such traditions and facts are merely derivative of particular modes of thinking which are now themselves contested. The hope for progress in theory building has thus given way to a feeling of retrogression. Olson and Onuf, for example, argue that the last fifteen years of the discipline and its theory has betrayed an air of uncertainty and slippage, and its overall development antithetic to a series of logical steps leading to greater discoveries and insights.[82] Grand theoretic traditions, long the aspirant of those in the discipline, appear to be withering. Increasingly, current wisdom seems to be toward contextuality where "a variety of religions, cultures, moral and ethical systems and histories ensures that there can be no universal view of the main issues of international relations."[83] Apparently, the world looks sufficiently different from, "say, Calcutta than it does from Moscow, Kabul, Tehran or Kansas" so that "people in different countries will have contrasting views of what the most important issues are, and of how these are to be dealt with."[84] Metanarratives, universal theory, as well as international theory, look to be doomed to the proclivities of individuation among countries and peoples. In fact, this is the explicit intention of the "post-structuralist practices of genealogy, deconstruction and intertextualism," which seek "to disturb, disrupt and challenge the universalist and rationalist claims and conventions, the 'natural truths,' the 'logocentrism' of existing schools of thought in international relations."[85] The result, celebrated by some, is a theoretical anarchy and relativism which, for those so disposed to a Cartesian anxiety, symbolizes the death of objectivity, rationality, and the eclipse of hope in discovering truth.

International Relations is thus in a period of metamorphosis, an evolution of sorts in which disciplinary boundaries are being questioned and redefined, our object(s) of study reanalyzed and challenged, and our modes of theory construction subjected to critical reflection. The point at which the study of international politics begins and ends is ever more blurred; what constitutes the appropriate object(s) of study—the nation-state, the transnational corporation, or some other actors or combinations therein—is ever more contentious. How, for example, do we relate the growth in interdependence, the cobweb-like interlocking of interstate relations through global finance capital, the globalization of production techniques and consumption patterns, to our traditional concerns with relations between nation-states, to the security problematic and war making? Are these questions any longer worthy of a central analytical focus in the discipline? Indeed, if we accept that the discipline of International Relations is now a combinatorial regime of empiricists, practitioners, and theorists who, as James Richardson notes, have research interests that range from "the origins of the modern state system to threats to the survival of *any* social and political system, from nuclear strategies to global inequalities, from close analysis of decision-making to the most general concerns of the philosophy of science," how, then, can the term *discipline* be "anything more than honorific?"[86] Like the apocryphal "Lernean Hydra: each time one conceptual head is lopped off, another two appear in its place," expanding exponentially the number of research agendas and issues that fall under the gambit of International Relations.[87] And beyond the immediate concerns of crumbling disciplinary boundaries, multiplying research agendas, and intellectual perspectivism, international theorists are also confronted by the pervasive sense of profound transformation in those structures and processes we have traditionally studied. The world has changed, we are told, and changed fundamentally. For James Rosenau, we struggle intellectually under the "pervasive presence of transformations in global life" such that "international politics" and "international relations" are obsolete terms to describe a world that is now beyond the nation-state and beyond modernity. And this, argues Rosenau, compels us to look toward the idiom of the *post*:

> If the social sciences are now marked by analyses of postcapitalist society, postcivilized era, postcollectivist politics, posteconomic society, posthistoric man, postideological society, postliberal era, postliterature culture, postmarket society, post-Marxists, postmaterialist value system, postmaturity economy, postmodernism, postorganization society, post-Christian era, postscarcity society, postsocialist society, posttraditional society, and postwelfare society, as well as postindustrial society, surely it follows that profound changes in world affairs can be regarded as constituting postinternational politics.[88]

"All that is solid melts into air," and all that international theorists once knew is no more.[89] For Rosenau, everything has changed except our way of thinking. "Much of what passes for theory in international relations today," he writes, "was designed for an era now passing into oblivion."[90] "Postinternational politics," it seems, has made for multiple realities that "coexist, collide, and interpenetrate."[91] The nation-state now exists as one among many transnational actors, "from multinational corporations to professional societies to international organizations to terrorists."[92] International relations have become a tangled muddle of numerous phenomena: the bipolar world, a multipolar world; power, a multifarious phenomenon no longer confined to the barrel of a gun; and sovereignty, an increasingly antiquated phenomenon no longer impervious to the whims of international capital or the taste cultures of global consumerism that sweep the globe via electronic images.

In a sense, then, these are the problems of international relations, problems that cause us consternation about where to begin our project, where to end it, how to understand, what tools to employ, what actors to focus upon, how to construct theory, what type of theory (universal, micro-specific, contextual, mesolevel, constructivist or positivist), what role and purpose for theory, how to represent multiple realities and systemic change, whether to simplify or complicate, to particularize or generalize. Amid such concerns theorists of international relations experience a crisis of contemplation, an anxiety over their theoretical tools of analysis and their ability to represent adequately increasingly complex global phenomena. But more than this, the project of theoretical endeavor is itself now contested. The so-called interpretivist turn and the challenge of postmodernism thus confronts International Relations with philosophical insurrections like none it has ever before seen. Confronting this challenge critically, understanding the battle lines of contention and the language of deconstruction is therefore the last line of defense save for the surrender of the discipline and theory to those who would see them dismantled.

Chapter Three
Sentinels of Dissidence
A Typology of Postmodern Theory

> The danger in which stands the "holy heart of the peoples" of the West is not that of a decline, but instead that we, ourselves bewildered, *yield ourselves to the will of modernity* and drive it on.
> Martin Heidegger

> We must recognize that words and things have come unstuck.
> John O'Neill

> That we disavow reflection is positivism.
> Jurgen Habermas

Introduction

Despite its proliferation throughout the social sciences and humanities in the past few decades, postmodernism remains a curious lexeme of essentially contested concepts, disparate ideas, obtuse meanings, and political agendas. Postmodernist writings can only be described as an intellectual maelstrom, and the postmodernist movement a diverse collection of followers who are neither united in intent, similar in focus or method, nor canonized in terms of theoretical precision. The nomenclature is confusing, fluid, and imprecise; the boundaries of conventional scholarship, theory, and understanding, blurred and porous. Debates about theory have given way to metatheory, metaphysics, and metahistory, leading to intellectual ruptures not perhaps seen since the Renaissance itself. Few, it seems, know what to make of the idioms and idiolects of the *post*, which, at various junctures, transpose from postmodernism to poststructuralism, postpositivism, postindustrialism, postphilosophy, post-Marxism, or *posthistoire*—to name but a few. Literature, art, aesthetics, politics, and the advent of discourse and dialogism are again the celebrated emissaries of a new means to knowledge and understanding. At the end of the millennium, we find ourselves engaged in a project that, depending on one's position, threatens either ruination or renewal.

This chapter attempts an appraisal of postmodern theory by exploring critically its various motifs and thematic features. It does so out of a desire to make sense of postmodernism and, more generally, to infer which of its many strands and perspectives might prove useful to International Relations. To this end, the chapter is organized into two main sections. The first attempts to situate and make sense of the phenomena of postmodernism by locating contextually its relationship to modernity. I do this by offering two interpretive discussions of the leitmotifs of postmodernism as popularly understood: postmodernism as negation and postmodernism as epochal change. These discussions provide a brief introduction to the aims, issues, and concerns of postmodernists and illustrates the scope of the postmodernist project. The second section then develops a taxonomic/classificatory system to tease out the contrasting epistemic motifs evident among postmodernists. These are then assessed critically and some tentative conclusions drawn as to which type(s) of postmodernism might prove germane for theoretical endeavor in International Relations.[1]

On Definitions, Discourse, and Debate

Despite the devout "hopes of many cynics, the allure of post-modernism" remains undiminished and the "salon lizards of theory," as John Bowers describes them, "are yet to move *en masse* to any newer, more attractive fad."[2] The problem thus presents itself of what to make of these new idioms, words, thought habits, theories, and of the new scholarship? How do we understand it, indeed can it be understood? The answers are by no means uniform. Charles Newman, for example, sees postmodernism as a kind of incomplete nonidea that exists neither as a "canon of writers, nor a body of criticism."[3] Harry Levin, by contrast, abjures postmodernism for its anti-intellectualism while Irving Howe thinks it a mass cultural phenomenon "impatient with mind." For John Gardner, on the other hand, it represents a new mode of hyperintellectualism.[4] As to what constitutes the precise essence of the postmodern, few can agree. As Dick Hebdige notes, "It becomes more and more difficult . . . to specify exactly what it is that 'postmodernism' is supposed to refer to as the term gets stretched in all directions across different debates, different disciplinary and discursive boundaries, as different factions seek to make it their own, using it to designate a plethora of incommensurable objects, tendencies, emergencies."[5]

While the postmodern lexeme is all about us, the object of classroom conversations, graduate papers, increasing numbers of dissertations, conference proceedings, and book titles, still it remains clouded in mystique and intellectually opaque. Offering a stipulative definition of postmodernism or attempting to study it objectively might thus prove more fruitless than productive.[6] For unlike intellectual movements before it, postmodernism is less doctrine, creed, or canon than it is millennial anxiety and a sense of change in the structure of feeling. Postmodernism is thus best viewed not as a statement of principles, methodological formula, or a grand theory so much as a cathartic apostasy, a renunciation of faith in modernism, rationality, science, technology, and the philosophy of presence (representation).[7] In its most immediate form postmodernism might thus be thought of as antimodernist, rejecting the tradition of Enlightenment thought but not necessarily the emancipatory rationale that informed it. Indeed, there is in postmodern writings a feeling of liberation, a celebration of renewal, a sense that boundaries everywhere are being transgressed, new social mores established, new political identities forged, and new histories in the making. This might account for the intellectual muddle and elasticity of the concept itself, where postmodernism signifies an intellectual premonition of imminent change or impending closure. So too might this explain why postmodern writings have been adopted in such disparate milieus, connoting the assemblage of stylistic expressions in architecture, for example, or the landscape of political-economic changes in the nature of production and consumption; the mediascape of images comprising the simulacra; the crisis of representation and the allegoric tendency toward sign and symbol; the transformation of time-space dimensions with the revolutions in communications and transportations; the deconstruction of text and subject and the rise of intertextualism and intersubjectivity; or the repudiation of modernist philosophy accused of being atonal, logocentric, instrumentalist, and rationalist. Thus might we conceive of postmodernism not as a theory or theories but, as Hebdige argues, "a space, a 'condition' . . . where competing intentions, definitions, and effects, diverse social and intellectual tendencies and lines of force converge and clash."[8] Postmodernism might thus be little more than a nonspace without meaning, a word that captures this sense of rupture and disjuncture, but whose parameters it cannot identify. Attempting to define or elucidate postmodernism might, then, be an activity presaged to failure.

But the question remains: what to make of postmodernism; how to understand it; what might it do to theory, knowledge, and scholarship? Despite the inherent fussiness of the concept itself, there are, I would suggest, two dominant motifs in postmodernist writings. These might be called negation or resistance through intellectual disturbance, and the notion of millennial anxiety through conceptions of epochal change.

Postmodern Theory as Resistance and Disturbance

Postmodern theory is not complacent. Disturbance, disruption, reinscription, and the penchant to rethink knowledge are common to its sense of self. This might be why so few disciplines since the 1970s have been untouched by the temerity of postmodernist writings and readings. Philosophy, politics, music, film, sociology, geography, literary criticism, development studies, as well as International Relations, all display postmodernist intrusion.[9] Infiltration and dissonance of seemingly unrelated debates and research areas bear witness to its disparate adaptation and adoption. Indeed, this is one of its unique features, its ability to be understood concurrently as a means of reading texts, a method for theoretical deconstruction, a form of political-economy, a variant of feminist writings, an epitaph to modernism, a post-avant-garde, postexpressionist form of aesthetics, or a new hyperconsumer culture riven by image.[10] By their very nature, postmodern writings display a predilection for eclecticism, tending to divaricate into numerous, and often unrelated, subject areas. But this has not been a process of melding into disparate intellectual milieus. Far from attempting to colonize existing territories, postmodernists have sought to "interrogate" and "disrupt" them. The underlying ideological matrix of postmodernism thus reveals its political strategy, an attempt to disturb the substructural basis on which modernist knowledge and boundaries are built. The greatest threat to modernist narratives and knowledge thus comes not from assaults on its epistemological edifice, but when its medium of communication, its assumption of intersubjective communicative rationality, and its rules of rationalist engagement are circumvented via deliberate confusion, imprecision, and textual chicanery. For modernists, the threat of postmodern discourse lies in its stepping outside the dictates of rationalism and its refusal to be rational, precise, and commensurate. By design, postmodern writings are thus cryptic in form, enigmatic and amorphous, a strategy that not only disrupts modernist narratives through language deracination, but insulates the postmodern conduit from external assault. As Donald Kuspit notes, postmodernists are protected by mystique, their writings rhapsodic, elusive, exhilarating, and used with license. Like a panacea, postmodernist literature is rich with linguistic parody, irony, meaning, and insight.[11] By admitting only to fecundity in dimensions, postmodern writings shelter from critique, disguise their place of origin and essential meaning, and make themselves aeolian by their transient discursiveness. The very word *postmodern*, for example, has become a "floating signifier," able to penetrate all facets of social theory by virtue of its imprecise dimensions and ability to assume innumerable meanings dependent upon the context in which it is employed. Postmodern discourse might thus be little more than textual and intellectual irreverence in an attempt to be a spanner in the works of modernity. Andreas Huyssen, for example, argues, less than kindly, that the use of eclecticism is a thinly disguised facade that spares postmodern theory the embarrassment of revealing its theoretical impression and meaningless nature. For Huyssen, postmodernism is little more than an "aesthetic simulacrum: facile eclecticism combined with aesthetic amnesia and delusions of grandeur."[12]

Such textual and intellectual sabotage, however, serve their purpose, perplexing modernists who often seem bereft of responses to it. Traditional theorists like Christopher Norris or Alex Callinicos, for instance, display bewilderment at the ethereality, theoretical brevity, and reluctance of postmodernists to enunciate their epistemic motif beyond the errant practices of deconstruction.[13] Above all they are disenchanted at the unwillingness of postmodernists to abide by established rules for intellectual engagement: how does one rationally assess postmodern theory when postmodernists eschew all references to rationalist discourse? But they miss the point. Confusion, dissonance, and disruption are the point of postmodern discourse.

Postmodernism can thus be understood as political resistance rather than theoretical innovation; a means of stepping outside the established practices of (Western) scholarship and infusing it with critical insight. The incorporeal nature of language destabilization, for example, allows postmodernists to attack the rigidities of modernist discourse, particularly the sanctums of logic and reason, and escape the "victimization" which they argue has led to their "exile," "marginalization," and "disempowerment." Ethereality therefore becomes a political act of nonconformity, and textual deconstruction a way of "undoing" and challenging the power hierarchy of modernist theory that presupposes conformity in method, logic, knowledge, and interpretation.

One of the primary objectives of much postmodernist scholarship thus concerns itself with a form of deconstructive pluralism, deliberately designed to destabilize, or at least to challenge, the system(s) of knowledge premised upon Western rationalism and derived from the Enlightenment. Where the project of modern political theory might be said to concern itself with the good society, to inventing rules, norms, standards, and defining objectives on the basis of some master blueprint or universal grand strategy, postmodern theory might be said to be its arch rival, committed to seeing an end to this (modernist) project. Yet the alternatives it offers are all but invisible, especially when its aetiological basis is hidden beneath a complicated developmental historiography punctuated only by a disposition toward continental philosophy (in particular, French poststructuralist theory). Instead, postmodernists prefer the ether of the unspecified to the vexed realities of inscribed practices, disciplinary specialization, or concision in method and technique, and appeal to an as-yet-unspecified set of other criteria as the appropriate vehicles for understanding postmodern theory. Consequently, postmodernism continues to suffer from ill-defined parameters that betray an incomplete conception of itself and an inclination to self-contradiction, discursiveness, irreverence, and complicated forms of expression and self-explanation.[14]

On this reading, postmodern theory displays a central matrix remarkably simplistic and myopic in its theoretical and practical intent: the theoretical intent of negation, and the practical intent of resistance. The postmodernist project, for example, is readily defined by its rehearsal of the litany of horrors and injustices carried out in the modernist era. Jim George, for instance, argues that postmodern theory is able to connect "the nightmarish dimensions of the Enlightenment dream" with the rise of the rational subject and the experiences of Hiroshima and Auschwitz. "The point," he notes, "is that a celebration of the age of rational science and modern society cannot simply be disconnected from the weapons of mass slaughter or the techniques of genocide": the "language and logic of liberty and emancipation," cannot be "detached from the terror waged in their names."[15] In this guise, postmodernism is understood as a deconstructive practice: "a textual activity, a putting-into-question of the root metaphysical prejudice which posits self-identical concepts outside and above the disseminating play of language."[16] The postmodernist project becomes an exercise in linguistic relativism through deconstruction, an attempt to tear apart and negate modernity and demonstrate the centrality of language in the construction of knowledge and truth. We can see this, for example, in the derisive language employed by postmodernists, who aim to repudiate oppositional and relational thinking, deconstruct logocentric practices, engage in transformative ontologies, disparage master narratives, make for a polyvocal understanding, revalorize dialogical approaches, map new taste cultures, present counter hegemonic views, and transfigure monological interpretations. This is a theoretical-textual process of "undoing," and a political process of resisting modernist practices, modernist theory, values, and interpretations.[17] Theory-knowledge, the precepts of truth, right and wrong, just and unjust, and other "logocentric" combinations along with "master narratives" premised upon rationalist argument are not merely questioned but delegitimized. This is not simply an attack upon discrete theories waged from an alternative theoretical standpoint, but a deconstructive effort to undo the activity of Enlightenment theory and knowledge. In this way, postmodernists can disparage modernist rationalism as instrumentalist, dismiss epistemology as foundationalist, and reject ontology as positivist. As the cherished centerpieces of Enlightenment thought and Western rationalism, these critical-intellectual tools are summarily dismissed as no longer useful and no longer legitimate.

One of the central theoretical matrices of the postmodernist project, then, is a repudiation of organonist thought systems: an attempt to deconstruct inscribed means of reasoning and logic indicative of Western philosophy. This, undoubtedly, is what makes postmodernists so conspicuous and their project both tenacious and tenuous. For while postmodernists are patently antimodernist, their very rationality and purpose is prescribed by the logic of modernity, whether as an alternative to it or a reaction against it. Thus, the antilogic on which postmodern theory is founded can itself be seen as the binary opposite logic of modernity, entrapping postmodernists within modernist logic if only because of their own antilogocentrism. This makes postmodern theory vulnerable not only to criticism that it is unable to escape the very logic it chastises, but also because those criticisms it levels against modernist discourse invariably repudiate postmodern theory too. As Kate Manzo observes, "Even the most radically critical discourse easily slips into the form, the logic, and the implicit postulations of precisely what it seeks to contest, for it can never step completely outside of a heritage from which it must borrow its tools—its history, its language—in an attempt to destroy that heritage itself."[18]

Postmodern Theory as Epochal Change

While we often think of the postmodern project as largely a deconstructive effort inspired by Continental theorists like Jacques Derrida, or a project of resistance to the "oppressive" discourses of modernity as with Foucault, postmodernism as a periodizing category and the theories it engenders are not so easily classified. What of those who claim the arrival of a postmodern era and a different set of sensibilities? Things are surely changing; we no longer inhabit an era understood as simply modernist, but one where hyperactivity in communications, transportations, trade, and electronic images presupposes a new set of political, social, economic, and transnational realities.[19] "That we live in postmodern times," notes Wendy Brown, "is nearly inarguable," albeit that there is no agreement "about the configuration of this condition, its most striking marker, implications, and portents."[20]

Recent history, of course, displays a strong proclivity for such conclusions. The eminent historian, Arnold Toynbee, for example, toward the end of the Second World War, concluded his magnum opus, *A Study of World History,* by noting that "the world had just entered the last phase of Western history—the 'post-modern' era, an age that would be marked by anxiety and despair."[21] This sense of millennial anxiety, of absolute historical breakage and rupture, of new ages and new associations have been endemic themes in the social sciences and humanities, reflecting, perhaps, not only a fascination with change, science, technology, and the speed of innovation, but a sense of new horizons as conceptions of locality and space have been obliterated with interplanetary travel, jet-setting tourists, indeed of interstate commuters who jet from London to Brussels to work and home again in time for dinner. Dazzled by such transformations, it is easy to speculate that we have entered a new historical phase, or at the very least that we are approaching the "end of [modern] history."[22] In the last few decades of the twentieth century, it has thus become common parlance to speak the language of "new," "changed," "transformed," or "reordered" realities. The world is now understood to be composed of new economic, political, and spatial configurations. Various authors write of the restructuring of global industry, the rise of transnational finance capital, the new international division of labor, the new international economic disorder, the end of Pax Americana and the rise of Pax Nipponica, the emergence of global civil society and the reordering of world capitalism.[23] "Technological developments," claims David Elkins, "have shifted the balance away from purely territorial political forms to a greater role for non-territorial organizations and identities." These, he argues, constitute a new logic, one that "reveals a future that is already happening," even though the discussion of which is hindered by "a vocabulary appropriate to the era now ending rather than the one being born or created or constructed."[24] Not surprisingly, the nation-state too is seen to be "withering away," its utility, sovereignty, and political jurisdiction compromised in an era that knows no boundaries and transgresses territorial borders by virtue of technological innovations that make for a transvaluation of political loyalties and identities.[25] For Elkins, this is an age that takes us beyond nations and beyond sovereignty.[26]

Along with these pronouncements of new and transformed realities, new theoretical methods have emerged whose aim is to understand these transformations in light of the workings of either capitalism, culture, consumption, aesthetics, production, communications, representation, or some combination therein.[27] The recent tirade of studies on world order transformation, communications, and changing forms of governance, for example, point to a sense of fundamental transition not only in social, political and institutional structures, but how these necessitate change in mediums of inquiry and the theoretical apparatus to explain and understand these transitions.[28] Many of these innovations, of course, are to be welcomed, deepening our theoretical understanding and knowledge. Yet to suppose the dawn of a "new" age or that this new age is manifestly different from the past is at best premature and at worst misconceived.

Most generations are apt to be consumed with their own self-importance and their sense of difference from previous generations. But difference, transformation, or change does not necessarily equate with new. If we are in a new postmodern era, to what extent is this merely the consequence of the modernist epoch maturing, growing, and expanding? The notion of new, often expressed by the prefix *post* signifying disjuncture and breakage, is specious. Social processes, economics, politics, and the human condition have not suddenly reinvented themselves in the space of a few short decades. Rather is the case that they have been subtly altered and affected by changing scientific innovations, technological progress, and attendant reorientations in knowledge and understanding. This is the way Anthony Giddens explains the so-called postmodern age, not as a new era but part of the unfolding tapestry of modernity, where the radicalization and universalization of modernity now make its consequences manifest.[29] Processes otherwise claimed as evidence of a "postmodern condition," then, are more appropriately explained as the consequences of modernity that, through reflexivity, continually transposes its form, effects, and style. Thus, for example, the new forms of cultural expressionism that postmodernists claim are a reaction against the monism of modernist universality are more likely the logical consequence of technological innovations that make the mass transmission of ideas possible, as with, for example, the explosion of niche magazines that cater to specific (mass) taste cultures. Likewise, the fragmentation of political movements and the growth of special interest groups that postmodernists insist represent a new political sensibility celebrating diversity might also be explained by the increasing spread and acceptance of liberal ideas that reject absolutism while embracing tolerance. So too, the innovative styles and objectives of literary texts which have been coterminous with challenges to traditional conceptions of the role and purpose of theory are likely not so much instances of postmodernist theory as they are a reflection of the depreciation of Western literary influences through greater cross-culturalism due to global advances in literacy, communications, and travel. Likewise, the advent of hyperconsumerism that postmodernists claim is a result of the "simulacra" and the fixation with image and style is more obviously caused by materialist saturation, mass consumption, and mass marketing techniques, and fabricated by the availability of the mass electronic and print medias. And far from the nation-state withering away in an era of globalization, it is more likely the case that we are witnessing the universalization of capitalism and of a liberal trade regime just as the nation-state too has become universalized as the preferred medium of territorial-sociopolitical organization. This is not "radical disjuncture" from previous historical experience, but the triumph of that experience on a global scale. The fact that Japanese wear Levi jeans while attending baseball games in Tokyo, or that the Chinese sample Big Macs in Beijing, or that a New Yorker can communicate via the internet with a South African in real time is more accurately explained by the spread of modernity, technology, and, perhaps, the Americanization of global cultural taste preferences than it is by declarations of new epochs, new cultures, and new worlds. In other words, talk of a postmodern age is merely talk of the consequences of modernity, particularly developments in its constituent parts, namely liberal democracy, industrialism, capitalism, technology, and science. What postmodernists mistake as new cultural forms or as new modes of production are really consequences of old and well-established modernist practices: a case of old wine in new bottles.

In their haste to proclaim a new epoch, postmodernists have thus been inclined to myopia and ahistoricism, forgetting how instrumental and interrelated is the past to the present. As David Harvey notes, while many now employ the popular idiom of postmodernism, "the conditions of postmodernity are still very much tied to [the] historical-geographical workings of capitalism's inner logic." But as he also warns, this makes the "rhetoric of postmodernism . . . dangerous for it avoids confronting the realities of political economy and the circumstances of global power."[30] Indeed, any statistical survey of global trends will still find a world far from global in its experiences, standard of living, literacy, and the provision of basic necessities. The dialectics of hunger and famine, for example, still make for a North-South global divide, as do those of literacy, numeracy, or disease epidemics like cholera, dysentery, and premature death through privation. And while the word *globalism* is bandied about to signify absolute transformation in the sites of power and state sovereignty, still we know through statistical observation of military power and economic might that America is the global hegemon, consumes upwards of sixty percent of the world's resources, is predominant in controlling the value of the world's currencies through cross-rates with the greenback, controls the vast proportion of the world's patents and patented technologies, supplies most of the world's leading software applications for business and commerce, dominates the world's pharmaceutical industry, is the leading producer of research in the social sciences and sciences, and is paramount in orchestrating a global liberal trade regime. For a world so supposedly "diffuse" and increasingly "plural," the concentration of economic, military, political, and technological power can still be related via such modernist concepts as power politics, realism, hegemony, and imperialism. If anything, there is a strong case for the conclusion that global power and wealth are more concentrated today than previously.[31] In what sense the global order is now a postmodern one resplendent with globalized plural identities, experiences, consumption patterns, or reading and writing habits thus remains extremely problematic. The experiences of modernization, the incidence of telephone communications, or the availability of modern medical expertise is remarkably dissimilar in Africa, large portions of Central and South America, or Eastern Europe for that matter. To suggest the advent of a postmodern age before the vast majority of humankind has yet to experience the effects of modernity through modernization seems premature and reflects how parochial have futurists and postmodernists been in cataloguing the "new realities."

For postmodernists who stress deconstruction and resistance, however, what is new about the postmodern epoch is not the centrality of power or production, but the devolution of a central, sovereign, and authoritative center of interpretation and meaning. As Richard Ashley notes, European "peoples and places . . . long certain of their absolute presence as a centre of meaning and origin of authority, [have] had to accommodate their situation in a wider world of contesting cultures that at once effectively resist and effectively penetrate the European territory of truth."[32] This, for Ashley, is the essence of a new postmodern sensibility, a kind of relativistic-plural world full of competing interpretations with no sovereign center. Yet this too might also be viewed as a stage in the development of modernity: the effects of modernization, for example, which colonizes increasing parts of the global political-economy and changes the spatial dimension of geographic, economic, and cultural relationships.

Regardless of their efficacy, the assumption of epochal change and new realities has spawned a whole series of theories also variously labeled postmodern. Most obviously, notions of a postmodern era have engendered new ways of doing theory. Issues previously thought unimportant have become central, conceptions of time and space have changed, new sets of questions and issues have been raised, and a whole host of theories have arisen to address these issues.

This process has been common enough in the social sciences: a movement away from essentialist grand-theoretic narratives toward multitheoretical perspectivism and "islands of theory." Arguably, this eclecticism in theoretical approaches and ideas itself constitutes a postmodern sensibility, the notion that things are too complex to be grasped by any one theoretical account. The late-modern world is now variously understood to be composed of interpenetrating and multiple realities, where complexity in social, economic, and political relationships are further compounded by a multitude of electronic images, disparate cultural influences, and changes in the dimensional referents of time and space due to advances in transportations and communications. What this represents for postmodernists is a profound shift in the "structure of feeling" in the culture of advanced capitalist societies.[33] As Jane Flax observes, "Something has happened, is happening to Western societies. . . . Western culture is in the middle of a fundamental transformation: a 'shape of life' is growing old. The demise of the old is being hastened by the end of colonialism, the uprising of women, the revolt of other cultures against white Western hegemony, shifts in the balance of economic and political power within the world economy, and a growing awareness of the costs as well as the benefits of scientific 'progress.'"[34] For postmodernists, the complexity of these realities discounts the utility of monotheoretical (essentialist) accounts. Instead, it suggests the need for multiple theoretical analyses that avoid reflection on any one dimension in favor of a reflexive understanding of relationships between social, political, and economic dimensions.

This trend is generally constitutive of the new forms of postmodern theory in political-economy. These tend to (1) subsume disciplinary boundaries; (2) concern themselves with technoscientific change and their economic, political, and social consequences in theses of the postindustrial society; (3) integrate into theories of commodity production and consumption a theory of aesthetics and cultural forms; (4) problematize claims and suppositions and expose them to critical analysis; (5) contextualize knowledge claims; and (6) in the context of deconstruction theory "obliterate the boundaries between literature and other disciplines" and reduce "all modes of thought to the common condition of writing."[35]

Thus, if we are to approach an understanding of postmodernism, we must first realize that no one understanding is sufficient. Certainly its dominant constellations exist as deconstructive antimodernist efforts, but this is not true of all postmodern theory or postmodernists. Increasingly, those who claim a postmodern heritage are not easily slotted into a deconstructionist mold, but concern themselves with objective changes in technologies, economics, political organization, culture, and their reflexive effects upon such things as interstate relations, interdependence, or consumption and production patterns. Consequently, the postmodernist lexicon is best understood as a generic shell that houses numerous commentaries on the condition of late-modernity, some from a deconstructionist/resistance standpoint, others from a position of documenting change. What unites these forms of analysis is that all of them are reacting to the modernist project and the latent processes of modernization, whether this be a political commentary on the "nightmarish dimensions of the Enlightenment dream," the consequences of changing social and political sensibilities in the era of mass communications, or on the end of the industrial era and the rise of a postindustrial one.[36] In short, these commentaries are both a postscript to the modernist era and a preface to the consequences of that era which are now becoming evident.

A reading of postmodern theory as epochal change thus proves instructive. In this context, postmodern theory acts as a sequential marker or periodizing category, a metaphor that is both emblematic of changes in culture, history, society, and thought, while perhaps also contributory to them.[37] Whether such changes are real or imagined, the point is moot. What is imagined today becomes tomorrow's reality, and a great deal of postmodern theory is directed toward capturing this sense of change in the "structure of feeling" which itself has reflexive implications for the way social and political relations are actually practiced.[38] The uniqueness of postmodern theory therefore resides in its reflexivity, its ability to offer commentary on these changes and make them real. My quibble with postmodern theory does not reside in these observations, but the extent to which these changes are the result of modernist attributes wrongly ascribed to a postmodern reality and detached from historical and genealogical moorings. To this extent, postmodern theory is oxymoronic, since the realities, changes, and sensibilities it deals with are themselves modernist in origin. Thus, while the two readings I have offered have obvious utility, by themselves they are unable to capture the depth of epistemological diversity within postmodern theory or the peculiarity of its inconsonant nuances. For this, a more substantial taxonomic system is required.

Three Typologies of Postmodern Theory

If postmodernists grapple with the modalities of late-modernity, they do so in multifarious ways, many of which seem unrelated and dissimilar. As Pauline Rosenau observes, there are "as many forms of post-modernism as there are post-modernists," making postmodern theory a diverse amalgam of contending interests and approaches.[39] Any classificatory scheme that attempts to order postmodern theory is thus prone to the dangers of oversimplification, not least because it will invariably reduce the breadth and diversity of postmodern theory to a few cursory categories. However, if we are to gain a systematic understanding of postmodernism and its diversity, then such typologies are not only heuristically necessary but indispensable.

The application of Weberian ideal types to postmodern theory is not new. Hal Foster divided postmodern theory into two schematic categories: a neoconservative and poststructuralist variety. Similarly, Pauline Rosenau wrote of affirmative and skeptical postmodernism; Richard Rorty of deconstructionist and bourgeois postmodernism; and Mark Hoffman of critical and radical interpretivism.[40] While classifications of this nature are useful, they also betray a number of problems inherent in the construction of schematic ideal types. First, most ideal types rely on simple dichotomized categories that are restrictive and exclusionary (as with the above). Theories and theorists are never as neatly compartmentalized or clearly defined as many historiographical-epistemological narratives would suggest. And still fewer intellectual movements, let alone the postmodern one, can be captured adequately by single variable categories like poststructuralist or bourgeois. Intellectual discourse and the manner in which ideas emerge, develop, and are employed, and of how they interact reflexively with other theories and change their systemic structure are notoriously complicated questions. Moreover, the inscription of particular theorists and theories into discrete intellectual boxes is an activity far from objective and often infused with subjective bias and interpretation.

I do not pretend to offer any alternatives to these dilemmas, but simply to acknowledge the weaknesses implicit in the construction of classificatory schemes. These weaknesses, however, do not detract from the overall utility of schematic typologies as heuristic tools. Their continued use throughout the social sciences bears testimony to this. Classificatory schemes and processes of theoretical taxonomy are pedagogically indispensable if we are to appreciate the constituent parts of theories, assess their usefulness, and utilize them. For this reason, I also intend to employ a classificatory scheme that identifies thematic ideal types in postmodern theory.

While the criteria for the construction of ideal types are often subjectively derived, in the case of postmodern theory a number of dominant thematic issues immediately suggest themselves. First, I have already identified the theoretical intent of some postmodern theories to negate and resist modernist discourse. Second, I have identified the use of postmodernism as a periodizing category denoting change in such things as culture, technology, science, politics, and economics. Third, I also indicated that new forms of theoretical analysis have arisen in response to these "new" postmodern realities, theories which attempt an understanding of postmodern dynamics and why they came about.

These expressed concerns allow for the identification of three broad, and by no means inclusive, categories of postmodern theory. These I have called (1) technological or productionist postmodernism, reflecting the themes of technoscientific changes and their reflexive social, political, and economic effects; (2) critical postmodernism, reflecting the growth of new theoretical mediums and new ways of doing theory, particularly those concerned with assessing critically foundational propositions and contextualizing knowledge; and (3) subversive or deconstructive postmodernism, reflecting the themes of negation and resistance.[41]

These can be summarized briefly:

Technological or Productionist Postmodernism: Technological or productionist postmodernism has a thematic matrix concerned with objective changes; that is, as a consequence of modernity and the spread and advance of science and technology, the traditional modernist dialectics of production and consumption, labor and capital, state and market, etc. have been transposed with reflexive effects upon cultural forms, economics, and politics. These effects are represented, for example, in theories of the postindustrial society, postmaterialist society, or postclass society. As such, technological postmodernists tend to be concerned with ontological issues, framed in terms of spatial and temporal transformations in the matrix of production, consumption, and the new political-economy of signs, symbols, and codes. They also respond to what is perceived to be the "radical indeterminacy" of the "new aesthetics," where traditional dialectics such as left and right politics, for example, become blurred "through the commutability of terms once contradictory or dialectically opposed."[42] Modernist categories like fashion, image, spectacle, art, politics, self, other, good, or bad, for example, all become lost amid a montage of hypercommunications that change the systemic basis of capitalist accumulation and the modernist logic of economy, culture, politics, and society.

Critical Postmodernism: Critical postmodernists seek to expose the foundationalist assumptions on which metatheoretical knowledge systems are constructed. It is a relatively benign form of postmodernism whose genealogy can be traced directly to the critical social theorists of the Frankfurt school.[43] Because of this, it is associated closely with many of the debates concerning the crisis in Marxist theory and post-Marxist discourse. Critical postmodernism is also concerned with the relationship between aesthetics and cultural forms and modes of production, attempting to construct a unified theory of aesthetics and culture within a Marxist epistemology (the work of Antonio Gramsci, for example).[44] As such, critical postmodernists tend to be concerned with methodological issues (the fact-value distinction of positivism, for instance), and their project sympathetic to epistemology, grand narratives, and foundationalist-objective thought.

Subversive-Deconstructive Postmodernism: Subversive postmodernism displays a thematic concern with negation and resistance to modernist practices and discourse, primarily via a deconstructive-textual analysis of logocentric practices, modernist knowledge systems, and language. In particular, subversive postmodernists attempt to demonstrate how all knowledge is mediated by language, and how the modernist referents of reality, truth, reason, and logic are fictive sociolinguistic constructs that act as mechanisms of social and individual control. Subversive postmodernism, through deconstruction, attempts to erect a "structure of resistance," attacking what might be broadly called the Western-Judaeo intellectual tradition and the politics of the Enlightenment.[45] Their project is thus anti-epistemological and targets Cartesian-Kantian epistemology and the notion of philosophical foundations in theory and knowledge. For subversive postmodernists, knowledge is located in the fact of discourse and dialogism and situated in subjective-individual, and not universal, sites.

Excursions into the Postmodernist Labyrinth: The Motifs of Postmodern Theory

Let us turn now to a critical exposition of these three motifs as they occur in the writings of a number of leading postmodernists. As I have already mentioned, however, this task is made discursive if only because postmodernist writings tend to operate amid a series of contending motifs by virtue of their penchant for eclecticism. Consequently, I intend to treat these motifs as porous codifications rather than monothematic categories into which postmodernists can be slotted. These motifs are therefore advanced for purely analytical and heuristic reasons in order to explore critically the epistemological and ontological constructions which underlie them.

Postmodernism as Technological Change

When writing about postmodernism, Fredric Jameson offers the mystic observation that it is both a new age as well as an inverted form of intellectual reflection. Postmodernism, he notes, "is what you have when the modernization process is complete and nature is gone for good."[46] It reflects an indulgent attempt at "theorizing its own condition of possibility, which consists," notes Jameson, "in the sheer enumeration of changes and modifications."[47] Here, the postmodern denotes change, difference, and historical movement, as well as new forms of intellectual reflection, new theoretical issues, and new forms of theory. Historical or epochal change and the new forms of theory that have arisen are not mutually exclusive but, as Jameson insists, causally connected: the latter consequent on the former. This betrays Jameson's Marxist origins, particularly his reductionist penchant for seeing intellectual change as the product of changes in the nature of capitalist relations of production. For Jameson, the postmodern era becomes not so much a new era detached from the previous, but, like Giddens's understanding, an era consequent on the manifestations of modernity, particularly those transformations evident in capitalism, science, and technology. In fact, Jameson writes of a third stage in the development of capitalism: a mature capitalism that displays an inner logic and whose rationality is defined by accumulation. This third stage incorporates into the Marxist production matrix culture and aesthetics, whereby there has occurred "some fundamental mutation of the sphere of culture in the world of late-capitalism, which includes a momentous modification of its social function."[48] Values, ideas, theory, production, class, and thinking itself are transformed by technoscientific advances, allowing late-capitalism to transpose itself into a truly global phenomenon in which the referents of time, space, place, and cultural difference are obliterated under its universalization.

Jameson approaches what I have termed a technological or productionist postmodernist: where postmodernism denotes a periodizing category expressing objective changes in technology, culture, society, and politics as a consequence of the modalities of late-capitalism. For Jameson, this constitutes "a moment in which not merely the older city but even the nation-state itself has ceased to play a central functional or formal role in a process that has a new quantum leap of capital prodigiously expanded beyond them, leaving them behind as ruined and archaic remains of earlier stages in the development of this new mode of production."[49] The postmodern era is one of new configurations, not least of them spatial, which transposes social orders, the role and power of the state, and affects cultural and political sensibilities.

However, it would be naive to suppose Jameson only a technological postmodernist. He also displays a keen understanding of how theory is transformed in the postmodern epoch. For example, he is intimately involved in transforming Marxist theory from its reductionist and essentialist economism into a reflexive theoretical understanding of the connections between cultural forms and political and economic structures. Thus, we can also see his writings contiguous with the motifs of critical postmodernism, particularly his attempts to integrate a cultural-aesthetic dimension into (post)Marxist theory and continue the critical theoretic tradition of the Frankfurt school. In fact, Jameson's project is readily understood as critical through his continued commitment to Marxist categories like class, mode of production, and capitalism. In Jameson's writings, these categories still assume a central ontological position as substructural and foundational elements responsible for social relations. These categories, as in all Marxist theory, remain central analytical tools in Jameson's effort to uncover the foundational elements responsible for postmodern life and to explain historical movement and transformation. Because of this, he insists that postmodernism "should not be thought of as purely a cultural affair."[50] Rather, he urges, "I must remind the reader of the obvious; namely, that this whole global, yet American, postmodern culture is the internal and superstructural expression of a whole new wave of American military and economic domination throughout the world: in this sense, as throughout class history, the underside of culture is blood, torture, death, and terror."[51] Jameson's response to the postmodern era, then, is to infuse Marxist theory with an understanding of culture and aesthetics while integrating them into a theory of the modes of production. This, for Jameson, explains not only the dynamics of capitalist accumulation and of technological and scientific innovation, but ultimately reveals capitalism and its economic-social matrix to be the driving force of history.

Scott Lash, on the other hand, takes a slightly different perspective. For Lash, postmodernism represents the cultural subterfuge of postindustrial society, particularly the deepening of commodification. Here, postmodernism is a cultural phenomenon with economic and political consequences where commodified images are performative of accumulatory practices for capitalism and where the "transvaluation" of image and aesthetics displace class culture.[52] The result is the transformation of the universal proletarian into a cognitariat, displacing its political activism with spectatorism that pluralizes left political culture.[53] Class culture ceases to exist, the dialectics of class and capital no longer drive history, and those social agents previously thought central in the historical dialectic are superseded in the postmodern age.

Charles Jencks has drawn similar conclusions but argues that different mechanisms have been responsible for these outcomes. Jencks, for example, conflates postmodernism as a cultural phenomenon with postfordism, an economic phenomenon, and reflexively implicates each in the other's change. Here, the postmodern condition represents kaleidoscopic and simultaneous changes "from mass production to segmented production; from a relatively integrated mass-culture to many fragmented taste cultures; from centralised control in government and business to peripheral decision-making; from repetitive manufacture of identical objects to the fast-changing manufacture of varying objects; from few styles to many genres; from national to global consciousness and, at the same time, local identification."[54]

This position is similar to Jameson's, locating the dynamic of postmodernity within technoscientific changes that have reflexive cultural and aesthetic implications. Jameson, for example, understands the postmodern era as merely a new mode of production, where production enters the ether of image, aesthetics, symbol, sign, and space.[55] "What has happened is that aesthetic production today has become integrated into commodity production generally: the frantic economic urgency of producing fresh waves of ever more novel-seeming goods (from clothing to airplanes), at ever greater rates of turnover, now assigns an increasingly essential structural function and position to aesthetic innovation and experimentation."[56] Jean Baudrillard goes even further, declaring that the dawn of the postmodern era with its technological implications marks the end of labor, the end of the era of production, and the end of political economy.[57] Baudrillard is one among many who welcome such innovations and transformations. These signal not merely a new economic dialectic, but a political and cultural one, where new political sensibilities symbolize the end of modernist referents like class, ascriptive and discriminatory gender roles, or socioeconomic hierarchies that privilege some while marginalizing others.[58] The postmodern condition is thus understood to be profoundly liberating, portending to a new era that offers more choice, more freedom, more consumption, and more possibilities for emancipatory politics.

Unique to all these interpretations is a celebration of the postmodern age as a global process, whereby social, political, and territorial boundaries are tumbling down and in their place a new transnational mode of sociocultural-economic production is emerging. Like the great historical transformations before it, this one too is greeted with optimism, beholding the promise of a technological fix to the problems of global relations, via, for example, the emergence of a global community through hypercommunications technologies such as the information super highway, or by promising to render war dysfunctional to the political economy of postindustrial states. In the new information age, states will acquire wealth not through territorial conquest, plunder and pillage, but by generating new technologies, new markets, new goods and services, and by achieving higher levels of education and innovating the technoscientific basis of the "new economy" to make themselves globally competitive. The language and discourse will be familiar to all, rehearsed daily by Wall Street barons, economists, and political leaders alike.

Amid these platitudes and announcements of new worlds, however, there also lurks a more pessimistic strand of writings that fears the postmodern age and its technological consequences. Those very processes otherwise identified as liberating, some argue are leading to greater misery, dehumanization, and cultural disintegration. Dick Hebdige, for instance, sees postmodernism as nihilistic and the postmodern age as modernist but "without the hopes and dreams which made modernity bearable."[59] For Hebdige, postmodernity is what comes after an age of illusion, optimism, and certitude, an age where the omnipotence of Faustian technology and its grounding in reason, science, and industry made possible the writings of grand narratives and emancipatory projects: Marxism, Freudianism, liberalism, new moral and social orders. The age of modernity was the age of illusion. Postmodernity, however, is the age of disillusion, bewilderment, and cynicism. Postmodernists now attack the age of reason, critique Enlightenment thought, and react to the excesses of utopian reason founded on the simplistic themes of truth, justice, and right.[60] Jean-Francois Lyotard, for example, insists that postmodernism constitutes a libidinal history that refuses to indulge in the complacency of knowledge, asserting instead that there exists no privileged standpoint for deciphering truth.[61] Postmodernists no longer see the pursuit of knowledge as a means to truth and certitude, but as an intellectual mode of production used for legitimation that masks the power it wields and those whom it serves.[62] Behind Lyotard's words lurks *The Will to Power* of Friedrich Nietzsche and the nihilism inscribed in the *fin-de-millennium*.[63] This is an epoch that comes at the end of history, a "twilight time of ultramodernism," for Kroker and Cook, where "the death of the grand referent of God" which so preoccupied Nietzsche anticipates the ruins of the "postmodern condition"—nihilism, that "lightning-flash" which illuminates the sky for an instant only to reveal the "immensity of the darkness within."[64]

Metaphors of this hue betray the pessimism inherent in the postmodern scene, one symbolic of a new dark age in the "dying days of modernism . . . as western culture runs down towards the brilliant illumination of a final burnout."[65] Many technological postmodernists thus encapsulate what Scherpe terms an "eschatological consciousness of the apocalypse," since they contemplate the end of modernity, the rise of cynicism, and the triumph of nihilism in the face of declining identity, purpose, and meaning.[66] This is the "age of *posthistorie,* the end of the world."[67]

The defining moment for technological postmodernists of this variety is the relentless advance of technological society and the subsumption of all forms of human and scientific rationality unto its logic. Arthur Kroker, for example, writes of the possessed individual, one entrapped in an eerie simulacra of virtual reality where all original experience has evaporated. For Kroker, postmodernism is a commentary on technology. It refuses "the pragmatic account of technology as freedom," progress, liberation, and development, and instead represents the "tragic description of technology as denigration."[68] The hitherto dominant dialectics under modernity—technological progress, freedom from the constraints of nature, economic growth, increased human welfare, and emancipation are now displaced; hope is gone. The new information age might thus be little more than the subsumption of liberal individuality where advances in technology deprives us of culture, feeling, and expression, and reduces us all to automatons. In the end, each of us is dehumanized, reduced to so many numbers as our taste preferences, consumption patterns, credit histories, social security payments, banking practices, and television viewing habits are recorded, analyzed, and manipulated by centralized bureaucracies and computers.

For technological postmodernists, then, objective changes in information, computer, communication, and production technologies, coupled with new taste cultures and political movements have transposed power relations, the workings of capital, relationships between states, and the importance of knowledge. This, for example, is the conclusion of Lyotard, who notes, "Our working hypothesis is that the status of knowledge is altered as societies enter what is known as the postindustrial age and cultures enter what is known as the postmodern age."[69]

Postmodernism as Critical Epistemology

Raymond Morrow rejects all these interpretations and argues that postmodernism is an intellectual mirage that masks a critical (leftist) form of epistemology. For Morrow, postmodernism is "what remains in the shambles of the Marxist and neo-Marxist theoretical positions, the best of what is left of the left."[70] Alex Callinicos explains postmodernist discourse in similar terms, seeing contemporary postmodernists as the leftovers of the "political odyssey of the 1968 generation." That generation has now entered middle age, the middle class, middle management, administrative and university positions, "with all hope of socialist revolution gone—indeed, often having ceased to believe in the desirability of any such revolution."[71] As Callinicos argues, "this conjuncture—the prosperity of the Western new middle class combined with the political disillusionment of many of its most articulate members—provides the context to the proliferating talk of postmodernism . . . [and] the *acceptance* by quite large numbers of people of certain ideas."[72] Callinicos dismisses postmodernism as a feel-good movement by those who wish to accommodate their political feelings with the excesses of their overconsumptionist lifestyle. By turning to the politically benign spheres of culture and aesthetics, Callinicos thinks postmodernism a veiled and pathetic attempt to rid the leftovers of the 1968 generation of their consumer guilt. Postmodern theory thus attempts to depict the consumption of cultural goods as a process of individuation, an individual act of uniqueness, difference, and dissimilarity, and a means of political disassociation from modernist mass production and conformity in style and design. But for Callinicos, this is only capitalism in a different form, and postmodernists, the embourgeoised ex-radicals of the 1990s. They are, in Callinicos's understanding, old guard traitors who grasp at an "aesthetic pose based on the refusal to seek either to comprehend or transform existing social reality."[73] The consumption of cultural goods becomes the palatable political act of resistance commensurate with a middle class lifestyle: "Resistance is reduced to the knowing consumption of cultural products."[74] Thus, as Callinicos argues,

> The discourse of postmodernism is best seen as the product of a socially mobile intelligentsia in a climate dominated by the retreat of the Western labour movement and the "overconsumptionist" dynamic of capitalism in a Reagan-Thatcher era. From this perspective the term *postmodern* would seem to be a floating signifier by means of which this intelligentsia has sought to articulate its political disillusionment and its aspiration to a consumption-orientated lifestyle. The difficulties

involved in identifying a referent for this term are therefore beside the point, since talk about postmodernism turns out to be less about the world than the expression of a particular generation's sense of an ending.[75]

While I have sympathy with this interpretation, I also think Callinicos's position belittles much post-Marxist literature and the insights it offers. Certainly, the 1968 generation is germane to an understanding of leftist postmodernism, but this is only one facet of its intellectual tapestry. First, we need to distinguish those conservative and proconsumptionist postmodernists who celebrate discursive styles and materiality and whom Callinicos makes the target of his criticism from those whom I have identified here as critical postmodernists. These postmodernists continue a leftist tradition of critical interpretivism under the banner of post-Marxism, particularly in their writings on capitalism and, more recently, on the politics of aesthetics and culture. Where I disagree with Callinicos is that I do not see the turn to aesthetics and cultural forms as something new, but rather the contemporary equivalent of the Frankfurt school of critical social theorists operative during the 1930s: those who retreated from the practical politics of socialist revolution because of disillusionment at the rise of German national socialism. The same is apparent of the 1968 generation: disillusionment at the failure of socialism and the triumph of capitalism, as Callinicos correctly points out, but not a moral ambiguity and resignation to consumptionism so much as a turn to theory and a theoretical critique of these phenomena.

Thus, I prefer to understand critical postmodernists as (post)Marxist political émigrés deprived of their historical destiny due to the triumph of neoliberalism and capitalism. These theorists have turned their attentions to articulating critical social and political theories that attempt to uncover the epistemic structures responsible for postmodern social, political, and economic life.[76] And just as the critical social theorists of the Frankfurt school did it by turning to the politics of aesthetics and culture, so critical postmodernists do the same today.

The distinguishing feature of critical postmodernists is their movement away from any praxiological intent toward theoretical endeavors: a position that Callinicos sees as an abrogation of moral responsibilities. This movement toward theory was partly necessitated by the various poststructuralist critiques of Marxist theory that emerged during the late 1960s and 1970s. In particular, Marxist metatheory was attacked vigorously for its reductionist, essentialist, determinist, and structuralist ontologies. The ensuing in-house debates, coupled with rapid changes in the global political-economy and the rise of diverse social movements cast still more doubt over the ability of Marxist metatheory to explain contemporary phenomena. The result, however, has been a theoretical reformulation of Marxist theory through critical epistemological and ontological debates. Post-Marxists have been at the forefront of these retheorizations, attempting a continuation of Marxist and critical theoretic traditions, but via new theoretical forms.[77] Subsequently, as Raymond Morrow has pointed out, the theoretical project of post-Marxism was reconceived as a fourfold project

> to regain a sense of the empirical importance of economic structures and state mediation, without relapsing into instrumentalist or structuralist reductionism; to develop a theory of cultural struggle which challenges static conceptions of hegemony and domination; to articulate a theory of cultural forms which could draw upon advances in semiotic theories of communication; and to provide an approach to the subject which preserved the agency structure dialectic and incorporated a theory of resistance . . . [that does not rely on] expressivist conceptions of totality and related understandings of ideology and subjectivity.[78]

Critical postmodernists, then, attempt to integrate into their theoretical conduit a theory of cultural forms and aesthetics while shedding the reductionism and structuralism of Marxist theory. For Perry Anderson, this was a reactive project illustrative of how the fortunes of theoretical work on the left are inversely related to the fortunes of left-wing politics at large.[79] Callinicos was therefore correct to suppose that critical postmodernism was born from the failure of left radicalism of the 1968 generation.[80] Those very conditions which made for a crisis in left-wing politics were, in retrospect, the making of leftist theory, channeling creative energies toward theoretical innovation and an interrogation of hitherto dominant narratives. Consequently, as Laclau and Mouffe observe, "left-wing thought today stands at a crossroads. The 'evident truths' of the past—the classical forms of analysis and political calculation, the nature of the forces in conflict, the very meaning of the Left's struggles and objectives—have been seriously challenged. . . . A question-mark has fallen more and more heavily over a whole way of conceiving both socialism and the roads that should lead to it."[81]

Critical thinking has been transformed. The simple slogans of class struggle and revolutionary emancipation have given way to more complex theoretical undertakings that challenge notions of patriarchy, gender, linguistics, science, and power. The patriarchal elitism of an all-male vanguard leading male workers from the factories to freedom is now understood as both hollow and just another form of domination. The sweatshops erected in Soviet Russia in the name of socialism, for example, were no different from those during the English industrial revolution. This does much to explain the current character of leftist postmodern theory that, by and large, has championed the "politics of inclusion" under the banner of "political correctness." Totalizing metanarratives conferring ontological centrality on certain key groups (the white male working class, for example) have been abandoned in recognition of the proliferation of social movements that now constitute the spectrum of left politics (feminists, ethnic and religious minorities, sexual minorities, ecological activists, human rights activists, the disabled, etc.).

Despite Callinicos's conclusions, then, critical postmodernists remain faithful to classical varieties of critical thought, but extend their purview to cultural and linguistic forms of analysis. The result is a more eclectic and less centered critical theory that assaults not just the practices of capitalism but the entire modernist edifice that valorizes such practices (cultural practices, aesthetics, patriarchy, etc.).[82] This is the sense in which Zygmunt Bauman conceives of postmodernism: "modernity conscious of its true nature" and reactive to its "diseased state," particularly universalizing metanarratives exclusionary of "marginal voices" and the suffocating mental straitjacket of scientific logic. The political compass of critical postmodernism is thus inclusionary and "marked by a view of the human world as irreducibly and irrevocably pluralistic, split into a multitude of sovereign units and sites of authority, with no horizontal or vertical order."[83] Consequently, contemporary critical theory abandons the pretensions of objectivity and refutes the existence of a realm of residual truth and meaning. Instead, the postmodern enterprise "reveals the world as composed of an indefinite number of meaning-generating agencies, all relatively self-sustained and autonomous, all subject to their own respective logics and armed with their own facilities of truth-validation."[84] Subjectivity, in other words, and a sensitivity to the milieu from which one views the world makes for a new identity politics (black politics, gay politics, green-politics, feminist politics, etc.), and with it the construction of intellectual spaces in search of their respective histories and experiences (black studies, gay studies, women's studies, etc.), or what some might term a kind of methodological individualism pushed to its extreme.

This position defines implicitly the relationship of critical postmodernists to radical politics, for they challenge the precepts of modernist discourse that, through objective and universal standards, inscribes inequality: the distinction between mass culture and the avant-garde, for example, the hierarchies of class and meritocratic practices, or the value patterns that reify science over the humanities, men over women, and facts over values. And it is these themes that feed directly into the epistemic motifs of subversive postmodernists and lead to the practices of deconstruction.

Postmodernism as Subversion

Subversive postmodernists attempt to dismantle these value-hierarchies and the belief that universalization can bestow justice through instrumental rationality.[85] They do so through the "politics of inclusion," or in more radical contexts, through deconstructing logocentric practices, binary logic, and the presumption that we can speak for the marginalized (other).[86] These deconstructive practices I have attributed to subversive postmodernists since they attempt to dismantle organonist knowledge systems that, by and large, have been the hallmark of the Western intellectual tradition.[87] In this sense, the project repudiates epistemology and attempts instead to establish a postfoundational view of the world. The champion of the American postmodern movement, Ihab Hassen, for example, argues that the intent of subversive postmodernists is the destruction of the Western *cogito:*

> It is an antinomian moment that assumes a vast unmasking of the Western mind—what Michel Foucault might call a postmodern *episteme*. I say "unmasking" though other terms are now *de rigeur:* for instance, deconstruction, decentring, disappearance, dissemination, demystification, discontinuity, *difference,* dispersion, etc. Such terms express an ontological rejection of the traditional full subject, the *cogito* of Western philosophy. They express too an epistemological obsession with fragments or fractures, and a corresponding ideological commitment to minorities. . . . To think well, to feel well, to act well, to read well, according to this *episteme* of unmasking, is to refuse the tyranny of wholes; totalization in any human endeavour is potentially totalitarian.[88]

This project attempts an "explosion of the modern episteme, in which reason . . . [is] blown to pieces."[89] Consequently, the entire modernist edifice that is valorized by reason and rationalist discourse is challenged. Subversive postmodernists, for example, celebrate difference, discursive practices, and repudiate ideas of universal truth claims, rationality, or representationalism. Rather, the world is seen from a relativist position, with no single arbiter or knowledge system able to judge between truth claims. This assaults modernist theory and destabilizes the idea of logic and reason as the road to truth, fact, knowledge, and ultimately to certitude in our understanding of the physical and social worlds. Faith in science and theory-knowledge is eroded. For subversive postmodernists, truth is in the eye of the beholder, not the test tube of a scientist, the theory of a mathematician, or the methodology of rational argument.[90] Interpretation replaces absolute knowledge and epistemology, where, for example, physics too becomes "only an interpretation and arrangement of the world . . . and *not* an explanation of the world."[91]

This extreme position is evident in the unruly mixture of Continental poststructuralism and American philosophical pragmatism that emerged throughout the 1980s. Richard Bernstein notes that this made for an era filled with suspicion toward "reason, and of the very idea of universal validity claims that can be justified through argument." The entire Enlightenment project and its legacy have come under attack, where in postmodernist circles there is a "rage against humanism" and a movement seeking the delegitimation of European modernity.[92] David Harvey maintains that this movement seeks an end to the age of reason, and rejects "any project that . . . [seeks] universal human emancipation through mobilization of the powers of technology, science and reason."[93] For subversive postmodernists, these modernist referents are not the agents of liberation, but things to be liberated from.

The deconstruction of modernist discourse, logic, and reason—and with it the attack upon and repudiation of epistemology—are thus the major occupations of subversive postmodernists. Richard Rorty attributes these deconstructive practices to the Cartesian-Kantian traditions of philosophy. These, Rorty argues, attempted to escape from history by externalizing and objectifying reality in order to erect a foundationalist transhistorical knowledge.[94] Antithetic to this tradition, postmodernists have rediscovered contextualism and, like Dewey, Wittgenstein, and Heidegger before them, attempt to teach a historicist lesson: that knowledge in all forms and varieties is contaminated by the language used to describe it, by ideology, by historical milieu and culture.[95] Modernist narratives of the universal and transhistorical genre are, accordingly, rejected. Lyotard, for instance, argues that we can no longer "organize the multitude of events that come to us from the world . . . by subsuming them beneath the idea of a universal history of humanity."[96] "Totalizing narratives" not only exclude marginal voices but also assume the ontological centrality of certain groups, creating a theoretical exclusivity in the way specific groups are made the targets of emancipation or the objects of narratives.[97] Feminists, for example, point out that the history of humankind has been told as the history of mankind, North American Indians that American history has only narrated the history of white European settlement of "unoccupied" lands, and peoples of the Southern Hemisphere, that so-called world history has been told from the perspective of eurocentric narratives of European expansionism and colonization. Modernist theory is therefore charged with becoming overly myopic, where the exclusivity of theoretical categories like working class or white males, for example, become the sine qua non for justice and liberation, or the privileged subjects of historical narratives.[98] Learned traditions, in other words, are merely the textual inscriptions of those who have been privileged enough to write: white males of largely European descent who, either wittingly or unwittingly, have replicated and legitimated the social and political order from which their privilege is derived. For subversive postmodernists, the social sciences and humanities are merely representations of these privileged narratives, or, more correctly, fictions evolved as practices, whose reality is only so because so many are duplicitous, or simply duped, into replicating these practices that these become coterminous with the events and facts of the social and political world. In this way, subversive postmodernism is more properly understood not merely as a site of critical reexamination, but one of deconstruction, intertextual readings, dissident thought, and a relocation of the temporal plain of perception to include such mediums as place, space, and contextualism as well as gender, identity, signs, symbols, and images as ingredients in the intersubjective construction of truth, meaning, and reality. Boundaries otherwise used as means of demarcation and intellectual ordering devices are understood by postmodernists as mediums of modernist exclusion, mechanisms of marginalization that have silenced voices or, worse still, been used in the service of specific interests to plunder and pillage peoples of wealth and well being. For subversive postmodernists, the point is a political one, as Chris Brown notes: "In the twentieth century the instrumental rationality of the West has so often found itself at the service of dubious causes that it has become itself politically suspect."[99] The once-privileged status of Western thought is no more, but collapsed under the mantra of its own contradictions which, postmodernists claim, opens up new sites of thinking space and leads to dialogism. For postmodernists, this is a place where "we can learn things about ourselves by studying our history and reading our literary inheritance . . . *[but only after] we have removed the monolog-*

ical tendencies past readings have assigned to these genres" (my emphasis).[100] History, in other words, is to be rewritten, or at least written from the perspective of those who have not written it before: women, people of color, gays and lesbians, indigenous peoples, and so forth.

The project of subversive postmodernists has thus been to deconstruct privileged representations, totalizing emancipatory projects and metadiscourses. Instead, they champion "discontinuities" and seek to include otherwise marginalized voices in multifarious discourses that are tempered through relativity in language, interpretation, culture, and history. At base, this is a reaction to the (non)history of silence and an attempt to speak, write, and be read as people of color, lesbians, women, feminists, gays, Japanese Americans, or any number of "other" voices expunged from mainstream history. Identity politics is thus the most obvious outgrowth of subversive postmodernism, where, argues Stanley Aronowitz, the effects "of de-territorialization of production on the patterns of everyday life," makes for a lost sense of place, purpose, and meaning. "In the absence of orientating instruments, to avert existential bewilderment," and substituting (poorly) for more comprehensive political analysis," subversive postmodernists "resort to fierce assertions of 'identities' in order to know/invent who, where, and what they are."[101] This, notes Wendy Brown, is as "much a signifier of powerlessness as a redress of it," an attempt to reclaim the "integrity of communities producing identity," rather than to have them submerged beneath the "boundless commodification of cultural practices" or the "cross-cultural meldings and appropriations" of late capitalism, where, for example, underwear is sold to us by the "all American white, heterosexual, middle class, blond haired, blue eyed boy next door." The lesson is as simple as it is profound. We are not all heterosexual, white, middle class, male, or American; rather, what we all are is *different*. Yet, as Brown also notes, "identity politics permits positioning without mapping, a feature which sharply distinguishes it from (Marxian) class analysis and reveals its proximity to (liberal) interest group politics."[102] In the end, then, identity politics might be less inspired by postmodernism than a symptom of its disorienting effects and its dismemberment of meaning, place, origin, and purpose.

Regardless, the constitutive elements of subversive postmodern politics are found in its celebration of diversity, "in the regional cultural diversification accompanying the relentless process of global integration, and in the discovery of differences infinitude." These are exaggerated in topographical articulation and complexity, where plurality and difference mean politics, society, and economics are "no longer reducible to class society or interest based politics," but, at the same time, "is never innocent of power and stratification."[103] For some, this might be little more than a new ageism, the me generation, for example, or the perversion of liberal individualism into a kind of hyperindividuality. Whatever the case, monological interpretation, collective politics, or the politics of mass loyalty and mass identity give way to complex individuation, crisscrossing identities, and multiple perspectivism. More importantly, this conception signals a loss of faith in the idea of common destiny or collective purpose, where history is stripped systematically of progress, God, teleologies, iron laws of development, or any other reason so that humans beings become the sole creator and repository of all that there is: a kind of species-centrism where there is no ultimate essence other than ourselves.[104] Postmodern theory thus becomes the infinite task of "complexification" and not, as with modernist theory, a process of simplification and metatheoretic generalization:[105] Universalism is abandoned for particularism, macrotheory for microtheory and micropolitics, and the dimensional referent of time (history) is now interspersed with place, space, and identity to emphasize complexity and contextuality.[106]

Contextuality, particularism, and relativism become the analytic nostrums that separate the grand designs of modernist discourse from the specificities of poststructuralism. This has enormous consequences for the way postmodernists engage in, utilize, and understand the aims of theoretical activity, and in the way they conceive of and explain, for example, the workings of power, capitalism, oppression, or emancipation. Unlike the structural monism of much Marxist and neo-Marxist literature, postmodernists view the modalities of power and oppression as intricate, localized, and divergent. Michel Foucault, for instance, combined a poststructuralist account of power and oppression with a postmodernist critique of rationality and science, and abandoned grand narratives for particularistic historical genealogies. Unlike his structuralist predecessors, Foucault depicted power as irreducibly plural, thriving at the microcosmic levels of society. And grappling with the modalities of power and discourse politics, he argued, was the problem that had to be solved.[107] Foucault's work, then, was an attempt at understanding the "political status of science and the ideological functions which it could serve."[108] And his historical genealogical documentaries were extensions of this project, attempts at demonstrating "how objectifying forms of reason (and their regimes of truth and knowledge) have been made": that, in fact, they are historically contingent rather than naturally inscribed.[109] His genealogical accounts of power in the prison and asylum, for example, reoriented political theory away from an a priori assumption of its imposition to a precise account of how power is made, matures, and infects. The political and social problematic of power is thus diffused and no longer contained by modernist referents like the state or the sovereign, but, instead, reveals itself to be everywhere. Power is in gender, class, race, ethnicity, and sexuality; in speech, writing, discourse, representation, and reason; in families, curricula, bodies, and the arts. Every facet of the social and political become sites of power, struggle, and resistance so that all is politicized, eroding all constructed boundaries that otherwise define, describe, and name social, political, and economic entities/concepts.[110] This is theory from the bottom up: genealogical, meticulous, and incisive of the workings of power in institutional, societal, and individual bodies. So too is it subversive, both in its political ambitions and its implications for modernist theory, seeing truth and knowledge as socially constructed and performative of oppressive tasks. This is what Lyotard meant when he wrote of the terror of theory: theory used as power, knowledge used to oppress, truth used for legitimation.[111]

Given this conception of theory, it is hardly surprising that faith in theory-knowledge has been eroded and its deconstruction sought, principally through linguistic analyses and the pejorative use of language games. Language has proved the ultimate weapon for subversive postmodernists, enabling the "destabilization" of the very nexus of representation and communication that otherwise makes theory-knowledge possible. Consequently, theory itself is now problematized by subversive postmodernists, as textural analysis acquires a political utility in its demolition of modernist theories of representation.[112]

This demolition has proceeded along two avenues. First, subversive postmodernists have inverted the classical subject-object divide upon which modernist-scientific inquiry proceeded to represent reality; a simple process of problematizing the role of the subject as neutral and of the a priori existence of the object (reality). As Michael Ryan notes, the postmodern movement has discovered "that what were thought to be effects in the classical theory of representation can be causes; representations can create the substance they supposedly reflect."[113] In other words, the observatory act is no longer considered neutral but proactive, which, for postmodernists, inevitably changes the significance and political capacity of theory.

Secondly, assumptions of communicative rationality have been challenged by destabilizing language and attacking the possibility of accurate representation and communication. Modernists like Habermas, for example, insist upon the fixity of meaning in language and upon communicative rationality, where speaker and hearer are rationally committed to the task of reciprocal understanding.[114] Similarly, Robert Brandom argues that "the essential feature of language is its capacity to represent the way things are," to "take truth to be the basic concept in terms of which a theory of meaning, and hence a theory of language, is to be developed."[115] Subversive postmodernists, however, reject this and see language as socially constructed, at best a partial and imperfect intermediary between subjects. Language is unstable: "no statement ever has a determinate meaning," no word a fixed denotation, all referents are transient, and meaning is an interpretive enterprise that varies from subject to subject.[116] The authorial point of view, for deconstructionists, cannot be related to readers since text and subject are not as one but separate and the act of reading, as of writing, is an intertextual and intersubjective process that is multilayered and unique to each text and reader.[117] As Harvey notes, "Writers who create texts or use words do so on the basis of all other texts and words they have encountered, while readers deal with them in the same way." Acts of reading and writing become a "series of texts intersecting with other texts, producing more texts," such that this intertextual weaving takes on a life of its own.[118] The postmodern condition, then, is one where universal language is dead and sites of specialized languages have emerged: the university, the workplace, the bureaucracy, so that effective communication can never be guaranteed and radical misunderstanding results.[119] A crisis of representation ensues.

Subversive postmodern theory thus "provides a critique of representation and the modern belief that theory mirrors reality, taking instead 'perspectivist' and 'relativist' positions that theories at best provide partial perspectives on their objects, and that all cognitive representations of the world are historically and linguistically mediated."[120] In North America this position is best exemplified in the work of Richard Rorty, where knowledge approaches what Rorty calls a postphilosophical culture, a postrepresentational view of knowledge that is prepositional and nonfoundationalist.[121] Knowledge, particularly that type of knowledge generated in the social sciences and humanities, is not approached as a confrontation between the knowing subject and the object of inquiry (knowledge simply seen as the mirror of nature, for example), but as an ongoing conversation between knowing subjects. In other words, knowledge is rooted in a socially constructed discourse, and attempts to move beyond this, as with the Cartesian-Kantian traditions of inquiry that established Western philosophy-as-epistemology, are fallacious.[122]

The abandonment of accurate representation as the touchstone of knowledge is, to say the least, unsettling, repudiating the modernist habit of assuming a realm of reality and truth outside the subject and our language. Postmodernists ask us to rely on a theory-knowledge generated merely by chatting "away in a post-Wittgensteinian room whose mirrors reflect nothing but the lost contexts of . . . [our] own good sense."[123] As Trimbur and Holt observe, "to imagine human culture and the quest for knowledge as a conversation between persons instead of a confrontation with reality may appear to lock us in a 'prison house of language,' a hermeneutic circle that offers no release, no standpoint to get outside our discursive practices in order to show how things really are."[124] Subversive postmodernists, however, dismiss these concerns. In the writings of Derrida we find a deeper malcontent and a resolve to slay the "Hydra of Western logocentrism."[125] Derrida's deconstructionist project aims to "uproot," "decompose," "undo," "dismantle," and "overturn" Western metaphysics through textual analyses of philosophical writings.[126] The aim is not, it should be noted, a complete dismissal of Western rationalism, since Derrida recognizes this to be impossible, but an attempt "to transform [such concepts], to displace them, to turn them against their presuppositions, to reinscribe them in other chains, and little by little to modify the terrain of our work and thereby to produce new configurations." Derrida hopes this will coalesce into a "structure of resistance" to the dominant mode of conceptuality which, to date, under the auspices of Enlightenment thinking, has led to the violence of exclusion, in which certain groups, peoples, voices, thoughts, and modes of conceptualization have been marginalized, exiled, and disenfranchised.[127]

The defining moment for subversive postmodernists obviously rests in the political act they recommend: resistance. The politics of negation dominates their agenda, particularly the want to tear down the modernist edifice and subvert its practices. However, subversive postmodernists are not consistent in this project but contradictory, pragmatic, and opportunistic. As Pauline Rosenau notes, postmodernists are not "concerned with categorical epistemological rigor or total coherence," and "relinquish intellectual consistency in exchange for political relevance." Witness, for example, the way subversive postmodernists portend to be avowedly antitheoretical, a position which is not only deduced from theoretical activity but presented as part of a theoretical discourse and comprised of theoretical propositions.[128] As Norris sardonically observes, the act of theoretical negation is itself a "form of theoretical endeavour, including such attempts to discredit other kinds of theory while smuggling one's own back in, so to speak, by the side entrance."[129] Many of the charges laid against modernist theory thus seem somewhat futile since they also implicate postmodernists in similar theoretical crimes. To denounce truth claims or foundationalist theory and epistemological philosophy, for example, is an inherently foundationalist position presupposing some singular and superior insight beyond modernist understanding—dare one say an appeal to a higher realm of truth and a better conception of the good? Similarly, denouncing reason and logic while engaging in a meticulous discourse that is well reasoned, logically rigorous, and cumulative in its critique suggests the very use of those tools they attempt to destroy. Further, by attacking value hierarchies subversive postmodernists champion the cause of the oppressed, marginalized, and the disempowered, displaying a keen awareness of right from wrong, good from bad, and a zealous preoccupation with such modernist themes as social justice, emancipation, and liberation.[130] And if, as subversive postmodernists insist, language is imprecise, effective communication is impossible, and culture is running down toward allegoric illiteracy amid a simulacra of electronic images, it seems highly unusual for so much effort to be placed on the enunciation of postmodernist theory and its communication through language and the written word; writing and reading for subversive postmodernists should surely be a barren and improbable task. Why, we might ask, do postmodernists feel the need to deconstruct modernist knowledge systems if language is so imprecise and communication so ineffective?

Contradictions of this type inflame the passions of those who would see an end to postmodernism. Christopher Norris dismisses postmodernism as quasi postural political correctness interspersed with "deconstructionist word spinning nonsense."[131] This sentiment is shared by Eric Hirsch who objects to the "decadence of literary scholarship" and the debasement of scholarship and language through "anti-rationalism, faddism, and extreme relativism."[132] For Hirsch, "Scholars are right to feel indignant toward those learned writers who deliberately exploit the institutions of scholarship—even down to its punctilious conventions like footnotes and quotations—to deny the whole point of the institutions of scholarship, to deny, that is, the possibility of knowledge. It is ethically inconsistent to batten on institutions whose very foundations one attacks. It is logically inconsistent to write scholarly books which argue that there is no point in writing scholarly books."[133] Such farcical and light-minded playfulness Alex Callinicos attributes to a Western intelligentsia suffering from an apocalyptic mood as they confront the end of the millennium. He blames, in particular, two French theorists, Derrida and Foucault, who, through stressing the fragmentary, plural, and heterogeneous character of reality, have attempted to deny "human thought the ability to arrive at any objective account of that reality and reduced the bearer of this thought, the subject, to an incoherent welter of sub- and trans-individual drives and desires."[134] The success enjoyed by postmodernists, he concludes, is "quite out of proportion with any slight intellectual merit their work might have."[135]

The success of postmodern theory seems all the more amazing when one considers its spurious relativism. Derrida and Foucault, for example, abandon objectivity, embrace perspectivism and relativism, and deny the privileging of any one narrative over others. Yet, both these theorists proceed to insist that we should reject modernist for postmodernist narratives and adopt a postmodern interpretation of the world. This position is no less absolutist than the one expounded by their modernist counterparts. As Eric Hirsch observes, for postmodernists, "All principles are subject to a universal relativism except relativism itself," which leads him to ask, "But whence comes *its* exception? What is the sanction, in a world devoid of absolutes, for *its* absoluteness? We are never told. This question, so absurdly simple, yet so embarrassing to relativism, is never answered by even the most brilliant of the cognitive atheists."[136]

Toward an Understanding of Postmodernisms

Despite Hirsch's insightful comments, this perhaps is not the way to judge the agency of postmodern theory and its effects upon theoretical discourse. We cannot, as is clear from the foregoing, speak of a singular postmodern theory and dismiss all for the shortcomings of one particular strand. As Jameson noted, "No one postmodernist can give us postmodernism."[137] Rather, I think it best to assess postmodern theory in terms of its effects on our sensibilities in the era of late-modernity where the modernist referents of science, industry, and technology, and faith in the application of reason and logic experience a crisis of confidence; where the modernist project is now questioned; and where the end of the millennium suffers from malaise. These events, be they real or imagined, allow us to understand the revisionist concerns of subversive postmodernists, the catalogue of technological innovations recorded by technological postmodernists, and the search for new understandings by critical postmodernists.

John O'Neill sees in these concerns the ongoing battle between the division of our reason, "divided once and for all into the subrationalities of science, art, and ethics." Yet, he notes, we have not experienced any settlement in this process. "On the contrary, our science tries to rule our politics and economy, while our economy largely dominates our art and morality, if not our science. At the extreme edge, our art and morality try to impose their rule upon our science and political economy—but they generally lack the stamina."[138]

In some ways the postmodernist project is a contribution to understanding this interstitial battle between the subrationalities of art, science, ethics, politics, and economics; a contribution to exploring the human condition and its various constituencies in search of new meaning and understanding. This project, however, is not dissimilar to the one upon which those modernist institutions, the social sciences and humanities, were founded originally. Thus, we should not think of postmodern theory as separate to, distinct from, or outside of the modernist-Western tradition as some postmodernists insist, but as part of its unfolding genealogical tapestry and implicated in its project. What distinguishes subversive postmodernists is their revisionist disposition toward modernity: their search for "thinking space" as they reflect on the modernist experience and their willingness to exploit the crisis of modernity and contribute to it. There is no constructive endeavor, only a celebration of the loss of certainty, where, argues John O'Neill, "Men (sic) are no longer sure of their ruling knowledge and are unable to mobilize sufficient legitimation for the master-narratives of truth and justice." By relativizing all that is offered as knowledge and theory, subversive postmodernists rejoice in the loss of authority that hitherto marked modernist institutions.[139] In other varieties, however, technological postmodernism might well prove a vehicle for not only alerting us to sweeping change, but of theorizing its objective effects upon our social, economic, and political institutions and for remaking a new social science cognizant of postmodern dynamics. Or, in the case of critical postmodernism, we might understand it as an avenue for conceptualizing the heightened engagement between cultural and aesthetic sensibilities and their incorporation into commodity production. In this context, technological and critical postmodernism have obvious utility to the study of international relations, albeit that at present there is little sign of their application in the discipline.[140]

To what end these approaches will prove beneficial, however, to what end their concerns and depictions of current realities prove accurate remains problematic. What does seem obvious, though, is the continuing desire for understanding, the need to examine, comprehend, and make sense of events and, consequently, the need for theoretical endeavor. Despite "nihilistic despair" or charges of epochal change, most of us will wake up tomorrow confronted by a world much the same as today, one that experiences the recurring problems of inequality, injustice, war, famine, violence, and conflict. Various problems will emerge and solutions to them will be sought. These, surely, cannot be deconstructed as the subversive postmodernists insist, but only reinscribed as new questions. And while we might problematize current knowledge and interpretations, question our faith in science, reason, and logic, or reinscribe questions in new contexts, to suppose these endeavors contrary to the activity of theory and the search for meaning and understanding seems plainly absurd. If we abandon the principles of logic and reason, dump the yardsticks of objectivity and assessment, and succumb to a blind relativism that privileges no one narrative or understanding over another, how do we tackle such problems or assess the merits of one solution vis-à-vis another? How do we go about the activity of living, making decisions, engaging in trade, deciding on social rules or making laws, if objective criteria are not to be employed and reason and logic abandoned? How would we construct research programs, delimit areas of inquiry or define problems to be studied if we abandon rationalist tools of inquiry?

Perhaps if only for the fact of its abstractness, postmodern theory has enjoyed a certain aloofness in the social sciences and humanities, often sheltered from critical analysis because of its obtuse language and ethereal forms of representation. In some respects, of course, this has been intentional. Subversive postmodernists, in particular, have tried deliberately to distance themselves from orthodox scholarship and, through their confrontationalist and aggressive styles, have managed to subdue opposition that would otherwise be vocal. Orthodox theorists, confused both by its nomenclature and their discursive styles, have been defensive and reticent to analyze systematically postmodern theory, confusing the motifs of one particular strand with all postmodernisms. Dialogue between these schools has thus been mute.[141] And while this might reflect the unwillingness of postmodernists to respond to criticism, it also reflects the brevity of criticism to come from orthodox theorists, many of whom are plainly on the defensive. Rarely have modernists known how to respond to allegations that implicate them and the age of reason in mass slaughter and genocide, the active marginalization of minority groups, the oppression of women and nonwhite peoples, the disfiguration of the environment, the brainwashing of subjects into prespecified modes of conceptualization that serve instrumentalist purposes, and the degradation of knowledge and universities to proactive instruments of social control and legitimation. Both Richard Ashley and Robert Walker, for example, charge that positivist/structural realists have tended to act as gatekeepers to their discipline, and, in the process, have been apt to "conspicuous displays of violence" against "students, junior faculty, scholars of color, feminists, and other disciplinary marginals."[142] Much of the postmodernist conduit along with these allegations has simply been dismissed as politics from the fringe. Few have seen the need to analyze critically postmodern theory; most have left it alone in the hope it might go away; and nearly all have been baffled (and some intimidated) by its imperceptible vernacular. The lack of vigilance or, more precisely, the surrender of conventional standards of appraisal have enabled subversive postmodernists to infiltrate nearly every imaginable theoretical discussion, and modernists to dismiss all postmodern theory on the basis of the actions and writings of a few.[143] Indeed, of those who have tried to resist the postmodernist tide or even subject it to critical analysis, the cult of political correctness accompanying it has stigmatized its detractors as vagabonds of reason and oppression.[144] The "terror of theory," it seems, has also used in the service of postmodernism.

As a preliminary offering, this chapter has attempted to transcend this gulf of nondiscourse. If nothing else, I trust it behooves readers to a judicious examination of the alternatives and their implications before we pronounce the death of the age of reason and the closure of the Enlightenment project. I for one am not prepared to make the mighty jump from modernist to postmodernist theory without first understanding what such a move would mean for international theory and the discipline of International Relations, yet I also appreciate the sense of change and disjuncture that permeates all facets of our social existence and ostensibly changes the nature of political discourse. The next stage in International Relations, to borrow Linklater's phrase, must thus concern itself with such an examination if intellectual discourse in the discipline is to be saved from a series of discrete debates conducted in isolation from one another, where modernist and postmodernist perspectives speak only to themselves and not to each other.[145] Save for this, perspectivism and islands of theory threatens to make International Relations the anything-goes discipline. At least with a preliminary classificatory scheme with which to approach the plethora of theory labeled postmodern, the task of assessing its relevance to international relations and understanding its sites and sources of origin might now begin.

Chapter Four

Richard K. Ashley and the Subversion of International Political Theory
The "Heroic" Phase

> Madness is to think of too many things in succession too fast, or to think on one thing exclusively.
> Voltaire

> A spectre haunts Europe: the dissident.
> Julia Kristeva

> Words wreak havoc when they find names for what had previously been lived namelessly.
> Jean-Paul Sartre

> I have seen young people, and older people too, who are good democratic liberals, lovers of peace and gentleness, struck dumb with admiration for individuals threatening or using the most terrible violence for the slightest and tawdriest reasons.
> Allen Bloom

Much as political theory is now haunted by the spectre of the dissident, so too is international political theory. Intellectual dissidents now comprise a significant number of theorists in the discipline. Their work, although not as widely read as the ubiquitous rehearsals of neorealism and neo-liberalism, is certainly infamous. In the space of only a decade, the study of international relations has "come under the influence of continental philosophical and intellectual practices"—belatedly for some, and unfortunately for others.[1] Where previously the study of International

Relations was the preserve of positivist- and empiricist-based pedagogical practices, theoretical debate now slides between affirmations of Kuhnian theories of knowledge development and intertextualism, as well as feminist psychoanalytic theory, semiotics, genealogy, and deconstructionism.

In International Relations the undiminished allure of postmodernism is plainly attributable to two theorists, Richard Ashley and, to a lesser extent, Robert Walker.[2] Since the early 1980s their intellectual contributions have made dissident writings a veritable cottage industry. Few students of international relations are today unaware of the new reflectivist trends in theorizing. Most distinctive, however, have been the writings of Richard Ashley. These have not only widened the scope of international political theory but have also brought seemingly alien concepts and theoretical tools to its study. In particular, Ashley has brought to the discipline constructivist theoretical accounts of the state, political power, the practices of realpolitik, and raised questions of the Enlightenment's authority over the construction of knowledge, meaning, identity, and truth. Never before have international theorists been so assaulted by excursions into metatheory, especially when the depth of this excursion questions not only the ontological but also the epistemological and "axiological foundations of their scientific endeavours."[3] Not all have welcomed this examination nor the subsequent course of debate in the discipline. There are, as Yosef Lapid notes, those who proscribe "a rigorous philosophy-avoidance strategy" and who warn of the dangers of pursuing philosophy at the expense of "actual research."[4] Robert Keohane, on more than one occasion, has warned that the "postmodernist project is a dead-end in the study of international relations," and that it serves no useful purpose to conduct indefinitely "a debate at the purely theoretical level, much less simply to argue about epistemological and ontological issues in the abstract." For Keohane, such debates "would take us away from the study of our subject matter, world politics, toward what would probably become an intellectually derivative and programmatically diversionary philosophical discussion."[5] Yet philosophical insurgencies abound, reminding us that "those who try to ignore philosophy only succeed in reinventing it."[6] In this respect, Ashley can rightly be thought of as a pioneer, delineating an intellectual space that, in his own words, exists on the margins and border lines of the discipline, yet one which now enjoys a considerable following. Indeed, the new-found prominence of theory in the study of international relations is, in no small measure, a consequence of the metatheoretical excursion launched by Ashley. His assault upon neorealism and the shibboleths of reason, logic, positivism, and science has fulfilled his original calls for "a methodologically more demanding science: a science that expands the range of allowable criticism, and sharpens the standards of theoretical adequacy, by institutionalizing the expectation of continuous critical reflection on the historical significance and possibility of our attempts to arrive at objectivist conclusions."[7]

To this end, Ashley has expanded the domain of discourse in International Relations, causing us to re-examine our theoretical tools of analysis and the assumptions on which they are based.[8] Yet despite this not inconsiderable achievement, his work has rarely been subjected to critical inquiry let alone comprehensive exegetic analysis. This, to say the least, is unusual given the gravity of Ashley's writings and their implications for the discipline. Of those who have attempted to appraise Ashley's work, not only are their contributions all too brief, but their number unusually sparse.[9] This might be explained by the fact that postmodern thinkers "are more often attacked than read."[10] Rather than an occasion for productive dialogue and diligent attention to the theoretical intricacies of contending approaches, the Third Debate seems more a battleground between the deaf.[11] Scholars frequently talk past one another, accepting theoretical incommensurability much as they accept national borders as a means of demarcation between different value and belief systems. Robert Gilpin can thus largely dismiss Ashley's discourse, not in terms of the weaknesses implicit in its postulates, but by virtue "of the opacity of much of Ashley's prose," the needless jargon he employs, and the fact that Gilpin has "no idea what it means."[12] In this way, postmodernist approaches have not provoked meaningful or enlightening dialogue as much as they have "heat, venom, and nonproductive controversy."[13] And when critical appraisals of postmodernist approaches in International Relations have been attempted, for James Der Derian most have "arisen as much from confusion and wilful ignorance as from disagreement."[14]

This chapter, as with the following, aims to correct these past mistakes by analyzing critically and exegetically the work of Richard Ashley. My analysis focuses exclusively on Ashley,[15] not because other theorists are of lesser importance, but because Ashley is the preeminent and defining voice of a postmodernist perspective in international theory today. His work is thus emblematic of a tradition of scholarship now endemic to the Third Debate and postmodernism in International Relations.

Before I begin, however, a few remarks are in order about my method of analysis. Following Ashley's own intellectual evolution and metamorphosis, I treat Ashley's work programmatically and episodically. In this chapter I concentrate on Ashley's formative works, or what I shall characterize as Ashley's "heroic" episode, and analyze thematically his motifs of technical rationality, structuralism, economism, and reductionism.[16] My reasons for doing so are fourfold. First, apart from *The Poverty of Neorealism*, Ashley's early works have been generally ignored, detracting from a perspicacious understanding of the evolution of his ideas. Second, this has fostered the false impression that his work is a unitary exercise founded upon the rejection of structural realism. While this is true to some degree, it understates the real intent and scope of Ashley's project. When considered collectively, for example, Ashley's early works are as much a polemic against economistic, structuralist, and reductionist forms of theory as they are a rejection of neorealism itself. Third, Ashley's writings should not be considered separately but as a series of interrelated efforts more accurately understood as a project.[17] In this regard, his early writings need to be seen as contiguous efforts, each concerned with validating one particular aspect of his overall program. And fourth, I review his early works since I believe them to be the more substantive, original, and useful of his contributions, especially Ashley's insightful critique of the structuralist turn in international political theory.

The Heroic Ashley: Against Technical Rationality

Ashley's earliest work, *The Political Economy of War and Peace*, upon first reading appears to bear no relation to his subsequent concerns.[18] It was, he wrote, a book "about the sources of conflict and violence among today's major military powers: the Chinese People's Republic, the Soviet Union, and the United States." Its focus, he added, addressed the issues of the balance of power, the modern security problematique, and the dynamics and dilemmas of military rivalry. Its approach Ashley termed international political economy, and its contents considered "the processes of growth—differential, technological, economic, and population growth in a world of finite resources and unevenly distributed capabilities."[19] Ostensibly, the study purported to be orthodox, the methodology empirical, and the objective laudable: the search for a lasting peaceful order.[20] Books, however, can never be judged by their covers, nor should their contents by the prefatory remarks that introduce them. While Ashley's book was about all these things, they were neither the purpose of, nor point to, his study. Rather, they were exemplars, demonstrative subjects used to illustrate the consequences of a particular mode of conceptualization that Ashley termed technical rationality. The latter became and remains Ashley's intellectual raison d'être, the defining purpose and motivation of all his works. And for this reason *The Political*

Economy of War and Peace remains central to any appreciation of Ashley's intellectual development, since it foreshadowed and defined his subsequent project and the path it would take. In fact, the works that followed were merely augmentations, logical extensions, and refinements of Ashley's crusade against technical rationality that would eventually lead him to reject rationality altogether and adopt a subversive philosophy.

In this first, "heroic" episode, Ashley's project was comprised of three constellations: the first was his attack against the superstructural edifice of technical rationalism; the second attacked the substructural foundations of instrumentalist logic when he argued the case against economism and reductionism; and the third extended this critique to attack structuralism. His rejection of neorealism was therefore only incidental, predicated not on the nature, logical consistency, or efficacy of neorealist theory per se, but upon neorealism as the exemplar par excellence of technical rationalism and structuralist theory.

It is thus that I approach his works both episodically and thematically, and his writings as an interrelated program unified by their rejection of technical rationalism. The latter, Ashley believed, inspired an instrumentalist grammar of thought that reduced scholarship to the design of research programs whose sole objective was the analysis and solution of discrete problem situations. This enterprise, he wrote, tended "to conceive of life as consisting of so many more or less discrete problem situations; . . . defined in terms of certain given purposes or needs, certain obstacles to or limits on the realization or satisfaction of these, and certain means by which the obstacles and limits can or might be overcome."[21] Technical rationality tended to lure the pursuit of knowledge into this service, denying any "rational purpose for knowledge and skills except insofar as they orient the development, application, or strategic manipulation of means to solve problems and serve ends."[22] Ashley's polemic was therefore directed against the construction and use of theory for purely instrumental purposes. Perhaps reacting to the remains of the behaviorist revolution, Ashley was at pains to reject such pragmatic and utilitarian theoretical enterprises in part because theory lost its critical function and became simply a nonreflective problem-solving tool.[23] Doubtless Ashley was also reacting to what Richardson describes as the discipline's "excessive reliance on the style of theorizing derived from economics" and "a one-sided emphasis on rational choice models."[24] As far as Ashley was concerned, rational choice and utility theory[25] made the study of international relations a technocratic exercise. In this way, theorists were less concerned with the theoretical task of explaining the complex multilevel phenomena of international relations as they were with developing parsimonious models drawn from empirical observations of the patterns of behavior, historical repetitions, or structural attributes of discrete subject areas.[26]

Ashley outlined this methodological schema in the case of the security problematique where technical rationality inspired a grammar of thought that attempted "to systematically join insights from several different traditions, each focusing upon particular sectors or levels of activity, and each offering generalizing knowledge claims regarding certain patterns and processes."

Moreover, Ashley noted, "each assumes that the patterns it identifies reflect the technical-rational choices of people acting within certain kinds of problem situations." The aim of this knowledge was thus purely instrumental: "as a knowledge of . . . [a] particular domain is enhanced and applied, people will be better able to make rational choices that solve or manage the problems that beset them."[27] The job of the social scientist was therefore reduced to that of technician whose task was to ensure improved knowledge and the resolute application of that knowledge as a means to greater control and the creation of a "more encompassing political order."[28]

Such an approach has long comprised the theoretical ambitions of scholars of international politics. Hans Morgenthau, for instance, had urged that we "put ourselves in the position of a statesmen who must confront a certain problem of foreign policy under certain circumstances, and [that] we ask ourselves what the rational alternatives are from which a statesmen may choose who must meet this problem under these circumstances, . . . and which of these circumstances he is likely to choose." For Morgenthau, it was "the testing of this rational hypothesis against the actual facts and their circumstances" that would give "theoretical meaning to the facts of international politics."[29] This approach proved attractive, dominating theoretical research for many years to come. Ashley, for example, argued that Stanley Hoffmann's imaginative reconstruction and Thomas Schelling's vicarious problem-solving were complementary extensions of Morgenthau's approach and technical rationalism. This was also true of "Ernst Haas and his assumptions about welfare-oriented technocrat-politicians"; of "Keohane and Nye with their arguments about the choices of state bureaucracies engaged in transgovernmental politics"; as well as Graham Allison with his attempt to locate rationality within bureaucratic players in a central competitive game.[30] Ashley thought all these approaches were essentially the same since they all assumed that "the actualities of international relations" could "be understood in terms of the interactions, aggregations, and recombinations of individual technical-rational choices."[31]

Ashley rejected this approach not only for its utilitarian and instrumentalist rationality but also for its hegemonic dominance, particularly its ability to exclude and delegitimize other knowledge systems. More obviously, though, Ashley opposed the delimiting task proscribed the social scientist by technical rationalism, a task instrumentally conceived in order to capture social laws or general social principles as a means to "solve (analytical) problems, close (theoretical-empirical) gaps, and bring social reality (intellectually) under control." And to the extent that knowledge and scholarship were seen simply as a means to inform and solve particular social problems, and their worth judged on this basis, then in Ashley's view this made the dominance of technical rationality all the more plain and its effects the more insidious.[32]

Ashley's concerns and the debate they inspired will be familiar, albeit presently conducted under the positivist versus postpositivist rubric. Indeed, technical rationality has become one of the central motifs that currently informs the parameters of discourse between contending schools of thought in the field. We need hardly recall, for example, Robert Keohane's recent chastising of the reflective approaches for their failure to approximate rationalistic premises and impart "a clear reflective research program." For Keohane the nonrationalist approaches are less well specified as theories, too preoccupied with epistemological and ontological debates and therefore display "little prospect of becoming a comprehensive deductive explanation of international institutions." Rationalistic theory, he argues, offers such an explanation and is able to "specify the characteristics of a given institutional situation" and "anticipate the path that change will take." Reflective theory, on the other hand, offers us the machinations of self-doubt, philosophic speculation, and from the point of view of empirical theory, inconsequential, untestable, nonoperational, and nonuseful conjecture. His remarks clearly expose the chasm between these two contending schools, demonstrated, for example, when he insists that interpretive scholars are yet to illuminate important issues in world politics. The inference is quite apparent: reflective approaches are less than worthy of the title theory, and their project something other than useful and legitimate if not formalized and presented as a research program germane to predictive and problem-solving tasks. Under the regime of technical rationality,[33] legitimacy for the reflectivist approaches rests in their renouncing the margins and adopting a research program with testable theories and an explicit research scope that leads to systematic empirical investigations.[34]

The problem of course is that Keohane's recommendations not only disparage the hermeneutic epistemology of the reflectivist approach but also recommend its complete overhaul and substitution for a positivist one![35] And this was precisely Ashley's point and his reason for rejecting technical rationality. The grammar of thought which it inspires acts as an intellectual hegemon and a self-appointed arbiter of what is, and what is not, legitimate theory, research, and knowledge. James Der Derian makes a similar observation of Keohane's arguments, noting that within them there "lies an implicit imprecation: if one is to find a 'genuine research program' it is better to take the enlightened road of rationalist reflection than the benighted wood of poststructuralist reflexivity."[36]

Ashley's observations were not meant as arcane reflections on the territorializing abilities of one particular knowledge system, however. He believed they had very real implications for the way in which global politics, security, trade, or decision-making processes were conducted. And it was through these concerns that his alternative theoretical vision would come ultimately to confront neorealist theory. His explorations of the security problematique, for example, were meant to be illustrative of but one "protracted climactic scene in the tragic drama of technical rationality's ultimate failure."[37] The constellation of global order embodied in the state system and thus the modern security problematique, for example, Ashley attributed "not to natural law and not to historical accident, but to the culminations and the interactions of processes framed by a technical-rational grammar of thought."[38] Within the "violence prone [state] system," he noted, it was impossible to "contemplate peace within a grammar of thought that frame[ed] choices in a way producing the absence of peace."[39]

Against technical rationality Ashley therefore aspired to create a more encompassing and liberating form of reflection, to open up a new, more expansive rational logic as a means to escape the delimiting options conferred by instrumentalist thought. He also wanted to demonstrate the capacity for reflective political agency, to change structural conditions rather than merely react to their circumstances. This alternative form of reflection he clumsily termed rationality proper. Unlike technical rationality, it was cognizant of history, the historical conditioning of reality, and of a differentiated reality. It attempted to embed and subordinate "technical rationality within a richer logic that problematize[d] the elements of technical-rational problem-solving."[40] The aim was to escape finitude in knowledge and understanding, at least as proclaimed by the shibboleths of technical rationalism, and restore to the task of knowledge generation a sense of ongoing reflection. All knowledge had therefore to be situated within historical contexts, and its meaning and efficacy restricted to that milieu. History, in other words, could not be understood as a series of structures imposed from above, and truth as an autonomous referent detached from historically specific conditions, but as a series of perpetually changing sociopolitical practices and modes of thought modified by agents within interrelated, but historically distinctive epochs. This clearly established Ashley's opposition to structuralist theory, since the latter discounted the role of political agency, failed to understand history as the processual outcome of structured interactions between subjects and structures, and foreclosed political/historical options via structuralist determinism.[41] In contrast, Ashley understood history as knowable only via "an attempt to import the larger historical reality" so as "to engage, criticize, and synthesize competing vantage points associated with other aspects of reality." By doing so, Ashley could avoid "invoking the assumption that there exists some fixed, final, and potentially knowable structure predominating over the whole of reality."[42] The difference between these two perspectives was therefore ontological. Technical rationality proclaimed "human freedom by denying the determinist influences of historical processes" yet was entrapped in history and unable to imagine or criticize it. Rationality proper, on the other hand, commenced "the search for human freedom by allowing that human beings . . . [were] distinctly unfree of historical-processual influences" and embedded in community constituted by tradition.

The distinction rested on the ontological conception of history. "Technical rationality sees history episodically, as a sequence of discrete . . . problem situations. It see [sic] reality as segmentable . . . into a number of bounded . . . problem domains. . . . Rationality proper sees history processually. It allows that the segments of reality are processually created, interdependent, and susceptible to change."[43] Truth, knowledge, and reality were therefore different creatures depending upon one's ontological conception of history: "Technical rationality assumes the autonomy of systematic knowledge, [and] sees truth in the actual dominant patterns of the historical moment. . . . Rationality proper strives for autonomy and truth by seeking . . . an intersubjective consensus through the . . . exchange of communications and criticisms among people . . . situated within, and having varying vantage points upon, the whole of actual and possible human experience."[44]

Ashley's approach therefore reified historicity, making knowledge contingent not only on the historical milieu it occupied but also on the cultural vantage point from which it stemmed. The methodology was contextualist and designed to escape the structuralist logic that dominated social and political theory throughout the 1960s and 1970s. It was also idealistic, aspiring to erect a "rationality proper" that would inform an emancipatory logic. The latter Ashley implored of the transnational communities of social science who, he argued, represented "a likely point of departure for [the development of an] emancipatory praxis."[45] Indeed, Ashley was optimistic that technical rationality's dominance would decline. This he believed was coming about due to technological changes that would allow greater latitude for effective expression: first, in the developments in global communications and information processing technologies; second, through growing global interdependence and cross-culturalism; and third, in the growth of a multifaceted, transnational social scientific community that was "already exhibiting a modest commitment to the seeking of autonomy through the criticism-conscious pursuit of some intersubjective consensus across social, political, and economic divides." While these developments did not guarantee the subordination of technical rationality, they did present "opportunities unlike any previously experienced in the history of humankind."[46] More importantly, they were occurring at precisely the same time as was the interpretivist and poststructuralist turn in political theory in the United States. The latter Ashley not only foresaw, but would eventually contribute to and exploit. And this, more than any other single event, provided Ashley with the intellectual-theoretical wherewithal to challenge what he saw as the "acme of technical rationality": "world empire via massive violence." At the very least it would furnish him the theoretical means to unmask the "false logic" of technical rationality. And, it need hardly be noted, this became Ashley's preoccupation: an "heroic" effort to speak with a sovereign voice and invoke an alternative means of thinking, conceptualizing, theorizing, and of political praxis. His project was therefore begun, his course of action defined, and the method implicit. The arguments and allegations would become legion, and all of them sounded from this beginning:

> . . . technical rationality is a false logic. . . . It is a false logic because it is at once a creative logic and a logic totally in awe of its creations. It is a false logic because it serves human purposes without questioning their sources and creates new needs in ways it refuses to see. . . . It is a false logic because it orients attempts to solve problems in fragments, frames social action such that it institutionalizes limitlessness in society's manifest structures and forms, and thereby implicates all aspects of a finite world in every seemingly isolated problem situation. It is a false logic because its equates autonomy with an unobtainable independence and mastery over the environment. . . . It is

a false logic because, in its celebration of autonomy and its equation of autonomy with power, it finds lasting success by persistently subordinating the many to the solutions of the few.[47]

With the objectives and targets of his project defined, and the obsessions of his ideological ambitions implicit in his call for an emancipatory praxis, all that remained was an ongoing "heroic" commitment to their realization. In the context of international theory, that commitment would continue by his connecting realism (specifically neorealism) to technical rationality, positivism, economism, reductionism, and eventually to structuralism.

Against Technical Rationality, Positivism, Economism, and Structuralism

The four articles considered here comprised Ashley's most ingenious and certainly his most erudite period.[48] Each was concerned with validating a particular aspect of his ideological program. *Political Realism and Human Interests*, for example, extended his critique of technical rationality to the domain of political realism. *The Eye of the Power: The Politics of World Modeling* vilified the paragon of technical science presumed in attempts to model world order and calculate interests, costs, benefits, and outcomes while situating its epistemology within positivism and its technical rationality in a Benthamite panopticon preoccupied with control. The *Three Modes of Economism* attacked the economization of theory, the infusion of econometric logic into the determination of social and political relations, and the reduction of all things political to the logic of economy. Finally, *The Poverty of Neorealism* was the conduit that synthesized all these concerns, the climatic presentation that charged neorealist theory with a legion of theoretical crimes: first, in its penchant toward structuralism; second, its technical rationalism embodied in its instrumentalist utilitarianism; and last, in its reductionist econometric logic that reified positivism and science to the detriment of a reflective, critical-hermeneutic understanding of international politics.[49]

While thematically discrete, all these articles were interrelated—cumulative projects designed to challenge orthodox international political theory. In this respect, they were hardly unique. All of Ashley's contributions have attempted to problematize orthodox interpretations of international politics. What distinguished these earlier attempts from his more recent contributions was their grounding in rationalist epistemology. Despite his incredulity toward modernist metanarratives and their positivist foundationalism, his work derived entirely from modernist-Enlightenment thinking. In *Political Realism and Human Interests,* for example, the writings of Jurgen Habermas, one of the leading champions of Enlightenment thought, were used to distinguish between what Ashley termed a technical and a practical realism.[50] The latter Ashley understood as containing "genuine antinomies—some critical tensions" that made it, at least potentially, a vital, open ended tradition.[51] Practical realism, he wrote, had a practical cognitive interest: "This is an interest in knowledge as a basis for furthering mutual, intersubjective understanding. It guides knowledge toward the development of interpretations that make possible the orientations of action within common traditions."[52] Technical realism, on the other hand, had a technical cognitive interest: "This is an interest in knowledge as the basis for extending control over objects in the subject's environment (possibly including strategic dominance over other human beings). It guides knowledge to obtain information that expands . . . powers of technical control. The technical cognitive interest . . . finds its foremost philosophical expression in positivism."[53]

As always, the point of his critique was to contextualize knowledge and demonstrate the fallacy of positivistic social science and technical realism. "Knowledge," he wrote, "is not constituted objectively. It is not constituted as a universe of facts whose lawlike connection can be grasped descriptively." Instead, the illusion of objectivism, of knowledge inductively generated via the positivist pretense of a posteriori value-neutral observation, had to "be replaced with the recognition that knowledge is always constituted in reflection of interests."[54] Ashley's dilemma, then, was Habermasian in nature: "How to progress beyond this position without reducing the relation between knowledge and interests to Mannheimian simplisms?"[55] (For example, Robert Cox's reductionist adage that "Theory is always *for* someone and *for* some purpose"[56]). Stated in another way: how is realism to "reconcile a practical interest in intersubjective understanding, on the one hand, with the mutually objectifying instrumentalism of power politics, on the other?" Ashley's solution (borrowed, in part, from Habermas) was hermeneutic interpretivism, or practical realism: a tradition derived from subjectivities who "maintain a consensus of coreflective self-understanding."[57] The idea was deceptively simple: to situate all knowledge and understanding in the series of social relations constituted by the historical traditions established by subjective practices.[58] The aim of knowledge had therefore to be "the attainment of possible consensus among actors in the framework of a self-understanding derived from tradition."[59] Practically speaking, this meant "the integration of society, the maintenance of order, the mutuality of interaction, and the avoidance of severe, dislocating social conflict."[60] In this way, valid knowledge for practical realism entailed "not so much an improved capacity to control one's object environment, but an improved capacity to be and behave as a worthy member of one's traditional community, with its intersubjective and consensually endorsed norms, rights, meanings, purposes, and limitations on what the individual participants can be and might become."[61]

This hermeneutical method of inquiry approached texts interpretively, not in a postmodernist sense of interpretation detached from empirical verification, but one that tests the hypothesis of texts against practice. As Ashley put it, "Every interpretation is tested, as it were, insofar as it generates expectations for practice, including language, that can be gauged against actual practices." Consequently, "a disappointment of expectations signals the failure of interpretation and a need . . . to carry the dialogue forward. . . . Only when the interpreter's expectations close on actual practice can it be said—and then always provisionally—that the interpreter has succeeded."[62]

As an example of practical realism and this hermeneutic attitude, Ashley cited the work of Hans Morgenthau,[63] who urged that we "retrace and anticipate . . . the steps a statesman—past, present, or future—has taken or will take on the political scene. We look over his shoulder when he writes his dispatches; we listen in on his conversations with other statesmen; we read and anticipate his very thoughts."[64] Morgenthau's realism was interpretivist to the extent that it recognized that realist practices were socially located; that they reflected, and were contingent upon, the actions of agents acting within historical traditions to give them meaning and reality. And Morgenthau's approach was practical realism to the extent that it recognized that "no study of politics . . . can be disinterested in the sense that it is possible to divorce knowledge from action." Far from being esoteric-philosophic reflection, then, practical realism displayed a practical cognitive interest, albeit articulated via a hermeneutic logic.[65] It was not an instance of theory detached from practice any more than it was observations of practice detached from theory. On the contrary, it reflected the intersection between action and knowledge, synthesizing these two categories into one to produce a praxiology of international politics. And Morgenthau's hermeneutic praxiology was, according to Ashley, a form of textual interpretivism where theoretical insights vented practice, informing the conundrums of foreign policy, statesmanship, diplomacy, and statecraft while realist practices vented theory, providing the empirical referents to test texts and, through a perpetual state of modification, adapt theory to the modalities of specific historical circumstance. So important was Morgenthau's hermeneutic attitude that, for Ashley, it explained why *Politics Among Nations* was still prescribed reading among foreign service officers, for it not only recognized their political agency, albeit restrained by the traditions in which they operated, but provided the nearest thing yet to a practical-theoretical manual of instruction, not about the facts of international politics, but about the processes contained within them and derived from the reflexive intersection between action and knowledge. And this is what made practical realism an "open-ended tradition," where international politics reflected the dynamic interplay of instrumental power politics amid hermeneutic interpretation. History, in other words, was explained as process, the outcome of coaction among agents (or as Ashley termed them, subjectivities) operative within tradition, and not as the mechanistic effects of metaphysically conceived systems or structures. This is what made practical realism, and thus Morgenthau's approach, attractive to Ashley: their refusal to foreclose history through any kind of structuralist determinism. Instead, the partial autonomy implicit in practical realism allowed room for practical action, which, in Ashley's view, was coterminous with an emancipatory logic and reflective progress.[66]

The distinction between practical and technical realism was important for Ashley since the former did not portend to transhistorical foundationalism, truth, certitude, or fact. Practical realism understood fact and reality as merely historical dialogical readings, and theoretical-narratives as historical documents of interpretation. Ashley, for example, reminded us of Morgenthau's contention that no fixed, once-and-for-all operational definition of power and national interest was possible. The contents, characteristics, and nature of these terms "at any moment depend upon the political and cultural environments, the political and cultural context within which foreign policy is formulated."[67] Morgenthau, as Ashley was keen to point out, simply recognized that things change, that history was not just repetition with new players, that knowledge was not immutable, and that fact and reality were as much determined by one's cultural, aesthetic, and historical vantage point as they were by supposedly objectifying forms of reason.

Against this belief, however, Ashley confronted the dominance of technical realism where a "very considerable proportion of North American international politics research . . . [had] been tidily confined within the logic of economy." Neofunctional integration theory, along with "deterrence theory, game theory, and so-called 'strategic thinking,' . . . operated entirely within the model of technical rational action," a condition Ashley depicted as the economization of politics.[68] His opposition to this stemmed from a well-established intellectual tradition. Morgenthau, for instance, had objected to the use "of the tools of modern economic analysis . . . to understand international relations. In such a theoretical scheme," he had written, "nations confront each other not as living historic entities with all their complexities but as rational abstractions, after the model of economic man."[69] Before him E. H. Carr had also addressed the illusion of a divorce between politics and economics and of the infusion of economic rationality into the study of political phenomena. Carr had insisted that economic forces were in fact political forces.[70] Similarly, the masterly study by Karl Polanyi, *The Great Transformation*, traced the tumultuous consequences of a world turned upside-down where "instead of economy being embedded in social relations, social relations . . . [were] embedded in the economic system."[71] For Polanyi, this great transformation was tantamount to the usurping of social needs in the name of economic rationality with consequences that obliterated international order, first in the Great Depression of the 1930s and then its political ramifications in Germany and world war. Ashley did no more than take his lead from these three theorists in particular, seeing economism and its theoretical offsprings of rational choice theory and neorealism (or technical realism), manifestations of a single nemesis—technical rationality. All these, he said, derived from a technical cognitive interest which remains "the knowledge-constitutive interest of the empirical-analytic sciences" expressed as positivism.[72] The objective of his project had therefore to be a thorough critique of positivism, especially its pretense to science, empirical value-free knowledge, and its vapid manifestations in structuralist and reductionist economistic theory.

Ashley's main target in this undertaking was Kenneth Waltz and his work, *Theory of International Politics*.[73] Ashley chastised Waltz's instrumentalist approach to theory, where a theory's usefulness was assessed in terms of its "capacities to *orient purposive-rational attempts to exert control over an objectified reality*." Waltz clearly displayed a technical cognitive interest, for example, when he noted, "The urge to explain is not born of idle curiosity alone. It is produced also by the desire to control, or at least to know if control is possible."[74] This conception of theory was said to conceal a deeper political significance that, by making theoretical endeavor conditional upon purposive-rational control, established "expectations as to the kinds of research practices that were warranted, comprehensible, appropriate, and worthy of community [read financial and institutional] support."[75] "Appropriate" or "legitimate" theory sought to solve problems and enhance control while "inappropriate" theory problematized knowledge and engaged in rank speculation. Reason had been reduced to purposive rationality and action was now gauged solely in terms of the efficiency of means, disparaging human reflective capacities that might transcend the technical interest in control.[76] The root of this problem derived from neorealism's positivist epistemology. As Ashley noted, "Neorealist theory . . . [was] theory of, by, and for positivists."[77] And positivist epistemology, or more precisely the technical rationality inherent in positivism, tended to "inhabit the domain of the is rather than the domain of the ought" where its truth required no normative defense.[78] Hermeneutic reflection or interpretation, questions of values or issues of epistemology or ontology could therefore be jettisoned from positivist discourse. This was also true of neorealists who deflected criticism of their project by limiting "the range of theories about society that [could] be scientifically entertained."[79] Indeed, they could simply dismiss, or more easily ignore criticisms that derived from philosophic what-ought-to-be type arguments, asserting instead that their theoretical purview concerned only the facts of international politics and questions of what-is. The purpose of theory was thus self-evident. As Waltz noted, "by a theory the significance of the observed is made manifest."[80] Theory had only to bring parsimonious order to the complexity of facts and phenomena that constituted international politics, and, by virtue of this knowledge, influence and control over them might be extended.

Ashley's more immediate criticism of Waltz, however, rested on his rejection of structuralism. More precisely, it rested on the duplicitous way Waltz had fused an instrumentalist, utilitarian, positivist conception of theory to a structuralist understanding of international politics. Waltz, he claimed, had used a form of structuralist sophistry by assuming the state to be "*ontologically* prior to the international system," and by ascribing to the state a generative structuralism in the creation of the international system and the condition of anarchy.[81] This was an instance of statist economism, where states were infused with a technical-economic rationality and the international system was said to be "an emergent property, a consequence of the coaction of a multiplicity of unitary, complete, and egoistic states oriented according to the logic of raison d'etat.[82] Ashley, of course, thought this argument fallacious. The state-as-actor assumption, the epistemological linchpin of neorealist theory, was merely "a metaphysical commitment prior to science and exempted from scientific criticism." Despite its pretensions to science, neorealist theory rested entirely on normative supposition: the ontological presumption of the state-as-actor which, despite its ontological centrality, remained an untheorized category. In fact, this neorealist move was "a sleight of hand, for despite its statism, "neorealism . . . [could] produce no theory of the state capable of satisfying the state-as-actor premises of its international political theory."[83]

Ashley also thought Waltz's inverted structuralist assumptions illogical. For example, once the utilitarian-rationalist state-as-actor (the parts) had generated the anarchic international system (the whole), the logic of Waltz's generative structuralism—the causal effects of the parts upon the whole—ceased to operate. In fact, Waltz inverted this structuralist causality, granting to the anarchic international system "absolute predominance over the parts."[84] Ashley was thus the first to identify what others would come subsequently to recognize, that Waltz's neorealism suffered from ontological confusion and contradiction, emasculating cause and effect beneath a top-heavy structuralism after having explained the process as bottom up—generative—structuralism, and all of this premised upon the ontological assumption of the state. But perhaps Waltz's greatest mistake, for Ashley at least, lay in the way he depicted structure as ontologically independent of its generating agents—human subjectivities. Neorealism denied the "historical significance of practice, the moment at which men and women enter with greater or lesser degrees of consciousness into the making of their world." No longer were men and women free agents, but "some idealized *homo oeconomicus*, able only to carry out, but never to reflect critically on, the limited rational logic that the system demands of them."[85] Likewise, by infusing the state-as-actor with contrary-differentiated-competitive interests, Waltz denied states the ability to engage in unified coaction that might bring about systemic-system change. All that was left was a stagnant ahistorical and apolitical structuralist model, unable to account for historical movement or provide latitude for international collaboration, transnational learning, or conscious political agency.

Ashley correctly characterized this as crude structuralist determinism articulated via the logic of economy, where international politics was understood in reductionist fashion as the interstitial points of engagement between structurally determined entities—states—motivated by the abstract logic of utilitarianism. Ashley therefore rejected neorealist theory on the basis that it was top-heavy structuralism and not a theory of international politics per se. Rather, neorealist historicism was said to deny politics, or "more correctly, neorealism reduce[d] politics to those aspects which . . . [lent] themselves to interpretation exclusively within a framework of economic action under structural constraints."[86] This, it need hardly be said, was the elemental fault in neorealist theory as far as Ashley could see. "Absent from neorealist categories . . . [was] any hint of politics as a creative, critical enterprise, an enterprise by which men and women might reflect on their goals and strive to shape freely their collective will." Waltz's structural realism was thus an "orrery of errors."[87]

> Far from expanding discourse, this so-called structuralism encloses it. . . . Far from penetrating the surface of appearances, this so-called structuralism's fixed categories freeze the given order, reducing the history and future of social evolution to an expression of those interests which can be mediated by the vectoring of power among competing states-as-actors. Far from presenting a structuralism that envisions political learning on a transnational scale, neorealism presents a structure in which political learning is reduced to the consequences of instrumental coaction among dumb, unreflective, technical-rational unities that are barraged and buffeted by technological and economic changes they are powerless to control.[88]

This was "statism, utilitarianism, positivism, structuralism, and statism yet again," a strange unity of contrarieties where "absurdities abound."[89]

Ashley's "heroic" project was now complete. The paragon of international theory, neorealism, had been attacked and its epistemic basis problematized. There was one problem however. Where Ashley's "heroic" strategy had intended a revolutionary reconstruction of international theory, his efforts had largely failed and were "marginalized" by the extremity of his own discourse. International theory remained committed to technical theory and its preeminent practitioners unconvinced by Ashley's critique. If Ashley's project had intended to destabilize orthodox theory and reorient theory in reflection of an emancipatory interest, then he had been only marginally successful. It was time to try new strategies.

Observations on the Death of a "Hero"

The "heroic" Ashley no longer lives, but, according to Ashley, lies dead and buried beneath the rubble of a "sovereign knowledge." At his request, his early works are now largely ignored, indeed derided by a self-reflective autocritique.[90] In their place the works of a new neo-Nietzschean Ashley have arisen, one more radicalized, flamboyant, and infamous in style and rhetoric. He now shuns his early works for their ideological epistemology and for what he calls their heroic strategy. Yet, he was not wrong, he writes, for he was still a dissident, but a dissident imprisoned in a false logic, method, and tradition.[91]

That tradition was rationalist and bound to the Enlightenment project, and adopted by Ashley because of its emancipatory problematic: an heroic strategy committed to the principles of truth, justice, and liberation. His mentor in this undertaking was Jurgen Habermas, who, he acknowledged, exerted an important influence over his work.[92] Indeed, his entire methodological formula cum emancipatory project was vintage Habermas, imported into international theory and used in his crusade against technical rationality and its omnipresence in positivist-structural-realism.

Like Habermas, Ashley's "heroic" project challenged the community of science, the substitution of hermeneutic social theory for positivism, and sought to realize progress through emancipation.[93] All humankind, he noted, had "an emancipatory interest—an interest in the unrestrained, communicative exercise of reflective reason—because, amidst the exigencies of man's struggles for self-preservation, only reflection on the self-formative process of the human species . . . makes possible the autonomous, self-conscious development of life."[94] He thus asked his readers to join him and struggle as well against the self-enclosure imposed by a technical-rational grammar of thought, and to erect instead "a reflective reason in light of needs, knowledge, and rules" so as to achieve human autonomy and self-understanding. Much like his mentor, Ashley's knowledge-guiding interest was emancipatory, and his project a critical one, partly inspired by the politics of the Frankfurt school and Marxist epistemology.[95] But while his ambitions were Marxist in origin it would be wrong to assume Ashley's heroic phase as wholly modernist. Though inspired by the Enlightenment project, many of his methodological techniques and modes of criticism derived from poststructuralist thought, creating obvious tensions and contradictions in his scholarship. What was peculiar therefore about Ashley's "heroic" phase was his attempt to realize modernist ambitions but through postmodernist means.[96] Habermas, for example, slowly gave way to Foucault, and what started out as an emancipatory project inspired by Habermasian logic, became increasingly a Habermasian project informed by Foucauldian theory. By 1984 with the publication of the *Poverty of Neorealism*, this transformation was all but complete and the contradictions evident.[97] International theory was now witness to the perverse amalgamation of two opposed epistemologies. Single-handedly, Ashley had made Habermas and Foucault political bedfellows. Understandably for orthodox theorists this combination proved unfathomable and Ashley's discourse too erratic to maintain their interest. Consequently, most observers gave up on Ashley, surrendering his scholarship to his enigma where it was free to roam the discipline unrestrained by critical analysis.

My preceding chronological narrative, however, makes it possible to wipe away Ashley's enigmatic aegis and assess the merits of his scholarship. It is for this reason that I have characterized Ashley's "heroic" phase as critical-epistemological postmodernism where epistemology accommodates Ashley's "heroic" cum modernist search for truth, allows a contingent foundationalism and universal ethical commitment to emancipation, while postmodernism accommodates many of his theoretical techniques and especially his political acumen that derived increasingly from a poststructuralist sensibility.[98] This typology also disentangles Ashley's substantive beliefs from his pragmatic politics, exposing his use of poststructuralist theory a strategic means of articulating his modernist agenda. In other words, poststructuralism became an exploitable vehicle through which Ashley could promote his political and theoretical ambitions. Thus, for example, he could aspire to a modernist constructivist project, a sovereign project spoken with a "sovereign voice," while employing poststructural theory to dismiss positivism for its pretense to truth and foundationalism. And while he displayed a modernist conception of philosophy-as-epistemology, a foundationalist enterprise whose object was to discover universal truth, the use of poststructural theory lent credibility to his enterprise as a contextualist and contingent one. Indeed, poststructural theory allowed him to caution against universalism, supposing that while we could not "fashion a pure universalism (a pure rationalism, a pure empiricism) uncontaminated by the particular culture in which we are located," we could instead "fashion a pure contextualism . . . a pure interpretivism" mediated by history, culture, and aesthetics, but whose objective remained a transformational critique.[99] If the logic seems obtuse, it was, and Ashley was quite aware of this, justifying this rather discrepant combination of modernist ambition with postmodernist means in terms of his steadfast commitment to transformational politics.

As we have seen, however, even Ashley could not maintain this elaborate and contradictory charade indefinitely and was forced eventually to bury the "heroic Ashley." Before we do the same, though, it is perhaps worth pondering Ashley's "heroic" phase if only because of the insights it offers as to his motivations and subsequent conversion to subversive postmodernism. For while Ashley was adept at blurring modernist and poststructuralist epistemologies, his "heroic" phase remains distinctive if only because of its blatantly ideological commitment to insurrection and the strategic use of theory to that end. More importantly, what this suggests of Ashley's "heroic" scholarship was a constructivist ethic and a commitment to the idea of theory because of its centrality in informing political praxis. Unlike his more recent deconstructionist offerings where he attempts to destabilize the very idea of theory, the "heroic Ashley" was committed to a transformational reconstruction of international theory, hoping to reconstitute its cognitive interest away from technical control and toward an emancipatory praxiology. The battle, therefore, was over the ideological use to which theory should be employed, not the efficacy of theory itself which now seems to concern him. The distinction is important and explains the otherwise contradictory ambiguities that have so confused other commentators of Ashley's work. It reveals Ashley's heroic phase to be more rationalist than poststructuralist, yet strategic in its use of poststructuralist techniques to support his ideological project. With this in mind, I want to exhume the "heroic Ashley," engage in a little archaeological dig and postmortem as it were, in order that we might not only find the reasons for his demise, the rationale for his suicide, but also the basis for his reincarnation in another medium.

A Postmortem of Ashley's Heroic Scholarship

At the beginning of this book, I noted that my approach to Ashley sublimated his theoretical constructs beneath his political program. We can perhaps now begin to see why this approach was implicit in Ashley's scholarship by demonstrating the conduit between his political beliefs and their theoretical expression. The first demonstration of this lies in the way Ashley's "heroic" scholarship utilized theory in terms of a means-ends rationality, that is, theory was prized but only insofar as it might realize the promise of the Enlightenment. This betrayed an instrumentalist conception of theory as an entity able to be captured and used in the service of specific rationalities. More importantly, it provided Ashley with a twin-edged sword: first, as a means of attacking positivists on the basis that they exploited theory in reflection of their technical-instrumental interests in control, while, secondly, demonstrating to Ashley that, if captured, theory could also be used in promotion of a progressive agenda. Arguably this insight not only defined his approach to theory but also surrendered it to the battleground of ideology, to be fought over and manipulated in reflection of particular interests. In this sense Ashley was about to do to theory what he had originally professed to avoid: reduce theory to a Mannheimian simplism and constitute a knowledge in reflection of a specific (emancipatory) rationality.[100] Consequently, Ashley's "heroic" scholarship was no different to positivism, objectifying theory and scholarship and rendering them instrumentalities of a power-knowledge—a betrayal of his mentor's approach to theory. This had fairly obvious implications for theory, not least of which was its abuse when used in reckless fashion in support of ideological ends. Ashley, for example, could combine opposing epistemologies in the construction of a new critical theory, but in doing so forsake the yardsticks of rationality and consistency and the sanctity of theory for purely partisan ends. Likewise, rather than preserve the institution of theory on the basis of its contribution to knowledge or its efficacy in contemplation, its purpose had always to be inscribed in reflection of interests and accepted or rejected on the basis of its relationship to one's own political agenda. There was no point to theory and knowledge except insofar as they served ideological ends. If this was true of positivism as Ashley insisted, then it was also true of Ashley. The label that best explains Ashley's "heroic" motivations and rationality, then, is transformationary or revolutionary and it is in this context that I interpret his "heroic" scholarship and explain the denigration of theory.

Ashley was careful, however, to conceal the duplicity of his theoretical enterprise to his transformationary program. We thus have to read Ashley with an eye to his sophistry, aware that he too is engaged in a positivist project of sorts: the construction of theory in reflection of a transformationary ambition. In his attempt to forge a "rationality proper" and escape the war-prone logic of technical rationality, for example, he appeared the great integrationist and protector of the realist tradition, not a deconstructionist but a synthesist striving to preserve it. Indeed, when reinterpreting the work of John Hertz, Ashley implored us to preserve practical realism, "not to deny or replace realism, but to find in the realist dialogue the basis for a new synthesis" where "technical interests in control no longer subordinate . . . reflective reason."[101] For Ashley, once this synthesis was realized, reflective reason or "rationality proper" would guide humankind away from hierarchical social relations of domination and deliver us to the good society. We had only to free ourselves of this mode of conceptualization, emancipate our minds, and collectively aspire to a just world order.

Realizing this synthesis, however, required more than theoretical argument; it required political action albeit theoretically informed and inspired. Theory had a rational-purposive function—the investigation of and contribution to, "the prospects for emancipatory politics in the late twentieth century." Its role was political, involving a "ceaseless analysis, vigilance and will to subversion," so as to open up "alternative spaces, for the constitution of alternative subjects, for the making of alternative worlds."[102] Political transformation was the objective, and theory a practical means of contributing to its realization. While theoretical critique(s) would shatter the ideological illusions of realism, praxis would transform and usurp the material basis on which realism rested and its practices legitimized. "In the end," Ashley wrote, "the only kind of criticism that would do away with realism is a global revolutionary change that would put an end to the current order of domination without establishing a new one in its place. In the end, this, and only this, is the kind of falsifying evidence that realism will recognise."[103] In Ashley's grand plan, realism was only an incidental casualty, a manifestation of the real enemy—technical realism—and to fight realism without assaulting its epistemological essence—its material basis—would all but leave it intact.

Like all transformationalists, Ashley's ambition was fed by a quixotic idealism, a faith that the revolutionary act would not only transform existing social relations but kindle a new moral order and a higher state of being.[104] His position reflected the perennial realist/idealist dialectic in international theory. Antithetic to the realist tradition where mankind was entrapped in the Hobbesian state of nature—"a perpetual and restlesse desire for power after power"—Ashley embraced a Rousseauian cum Marxist position, where humankind was understood as a pristine being corrupted by societal tyranny.[105] Ashley's "heroic" project therefore displayed all the trappings of the idealist tradition: a reactionist stance against the current global order, a dissatisfaction with the nation-state as the basic unit of global organization, and a commitment to transformational politics and the creation of new forms of global order founded upon unity, harmony, inclusiveness, and peace. At base, Ashley believed it was the nation-state that was the source of war and conflict. More precisely, it was the state combined with technical rationality that, in a world of finite resources, created competitive dynamics between states and resulted in differential technological and economic growth patterns, unevenly distributed capabilities and a global system prone to war.[106] This explains why Ashley understood realism as a symptom and not the source of conflictual politics and why a theoretical deconstruction of realism and neorealism would never suffice as a transformational strategy. In the end, only the obliteration of the state itself would allow humankind freedom from the territorial logic of the state-as-actor. Only then would we escape the cartographic abstractions that divide humankind, the perceptions of insecurity they incite, and the realist narratives they necessitate. Only then would humankind achieve self-realization.

Ashley's commitment to transformational politics necessarily made his scholarship secondary to that goal. Many of the ambiguities and contradictions in his scholarship could therefore be explained in terms of pragmatic opportunism. For example, while Ashley opposed technical realism he preserved practical realism, arguing that the latter's cognitive interest in instrumental power politics was useful for revolutionary purposes and its intersubjective understanding helpful in realizing an emancipatory problematic. The job of the revolutionary, he noted, was not to repudiate the community of power politics and abnegate a revolutionary resource, but to exploit and strengthen this community and do "violence to a tradition notorious for its celebration of violence."[107] Making new worlds apparently required the use of old tools and Ashley was not averse to the appropriation of violent means to that end. It was therefore ironic that Ashley should have been so outraged by those "conspicuous displays of violence" against "students, junior faculty, scholars of color, feminists, and other disciplinary marginals" that he alleged of realists, when he himself was so quick to advocate revolutionary violence on a global scale.[108] Indeed, Ashley's condemnation of so-called technical theory seemed curious in view of its commitment to the aversion of international violence through greater theoretical insight, informed practice and enhanced control. Calling for massive revolutionary action to correct the abstract, if not fictitious, violence of technical rationality was thus a contrived and spurious justification at best. Likewise, while committed to global transformational change—a universal project or master-narrative by anyone's definition—he attacked positivist theory for its metatheoretical commitments and universalist aspirations. Universalism in pursuit of an emancipatory problematic was perfectly acceptable, but in pursuit of science whose cognitive interest was control, Ashley labeled it dangerous. Moreover, while he derided realism's technical interest, he failed to acknowledge that his own emancipatory interest shared many of the same commitments. Ashley's ambition to erect a reflective knowledge, for example, could also be seen as a quest for technical knowledge, especially since reflective knowledge sought to engineer, or at the very least contribute to, the technical project of global transformation. Reflective knowledge was not benign as Ashley freely admitted. It had a "practical cognitive interest" that endeavored to facilitate an interpretivist or contemplative space and apprise subjectivities of the means to political action. Surely this also was a masterplan to shape the course of history, a desire to control and technically manipulate historical events and secure outcomes much like the community of science. Similarly, while Ashley advocated contextualism and rejected absolutism in knowledge, his project was clearly foundationalist if not absolutist. It had to be, or how else could Ashley claim emancipation ontologically and ethically superior to all other cognitive interests? And while he rejected structuralism for its analytical shortcomings, his own critique relied upon structuralist conceptions of power and oppression; understood the state as a structural entity constituted by practice; used structural categories like class to objectify interests; and used structural notions of instrumental power politics as a means of informing political praxis.

These anomalies tell us much about Ashley's "heroic" scholarship. First, they tell us that Ashley's commentaries were not attempts at constructing a theory of international politics. More likely, they were attempts at contributing to politics, projects that aimed at realizing a political praxis by providing a theoretical medium to legitimize and sanction political action. More gratuitously, we might interpret them as crude revolutionary documents—a sort of call to arms. Ashley's focus upon political agency, indeed its centrality in his discourse, is more appropriately understood in terms of its political utility than its theoretical poignancy. After all, if one is to effect, or at least contribute (theoretically) to the possibility of political transformation, one need first demonstrate that this is (1) desirable; (2) necessary if freedom and emancipation are to be achieved; and (3) possible inasmuch as human agents are able to mold their political realities. Thus, by reifying the agency of subjectivities, Ashley could critique structural realism's cognitive interest in control as an attempt to delimit political-agency (an attempt to preserve the constellation of global order), and at the same time, offer a theoretical rationale or legitimacy for transformational politics, and a theoretical knowledge on which to base it. Second, this tells us that Ashley's discourse was not dispassionate intellectual inquiry, but ideological belief forcefully expressed in pragmatic discourse where the ends justified the means. Ashley was not attacking a theory or theories per se, but the configuration of global order. Far from being a benign theory of interpretation, structural realism represented the interests of state and class, according recognition to, and allied with, "those class and sectorial interests . . . congruent with state interests and legitimations." The fight for freedom or Ashley's "heroic" strategy thus lay in demolishing realism and neorealism, not because they were theoretical categories of positivism, but because in reality they obstructed and denied "recognition to those class and human interests" opposed to the reason of state.[109]

The argument, of course, was purely Marxian. Where Marx saw ideology as "the false system of thought elaborated by the ruling class to justify its rule in the eyes of the ruled, while hiding its real selfish motives"—a false consciousness—Ashley depicted realism in the same manner: an ideological mask erected by the oppressors and serving the interests of the transnational ruling elites.[110] Realism was simply a technical competence model facilitating the repression of opposition forces who threatened the constellation of global order.[111] Realism, he noted, was "the ideological apparatus of a global professional community, the community of competent statesmen" who, through their actions, "ideologically reproduce a tradition that constitutes important aspects of the world"; a tradition of "silences, omissions, and failures of self-critical nerve" that together joined "in secret complicity with an order of domination that reproduce[d] the expectation of inequality as a motivating force, and insecurity as an integrating principle."[112] So long as the world remained a "hierarchical order of domination, the dominant . . . would . . . always retain an interest in realist concepts and claims, and being dominant," they would try "to make the world in reflection of those concepts and claims."[113] Ashley as "hero" thus issued forth "a promise of an abstract freedom that comes to those who repudiate neorealist commitments."[114] The "heroic" strategy was merely a transformationary one, premised upon a critical epistemology that claimed truth, and for those who followed it, freedom and emancipation. Only a critical-theoretic interpretation could shatter the ideological blinkers of neorealism's false consciousness, "play havoc with neorealist concepts and claims," and "crack them open."[115]

The gulf between Marx and the "heroic" Ashley was thus not as wide as Ashley would protest. To be sure, the language was slightly different, the project less overtly stated, but the ambitions virtually synonymous. Yet it would be incorrect simply to label Ashley's project a Marxist one. Unlike Marxist theory, he refused to offer a unified theory of the interconnections between capitalism, states, and violence, for example. Indeed, he was positively shy when it came to discussing issues of capitalist modes of production as instrumental forces in history.[116] His discussions of power, for example, are noticeably aeconomic, refusing to observe what seem patently obvious associations between exploitative economic relationships and the structure of North-South relations, or the effects of differential growth patterns on military-power capabilities. Ashley's critical epistemology all but abandoned categories of economic imperialism, capitalist practices of accumulation, or issues of the global division of labor, pretending that these objectified realities were only representations manifested by dominant interests. In doing so, however, Ashley was strangely reticent to identify these interests explicitly, let alone ascribe to them some economic motif that might explain their epistemological basis in relation to the operation of political power. One can only assume that, like Foucault, Ashley understood the operation of power to be diffuse, abstract, and ethereal. Yet, as Tony Porter points out, Ashley's approach was also extremely elitist, crediting the play of international politics, diplomacy, statecraft, and international institutions, the exclusive preserve of a few intellectuals and statesmen.[117] In Ashley's appraisal, "Statesmen and intellectuals create not only an ideology . . . but equally create the state structures, their foreign policies, and the sense of community and xenophobia that citizens experience." That this borders on a paranoid disposition toward conspiracy theory should be obvious, and that it contradicts Ashley's attempt to inflate the agency of subjectivities should be even more obvious. Those that he calls marginalized in the discourse of international politics are made more invisible by his own disposition toward elite theory as an explanation of international relations. If only the world were so simple, Ashley might have a modicum of theoretical relevancy.

In all these ways Ashley's discourse was only partially Marxian. It is probably more appropriate to ascribe his emancipatory interest to a humanist philosophic tradition replete with idealist accouterments that, together, marked the beginnings of a new neoidealist movement in international theory.[118] At the same time, however, it was Ashley's genius at covertly repackaging and reintroducing Marxian themes into the North American international relations discourse that popularized his work. He managed to blunt the overt ideology of previous Marxist and neo-Marxist approaches—various new left theories of the early 1970s whose penchant for economic reductionism explained everything in terms of capitalist modes of production, for example[119]—and revise these offerings by discarding their economism and introducing contextualist and poststructuralist techniques. This achievement was significant, seeding a strong critical tradition in North American international relations scholarship that, arguably, had been absent for too long. The irony, though, was that while Ashley now claimed his critical approach free of totalitarian narratives, patriarchal insensitivity, eurocentricity, and historical determinism, and contextually sensitive to the cultural and specific histories of marginal groups, this was only an illusion. Ashley still made absolutist claims, operated from a foundationalist position, disparaged alternative interpretations that failed to conform to antipositivist critical theory, and in reifying contextualism made claims to a new methodological master narrative! The illusion was a political sleight of hand, expertly executed in the hope that his ideological project might see an end to neorealism, and, in its own small way, contribute to some romantic notion of emancipation. But more than this, Ashley displayed his mastery for overblown rhetoric that was issued as part of a "political campaign to persuade [others] . . . in international studies to come over" to his "version of dissidence."[120]

It would be wrong, however, to dismiss Ashley's "heroic" phase entirely, for he succeeded in highlighting many of the epistemological and ontological premises on which realist and neorealist orthodoxies were constructed. In the case of neorealist theory, he provided a necessary corrective to its excessive structuralism, highlighting its determinism and inability to explain adequately agency, change, or history. Ashley also demonstrated the fallacy of applying microeconomic tools of analysis to the study of political phenomena and explaining what are inherently complex relationships in terms of the logic of economy. Similarly, his critiques of world modeling research succeeded in highlighting its political content and complicity in the maintenance of social orders. He made such theorists ask basic questions of their project, insisting that they "locate, interpret, problematize, and define the limits of their" research so as to expose "its rules, expectations, conscious claims, explicit premises, implicit presuppositions, mystifications, and lapses."[121] In this he not only challenged these research projects but made theorists aware of the political functions theory performed and how supposedly objective theory was often normatively derived. So too, his taking to task neorealist theory for its overly circumspect understanding of the state and his attempt to retheorize it in reflection of power interests and theories of representation has only strengthened our understanding of what in international theory is our central analytical construct—the state-as-actor. All these commentaries were insightful. Indeed, his critique of instrumental-technical-rationality and positivism, a concurrent theme throughout all his works, acted as a catalyst to the development of postpositivist perspectives in the discipline. Almost single-handedly Ashley's theoretical agenda defined the course of research most critical theorists would pursue. In fact, it would be no exaggeration to claim that Ashley's "heroic" scholarship began the Third Debate, bringing to the discipline a period of introspective reflection that, in many ways, has strengthened theory and the quality of research. Undoubtedly, the discipline has benefited from these developments. We now have a more informed understanding of agency thanks to Ashley's importation of poststructural and structurationist theories. Agents and structures are now coactively understood and analyzed through the mediating influences of culture, specificity, and tradition.[122] Ashley's interpretivist presentation of practical realism and his reconceptualization of Morgenthau, for example, demonstrated the utility of a hermeneutic-structurationist realism as a means of comprehending how practice and structure are constituted through agency and tradition. Likewise, theory in the discipline has become more sophisticated, having jettisoned many of its banal generalities in favor of greater precision and complexity. The breadth of theory, its concerns and scope, have dramatically increased and now incorporates feminist, Third World, environmental, and other previously marginal perspectives along with traditional concerns.[123] Many of these developments we can trace to the critical perspectives pioneered by Ashley.

Ironically, however, while orthodox practitioners have generally welcomed these developments, for Ashley it signaled the failure of his project and an end to his "heroic" strategy. Modifications to orthodox theory were never his intentions so much as its downfall and eradication. It was time to try new tactics.

Chapter Five
Continental Drift
Ashley and Subversive Postmodernism

> A good war makes sacred almost any cause.
> Friedrich Nietzsche

> Yet is there not a danger that instead of being a window through which the world may be seen more clearly, the new approaches may be something more like a looking glass in which we see only ourselves deeply engaged in methodological and theoretical controversies which become less and less intelligible to those who determine the policies on whose wisdom survival depends?
> William C. Olson

> The crisis consists precisely in the fact that the old is dying and the new cannot yet be born; in this interregnum a great variety of morbid symptoms appears.
> Antonio Gramsci

Much like his "heroic" strategy, Ashley's poststructuralist writings also attempt to realize emancipation, but by offering "radical reflections about difference and freedom" and by opposing "all forms of rationalistic and totalistic thinking and practice." The implicit imprecation in postmodernist thinking, as John McGowan points out, is that modernity "perhaps fostered by insecurity about legitimating principles," displays an "increased intolerance . . . of differences within the social whole," moving with ever increasing certitude toward "Weber's 'iron cage,' Adorno's 'administered society,' and Levi-Strauss's 'monoculture.'"[1] Thus, no longer is the emancipatory ethic defined in relation to economistic and moral rationalities (freedom from capitalist exploitation, for example), but by cultural and aesthetic sensibilities alarmed at the banal conformity imposed by universalism and amid which the subject has been made destitute of difference, creativity, and "thinking space." From this, postmodernists insist, thinking practices must be liberated, differences recognized, discontinuities celebrated, and the inscribed modes of thinking inspired by reason, obliterated. And while redefinitions of the nature of oppression have changed the rationale for emancipation, so too have they wrought change in the strategic mechanisms of achieving it. Michel Foucault, from whom Ashley appropriates much of his theory, has redefined the very essence of emancipation by reconceptualizing power and oppression. Modernist conceptions of power anchored in macrostructuralist economistic categories like ruling class and capitalism, or juridical categories like law, moral right, and political sovereignty are rejected. Power is understood now genealogically as a microphenomenon of disciplinary matrices that operate in a variety of institutional settings, "not through physical force or representation by law, but through the hegemony of norms, political technologies, and the shaping of the body and soul."[2] A genealogical archaeology of power therefore explores the cultural and aesthetic dimensions from which thinking practices arise, and understands subjects, the product of scientific-disciplinary mechanisms fabricated by processes of normalization which are then subsumed amid culturally determined patterns of thinking: a sort of mental imprisonment. Power becomes an asymmetrical and relational entity, highly indeterminate in character and exercised from innumerable points such that there is no source or center of power to contest.[3] Mass struggle in the name of alternative rationalities (Marxism, liberalism) becomes superfluous when in (post)modern society power is so diffused. Indeed, universal emancipatory schemes advanced in the name of reason, postmodernists argue, are symptomatic of power/knowledge that, in the end, reproduce merely new forms of domination.[4] A new micropolitics of resistance is therefore called for, a discourse politics that acts as "a point of resistance and a starting point for an opposing strategy." Discourse politics, like Derrida's deconstruction, "attempts to contest the hegemonic discourses . . . of normal identities" and to subvert "the norms of what is rational, sane, or true" by speaking from outside these rules and from the margins.[5] In this way, Ashley hopes that "practices might be resisted or disabled; boundaries might be put in doubt and transgressed; representations might be subverted, deprived of the presumption of self-evidence, and politicised and historicised; new connections among diverse cultural elements might become possible; and new ways of thinking and doing global politics might be opened up."[6]

This program is made necessary by what Ashley understands as the failed promise of the Enlightenment. "Despite modern discourse's heralding of reason as a critical emancipatory force" that would "break through all traditional barriers and expose every ideology for what it is," the regime of modernity has cemented reason in "an indispensable ideological limit, a sovereign voice that is itself immunised from reasoned criticism."[7] Consequently, reason too must be disturbed and deconstructed if emancipation is ever to be realized. Reason, Ashley argues, like any other knowledge system, produces certain historical outcomes through its theoretical practice, and hence the realities we observe are not immutable, unproblematic sovereign sites, but arbitrary social constructions articulated through particular thought practices. Where some see this interpretivist stance as dangerous and destabilizing, challenging the very motif of Enlightenment thinking, Ashley thinks it profoundly liberating, demonstrating not only how tenuous are current realities, but how numerous are the possibilities for alternative future worlds and histories. In the case of state-centric global organization, for example, Ashley notes,

> By carefully analyzing the *workings* of theoretical discourse on the anarchy problematique—the knowledgeable practices by which it controls ambiguity and disciplines the proliferation of meaning—we may gain some insight into how the predicament it portrays and takes to be foundational is actively produced in history and through practice. By showing how, on the plane of theory, these knowledgeable practices might be exposed as arbitrary and rhetorical rather than unproblematic, we may catch a glimpse of how in history the anarchy problematique might come to be understood, not as a necessary condition that the realistic conduct of politics must take to be beyond question, but as an arbitrary political construction that is always in the process of being imposed.[8]

By doing this, Ashley hopes that we can "begin to see how these practices of imposition might be resisted" and the anarchy problematique transgressed. Ultimately, "explorations of new practices—and, with them, new modes of global political seeing, saying, and being—might thereby become possible."[9]

Obviously, then, the difference between Ashley's "heroic" and poststructuralist strategy is not to be found in his ambition (this remains contiguous—global transformation), but in his targets and methodology. Under his heroic strategy his targets were technical rationality and positivism but attacked using a rationalist discourse. In his subversive phase, these targets are broadened to encompass modernity and rationality, and the strategy is to subvert the logic of modernity, depriving it of those "techniques, strategies, and rituals by which practices are disciplined, resistances are tamed, regions of silence are imposed, boundaries of practice are secured, subjects are legitimated, order is normalized, and domination is violently projected in the world."[10] By operating at "places of closure," at those sites where the Enlightenment's authority over the construction of knowledge, truth, and meaning has closed off reason as an unproblematic sovereign site, Ashley aims to disturb "the placid unanimity of the current Western order" by turning its own discourse against itself.[11]

This strategy I have termed subversive, since it seeks to decenter reason and the representations on which international theory are constructed and world politics conducted. Yet Ashley seeks to do so from a nonposition, refusing to speak in "a sovereign voice . . . of interpretation and judgment from which truth and power are thought to emanate." His purpose, he insists, "is not to announce a new and powerful perspective on global politics," nor is it to "impose a standard and pass a judgment." Dissidents "stake out no territory to be defended" and issue no "manual of war by which soldiers of a new mode of global or political theory might be taught to seize, defend, and extend a domain." In fact, Ashley issues "no promises" and "bears no flag."[12] Rather, he argues, what he does offer is a means to chaos and anarchy in theory by contributing to the crisis of representation in modern discourse.[13] In international theory this is achieved primarily through attacking the anarchy problematique, depictions of the global arena as a residual, natural, and primordial sphere as well as the arbitrary demarcations that divide domestic from international and state from society. Through discursive textual analysis and rhetoric Ashley problematizes these representations—indeed all monological interpretations derived through the application of reason—and advances, instead, the idea of multiple realities through interpretivism and thus the relativity and instability of truth and meaning. What he has shown, he notes, is that "in theory as much as in any other domain of modern culture, it is impossible to arrive at any stable representation of the state and domestic society as a well-bounded sovereign identity, an unproblematic origin, a final ground upon which a rational understanding of international politics might be built."[14]

Here we observe the encroaching shadow of Foucault on international theory as Ashley imports his genealogical attitude.[15] No longer can international theory be an exercise in "apocalyptic objectivity," where reality can be captured in a "singular narrative, a law of development, or a vision of progress toward a certain end of humankind." On the contrary, "there are no constants, no fixed meanings, no secure grounds, no profound secrets, no final structures or limits of history." In the end, Ashley maintains, there is only interpretation, where history "is a series of interpretations imposed upon interpretations—none primary, all arbitrary" and all without essential meaning.[16] Within this meaningless edifice, the job of the theorist cannot be to understand, discover, or resolve the meaning, purpose, or truth of history, but only to contemplate how, through clashes of historical practices, the imposition of structure might be resisted. World politics, in other words, is perceived as the never completed "historical emergence, bounding, conquest, and administration of social *spaces*" or "a still-contested product of struggle to impose interpretation upon interpretation" where nothing is finally stable.[17]

To highlight this point, Ashley studies the imposition of structure that occurs in the context of realist narratives. These, Ashley argues, invoke "a Western rationalist understanding of a domestic *community-as-presence* in order to differentiate a field of international political practice recognized as a primordial *absence-of-community*." In doing so, realist narratives sustain an artificial representation of the international sphere as a realm of necessity that exists independently of knowledge, will, and practice.[18] This double move, as Ashley terms it, imposes silence "by occulting the community of international politics" and "misrecognizing it as a natural sphere." Consequently, this "excludes from active political discourse the strategies and procedures by which the margins of domestic and international society are produced, [how] the sphere of international politics is constituted and normalized, and [how] the prevailing subjectivity of modern statesmanship is empowered."[19]

The effect of realism is thus to render silent the genealogical "proposition that political realism is itself the voice of a specific historical mode of international community that has sustained a tentative hold on international political space": the European-born global order that now has a transnational reach.[20] Subsequently, our object of study, the modern sovereign state, is for Ashley never more than an effect of realist practices. And this, he argues, explains the pervasive and recurrent presence of realist doctrine in international theory; it complements, legitimizes, and reproduces the modern state system thereby validating the current configuration of global order and those subjectivities (statesmen and transnational elites) empowered to administer it. Ashley is therefore forced to the conclusion that "realism will always be the name of the discipline of the state, as it will also be the name of the state of the discipline."[21] Realism and realists alike are accredited with an insidious, almost conspiratorial, quality: "Realist power politics does not identify with the state; it produces the effect of the state. The state is not a fiction that realists reify; the state is a fiction that people know to be necessary because realist practices work to construct people who will know that they would be imperiled were they not willing to participate in its writing."[22]

It is not surprising therefore that Ashley does "not seek theoretical engagement with an established discipline" that propagates this order, but an exposé of how the "discipline itself sustains orders of domination, control and exclusion" and why these should be questioned, subverted and overcome.[23] And this is the purpose of his project: a commitment to disruption, instability, and transformation in order that the elusive quest for emancipation, to borrow a positivist metaphor, might yet be realized if modernist theory in its various positivist, realist, and structuralist forms can only be subverted and dismantled. Freed of reason, of presuppositions that seemingly delimit the ability of agents to effect change and take control of history, transformation might yet be effected. If Ashley can first liberate the mind from this mental imprisonment, "forestall the further spread of [the] rationalist order," then might he liberate the body from its physical inactivity and see the emergence of new worlds and histories.[24] What we witness in Ashley, then, is not a theory of world politics or a tool of analysis to foster greater understanding, but, as with his heroic strategy, a means to transformation and ideological insurrection, a strategy to overturn, destroy, and then make anew the discipline and its theory in forms that few would recognize.

Assessing Ashley's Poststructuralist Challenge: The Politics of Rhetoric and Interpretivism

In the space of only a few short years the poststructural challenge to international theory has risen to prominence. What once was a "marginal" activity dispensed by an "exiled" few now attracts numerous cohorts who issue their attacks against the discipline from within its hegemonic center. For Ashley and Walker, this signals "a crisis of confidence, a loss of faith, a degeneration of reigning paradigms, an organic crisis in which, as Gramscians would say, 'the old is dying and the new cannot yet be born.'"[25] Needless to say, both Ashley and Walker celebrate this trend. For them, "the game is pretty much up," and "the crisis of international studies" merely reflects a whole series of crises in modern culture: "a crisis of patriarchy, a crisis of governability, [and] a generalized crisis of representation."[26] Whether in the proliferating works of dissident thought, in the informal xerox-circuits of the field, or in the seminar papers of graduate students, Ashley and Walker "detect an increasing volume and variety of work whose principal business is to interrogate limits . . . and to think *other*-wise." Despite the "oppressive" legacy of positivist social science, these happenings, they insist, "indicate the opening up of international studies into a boundless space of freedom," where marginality is fast becoming the norm and where the "cocksure voice of sovereign judgment" now trembles in self-doubt.[27]

Doubtless, Ashley and Walker overstate the success and attraction of postpositivist approaches for political reasons. Yet there is also much truth in what they claim; the lexicon of poststructural theory has indeed become commonplace in the field and far from a marginal or ostracized activity. The discipline's most eminent journals, for example, commonly feature articles with a postmodernist perspective. Indeed, the willing complicity of disciplinary journals to publish these perspectives has, ironically, been one of the main vehicles by which Ashley and Walker have promoted and popularized their agenda.[28] This fact alone would seem to make a mockery of their allegations of victimization, and how, under "the threat of some deprival of status, tenancy, or right to speak, be heard, and earn a living among the ranks of the profession," so-called disciplinary marginals are "coerced into submission."[29] Such threats are surely more imagined than real, and the suggestion of coercion almost ludicrous when one considers how those who "think other-wise" have been so prolific in filling the discipline's learned journals, conferences, and graduate seminars with voluminous postmodernist literatures. One can either be victimized or successfully published, but scarcely both. The absurdity of this suggestion, however, seems to have escaped Ashley and Walker, who list a litany of charges against realism and realists, of intimidation, coercion, and exclusion, but communicate these repressive horrors via a special issue of *International Studies Quarterly*, the discipline's flagship journal.[30] Apparently, those inclined to "conspicuous displays of violence" fail to count censorship among their tools of repression and banishment. Cries of victimization thus ring hollow when they are so well heard, so often repeated, and given so much freedom to be expressed in so many publications.

Arguably, however, such allegations are merely ambit claims, grounded not in fact so much as political ambition. The efficacy of these allegations are thus extraneous when we realize that the motivation for making them derives from the political advantages they obtain against external criticism. Consider, for example, how scholarly debate or critiques of postmodernist approaches are never that for Ashley and Walker, but crimes of marginalization, attempts to silence, strategies of territorialization that seek to close off debate, or threats of professional denunciation. Michael Walzer's critique of Foucault, for instance, is dismissed by Ashley and Walker for its imposition and observance of ethical thought and conduct "defined and justified from the standpoint of a sovereign centre of judgment." Walzer becomes the villain, a totalitarian monster who would impose moral and ethical criteria upon his victims by intimidating would-be readers through the suggestion that Foucault's radical abolitionism approaches nihilism and ethical relativism.[31] Differences of opinion and debate, let alone critique, become impossible under circumstances where all would-be opponents are tainted with such totalitarian and villainous intentions. If understood as a strategy of deflection and deterrence, however, this tactic serves Ashley and Walker well, creating a sort of hermeneutic truth that always presumes the guilt of detractors: a protective cocoon that shelters postmodern approaches from outside examination. In this way, Ashley and Walker have been able to dismiss rationalistic/modernist critiques of postmodernism, insisting that postmodernist perspectives can be assessed only in terms of their own discourse, but have then proceeded to dismiss Enlightenment thinking in terms of a postmodern discourse! And herein lies the novelty of these self-serving political strategies: they seemingly validate poststructural theory by removing its theoretical conduit from the realm of rationalist/modernist debate and therefore beyond the reach of those who, through the force of rationalist argument and logic, would expose the poverty of much postmodern theory. The great advocates of discourse and free thought thus turn out to be as intolerant of difference as they would have their opponents to be.

Doubtless, this is a clever tactical device but hardly sufficient to warrant postmodernists' permanent residence among those who count themselves as theorists of international relations. If understanding and explanation are to be advanced, postmodernism too must expose itself to the rough and tumble of critical examination. Prespecifying the terms of this analysis by attempting to disarm those who use the tools of rationalist discourse suggests only that postmodernists are not yet prepared to debate issues of epistemological difference or to expose their intellectual canons to those of the Enlightenment.

To admonish postmodernists for these intellectual shortcomings, however, is to be accused of issuing threats. Yet these too have come as much from the postmodernist side of the debate as they have from the orthodox. The sense of intimidation and exclusion has been borne equally by orthodox practitioners confronted with allegations of their duplicity in violence, marginalization, racism, patriarchy, and assorted other crimes and misdemeanors. As Robert Gilpin points out, to believe Ashley is to believe that realists, realism, modernists, and those who profess rationalistic thinking practices "are all card-carrying members of an insidious and rather dangerous conspiracy that, like Socrates, is indoctrinating youth (read graduate students) in false and dangerous ways of thinking."[32] For Gilpin, Ashley has assumed the mantle of a kafkaesque prosecutor who, in a self-enclosed, self-absorbed treatise, insulated as much by obtuse logic as needless jargon, has accused realists and modernists alike with intellectual treachery that approaches a pernicious evil. Collectively, however, such allegations have served their purpose, intimidating those who would protest against the protesters by closing off, silencing, or ascribing pejorative overtones to certain topics, debates, or issues now considered modernist, hierarchical, statist, sovereignist, realist, patriarchal, technical, structuralist, objectivist, positivist, foundationalist, or rationalist. These words are now lumped together into an amorphous whole, assumed inseparable and issued in condemnation. As Gilpin again notes, this "is polemical innuendo designed to scare easily corruptible graduate students away from the likes of such alleged protofascists as Bob Keohane and George Modelski."[33] And this, I think, is the crux of the matter: political sophistry disguised as theoretical discourse. Ashley, along with Walker, has executed an exceedingly clever political maneuver by invoking the theme of victimization, allowing them the freedom to allege horrendous crimes but in the absence of any substantive evidence. Indeed, this has become a trademark of their discourse where, against alleged intellectual treachery, they assume the moral highground, all the time sheltering from the probing eye of criticism by labeling themselves victims. Only the truly treacherous would dare bully the victim, subject them to yet more heinous ridicule, "violence," and "threats." Only the truly foolish would dare incur the wrath of the new vigilantism of political correctness. Presented with such options, few have felt compelled to reply to the likes of Ashley and Walker, and those who have are roundly dismissed for their intellectual impurity and moral culpability.

The politics of rhetoric and interpretivism, then, far from promoting the idea of plurality of meanings and an openness to dialogue, in practice have been exploited by Ashley to precipitate intellectual closure. What might have been a genuine intellectual tool for disturbing and disrupting the complacency of modernist narratives has, in Ashley's hands, been molded into a self-serving political tool that functions to close down discussion and ward off dissent.[34] Yet this had to be the case since to invite scrutiny would expose other contradictions and anomalies implicit in Ashley's poststructural theory.

Questions of Relevance, Rhetoric, Fiction, and Irrationalism

While Ashley's rhetoric serves to effect a number of political moves, it also helps conceal a series of blatant weaknesses implicit in his poststructural theory. The first of these we might identify as the rhetorical invention and reification of fictitious enemies, a mechanism that not only validates Ashley's project but gives it meaning. Frequently, for example, what Ashley purports to be attacking turns out to be a fictitious, or at best grossly exaggerated, entity. In his adoption of the "megahistorical unit, modernity," for example, Ashley presupposes an homogeneous, coherent phenomenon able to be studied—a suggestion most would find outrageous. As Tony Porter notes, "giving coherence to such a phenomenon requires doing violence to its diversity." Enlightenment thought can no more be reduced to a symmetric intellectual tradition or historical moment than can postmodernism.[35] Indeed, emasculating such an intellectual potpourri of ideas whose only similarity is dissonance seems peculiar considering Ashley's persistent commitment to venerate difference and discursive practices. To suppose that liberalism, Marxism, conservatism, fascism, leninism, or assorted other -isms that fall under the modernist rubric are contiguous is as preposterous as conflating Derrida with Foucault, Lyotard, and Baudrillard. Yet the hubris of Ashley's entire poststructural theory rests on such simplification and not only with the concept of modernity. Positivism, realism, or technical rationality, for instance, are all reduced to overly simplistic caricatures, assumed ubiquitous, and distilled into three or four rudimentary propositions that Ashley then sets about deconstructing. Technical rationality simply becomes nonreflexive problem-solving; positivism, a system of thought that divides subject from object and fact from value; while realism is reduced to the ontological presumption of the state-as-actor. While simplicity has unquestionable heuristic value, crude reductionism for the sake of political opportunism is plainly defamatory. Rather than parsimonious theory, what Ashley delivers is a series of fictitious straw men, theoretically fabricated along with crude ontological and epistemological presumptions that render them congenitally deformed and thus susceptible to Ashley's poststructural interpretivism.

In reality, of course, no such caricatures exist. Positivists, realists, and modernists alike are considerably more complex, divergent, and reflexive than Ashley would have us believe. In the case of realism, for example, Ashley conflates the writings of Kenneth Waltz, Robert Keohane, Stephen Krasner, Robert W. Tucker, George Modelski, Charles Kindleberger, and

Robert Gilpin, disregarding the disparate set of professional and political perspectives that makes each one distinctive and debate among them ferocious.[36] However, it is on the basis of these exaggerated caricatures that Ashley's raison d'être for poststructural theory and political transformation ultimately rests.

Perhaps more alarming though is the outright violence Ashley recommends in response to what at best seem trite, if not imagined, injustices. Inculpating modernity, positivism, technical rationality, or realism with violence, racism, war, and countless other crimes not only smacks of anthropomorphism but, as demonstrated by Ashley's torturous prose and reasoning, requires a dubious logic to make such connections in the first place. Are we really to believe that ethereal entities like positivism, modernism, or realism emanate a "violence" that marginalizes dissidents? Indeed, where is this violence, repression, and marginalization? As self-professed dissidents supposedly exiled from the discipline, Ashley and Walker appear remarkably well integrated into the academy—vocal, published, and at the center of the Third Debate and the forefront of theoretical research. Likewise, is Ashley seriously suggesting that, on the basis of this largely imagined violence, global transformation (perhaps even revolutionary violence) is a necessary, let alone desirable, response? Has the rationale for emancipation or the fight for justice been reduced to such vacuous revolutionary slogans as "Down with positivism and rationality"? The point is surely trite. Apart from members of the academy, who has heard of positivism and who for a moment imagines that they need to be emancipated from it, or from modernity, rationality, or realism for that matter? In an era of unprecedented change and turmoil, of new political and military configurations, of war in the Balkans and ethnic cleansing, is Ashley really suggesting that some of the greatest threats facing humankind or some of the great moments of history rest on such innocuous and largely unknown nonrealities like positivism and realism? These are imagined and fictitious enemies, theoretical fabrications that represent arcane, self-serving debates superfluous to the lives of most people and, arguably, to most issues of importance in international relations.

More is the pity that such irrational and obviously abstruse debate should so occupy us at a time of great global turmoil. That it does and continues to do so reflects our lack of judicious criteria for evaluating theory and, more importantly, the lack of attachment theorists have to the real world. Certainly it is right and proper that we ponder the depths of our theoretical imaginations, engage in epistemological and ontological debate, and analyze the sociology of our knowledge.[37] But to suppose that this is the only task of international theory, let alone the most important one, smacks of intellectual elitism and displays a certain contempt for those who search for guidance in their daily struggles as actors in international politics. What does Ashley's project, his deconstructive efforts, or valiant fight against positivism say to the truly marginalized, oppressed, and destitute? How does it help solve the plight of the poor, the displaced refugees, the casualties of war, or the émigrés of death squads? Does it in any way speak to those whose actions and thoughts comprise the policy and practice of international relations?

On all these questions one must answer no. This is not to say, of course, that all theory should be judged by its technical rationality and problem-solving capacity as Ashley forcefully argues. But to suppose that problem-solving technical theory is not necessary—or is in some way bad—is a contemptuous position that abrogates any hope of solving some of the nightmarish realities that millions confront daily. As Holsti argues, we need ask of these theorists and their theories the ultimate question, "So what?" To what purpose do they deconstruct, problematize, destabilize, undermine, ridicule, and belittle modernist and rationalist approaches? Does this get us any further, make the world any better, or enhance the human condition? In what sense can this "debate toward [a] bottomless pit of epistemology and metaphysics" be judged pertinent, relevant, helpful, or cogent to anyone other than those foolish enough to be scholastically excited by abstract and recondite debate.[38]

Contrary to Ashley's assertions, then, a poststructural approach fails to empower the marginalized and, in fact, abandons them. Rather than analyze the political economy of power, wealth, oppression, production, or international relations and render an intelligible understanding of these processes, Ashley succeeds in ostracizing those he portends to represent by delivering an obscure and highly convoluted discourse. If Ashley wishes to chastise structural realism for its abstractness and detachment, he must be prepared also to face similar criticism, especially when he so adamantly intends his work to address the real life plight of those who struggle at marginal places.

If the relevance of Ashley's project is questionable, so too is its logic and cogency. First, we might ask to what extent the postmodern "emphasis on the textual, constructed nature of the world" represents "an unwarranted extension of approaches appropriate for literature to other areas of human practice that are more constrained by an objective reality."[39] All theory is socially constructed and realities like the nation-state, domestic and international politics, regimes, or transnational agencies are obviously social fabrications. But to what extent is this observation of any real use? Just because we acknowledge that the state is a socially fabricated entity, or that the division between domestic and international society is arbitrarily inscribed does not make the reality of the state disappear or render invisible international politics. Whether socially constructed or objectively given, the argument over the ontological status of the state is of no particular moment. Does this change our experience of the state or somehow diminish the political-economic-juridical-military functions of the state? To recognize that states are not naturally inscribed but dynamic entities continually in the process of being made and reimposed and are therefore culturally dissimilar, economically different, and politically atypical, while perspicacious to our historical and theoretical understanding of the state, in no way detracts from its reality, practices, and consequences. Similarly, few would object to Ashley's hermeneutic interpretivist understanding of the international sphere as an artificially inscribed demarcation. But, to paraphrase Holsti again, so what? This does not make its effects any less real, diminish its importance in our lives, or excuse us from paying serious attention to it. That international politics and states would not exist without subjectivities is a banal tautology. The point, surely, is to move beyond this and study these processes. Thus, while intellectually interesting, constructivist theory is not an end point as Ashley seems to think, where we all throw up our hands and announce there are no foundations and all reality is an arbitrary social construction. Rather, it should be a means of recognizing the structurated nature of our being and the reciprocity between subjects and structures through history. Ashley, however, seems not to want to do this, but only to deconstruct the state, international politics, and international theory on the basis that none of these is objectively given but fictitious entities that arise out of modernist practices of representation. While an interesting theoretical enterprise, it is of no great consequence to the study of international politics. Indeed, structuration theory has long taken care of these ontological dilemmas that otherwise seem to preoccupy Ashley.[40]

Relativism, Nihilism, and Antifoundationalism

While the relevance of Ashley's poststructuralist theory is cause for concern, more disconcerting is its implicit nihilism. Not unexpectedly, Ashley rejects this, insisting that his discourse is not nihilistic but antifoundationalist. Upon closer inspection, however, this position proves both unsustainable and self-defeating. By rejecting foundationalism and all truth claims derived through the application of reason, Ashley unwittingly abandons theory, knowledge, and human practices to the ether of relativism and subjectivism. And by insisting that there "is no extratextual referent that can be used as a basis for adjudicating theoretical disputes," Ashley depreciates thought, theory, and knowledge to the particular outcomes of certain linguistic, interpretivist, and textual techniques.[41] Ashley is thus forced to conclude that truth, purpose, and meaning can only be textually inferred and never universally or eternally proclaimed. One theory becomes as good as any another theory and a particular truth claim no better or worse than other truth claims. Objective evaluation becomes impossible and, with it, any claim to a science of international politics. All that we might hope for is a subjective interpretivism, where, amid a vacuous intersection of texts, we each reach our own conclusions.

This position is both alarming and perplexing: alarming in that it moves us closer to the abyss of ethical relativism and perplexing since it undermines the intelligibility, legitimacy, and logic of Ashley's own writings. As Chris Brown notes, postmodern approaches end up destroying themselves. Demolishing the thought of modernity by rejecting foundationalism is a self-subverting theoretical stance since it prevents "any new thought taking the place from which the old categories have been ejected."[42] Tony Porter is even more adamant, noting that the poststructural rejection of foundationalism inevitably reduces concepts like truth and reality to subjective intertextual interpretations. Intellectual thought, let alone the possibility of an intersubjective consensus on issues like purpose, meaning, ethics, or truth, becomes impossible. Rather than create new thought categories or knowledge systems, poststructuralists simply devolve knowledge into a series of infinitesimal individual interpretations. Yet the issue is at best a mute one. Refuting the notion of truth is nonsensical. As William Connolly observes, "Do you not presuppose truth (reason, subjectivity, a transcendental ethic, and so on) in repudiating it? If so, must you not endorse the standard unequivocally once your own presupposition is revealed to you?" Obviously, notes Connolly, the answer is a resounding "yes, yes, yes, yes."[43]

Nonsensical or not, such arguments have proved useful for destabilizing modernist narratives. Yet they invariably do the same to poststructural theory, depriving it of any nontextual means of establishing its own legitimacy and therefore forcing it to use these same discursive techniques to fortify itself. Ironically, then, the logical corollary of this endless textual deconstruction is that Ashley, like all poststructuralists, merely succeeds in deconstructing himself, having deprived himself of all referents that might establish his nontextual authenticity or the political and ethical validity of his discourse. By eschewing all foundations, all criteria of assessment, any referent that might establish the superiority of particular truth claims, or the ethics of certain politics, Ashley unavoidably slides into the murky waters of ethical relativism and perspectivism.

This is a curious position, however, especially when Ashley is adamant that an emancipatory interest is ethically superior to a technical interest, that poststructural readings are better than modernist narratives, that modernist sensibilities commit crimes of violence and exclusion while postmodernist practices offer "boundless freedom" and inclusion, and that hermeneutic (classical) realism is preferable to structural realism. It seems plainly absurd that Ashley can both advocate an ethical politics while castigating foundationalist epistemologies. This is either outright confusion on Ashley's part—or political deception where he wants to have his cake and eat it, too.

Likewise, we might also question the extent to which understanding, political advocacy, let alone substantive action, is available to those who follow Ashley's poststructural approach. To what extent, for example, does Ashley's interpretivist view of history, truth, and meaning reduce his discourse to a series of solipsistic statements? When Ashley writes, "Nothing is finally stable. There are no constants, no fixed meanings, no secure grounds, no profound secrets, no final structures or limits of history," isn't he really saying that we can know nothing other than what we know personally? Intersubjective action, meaning, let alone community, would surely be impossible if we were to accept Ashley's narcissistic view of the world.[44] And doesn't this make pointless, then, the act of writing, reading, or communication? If no text is ever completed or has fixed meanings but, instead, is a series of random interpretations, "none primary, all arbitrary," why does Ashley bother to commit his thoughts to writing since they can never be communicated, only misinterpreted? As Spegele notes, "This position is self-refuting. If all texts are incomplete, all meanings pluralistic and all interpretations arbitrary, these criteria would apply to Ashley's texts as well. If the situation were as Ashley describes it, there could never be a clearly discernible connection between author and text or between text and world: language would be purely self-referential, and all interpretations would be equivocal. The very notion of text would collapse."[45]

Indeed, if, as postmodernists insist, there is nothing outside the text, then the text can only ever be understood in relation to other texts, and discourse is reduced to an endless intertextual conversation. This, however, is hardly a satisfactory position. Chris Brown, for example, asks, "If the chain of texts is not predetermined, does this mean that any text can be read in the light of any other text or set of texts?"[46] Is Ashley suggesting, for instance, that a reading of Waltz and Barbara Cartland would be a legitimate intertextual discourse on international relations? To quote Brown again, "are there limits here, and if so, how can they be justified" in the context of a nonfoundational intertextual discourse? And in the context of Ashley's relativity and interpretivism, why should we believe Ashley's evaluation and reading of Waltz to be authoritative, let alone definitive? After all, Ashley denies Waltz sovereignty over the interpretation of his texts, arguing that there are no true readings, only interpretations. In short, if we believe Ashley, we arrive at a world where the "object of knowledge—the 'transcendental signified'—disappears from view," while the "knowing subject also disappears" and the "'author' of the text becomes redundant."[47] This is a world rife with relativism and nihilism where the foundations on which we might make ethical evaluations have been denied us by Ashley's illogical and self-defeating rhetoric. In the end, Ashley's discourse is destroyed not by external criticism but by the weight of his own ill-conceived theoretical musings. Having divested himself of any epistemological ledge on which to secure his footing, let alone communicate his thesis, Ashley inevitably falls into his own linguistic traps. Well might we question then the ability of Ashley's poststructural challenge to move beyond rhetoric and toward substance.[48]

Questions of Intellectual Propriety in the Importation and (Mis)Representation of Ideas

In the *Modern Day Dictionary of Received Ideas,* the word *postmodernism* is afforded the following definition: "This word has no meaning. Use it as often as possible."[49] Undoubtedly this is fallacious, yet in the context of Ashley's usage, deservedly so. Rather than precision, consistency, or articulation of the core concepts and values of postmodernism, Ashley has engaged in a highly selective importation of specific ideas bereft of their context and accompanying theoretical baggage. Specifically, Ashley has pillaged the deconstructive elements of postmodernism while leaving unexamined its otherwise useful, and more applicable, insights into political-economy. And for good reason. Deconstruction has accommodated Ashley's transformationary ambition while depreciating the requirements of logic, consistency, and erudition. In Ashley's usage, postmodernism has become a pseudonym for intellectual anarchy where rules no longer apply and where, in the name of ideological insurrection, transformation, and future worlds, anything goes under the logos of deconstruction.

Consequently, postmodernism as written by postmodernists and postmodernism as written by Ashley are not to be confused for the same thing, but represent two very different ventures. Consider, for example, Ashley's rejection of rationality. His project, quite explicitly, is to "forestall the spread of the rationalist order" so that we might engage in the "making of alternative worlds."[50] Rationality is the nemesis and postmodernism is said to reject it. Yet this is rarely the case, especially if one considers the writings of Michel Foucault, who steers a middle ground on the question of rationality, seeing the "uncritical acceptance of modern rationality and its complete rejection as equally hazardous."[51] As Foucault notes, "It is extremely dangerous to say that Reason is the enemy that should be eliminated" while "it is just as dangerous to say that any critical questioning risks sending us into irrationality." For Foucault, critical thinking has to live on the borderlines of these tensions and theorize the "revolving door of rationality that refers us to its necessity, to its indispensability, and at the same time to its intrinsic dangers."[52]

The subtlety of these intellectual nuances, however, are lost on Ashley. There is no critical questioning of rationality, only its complete rejection. Where Foucault came to appreciate the "critical impulse in the modern will-to-knowledge," embracing many of the elements of Enlightenment thought, Ashley seems unaware of this, suggesting that Foucault and poststructuralist thought are dogmatically anti-Enlightenment and antimodernist. This simply is not true, indicating either a poor understanding of poststructuralist theory or dramatic license to rewrite (or textually reinterpret?) Foucault's writings. Thus, where Foucault was reasoned and perspicacious in his revisionism, Ashley takes a carte blanche stand against modernity, a sledge-hammer approach that seeks to destroy all and sundry in a rather violent and pernicious assault. Where Foucault sought new theory and new approaches, Ashley seeks only deconstruction through rejectionism. And where Foucault sought to construct new notions of identity, Ashley offers only an old-guard commitment to political transformation. The contrast could not be starker. Rather than a commitment to understanding the world, the likes of Ashley and Walker seek only to change it, as one reviewer recently remarked.[53] This is not theory but doctrinaire transformationary ambition disguised in the new language of postmodernism.

We should not be surprised by this however. Intellectual importations are not new in international theory. What is new, though, is the highly selective pilfering of certain ideas that, in the end, disfigure the theory they portend to represent while laying false claim to the kudos of its title. As Roger Spegele points out, Ashley would like to lay claim to the title poststructuralist while pretending that the importation of "deconstruction allows the suspension of rules of logical consistency." But this is not at all apparent in the writings of poststructuralists such as Foucault, Jean-Francois Lyotard, Jacques Derrida, or Baudrillard, who, regardless of the efficacy of their political views, all offer highly reasoned, logically coherent treatises.[54] Similarly, it is not apparent that these postmodernists dismiss moral foundationalism as an epistemological basis from which to advance an ethical critique of modernity. Yet Ashley insists that poststructuralism rejects universality and is antifoundationalist which "makes the very point of moral reasoning unintelligible." Even more absurd though, as Spegele points out again, is that after rejecting the Enlightenment, epistemology, language, and history, Ashley then "implies that his own project is one which seeks to develop a radically new conception of international relations based on a new epistemology and new notions of language and history." For all his postmodernist pretensions, "the end result is a conception of international relations deeply entrenched in the very tensions and difficulties of the Enlightenment against which . . . [he] rages so intemperately."[55] Postmodernism is not used so much as exploited; its title appropriated because of its utility in securing Ashley's political/ideological ambitions.

This point is highlighted in Ashley's apparent use of discursive techniques to deconstruct logocentric hierarchical practices that reify binary oppositions and condition thinking in speech/writing. Derrida invented such a strategy to expose the blind spots created in certain philosophical oppositions as between that of presence and absence or subject and object, for example. Yet Ashley and Walker appropriate this technique not to highlight these blind spots or deconstruct oppositions, "but to reconstitute them into ideological splits which pit dissidents against non-dissidents" and help them "achieve certain prior political aims."[56] Spegele sees this as an attempt to authenticate a certain ideological agenda which puts "dissident theory on the 'right side' of . . . [this] newly reconstituted ideological divide—the side of feminist movements, ecological movements, workers' movements, etc." Rather than obliterating binary oppositions, Ashley and Walker heighten them, hoping to demonstrate to prospective readers the superiority of their discourse compared to others. Dismissing modernist, positivist, realist, and scientific theory for their foundationalism and universality, then, is a derisive tactic and implies that dissidence is the new sovereign "terrain from which to view all others" and that what they have "discovered [is] the one true language outside language itself" that can arbitrate between truth claims. In the end, the very cartesianism Ashley and Walker profess to escape engulfs them; the differences they pretend to avoid they reify; the oppositions they want to deconstruct they reinvent as ideological splits; and the foundationalism and universality of modernist theory they chastise, they end up embracing in order to justify dissident thought.[57]

Continental Drift

Given these apparent weaknesses, one of the great remaining mysteries surrounding Richard Ashley's scholarship—indeed the postmodernist/poststructuralist movement generally—is the question, "Why?" Why the shift from modernist epistemologies to postmodernism? Why the progressive abandonment of Marx and Habermas for Derrida and Foucault? Why the rejection of rationalist for antirationalist discourse? And why the turn to deconstruction? In short, how might we account for the remarkable growth in postmodernist/poststructuralist theory and its adoption and popularity in numerous issues areas and academic disciplines? Allan Bloom suggests that the answer lies amid the debris left in the wake of Marxism's crisis and intellectual disintegration.[58] For Bloom, the old Marxism with its embarrassing economic determinism and ahistorical structuralism, grew increasingly vulgar, losing its theoretical credibility and political poignance. For a great many Marxists, Bloom suggests, Marx became boring, his intellectual deeds prosaic, no longer exciting the minds and souls of left intellectuals. Where once the *Manifesto* might have inspired, in the contemporary world it seemed naïve, and the rewards of reading *Capital* insufficient to warrant "the hard work it demands to be digested."[59] Consequently, Bloom argues, the eponymous hero of the Left, Marx, succumbed to an intellectual death, and those who for so long nourished themselves on his works were forced to turn elsewhere for intellectual gratification.

Marxism finally died, at least in the sense in which old-style Marxism had credibility as a worldview, could sustain a mass movement, incite revolution, provide solace for the oppressed and marginalized, or a critical metanarrative to explain history, purpose, and destiny. The Left was thus without an emissary, bereft of an intellectual system of thought otherwise able to unite progressives under a single metatheoretic edifice. Within this intellectual vacuum appeared Nietzsche, not by accident but sponsored by what Bloom terms a "mutant breed of Marxists" who sought to derationalize Marx and turn "Nietzsche into a Leftist."[60] Nietzsche, it was thought, would do for cultural analysis what Marx had done for economics, and the grafting of Nietzsche's cultural politics onto Marx has, according to Bloom, "strengthened Marx's position" while killing off vulgar

Marxism. "Nonvulgar Marxism is [now] Nietzsche," yielding a new and peculiar breed, leftist Nietzscheans with Marxist agendas.[61] The precise etiology of events, of course, Bloom admits to being confused by. What we are witnessing, he writes, is either the progressive "Nietzscheanization of the Left" or the Marxianization of Nietzsche. Regardless, the outcome is much of a muchness, with Nietzsche and the intellectual Left uniting in a way few previously would have thought possible or desirable. Thus, perhaps inspired by the need to revitalize Left critical-theory and politics and once again make it intellectually and politically viable, the Left have allowed themselves to be proselytized to the writings of a new emissary, Nietzsche, and now celebrate his pragmatism and political expediency. This newer breed of radical, as Bloom calls them, wills chaos and sees violence containing a certain charm of its own. But where vulgar Marxists saw history teleologically, automatically culminating with the new order, the newer breed understands that the "new order is not waiting, but has to be imposed by the will of man."[62] And it is this "will" which we can understand as the acts of deconstruction and destabilization, new-old political stratagems of transformation and revolution that appropriate Nietzsche's will to power and his individualist narcissism hoping that these will finally prove the chimera that realizes the new order.

The crisis in Marxism is thus as good a place as any in which to situate the genesis of postmodern theory. More importantly, it perhaps helps define those motives that caused Ashley to abandon epistemological for subversive postmodernism. Ashley was not alone in recognizing that Marxism's scholarly utility and intellectual credibility were declining. The New Left revivalism of the 1960s had exhausted itself by the late 1970s and was reflected in the rising political fortunes of conservative and reactionary political parties. Doubtless for many, Marxism's ideological veracity remained, but its strategic and political utility to left political movements became problematic. Consequently, like most left intellectuals during the 1980s, Ashley too experienced a continental drift, embraced Nietzsche for his pragmatism and succumbed to the allure of postmodernism.[63] Whether these intellectual transformations were truly that or merely pragmatic acts of political opportunism to achieve old ideological ends remains problematic. In the case of Ashley we can certainly interpret them as a function of the latter; so too, however, might they be a function of the former. Neither can be ruled out entirely. Yet, in as much as Ashley's political program shows considerable continuity, albeit transfigured with new language and intellectual tools, his commitment to the new interpretivism should be viewed with suspicion.

By Way of Conclusion

Richard Ashley concluded his *Poverty of Neorealism* with an obligatory autocritique, ostensibly to point out weaknesses in his critique of positivist theory.[64] It is, perhaps, fitting that I should do the same, highlighting some of the limitations implicit in my critique of Ashley.

First, I must acknowledge that any theoretical critique of Ashley's project, including this one, is destined to failure, at least in its ability to affect the course of debate within postmodernism. This problem is not endemic to the nature of the critique(s), but reflects the fact that postmodern theory is as much driven by ideological commitment as by theoretical innovation. Moreover, within international relations theory the postmodernist perspective exists independently of contending approaches, hermetically isolated if only because of its specialized nomenclature and distinctive ideological hue that encloses participants in a select and self-absorbed theoretical-ideological discourse.[65] Membership to this discourse is exclusive and limited to those who promise to take up the faith and propagate it, not question it critically. Thus, regardless of how erudite critiques might be, or how serendipitous critical analysis proves, we can scarcely expect Ashley to be convinced by intellectual musings when they are contrary to his political ambitions. For in Ashley's writings we are confronted as much by ideological intransigence as we are debate over ontological and epistemological issues. The postmodernist/modernist divide is more ideological than theoretical, a battle not between contending ontologies so much as between political loyalties. The facade of ontological and epistemological debate has thus been used deceptively to shield the underlying ideological axis upon which these debates ultimately rest. For this reason, we should not be surprised that postmodernists remain unconvinced by modernist theory, or vice versa, or that each is largely uninterested in the others perspective, theory, or arguments. Those views, theories, or paradigms not in accord with one's own worldview or basic values are rarely considered, let alone studied. And while Ashley would have us believe that these failings are the exclusive preserve of modernist/positivist theory, postmodernist theory too is just as guilty, having evolved in isolation, cocooned by technical nomenclature, reticent to engage contending perspectives in useful dialogue, and trigger happy in rejecting opposing perspectives without first understanding them.

Of course serious theoretical engagement was never possible. Crude theoretical caricatures and fallacious argument amid outrageous allegations served only to isolate these differing perspectives as so many more islands of theory. Postmodernist perspectives like Ashley's have thus survived and prospered if only because they have been left alone to do so.

The second limitation my critique faces derives from its rationalist epistemology and the assumption of similar virtues in those theories it has engaged. In particular, I have assumed a commitment to theoretical endeavor as a means to greater understanding, and, secondly, assumed that this endeavor is utilitarian in terms of its aim to better the human condition. This is why we do theory. Indeed, I have assumed that there is a certain orderliness and purpose to theory predicated upon a rationalist tradition of inquiry and the enhancement of that tradition through contributions to knowledge. The immediate problem, though, is that many of these assumptions and commitments are not shared by Ashley. On the contrary, they are the objects of his derision. My critique, for example, has suggested that Ashley not only rejects these rationalist sentiments but has actively sought to undo them through contributing to, and exploiting, intellectual and theoretical turmoil in the discipline. Specifically, I have argued that this is part of Ashley's broader political strategy that aims to undermine the metatheoretical fiat on which international political theory is constructed and replace it with an ideologically conceived set of political programs. Conventional critiques of postmodernist approaches are therefore limited by the fact of theoretical incommensurability and dissimilar aims and objectives. Moreover, there is no immediate solution to this dilemma save the force and quality of argument. Yet this more than anything else might prove Ashley's nemesis, for despite all the rhetoric of new theory, new perspectives, new identities, and Ashley's wish to be judged by different criteria beyond the fray of orthodox international theory, even Ashley's offerings must eventually "stand, fall, or languish in competition with established theories . . . and compete with them at the level of affirmative constructions."[66] But by Ashley's own admission, he can offer us very little if, indeed, anything at all: "The task of post-structuralist social theory is not to impose a general interpretation, a paradigm of the sovereignty of man, as a guide to the transformation of life on a global scale. In contrast to modern social theory, poststructuralism eschews grand designs, transcendental grounds, or universal projects of humankind."[67]

This we might interpret as faceless description without meaning, comment without purpose, and theory without reason. As William Connolly notes, Ashley creates a poststructuralism bereft of logic, direction, or mission, where "theory does not 'impose' a general interpretation; it does not offer 'a guide' to the 'transformation' of life 'on a global scale.'" Well might we ask, then, what does it do? After all, is this not the purpose of theory? Apparently not. It is enough for Ashley that we simply fret against transcendental grounds, universal projects, and grand designs. But, as Connolly observes, by imposing "this set of interwoven self-restrictions, Ashley may have reduced 'poststructuralism' to one perpetual assignment to 'invert the hierarchies' maintained in other theories. One might call this recipe for theoretical self-restriction 'post-ponism.' It links the inability to establish secure ontological ground for a theory with the obligation to defer indefinitely the construction of general theories of global politics. And it does so during a time when the greatest danger and contingencies in the world are global in character."[68] Connolly makes an excellent point, taking us closer to what I think is the crux of the matter: Ashley's latent positivism. In a curious way, Ashley's theoretical offerings can perhaps be explained if we understand him not as a postmodernist so much as a despondent positivist. At first, this suggestion seems ludicrous. But consider for a moment Ashley's defining preoccupations: an acute anxiety over the lack of any universal, foundational, nontextual referents able to arbitrate between truth claims, and undue concern with the necessity for secure ontological ground as a requisite for theory building. To say the least, these concerns display an excessive preoccupation with positivist precepts and correspondence theories of truth. More importantly, though, it extends the evidentiary requirements of the positivist canon by such an unreasonable measure as to obviate the possibility of it ever being satisfied. Thus, indirectly, Ashley's turn to subversive postmodernism is precipitated not by his attraction to it so much as the necessity of embracing it because of exacting positivist precepts. And this, in the end, unavoidably forces Ashley toward the chasm of nihilism and relativism precisely because of his imposition of overly rigid positivist criteria. What, for many, might have remained a mild case of Cartesian anxiety, a problematic question mark around the issue of ontological precision, for Ashley became a preoccupation that manifested into paranoia and ended in nihilism.

But regardless of the pathology or aetiological route that caused Ashley to arrive at subversive postmodernism, important questions of his thesis remain. How is this meant to help those on the margins, the poor, the weak, and the powerless, for whom Ashley professes great concern? How does it help those who seek answers as practitioners and theorists of international relations? If it is meant to empower feminists, scholars of color, and other persons who have suffered so-called disciplinary violence, how precisely does it intend to do this? If it cannot chart new directions and resists the modernist urge to guide and assist us in our dilemmas, refuses to confer general interpretations and enhance our understanding, how might it better our well being or resolve conflict and atrocity? What precisely does Ashley lay claim to do? Apart from seeking the closure of modernity, what does Ashley suggest we put in its place or is it simply a question of leaving empty the space vacated by modernist theory and knowledge?

These questions alone are cause for concern. However, as I have endeavored to demonstrate in this chapter, Ashley does not answer these questions but, instead, derides those who ask them. It is perhaps time to resist such derision and return to these questions, since in the absence of posing them we surrender the purpose of theory, its meaning, utility, and progress, indeed the study of international relations, to those who would pretend that these issues are no longer of any importance.

Chapter Six
Feminist Revisions of International Relations
Identity Politics, Postmodern(isms), and Gender

> ... International relations cannot be a theory of everything.
>
> Kenneth Waltz

> Now this is not the end. It is not even the beginning of the end. But it is, perhaps, the end of the new beginning.
>
> Winston Churchill

If the logical implications of Ashley's discourse prove less than sanguine, those who subscribe to his politics have nonetheless chosen to ignore them and push ahead with their respective programs. Indeed, in the 1990s, Ashley's would-be followers have created a veritable cottage industry of critical or subversive research agendas, all broadly concerned with disinventing International Relations and reinscribing its role, function, and purpose. One of the most forceful of such approaches has been feminist scholarship which has attempted not merely to "add women and stir," but demonstrate how women and feminist perspectives have been ghettoized and how the discipline and world politics have been encoded as masculine territory to exclude and repress women.[1] The task of feminist scholarship has thus been to demonstrate that International Relations is not a gender-neutral discipline and that realism and security politics derive from masculinist inscriptions that hide their epistemological essence by cloaking them in a realm of necessity and anarchy deemed to be beyond governance.[2] Feminist scholarship has thus been promoted as a necessary activity if the emperor is to be disrobed, "his" hidden practices of oppression and expulsion exposed, and international relations remade in a way that is sensitive to different ontological beginnings, questions, perspectives, and peoples. As Jean Bethke Elshtain argues, this project is made necessary because "professionalized IR discourse . . . is one of the most dubious of many dubious sciences that present truth claims that mask the power plays embedded in the discourse and in the practices it legitimates." This is not mere semantic squabbling over appropriate mediums of analysis, but for Elshtain, an attempt to rescue male practitioners of this discourse from "living out a perilous fantasy: the delusion that we have control over events when, in fact, we do not." Indeed, it is not the case that Elshtain condemns these practitioners for the scientific ways in which they think, but for the fact they do not think at all. Nor, she reminds us, is the increasing incidence of women in the academy reason to suppose that such discourses are being unwritten and apprised of new insight. On the contrary, women's increasing participation in international relations only confirms that many have been "prepared to take their place among the ranks of the purveyors of the hegemonic discourse—whatever it may be at any given moment in the academy and its journals."[3] Simply adding women to the realist/positivist/security equation is co-optation, not emancipation, so that the means to true understanding reside in formulating new equations and drawing upon the experiences of those whose histories and stories have otherwise been expunged from mainstream (or what Mary O'Brien calls malestream) discourse.[4]

For Elshtain, feminist analyses have thus emerged in the wake of those women who have managed to "escape the snare of these modes of professionalization and emerge from their training still able to grapple with the complexities of history, the vagaries of events, and the unpredictability of human passions," testament, she notes, "to a wider human attunement to *common* sense."[5] This is where contemporary feminist scholarship cuts into the Third Debate, chastising not only orthodox theory for "androcentric metatheoretical assumptions" evident "in the traditional definitions of the legitimate and substantive concerns of the discipline; that is, with 'high politics' or military security," but also "male scholars concerned with reflexivity" who have ignored the "relevance of philosophical debates within contemporary feminisms."[6] Christine Sylvester, for example, accuses the early phase of the Third Debate of excluding feminism, indeed for not even making Yosef Lapid's categorical list as one of its constituting -isms. "Women," she notes, "are beyond studied dissidence," and enjoy only "passing nods in the alternative international relations literature." This too is androcentric, masculine, and displays "shared understandings biased to one side" so that "even dissidence is more credible when it is represented to us mostly by men."[7] For Sylvester, it is not just the case that international relations has ignored feminist scholarship, but that the discipline is diseased by rampant sexism and misogyny, where it is all "too commonplace for self-defined critical social theorists to pay homage to the Critical Theorists, postmodernists and poststructuralists and to relegate the 'words of women to the after hours of academic work, to a hobby one never gets around to.'"[8] In fact, she suggests, there is "yet another sovereign voice singing IR, this time with dissident-sensitive lyrics that hint at but do not belt out a feminist message." Feminist writings and women have been equally "marginalized or preempted by those who plead for a more inclusive IR," do not "appear in the citation list of third debaters," or count "among the categories of contestation that Lapid notes."[9] Those males who otherwise claimed victimization because of their own intellectual dissent are now themselves accused of perpetrating crimes of exclusion, of ignoring the other "other" and operating in a "masculine territory" that belittles the contributions of feminist theory and women. Even the likes of Richard Ashley and Robert Walker, the very emissaries of dissidence, Sylvester condemns, when, as editors of the *International Studies Quarterly* special edition entitled *Speaking the Language of Exile: Dissidence in International Studies*, they address women but in a manner so cursory that the "dilemmas of gender are not considered important enough to warrant article-length treatment."[10] Likewise, when Andrew Linklater poses "The Question of the Next Stage in International Relations Theory,"[11] ostensibly to probe the possibilities of critical-theoretic, postmodern, and feminist perspectives, in Sylvester's eyes he merely perpetuates silence by making women invisible. "He says that women are among the excluded groups whose individual perspectives must be taken into account in developing critical theory. Nonetheless, feminists, and the 'women' they talk about, must be the illegitimate daughters of the really diverse ones because there is not one citation in Linklater's article to a feminist 'woman.' The postmodernists are cited. The critical theorists are cited. Feminist 'women,' however, have no names."[12] "Boys after all," it seems, "continue to be boys," which, for Sylvester, demands a new level of subversion beyond that proposed by male dissidents: dissidence from the (male) dissidents.[13] Under this new dissident dissidence, the real victims are women and feminist writings who now stand up to profess their victimization not just from the intellectual practices of orthodox theorists, but from those self-declared heretics like Ashley and Walker who now stand accused of being part of the tyranny of exclusion.

The Third Debate has thus evolved a new addendum, one where gender and identity politics questions even dissident thought, labeling it an equally suspect discourse propagated largely by white middle class heterosexual males. This represents a new, deeper, subversive tendency in dissident scholarship, perhaps more radical and more threatening than even Ashley's. This time the charge is not just that we have been thinking wrong, or not thinking at all, but when not thinking we have been actively constructing gender gulags, excluding women by segregating and denying them access to international relations. In its most overt form practitioners are charged with being misogynist, sexist, racist, and homophobic, a disposition in theory that manifests itself in to what Steve Smith describes as pomophobia, or what V. Spike Peterson laments as the failure of feminist literature to be taken seriously in International Relations.[14] For feminists, such a predilection represents an "androcentric system of thought inherited from early western state making[,] . . . revitalized in the Enlightenment," and now cemented in international relations as a form of "masculinism" but one which is "rendered so invisible as to be absent in even critical and postmodern accounts."[15] International Relations thus represents a form of professionalized bigotry, evolved through the natural outgrowth of unreflective men theorists who are wedded implicitly "to an unacknowledged and seemingly commonplace principle that international relations is the proper homestead or place for people called men." Men of all political stripes have, according to Sylvester, been winking at feminists as they walk by, failing to read them, appoint them, take them seriously, or acknowledge them.[16] In such a "chilly climate," women have been systematically "evacuated" from International Relations, forced into their assigned places at home, and even when they have managed to break free of such places, "their words have been lost, or covered-up and stored in the basement, . . . ignored because they are the views of people called women and 'women' have no place in the political places of 'men.'"[17] Of "all the institutionalized forms of contemporary social and political analysis," concludes R.B.J. Walker, International Relations is "the most gender-blind, indeed crudely patriarchal."[18]

At the center of this disciplinary bastion of male privilege and repression, feminists identify an unreflective male-body-politic, one unknowingly prone to gendered or masculinist worldviews because of their unconscious male-sexuality. Underpinning much contemporary feminist theory is an implicit assumption of innate difference between men and women, where social inequalities stem as much from the hormonal/anatomical attributes of men as they do from social institutions like patriarchy or the thought practices associated with rational or positivist-based epistemologies. For many feminists, the litany of allegations also derive from psychoanalytic interpretation, where, for example, the arms race, strategic and military studies, comparative force assessment, military-industrial complexes, or studies of the new surveillance technologies represent a male obsession with hardware and high politics characteristic of the egocentric, aggressive, powerseeking, rational man who unconsciously transposes his phallocentric desires into war-hunting-sport-fighting-power-seeking pursuits. Using a type of neobiological cum psychosociological logic, males are seen to project a testosterone-induced aggression/violence indicative of hormonal dispositions or imprinted primeval genetic memories to protect food sources or territory, for example. Or, as the case may be, some men never mature. They continue to play with dangerous toys—motorbikes, racing cars, weapons, and war—flirting with death.[19] For Helen Caldicott, some men simply display a fascination with killing. Why? Perhaps, she notes, "Because women know from birth that they can experience the ultimate act of creativity, whereas boys and men lack this potential capacity and replace it with a fascination with control over life and death and a feeling of creative omnipotence."[20] Women, on the other hand, are "allied to the life process" by virtue of "their hormonal constitution." "She is not afraid to admit she has made a mistake and is generally interested in life-oriented human dynamics. She innately understands the basic principles of conflict resolution."[21] Men, by contrast, when they make war do so for reasons of psychosexual virility, in order to demonstrate their sexual potency as aging, white, elite male decision makers. As Caldicott notes, "It is never the people who make the decision to kill who get killed. It is the boys who usually don't even know what a dispute is about, let alone understand the intricacies of international politics. [These] old men act out their fascination with killing, their need to prove their toughness and sexual adequacy by using innocent pawns."[22] Here, male aggression is ascribed to the deeply embedded psychodramas played out in male minds, the psychosociology of the male as a competitive sex predator, for example, and the fixation with phallocentric satisfaction.[23] Men theorists of international relations are still really boys playing with guns, tanks, and bombs, caught up in the activity of psychosexual play as they study or help prepare for, make, and fight wars. "Little boys with big toys" was the popular expression of the Campaign for Nuclear Disarmament (CND) and of the protests by women at Greenham Common against the deployment of Pershing and Cruise miles in the United Kingdom. For Caldicott, for example, the arms race was little more than an incidence of "missile envy," a competition between male superpowers intent on projecting their power as a phallocentric expression of their desire to compete and dominate. Indeed, for Caldicott, it is no accident that missiles and phalluses have a certain similarity in shape and appearance.[24]

While such renditions are, to be fair, extreme and few, there is a tendency among feminist theorists of international relations to meld a pseudopsycholanalytics with a textual interpretivism and arrive at discourses that posit sexual difference as a definitive explanation of the character of international politics by virtue of their domination by males. This also circumscribes the need for a feminist perspective/critique of the discipline and its theoretical approaches. Patriarchy, gender, and masculinism, for feminists, become as pertinent to understanding international relations as do strategic studies, nation-states, and military force. "A gender-sensitive lens," notes V. Spike Peterson, "illuminates mounting tensions and even contradictions between the 'deeper historical structures' of masculinism (bequeathed to us by the success of western civilization) and multiple transformations in 'events-time' (the dimensions of today's structural crisis)."[25] For feminists, gender is a "central facet of human identity," and identities are "constructed by others who have a stake in making up certain social categories and in trying to make people conform to them." In fact, for Jill Krause, gender is the ontological essence of self, being, and identity: "Our view of ourselves, how we relate to others and how we understand our world and our place in it are all coloured by our perception of ourselves and others as gendered individuals."[26] Gender, in other words, is an indispensable ingredient in the study of international politics, a means of understanding not just the systemic basis of the international system, but of the power structures imbedded in these relations. Without feminist perspectives, International Relations is adduced as being illegitimate, "dominated mostly by white, English-speaking background intellectuals, located mainly within the Anglo-North America academic establishment," and this dominated by men, asking questions and pursuing interests that affect them.[27] Gender, in other words, is both the problem in international relations (and International Relations) because of its untheorized, unconscious, unrecognized importance to the play of global politics and their analysis, and also the solution to these problems that, once out of the closet, will yet elucidate the systemic basis of aggression, war, identity, discrimination, power, and territoriality. The need for gendered perspectives and gender sensitive lenses is thus self-evident for feminists, representing "a more powerful variable than anarchy or power for understanding international relations."[28] "Gender," it seems, "makes the world go round."[29]

Gendering International Relations: Two Approaches

As one of the leading feminist theorists of international relations, Christine Sylvester is in no doubt as to what needs to be done: "It is time to stalk the shadows of the field and subvert and enliven, destabilize, disorder, disenchant, insecure, and homestead a field whose internal differences are so tied up with the voices of mainstream and dissident 'men' that they smack of debates within the hierarchy of one church."[30] Yet again, international relations is witness to a challenge, this time to a feminist "new beginning" to the new beginning called for previously by male dissidents.

But if the call to begin afresh the study of international relations resounds loudest among feminists, the respective approaches they proffer fall victim to radical disagreement. Postmodern feminism, feminist postmodernism, feminist empiricism, cultural feminism, or standpoint feminism, to name but a few, are among the many feminisms whose respective approaches either embrace women, reject their existence altogether, invoke the categories of gender, sexuality, patriarchy, or masculinism, or wish to repudiate all of these on the basis of their socially constructed nature. For feminists, the conundrum is manifest by problems of identity, representation, and language. Simply to "add women and stir" presupposes the subordinate importance of gender and, more importantly, that the category "women" is ubiquitous. For some feminists, for example, we can never really know "who are women," "where are women," or even "what are women."[31] Do women really exist or is the category "women" merely inscribed by patriarchal norms that represent little more than socially constructed fabrications? And if women do exist, does this singular noun presuppose a shared experience, a sisterhood, in short, a sex similarity? Attempting to dismantle the masculinist hegemony of International Relations thus proves discursive for feminists who tend to divaricate between two dominant schools of thought. These we might term constructivist or epistemological feminism, and the second essentialist, ontological or standpoint feminism.[32]

Epistemological Feminism

Christine Sylvester's work is indicative of an epistemological approach, melding a form of constructivist analysis with postpositivist and postmodernist theory so as to challenge all essentialist knowledge and categories. The centrality of sex and gender "beyond the role that *constructed* gender values and identities play in determining priorities and behaviour," Sylvester dismisses.[33] For her, "men" and "women" are understood "as socially constructed subject statuses that emerge from a politicization of slightly different anatomies in ways that support grand divisions of labor, traits, places, and power." If, Sylvester writes, "poststructuralism is known to 'resist or deconstruct common assumptions of culture,' and since men and women (and maybe even feminism) are examples of 'common assumptions of culture,'" then, for Sylvester, we must applaud efforts "to render 'questionable the possibility of locating a place from which to speak and act as a women knowing that all such places are socially and historically constructed, not given by nature.'"[34] Gender categories, in other words, are not permanent, immutable, determinant, and essential, but fluid, dispersed and relational. More important from Sylvester's perspective is an understanding of masculinism because it is this rather than essentialist categories like men and women that betray the theoretical moves and historical strategies that have displaced women from international relations. She thus refuses to speak of, for, or about "women" without placing that category in inverted commas since "women" do not really exist other than as categorical identities imposed upon anatomically distinct subjects. But rather than rejecting the category of "women" altogether, Sylvester chooses to use it if only because many women continue to self-identify with this category. Sylvester's is not, then, a feminist postmodernism estranged from foundational ontological discourse, displaying a "radical skepticism about the self, gender, knowledge, social relations, and culture," but a postmodern feminism that, while "skeptical about lines of thinking that unproblematically accept the meaningful existence of women, . . . does not run roughshod over people who find meaning in these subject statuses."[35] This is a self-declared middle ground, a "position of negotiation between standpoint feminism, with their conviction that real women exist[,] . . . and feminist postmodernist skepticisms," with its conviction that "women" don't really exist.[36] It rejects crude deconstructionism with its less-than-convincing pretensions to reform "various canons simply by flipping them over to expose the usually hidden instantiations of women." Telling stories or resurrecting voices otherwise silenced does not change the mantel upon which that silence has been imposed, but, for Sylvester, simply allows us to hear those previously silenced voices. For this very reason, she is skeptical "about abandoning 'women' as a false invention of sovereign 'man' without checking for the knowledges of life that these evacuated ones have learned and that we have ignored all along."[37] This, then, is an attempt at adding not only the gender variable, but a postpositivist position of (liberal?) tolerance for epistemological diversity that seeks neither to admonish as illegitimate certain perspectives or subject statuses, or claim some as ontologically central and foundational to the feminist canon.

In an attempt to do so, Sylvester turns to epistemological questions as a means of steering a middle course, wanting to disrupt the conventional self-images of the discipline, its assumptions, and theoretical perspectives, but not so as to "tyrannise some people while emancipating others."[38] To this end, she offers the parable of Ruby, a female elephant. "In a Phoenix, Arizona zoo, an Asian elephant named Ruby singlefootedly decenters conventional wisdom about the (seemingly nonexistent) relationship between visual arts and elephant proclivities. She paints abstract expressionist works. She is an aesthetic elephant," writes Sylvester. "Her 'strange' behavior partially transforms her keepers into epistemologists who ask: 'What does Ruby think or feel as she selects different colors from the paint palette offered by her caregiver? How does she know when her newest creation is finished and stops painting?' All around her," Sylvester suggests, "there are now imaginative reworkings of seemingly fixed identities: elephant becomes elephant-painter; zookeeper becomes zookeeper-art philosopher; visitors to the zoo become momentary art critics." For Sylvester, Ruby the elephant and those around her are instances of those who "homestead," meaning: those who "reconfigure 'known' subject statuses—such as 'elephant,' but also the commonplaces of human 'men' and 'women'—in ways that open up rather than fence in terrains of meaning, identity, and place."[39] And this, of course, is the objective of Sylvester's discourse, a repainting of the "canvas of IR" to destabilize meaning, place, and identity so as to produce new perspectives, new questions, and new meanings just as Ruby the elephant did in the Arizona zoo. Epistemology, in other words, is really a metatheoretical propensity toward contextualism and historicity in order to demonstrate constantly that things, ideas, facts, words, events, places, and actions are not always as they seem, that they are outcomes of the interstitial interplay of identity and gender, of masculinism, and of images and ideas dominated mostly by men who "homestead" them as their own. This is where postmodernism reveals its utility for Sylvester, exposing the "smokescreens" by which women have been "homesteaded" in separate, marginal places in international relations and the question of their marginal location settled "behind a smokescreen of transcendental imperatives." Postmodernism reveals the "histories of the screens and the smoke, in brilliant, eye-opening ways," that "deconstruct our identities and reconstitute them in expansive ways."[40] This is akin to a politics of disturbance "that unsettles realist-insinuating knowledges and ploughs up inherited turfs without planting the same old seeds in the field."[41]

Much like the perspectives of male postmodern dissidents, then, Sylvester too wants to render theorists "homeless from fixed and immobile research gazes," but not so as to "wander the streets lost," estranged and insecure in all knowledge.⁴² Constant insecurity in what we know and how we know it, after all, would be unproductive and aimless. By turning to "sociality" we can keep some insecurity at bay, "listen to others telling their stories in an identity-refracting way that reveals repositories of exclusion in our subjectivities and insecures that which seems to hold fast." These practices make for empathic group relationships, a "sociality" among like-minded subjectivities that, in the face of ontological homelessness and insecure knowledge provides "compensation" or what some might describe as a form of postmodern solidarity.⁴³ Above all, this sociality (solidarity) tends toward the formation of a conversation, not about international relations traditionally understood, but about "relations international"—a field about the "myriad positions that groups assume toward one another across the many boundaries and identities that defy field-invented parameters."⁴⁴ This is a new conversation informed by gendered perspectives, diverse subjectivities and identities, inclusionary of contending positions, but not fixed in its outlook, medium of analysis, or conclusions. Contrary to contemporary debates in International Relations that, for Sylvester, have been "narrow and encrusting of a politics in which 'men' control knowledge and 'women' are either out of place altogether or are issued visitors' passes that enable us to leave assigned homelands for temporary support roles in IR," Sylvester's canvas aims to be more encompassing, to "share space, respect, and trust in a re-formed endeavor that will hear the can(n)on shots of the past without assuming that one cannon is inevitable."⁴⁵ Multiple perspectives, opinions, approaches, methods, foci, issues, agendas, meanings, and identities will, for Sylvester, make for a better, gentler, nicer discipline. Her goals are plainly stated. While some militant feminists aspire to do "battle with 'men' for IR and killing them or the field in order to emancipate it," Sylvester strives for "emphatic cooperation," not a violent take-over.⁴⁶ "We want a different, difference-tolerant IR whose theories embed a range of mestiza consciousnesses and owlish sweeps of vision." This is a call to "shatter one's sense of men and women," to employ an "emphatic cooperative gaze" said to be able to "divest IR's nostalgic gender settlements of power by infusing them with knowledges that come from listening to and engaging canon-excluding and canon-including subjectivities."⁴⁷ The standard here is to "beware of colonial possibilities lurking in any recreated metaphor of 'Westward Ho!' and homestead differently."⁴⁸ The call is not to arms, but to "homestead" the first, second, and now the Third Debates, taking on the "gendered anarchies and reciprocities of a field, freeing prisoners from manipulated dilemmas and refusing divisive levels of analysis that have us not-seeing the lessons on cooperative relations that third world cooperatives and first world peace camps can teach."[49] "Relations international" looks, instead, toward the women of Greenham Common who "built empathy for difference through exercises that encouraged participants to listen to each other and cooperate, at minimum, by refusing to interrupt or to force conformity on others." At Greenham, notes Sylvester, there was "no directing, no breaking through, no need for a linear progression which gives the comforting illusion that one knows where one goes." Rather, there was a "disavowal of hierarchy and of 'tried and true' authority, task assignments, habits of deference, and modes of compliance in favor of cooperative anarchy."[50] As a model for "relations international," Sylvester celebrates the words of Gwyn Kirk who writes,

> At the peace camp each woman does what she thinks is necessary, so there are no rosters or lists of who has to do what. . . . This is very unfamiliar to some people, who exclaim in frustration "why don't they *organize* something?" To their credit, women at the camp have not given in to this demand but have created a space that allows many women to ask instead, "What do *I* want to do?" Some feel alienated and do not return, but others become much more autonomous and effective than they would if they merely followed other people's directives.[51]

This, for Sylvester, is an instance of "local homebred women" straddling "no-man's land to homestead on 'men's' and 'women's' assigned places in the Western Way of Security."[52] These are the "real" actors and subjects of "relations international," not prisoners' dilemmas or levels of analysis. Likewise, for Sylvester, "women cooperators in Harare," as they busy themselves "with paying their children's school fees, with lazy husbands drinking away the household income, with prices for their crops, [and] . . . with structural adjustment policies suggested by the World Bank, . . . belie any notion we might have that security studies can be restricted to some ubiquitous possibility of war between states. . . ."[53] "Feminist perspectives on security begin with women's own experiences of everyday life, and bodily danger and safety" argues Jan Jindy Pettman. To take "security seriously" is to focus one's lenses upon the experiences of women, their struggles to "homestead" politics, and their strategies to conduct politics in nonmasculinized, nonhierarchical, more inclusive, and sensitive ways.[54] As recurrent themes in Sylvester's writings, the calls to "unman" International Relations as masculine territory while demonstrating how pervasive is gender as a "filter of knowledge" reveals the objective intent and ambition of feminist postmodernism.[55] This is nothing short of a call to conduct and analyze international politics by other means, and in doing so to reconstruct theory, the discipline, and the subjects of our inquiry in ways that make subject genders the central analytical concern of theorists.

Standpoint Feminism

While Sylvester attempts to steer a middle course, accepting implicitly the legitimacy of all feminisms but rendering problematic notions of women as well as the imposed disciplinary parameters that define the research agendas of security studies, neoliberal institutionalism and neorealism, this is not true of feminists like Cynthia Enloe who do not question the existence of women but wants to make them ontologically central as the research subjects of International Relations. Her approach, as Marysia Zalewski notes, is ontologically assertive and takes the lived experiences of women seriously.[56] Change, for Enloe, can only come about if we relocate our ontological starting points and begin with those who experience international politics at the coal face, and from here work our way upwards to see how the superstructural edifice of international relations derives from the amalgam of actions constituted in the everyday practices of ordinary people. This is not ontological homelessness as proffered by Sylvester, but a neoessentialism that posits women as starting points for understanding the quintessential essence of international politics. Unlike Sylvester, Enloe feels no compulsion to deconstruct women and reconstruct them as "women," despite her understanding femininity and masculinism as socially constructed entities. Women, for Enloe, are also "women," the latter merely a socially inscribed category indicative of real women whose material realities and lived experiences are anything but problematic.[57] Enloe knows who women are, whereas Sylvester does not, refusing to start with "women" since, for her, this category is constantly changing, its composition in flux, populated by mobile subjectivities with multiple, socially fabricated identities. Thus, while men might be "men" and women might be "women," the point for Enloe is moot; both subjectivities have existed historically and the historical realities of their existence have tended to be defined by the oppression and control of women/"women" by men/"men." Singling "out women for ontological and methodological annihilation," Enloe thus dismisses as trite and unnecessary.[58]

Much as for Sylvester, long-established patriarchal hierarchies also explain the exclusion of women from international politics for Enloe. Men, comfortable within their patriarchal domains, have felt "particularly confident in dismissing feminist ideas. Rare is the professional commentator on international politics who takes women's experiences seriously."[59] Rather, insists Enloe, men ignore women, feminist perspectives, and make gender invisible by constructing a field whose lenses are so masculinized that "the workings of both femininity and masculinity in international politics" have become hidden from view.[60] "Realist International Relations theory," for example, feminists see as eliminating from view "all that is traditionally female" by premising its epistemological fiat on assumptions of "power, control, . . . domination and the obliteration of emotion and altruism."[61] Realism is the "S and M of international relations, neoliberal institutionalism is the set of street gangs that enforce the rule of honour among scoundrels and thieves." Such perspectives represent "the gender subterfuge, the furtive . . . den of drag," emasculating gender from international politics other than as a "naturally masculine" place for men.[62] Women and gender only feature in realist narratives, feminists argue, when the "gendered representatives of hearth and home" succumb to victimhood as "warring citizens . . . rape the enemy's women as part of war. People called women are thereby thrust into realist international relations. But they are not admitted into most realist studies of war."[63]

Enloe's project is thus to "cast doubt on . . . [these] comfortable assumptions," to expose the hidden workings of masculinity and femininity, the pervasive nature of gender identities, and to remake International Relations and international politics. Until now, "research and researchers have been tainted by entrenched misogyny and androcentrism (male centeredness)," resulting in a "distortion both of what is researched as well as the results of such research: knowledge."[64] For standpoint feminists, those who monopolize "the production and dissemination of knowledge will, in the end, determine what actually 'counts' as knowledge. Inevitably, that knowledge will reflect the interests and needs of the dominant or ruling group." And, since "men have historically produced most of the knowledge base currently employed," standpoint feminists claim that this knowledge is only partial, distorted, biased, misogynist, androcentric, and self-serving of the interests of men and the continuing oppression of women.[65] The vast majority of knowledge because of its "maleness" represents not mainstream but "malestream" knowledge which, in the eyes of standpoint feminists, renders it illegitimate, biased, and ignorant of the real realities that confront ordinary women out there at the coal face of international politics.[66] Hence the importance of, and need for, women-centered and -focused research. Standpoint feminism meets this challenge by giving an ontological "primacy to women . . . at the theoretical and practical level." In so doing, "it draws on a diverse body of literature containing many insights for international relations scholars."⁶⁷ Above all, it begins the process of remaking International Relations by homesteading "the field with knowledges that people called women develop as a consequence of being socially subordinate and excluded from centres of power."⁶⁸ The objective of standpoint feminism in Sylvester's estimation, for example, is "to explore and valorize these and other insights from the 'other side' and bring them to bear on fields that base their knowledge on the experiences of people called men." Indeed, for Enloe the object(ive) is even more poignant, cast in terms of an ontological superiority when she notes, "Women tend to be in a better position than men to conduct . . . a realistic investigation of international politics simply because so many women have learned to ask about gender when making sense of how public and private power operate."⁶⁹ Similarly, for Jacqui True, "Knowledge that emerges from women's experiences on the margins of world politics is actually more neutral and critical because it is not as complicit with, or blinded by, existing institutions and power relations."⁷⁰ Women, so the argument goes, "have a distinct moral language, one that emphasizes concern for others, responsibility, care, and obligation, hence a moral language profoundly at odds with formal, abstract models of morality defined in terms of absolute principles."⁷¹ Contrary to Sylvester's claim, this is not so much about bringing otherwise unseen perspectives to bear upon the "knowledges of men," but a better, superior knowledge and morality that surpasses that of men by virtue of its basis in the lived experiences of women. Regardless, the intimation here is of a qualitatively superior method of analysis, resident in gender subjectivities who, because of their oppression, marginalization, and exclusion from the power complexes of societies have keener insights into their workings. As Christina Hoff Sommers notes, standpoint feminists believe that they "have a epistemic advantage over men," because by "feeling more deeply, they see more clearly and understand reality better." Women, quite simply, "are better knowers."⁷²

For feminists the most immediate remedy to masculinist androcentrism in International Relations and global politics is, then, an empirical one: add more women and stir. Reconstituting International Relations in fundamentally new ways involves bringing more women into the academy and into positions of power in international politics. By adding more female researchers, for example, feminists argue that the proclivity to "malestream" theory can be checked by breaking down the boys' club syndrome.⁷³ Gender equity and affirmative action policies as a means to engineer socially an end to overt discrimination have thus been the first order of business. From here, feminist women, "less bounded by any narrow disciplinary lens," can then "examine insights from diverse locations, situate them in larger transdisciplinary contexts, and weave new understandings out of these multiple threads" by virtue of the "epistemic advantage" they enjoy over men knowers.[74] This, of course, is not just about more female representation as so-called empirical feminists would argue, but, from the perspective of standpoint feminists, about the ontological primacy of "women as knowers" combined with an attempt "to eliminate the fascism in our heads . . . build upon the open qualities of human discourse, and thereby intervene in the way knowledge is produced and constituted at the particular sites where a localized power-discourse prevails."[75] Equality in representation is only the first of many revolutions, a necessary but hardly sufficient condition to meet the challenges of thinking differently about how we think and know, and a recognition of how "gender both creates and reproduces a world of multiple inequalities that today threatens all of us."[76] Thus, "the task of ungendering power," notes Peterson, "is twofold—adding women to the existing world politics power structures and transforming those very power structures, ideologically and materially."[77]

This project has been common enough in International Relations, evidenced by increasing calls for more women researchers, more feminist analyses of international politics, and increased efforts to bring gendered perspectives and issues to bear upon the study of global events and processes. Yet, if these attempts appear diverse, all tend to be analogous, united by the common penchant to "reclaim the private." "The personal is political," writes Enloe, echoing the words of Susan Moller Okin.[78] "Feminist tracings of early state formation," for example, have sought to highlight the "emergence and consolidation of public political power and the centralisation of authority" which concomitantly "constituted a separate domestic or private sphere that came to be associated with women and the feminine."[79] This false public/private dichotomy feminists see as an artificial dualism intended to sideline women into domestic servitude while depoliticizing the domestic sphere. That the "personal is political," suggests Enloe, means "that politics is not shaped merely by what happens in legislative debates, voting booths or war rooms." Rather, men, "who dominate public life, have told women to stay in the kitchen, . . . [and] have used their public power to construct private relationships in ways that . . . [bolster] their masculinized political control."[80] Historically, men have thus appropriated public/political power, thereby denying women a legitimate political voice and making them dependent. New feminist understandings and research thus attempt to show how a reclamation of the private as political redefines the questions of International Relations and the research agenda's scholars should otherwise be engaged with. "Accepting that the political is personal prompts one to investigate the politics of marriage, venereal disease and homosexuality," claims Enloe, "not as marginal issues, but as matters central to the state. Doing this type of research becomes just as serious as studying military weaponry or taxation policy."[81] The cult of masculinity, as V. Spike Peterson terms it, extends down into the depths of what otherwise appears as natural or given. The "cult of motherhood" and the notion of "women's work," for example, represent patriarchal norms culturally ingrained in the modern nation-state that justifies "structural violence—inadequate health care, sexual harassment, and sex segregated wages, rights, and resources" for women.[82] Indeed, for Peterson, the state is complicit in structural violence, albeit indirectly, "through its promotion of masculinist, heterosexist, and classist ideologies—expressed, for example, in public education models, media images, the militarism of culture, welfare policies, and patriarchal law." Through "its selective sanctioning of nonstate violence, particularly in its policy of nonintervention in domestic violence," and through direct male brutality like "murder, rape, battering, [and] incest," Peterson claims that male domination is constantly reproduced, reaffirming the subjugation of women as "the objects of masculinist social control."[83] Reclaiming these "private spaces," events, and acts as public-political spaces demystifies the patriarchal base of the state and how it constructs and manipulates "the ideology describing public and private life." More importantly, this strategy opens up International Relations to a multiplicity of subjects, issues, and research agendas with all of them attempting to disrupt the boundaries imposed by the "radical bifurcation of asymmetrical public and private spheres"; so begins the project of "ungendering world politics."[84]

Despite the tacit pluralism in such ambitions, however, the focal point of feminist International Relations scholars remains an exposé of male violence as a "global war against women."[85] Realist theory, positivism, the conventional research agendas of security studies, the Enlightenment, modernity and rationality, or the precepts of state security, are all really the encoded masculinist ethos of multiple strategies to coerce, control, dominate, and subjugate women. This is not just male egocentrism manifest as chauvinism, but a functional element of class, state, international political, and capitalist reproduction that requires the domestic indenture of women. As Cynthia Enloe observes in the case of the diplomatic class, "Government men depend on women's unpaid labour to carry on relations with their political counterparts. So long as the conventional politics of marriage prevailed, no government needed either to acknowledge or to accommodate diplomatic wives and women careerists. They could use marriage both to grease the wheels of man-to-man negotiations and to ensure that no women reached positions of influence."[86]

National security too is understood as merely another foible for the maintenance of women in inferior and subservient positions. Just as states act as a kind of "protection racket" through an embedded sovereignty contract implicit in interstate relations, providing protection from outside threats and wielding absolute control over the legitimate use of force, so also do they extract protection payments internally from their citizens—especially women. "In the name of protection," notes True, "states demand the sacrifices of gendered citizens": mothers, for example, who provide the cannon fodder for state aggression by devoting "their lives to socializing these dutiful [male] citizens for the sovereign state as masculine deity." On top of this, women are also forced to seek refuge inside the institution of marriage, which, much like a protection racket, exercises a monopoly on legitimate reproduction and property inheritance. "Women," argues True, are forced to "seek security in marriage and the protection of a husband from the violence of other men or males in general, and from the economic insecurity of a international division of labour which devalues work associated with women." Not that this security is absolute, of course. Trapped in such private institutions, women must endure domestic violence, provide domestic and sexual service, and reproduce the household on a daily basis. The result, for True, is that the "limited security provided by 'protection rackets' allows men and states to consolidate their centralised authority over other men and states, but more importantly over women and nature on whom they are dependent as a source of exploitable resources, for the socio-cultural and biological reproduction of power relations."[87] National security is thus really about a series of gendered insecurities for women that, in subtle and sometimes overt ways, coerces them into socioinstitutional structures and practices that force them to serve the masculine state and men.

For feminists, however, these are merely political manifestations of a deeper, culturally ingrained means of thinking indicative of Western thought practices. As V. Spike Peterson notes, the subjugation of women through a "gender hierarchy is not coincidental to but in a significant sense constitutive of western Philosophy's objectivist metaphysics. Modernity's expression of that metaphysics, positivist science, (re)inscribes the identification of masculinity—as objectivity, reason, freedom, transcendence, and control—against femininity—as subjectivity, feeling, necessity, contingency, and disorder." The constitutive essence of Enlightenment thought and reason, in other words, is functionally dependent upon the objectification of women as "inferior," or of the "second order," to the more superior logos of "man." These represent a kind of "colonizing dualism" inherent in Enlightenment and Western thought, whereby, argues Peterson, the first term, man, "is assumed to be prior and superior to the second term," woman, "the latter perceived as threatening the values that the first asserts."[88] The whole of Western thought practices, especially modernist thinking, is thus rejected for its hierarchical tendency to place women in a culturally inferior light, a fact that for feminists is evident not only in the history of patriarchy, but in our very language, epistemologies, and unwritten cultural mores.

Whether, then, it is International Relations, the diplomatic corps, realist or neoliberal theory, positivism, or the nation-state—all are depicted as complicit in the oppression of women and, indeed, require their continued subjugation in order to reproduce the systemic power-political relations from which their authority emanates. The totality of Western (and non-Western) history can thus be told from a single standpoint, women. Witness the words of Sylvester on the evolution of the state, markets, and capitalism, for example: "States became war-constituted solidarities of men which transcended the realms of necessary labour where women dwelled. . . . The market system worked hand-in-glove with the state in demoting women and their activities to the sphere of private property. . . . States enshrined the rights of Man in the West, elsewhere through colonisation, and literally empowered men to own and control all manner of property, including women."[89] History, in all its epochs and places, is defined by its objectification of women, and "male dominance is perhaps the most pervasive and tenacious system of power in history."[90] The history of the world, it seems, has not been that of class struggle as Marx declared, but of gender struggle and gender wars.

Identity Politics, Gender, and International Relations: An Interim Assessment

Few in the social sciences and humanities will have missed the rise of what Sommers disapprovingly calls "militant gynocentrism and misandrism."[91] That feminist perspectives and feminist studies have had far reaching effects upon the academy and its knowledges is beyond question. In International Relations, gender perspectives have opened up important and hitherto neglected sites of inquiry. Studies into patriarchal structures like the military, the systemic exclusion of women and the phenomena of the glass ceiling, sexual intimidation, and the role masculinism plays in the conduct of international politics and military affairs have all been useful, revealing, and contributory to our understanding of international relations. So too, studies into the international political economy of global change, globalization, transnational corporations, the new Asian industrialism, and the exploitation of workers under the new international division of labor have benefited greatly from gender analyses highlighting the adverse and often different effects such phenomena have had on women and men. Yet, as Adam Jones concluded recently, despite their contributions, feminist "critiques are far from constituting an adequate account or even an inclusive framing of gender and IR. The wider task—theorizing and narrating the international politics of gender—remains."[92] For feminists who suggest that they have found better ontological viewing points from which to theorize the realities, causes, and issues of international politics, this is stinging criticism. Indeed, it renders problematic the "gender variable" as the principal ontological starting point for investigating international politics and makes apparent how premature are adages announcing that "gender makes the world go round." That feminist epistemologies, especially postmodern feminisms, are not above being problematic underscores how important is the need for further investigation before we all don postmodern gender lenses and view the world through this singular and unifocal lens.

Questioning Identity Politics

Critical research agendas of this type, however, are not found easily in International Relations. Critics of feminist perspectives run the risk of denouncement as either a misogynist malcontent or an androcentric keeper of the gate. At work in much of this discourse is an unstated political correctness, where the historical marginalization of women bestows intellectual autonomy, excluding those outside the identity group from legitimate participation in its discourse. Only feminist women can do real, legitimate, feminist theory since, in the mantra of identity politics, discourse must emanate from a positional (personal) ontology. Those sensitive or sympathetic to the identity politics of particular groups are, of course, welcome to lend support and encouragement, but only on terms delineated by the groups themselves. In this way, they enjoy an uncontested sovereign hegemony over their own self-identification, insuring the group discourse is self-constituted and that its parameters, operative methodology, and standards of argument, appraisal, and evidentiary provisions are self-defined. Thus, for example, when Sylvester calls for a "homesteading" of International Relations she does so "by [a] repetitive feminist insistence that *we be included on our terms*" (my emphasis). Rather than an invitation to engage in dialogue, this is an ultimatum that a sovereign intellectual space be provided and insulated from critics who question the merits of identity-based political discourse. Instead, Sylvester calls upon International Relations to "share space, respect, and trust in a re-formed endeavor," but one otherwise proscribed as committed to demonstrating not only "that the secure homes constructed by IR's many debaters are chimerical," but, as a consequence, to ending International Relations and remaking it along lines grounded in feminist postmodernism.[93] Such stipulative provisions might be likened to a form of negotiated sovereign territoriality where, as part of the settlement for the historically aggrieved, border incursions are to be allowed but may not be met with resistance or reciprocity. Demands for entry to the discipline are thus predicated on conditions that insure two sets of rules, cocooning postmodern feminist spaces from systematic analyses while "respecting" this discourse as it hastens about the project of deconstructing International Relations as a "male space." Sylvester's impassioned plea for tolerance and "emphatic cooperation" is thus confined to like-minded individuals, those who do not challenge feminist epistemologies but accept them as a necessary means of reinventing the discipline as a discourse between postmodern identities—the most important of which is gender.[94] Intolerance or misogyny thus become the ironic epithets attached to those who question the wisdom of this reinvention or the merits of the return of identity in international theory.[95] Most strategic of all, however, demands for entry to the discipline and calls for intellectual spaces betray a self-imposed, politically motivated marginality. After all, where are such calls issued from other than the discipline and the intellectual—and well established—spaces of feminist International Relations?

Much like the strategies employed by male dissidents, then, feminist postmodernists too deflect as illegitimate any criticism that derives from skeptics whose vantage points are labeled privileged. And privilege is variously interpreted historically, especially along lines of race, color, and sex where the denotations white and male, to name but two, serve as intergenerational mediums to assess the injustices of past histories. White males, for example, become generic signifiers for historical oppression, indicating an ontologically privileged group by which the historical experiences of the "other" can then be reclaimed in the context of their related oppression, exploitation, and exclusion. Legitimacy, in this context, can then be claimed in terms of one's group identity and the extent to which the history of that particular group has been "silenced." In this same way, self-identification or "self-situation" establishes one's credentials, allowing admittance to the group and legitimating the "authoritative" vantage point from which one speaks and writes. Thus, for example, Jan Jindy Pettman includes among the introductory pages to her most recent book, *Worlding Women,* a section titled "A (personal) politics of location," in which her identity as a woman, a feminist, and an academic, makes apparent her particular (marginal) identities and group loyalties.[96] Similarly, Christine Sylvester, in the introduction to her book, insists, "It is important to provide a context for one's work in the often-denied politics of the personal." Accordingly, self-declaration reveals to the reader that she is a feminist, went to a Catholic girls school where she was schooled to "develop your brains and confess something called 'sins' to always male forever priests," and that these provide some pieces to her dynamic objectivity.[97] Like territorial markers, self-identification permits entry to intellectual spaces whose sovereign authority is "policed" as much by marginal subjectivities as they allege of the oppressors who "police" the discourse of realism, or who are said to walk the corridors of the discipline insuring the replication of patriarchy, hierarchical agendas, and "malestream" theory. If Sylvester's version of feminist postmodernism is projected as tolerant, perspectivist, and encompassing of a multiplicity of approaches, in reality it is as selective, exclusionary, and dismissive of alternative perspectives as mainstream approaches are accused of being.

Skillful theoretical moves of this nature underscore the adroitness of postmodern feminist theory at emasculating many of its logical inconsistencies. In arguing for a feminist postmodernism, for example, Sylvester employs a double theoretical move that, on the one hand, invokes a kind of epistemological-deconstructive-anarchy-cum-relativism in an attempt to decenter or make insecure fixed research gazes, identities, and concepts (men, women, security, and nation-state), while on the other hand turning to the lived experiences of women as if ontologically given and assuming their experiences to be authentic, real, substantive, and authoritative interpretations of the realities of international relations. Women at the peace camps of Greenham Common or in the cooperatives of Harare, represent, for Sylvester, the real coal face of international politics, their experiences and strategies the real politics of "relations international." But why should we take the experiences of these women to be ontologically superior or more insightful than the experiences of other women or other men? As Sylvester admits elsewhere, "Experience . . . is at once always already an interpretation *and* in need of interpretation." Why, then, are experience-based modes of knowledge more insightful than knowledges derived through other modes of inquiry?[98] Such epistemologies are surely crudely positivistic in their singular reliance on osmotic perception of the facts as they impact upon the personal. If, as Sylvester writes, "sceptical inlining draws on substantive everydayness as a time and site of knowledge, much as does everyday feminist theorising," and if, as she further notes, "it understands experience . . . as mobile, indeterminate, hyphenated, [and] homeless," why should this knowledge be valued as anything other than fleeting subjective perceptions of multiple environmental stimuli whose meaning is beyond explanation other than as a personal narrative?[99] Is this what Sylvester means when she calls for a re-visioning and a repainting of the "canvases of IR," that we dissipate knowledge into an infinitesimal number of disparate sites, all equally valid, and let loose with a mélange of visceral perceptions; stories of how each of us perceive we experience international politics? If this is the case, then Sylvester's version of feminist postmodernism does not advance our understanding of international politics, leaving untheorized and unexplained the causes of international relations. Personal narratives do not constitute theoretical discourse, nor indeed an explanation of the systemic factors that procure international events, processes, or the actions of certain actors.

We might also extend a contextualist lens to analyze Sylvester's formulations, much as she insists her epistemological approach does. Sylvester, for example, is adamant that we can not really know who "women" are, since to do so would be to invoke an essentialist concept, concealing the diversity inherent in this category. "Women" don't really exist in Sylvester's estimation since there are black women, white women, Hispanic, disabled, lesbian, poor, rich, middle class, and illiterate women, to name but a few. The point, for Sylvester, is that to speak of "women" is to do violence to the diversity encapsulated in this category and, in its own way, to silence those women who remain unnamed. Well and good. Yet this same analytical respect for diversity seems lost with men. Politics and international relations become the "places of men." But which men? All men? Or just white men, or rich, educated, elite, upper class, heterosexual men? To speak of political places as the places of men ignores the fact that most men, in fact the overwhelming majority of men, are not in these political places at all, are not decision makers, elite, affluent, or powerful. Much as with Sylvester's categories, there are poor, lower class, illiterate, gay, black, and white men, many of whom suffer the vestiges of hunger, poverty, despair, and disenfranchisement just as much as women. So why invoke the category "men" in such essentialist and ubiquitous ways while cognizant only of the diversity in the category "women." These are double standards, not erudite theoretical formulations, betraying, dare one say, sexism toward men by invoking male gender generalizations and crude caricatures.

Problems of this nature, however, are really manifestations of a deeper, underlying ailment endemic to discourses derived from identity politics. At base, the most elemental question for identity discourse, as Zalewski and Enloe note, is "Who am I?"[100] The personal becomes the political, evolving a discourse where self-identification, but also one's identification by others, presupposes multiple identities that are fleeting, overlapping, and changing at any particular moment in time or place. "We have multiple identities," argues V. Spike Peterson, "e.g., Canadian, homemaker, Jewish, Hispanic, socialist."[101] And these identities are variously depicted as transient, polymorphic, interactive, discursive, and never fixed. As Richard Brown notes, "Identity is given neither institutionally nor biologically. It evolves as one orders continuities on one's conception of oneself."[102] Yet, if we accept this, the analytical utility of identity politics seems problematic at best. Which identity, for example, do we choose from the many that any one subject might display affinity for? Are we to assume that all identities are of equal importance or that some are more important than others? How do we know which of these identities might be transient and less consequential to one's sense of self and, in turn, politically significant to understanding international politics? Why, for example, should we place gender identity ontologically prior to class, sexual orientation, ethnic origin, ideological perspective, or national identity?[103] As Zalewski and Enloe ask, "Why do we consider states to be a major referent? Why not men? Or women?"[104] But by the same token, why not dogs, shipping magnates, movie stars, or trade regimes? Why is gender more constitutive of global politics than, say, class, or an identity as a cancer survivor, laborer, or social worker? Most of all, why is gender essentialized in feminist discourse, reified into the most preeminent of all identities as the primary lens through which international relations must be viewed? Perhaps, for example, people understand difference in the context of identities outside of gender. As Jane Martin notes, "How do we know that difference . . . does not turn on being fat or religious or in an abusive relationship?"[105] The point, perhaps flippantly made, is that identity is such a nebulous concept, its meaning so obtuse and so inherently subjective, that it is near meaningless as a conduit for understanding global politics if only because it can mean anything to anybody.

For others like Ann Tickner, however, identity challenges the assumption of state sovereignty. "Becoming curious about identity formation below the state and surrendering the simplistic assumption that the state is sovereign will," Tickner suggests, "make us much more realistic describers and explainers of the current international system."[106] The multiple subjects and their identities that constitute the nation-state are, for Tickner, what are important. In a way, of course, she is correct. States are constitutive entities drawn from the amalgam of their citizens. But such observations are somewhat trite and banal and lead International Relations into a devolving and perpetually dividing discourse based upon ever-emergent and transforming identities. Surely the more important observation, however, concerns the bounds of this enterprise. Where do we stop? Are there limits to this exercise or is it a boundless project? And how do we theorize the notion of multiple levels of identities harbored in each subject person? If each of us is fractured into multiple identities, must we then lunge into commentaries specific to each group? Well we might imagine, for example, a discourse in International Relations between white feminist heterosexual women, white middle class heterosexual physically challenged men, working class gay Latinos, transgendered persons, ethnic Italian New York female garment workers, and Asian lesbian ecofeminists. Each would represent a self-constituted knowledge and nomenclature, a discourse reflective of specific identity-group concerns. Knowledge and understanding would suffer from a diaspora, becoming unattainable in any perspicacious sense except in localities so specific that its general understanding, or intergroup applicability, would be obviated. Identity groups would become so splintered and disparate that International Relations would approach a form of identity tribalism with each group forming a kind of intellectual territory, jealously policing its knowledge borders from intrusions by other groups otherwise seen as illegitimate, nonrepresentative, or opposed to the interests of the group. Nor is it improbable to suppose that identity politics in International Relations would evolve a realpolitik between groups, a realist power-struggle for intergroup legitimacy or hegemonic control over particular knowledges or, in the broader polity, situations of intergroup conflict. With what legitimacy, for example, do middle class, by and large white, affluent, feminist, women International Relations scholars speak and write for black, poor, illiterate, gay, working class, others who might object, resist, or denounce such empathetic musings? The legitimacy with which Sylvester or Enloe write, for example, might be questioned on grounds of their identities as elite, educated, privileged women, unrepresentative of the experiences and realities of those at the coal face of international politics.

Celebrating and reifying difference as a political end in itself thus runs the risk of creating increasingly divisive and incommensurate discourses where each group claims a knowledge or experienced based legitimacy but, in doing so, precluding the possibility of common understanding or intergroup political discourse. Instead, difference produces antithetical discord and political-tribalism: only working class Hispanics living in South Central Los Angeles, for instance, can speak of, for, and about their community, its concerns, interests and needs; only female African Americans living in the projects of Chicago can speak "legitimately" of the housing and social problems endemic to inner city living. Discourse becomes confined not to conversations between identity groups since this is impossible, but story telling of personal/group experiences where the "other" listens intently until their turn comes to tell their own stories and experiences. Appropriating the voice or pain of others by speaking, writing, or theorizing on issues, perspectives, or events not indicative of one's group-identity becomes not only illegitimate but a medium of oppression and a means to silence others. The very activity of theory and political discourse as it has been understood traditionally in International Relations, and the social sciences more generally, is thus rendered inappropriate in the new milieu of identity politics.

Politically, progressives obviously see a danger in this type of discourse and, from a social scientific perspective, understand it to be less than rigorous. Generalizing, as with theorizing, for example, has fallen victim to postmodern feminist reactions against methodological essentialism and the adoption of what Jane Martin calls the instillation of false difference into identity discourse. By reacting against the assumption that "all individuals in the world called 'women' were exactly like us" (i.e. white, middle class, educated, etc.), feminists now tend "a priori to give privileged status to a predetermined set of analytic categories and to affirm the existence of nothing but difference." In avoiding the "pitfall of false unity," feminists have thus "walked straight into the trap of false difference."[107] Club words now dominate the discourse. Essentialism, ahistoricism, universalism, and androcentrism, for example, have become the "prime idiom[s] of intellectual terrorism and the privileged instrument[s] of political orthodoxy."[108] While sympathetic to the cause, even feminists like Jane Martin are critical of the methods that have arisen to circumvent the evils of essentialism, characterizing contemporary feminist scholarship as imposing its own "chilly climate" on those who question the methodological proclivity for difference and historicism. Postmodern feminists, she argues, have fallen victim to compulsory historicism, and by "rejecting one kind of essence talk but adopting another," have followed a course "whose logical conclusion all but precludes the use of language."[109] For

Martin, this approaches a "dogmatism on the methodological level that we do not countenance in other contexts. . . . It rules out theories, categories, and research projects in advance; prejudges the extent of difference and the nonexistence of similarity."[110] In all, it speaks to a methodological trap that produces many of the same problems as before, but this time in a language otherwise viewed as progressive, sensitive to the particularities of identity and gender, and destructive of conventional boundaries in disciplinary knowledge and theoretical endeavor.

Lurking behind such positions, of course, is the highly problematic assumption that a fundamental shift in the political, social, and economic worlds has occurred; that "people, machinery and money, images and ideas now follow increasingly nonisomorphic paths, and that because of this there is a "deterritorializing mobility of peoples, ideas, and images," one overcoming the "laborious moves of statism to project an image of the world divided along territorially discontinuous (separated) sovereign spaces, each supposedly with homogeneous cultures and impervious essences."[111] In this new world where global space-as-territory has been obliterated, where discrete national cultures no longer exist but are dissolved by cosmopolitanism and ubiquitous images peddled by hypermodern communications, all that remains as tangible referents for knowledge and understanding, we are told, are our own fractured identities.[112] While, for feminists, this is profoundly liberating, allowing them to recognize a "multiplicity of identities," each engaged in a "differing politics," it also betrays how narrow is the intent of feminist postmodernism, which stands for no other end except the eradication of essentialism.[113] Much as Ashley saw in positivism tyrannical structures of oppression, so in essentialism postmodern feminists see the subjugation of diversity amid universal narratives. Yet the reification of difference as the penultimate ontological beginning and end point seems disingenuous in the extreme. The question is not whether there are differences—of course there are—but whether these are significant for International Relations, and if so in what capacity? Historically, the brief of International Relations has been to go out in search of those things that unite us, not divide us. Division, disunity, and difference have been the unmistakable problems endemic to global politics, and overcoming them the objective that has provided scholars with both their motivating purpose and moral compass. In venerating difference, identity politics unwittingly reproduces this problematique: exacerbating differences beyond their significance, fabricating disunity, and contributing to social and political cleavage. Yes, we are not all the same. But the things that unite us are surely more important, more numerous, and more fundamental to the human condition than those that divide us. We all share a conviction that war is bad, for example, that violence is objectionable, global poverty unconscionable, and that peaceful interstate relations are desirable. Likewise, we all inhabit one earth and have similar environmental concerns, have the same basic needs in terms of developmental requirements, nutrition, personal security, education, and shelter. To suppose that these modernist concerns are divisible on the basis of gender, color, sexuality, or religious inclination seems specious, promoting contrariety where none really exists from the perspective of International Relations. How, for example, amid the reification of ever-divisible difference, do we foster political community and solidarity, hope to foster greater global collectivity, or unite antithetically inclined religious, segregationist, or racial groups on the basis of their professed difference? How this is meant to secure new visions of international politics, solve the divisions of previous disputations, or avert violent factionalisms in the future remains curiously absent from the discourse of identity politics.[114]

Methodologically, the implications of reifying false difference are also far from benign for International Relations, but betray a devolution of disciplinary knowledge and theory amid sundry narratives captive to personal "travelogues," attempts to recreate histories or enumerate a catalogue of previous "silences" simply on the basis that such has not been done before. The result is a type of agenda inflation, sprawling research topics that, from a more traditionalist perspective, would seem unrelated to International Relations. Consider, for example, Birigit Weiss, who attempted to extol the virtues of an identity-based research agenda for International Relations, suggesting that we think of "symbols such as phone boxes, mail boxes, or the little green man flashing electronically above pedestrian crossings. [These] are national (identity) symbols which we seldom notice as such," she writes. "Only: (sic) once we are away from home do we perceive them as different. First deduction. Being abroad we learn to know what home means." Travel, and the distance associated with it, for Weiss "helps us to define who we are (and where we come from)—which is a necessary condition for developing an international perspective." The old adage that "travel does round the individual" is now reiterated in postmodern form, and International Relations exalted to become "interNETional" or "intercultural" studies where, for example, Weiss notes that with the internet "one can travel from ocean to ocean, from continent to continent, from country to country and around the globe in one night—through cyberspace." One can only suppose that play on the internet assists in the formation of our personal identities, makes us better scholars, and that reflections on this can constitute discourse in "InterNETional" studies. As a final reflection on what "intercultural" as opposed to International Relations might look like, Weiss recalls the *Container 96—Art across Oceans* exhibition held in Copenhagen, where "artists coming from 96 seaport cities . . . created art works inside the containers. The visitors were able to 'circumnavigate the globe in just a few hours' and could 'take a walk from continent to continent, from climazone to climazone and from seaport to seaport and enter into visions and realities, as perceived by artists from near and far.'"[115] "In my view," Weiss writes, "this exhibition is an example for an alternative vision of international relations, and might help us look beyond the scope of the discipline."[116]

Similarly, Marysia Zalewski concerns herself "with the intersection between the international political economy and pregnant women's bodies," and addresses concerns such as the "ethics of 'quality-controlled babies,'" the relationship between eugenics and economic ideologies, and how the "ubiquitous use of ultrasound is incrementally erasing the presence of the mother" while "the fetus is imagined as a sort of extra-terrestrial floating in 'space.'" Her discussion is counterpoised against questions that reflect on popular cultural images like the movies *Three Men and a Baby*, *Junior*, and *Tootsie*. Ultimately, she is concerned with "what might happen when men can have babies? Or when the boundary between women and machine collapses? What might this do to our notions of subjectivity? Have reproductive technologies heralded the arrival of the posthuman body—the cyborg—at the end of the twentieth century?"[117] Likewise, Cynthia Enloe sees the purview of International Relations extending to such topics as the dating practices of American soldiers and the rumors surrounding "'barracks girls,' young British girls who leave home and in time become resident sexual partners of American male soldiers."[118] Issues and topics germane to International Relations Enloe extends to interracial liaisons and romances between African American GIs and British women; the sexual proclivities of U.S. soldiers; and observations that "Women can seem as much a threat as a comfort to the modern warrior. A women is to be destroyed just as the enemy is to be destroyed"; or that some soldiers are "far more ambivalent about women as a direct result of their militarized sexuality."[119]

While interesting, one wonders if the disciplinary parameters of International Relations are now so porous as to be meaningless. If, as Martin Griffiths and Terry O'Callaghan suggest, "Anyone can 'join' IR, regardless of their formal training," is there any longer an intrinsic meaning or purpose to what we do other than engage in academic musings for their own sake?[120] Does this mean, for example, that no formal training or grounding in world politics will suffice as preparation for studying them, that there is no core to our subject, no central concerns or recurring themes that warrant at least rudimentary attention if one is to have an elementary grasp of things international? The obliteration of intellectual boundaries, the suggestion that there is "no valid distinction between the international and domestic spheres,"[121] and that all issues are germane to International Relations supposes that we can not only "forget IR theory," as Roland Bleiker urges, but read, write, and research anything of nominal interest to us and call this international politics. Birigit Weiss's vision of container art exhibitions or Cynthia Enloe's reflections on the posthuman body—the cyborg—threatens not just to expand the vistas of our discipline but, in doing so, make us little more than a compendium of the visual arts, science fiction, identities, personal stories, and research whims whose intellectual agendas are so disparate as to be meaningless. Indeed, precisely how this makes for better knowledge and a better understanding of global politics or how such agendas or concerns are related to global events and processes, we are never told. The only objective evident in the new identity politics seems to be the "transgression of boundaries," where everything no matter how disparate is assumed to be related to international politics and where the purview of our disciplinary lenses are counseled to have no focus but be encompassing of all things social, political, and economic.

Feminist (Re)Visions of the Facts

Apart from the problematic nature of identity discourse as a theoretical avenue germane to International Relations, there is much else in postmodern feminist writings that are also questionable. Adam Jones, for example, is concerned about the exclusivity with which women are made the ontological essence of gendered analyses, creating skewed commentaries that, rather than frame the important question of gender in more inclusive ways, tends to imprison it amid a radical matriarchal discourse.[122] Unfortunately, this all too often leads to narratives and modes of analysis whose treatment of the facts in international relations is, at best, suspect. One of the recurrent themes in feminist analyses of international politics, for example, is that women everywhere suffer more violence, intimidation, torture, mutilation, and abuse than do men who otherwise perpetrate these crimes. When Ann Tickner attempts to draw attention to the "particular vulnerabilities of women within states," for instance, "the phrase 'particular vulnerabilities' suggests not just an analytically separable category, but a disproportionate degree of vulnerability."[123] Yet, if we look at the facts the contrary is true:

men direct the overwhelming majority of their violence toward other men. United States Department of Justice (USDJ) statistics for 1995 and 1996, for example, show that, "except for rape/sexual assault, every violent crime victimization rate for males was higher than for females."[124] Moreover, if the incidence of male-to-male prison rape is included in rape/sexual assault figures, then USDJ rape/sexual assault statistics for 1990 show that 130,000 women were the victims of rape, while male-to-male prison rape claimed 290,000 victims.[125] In terms of homicide victimizations, USDJ figures show that of the 21,937 homicides in 1994, females accounted for 20.4% or 4,489 of these, while males constituted 17,448 or 79.5% of homicide victims.[126] Inner city black male youths, in particular, have fatality rates approaching those for front-line soldiers during the Vietnam War and are significantly higher than those experienced by black and white female youths combined. As the statistician for the USDJ notes of national crime figures for 1996, in terms of victimization, "the young, blacks, and males were most vulnerable to violent crime." Similarly, British Home Office figures for 1992, show that young men "are more than twice as likely than are women to be killed by strangers" through acts of random street violence. It is young men, notes Lorraine Radford, "who are most at risk from 'stranger-danger,'" not women.[127]

Yet, according to V. Spike Peterson, "male violence constitutes a 'global war against women,'" perpetrated with state complicity because of patriarchal relations that invariably see women suffer far more than men.[128] In Peterson's estimation, women suffer a heavier burden than do men, suffer more emotional stress and bear the burden of patriarchal state expenditures that benefit men at the expense of women. "Systematic violence," things like "sexual harassment, battery, rape, and torture," Peterson and Runyan argue, "is the persistent price that women pay for the maintenance of large militaries."[129] The implication, of course, is that men pay no price and enjoy freedom from violence when, in fact, we know that hazing rituals, physical and verbal abuse, torture, and mental torment are daily occurrences throughout the armies of the world and these staffed almost exclusively by men. Human rights too suggest Peterson and Runyan, are compromised by militarization. "Amnesty International vividly documents examples of military and police forces around the world terrorizing, imprisoning, and even torturing women who seek information about family members who have 'disappeared' at the hands of government-sponsored death squads." What Peterson and Runyan forget to add, however, is that by Amnesty International's own estimation, the overwhelming number of political prisoners in the world who suffer cruel and inhumane treatment happen to be men;

that those who "disappeared" under Argentina's military junta and Nicaragua's and El Salvador's U.S.-sponsored death squads in the 1980s were disproportionately male; and that torture of political prisoners by sheer weight of numbers therefore concerns, disproportionately, the torture of male political prisoners.[130]

Even the traditional concerns of International Relations, war and conflict studies, are not spared from the biased framing of the gender variable. Cynthia Enloe, for instance, tells of the plight of women during the Bosnian war and how Bosnian, Serbian, and Croatian men used rape as an instrument of terror. By implication, however, we are left to assume that men in the Bosnian conflict endured no terror, brutality, or deprivations, but were simply the perpetrators of atrocities.[131] Similarly, in discussing the Gulf War, Enloe is highly exclusive in dealing with gender, adequately narrating the plight of female migrant workers in Kuwait who suffered atrocities like rape and torture at the hands of Iraqi troops, but neglecting the "wider Iraqi process of detention, torture, execution, and forced removal . . . of tens of thousands of Kuwaitis" that, "judging from the human-rights and media reports, [were] virtually all male."[132]

Narratives of this type reveal how exclusive has been the framing of the "gender variable" in International Relations, where men are characterized as a hegemonic gender-class whose interests, concerns, actions, and writings are opposed to the interests and well-being of women.[133] As Sylvester writes, "states and their regimes connect with people called women only to ensure . . . that the benefits of regime participation will flow from 'women' to 'men' and *not ever* the other way round."[134] With such a mindset, facts become superfluous to the argument(s), leading to a fallacy of composition where assertive prose is itself offered as evidence of the disproportionate level of burden or victimization that women suffer. Thus, for example, Jones is plainly bemused at Ann Tickner's assertion that women have been forced to enter "the military primarily in the lower ranks." But, asks Jones, "how *else* does one enter the military, except at the lower levels?"[135] Likewise, Peterson and Runyan assert that "the plight of both Third World and Western women has been exacerbated by the debt crisis."[136] Third World and Western men, apparently, were untouched by this same debt crisis. And when commenting on the migration south of the border of "the jobs of many working-class women in the United States," Peterson and Runyan announce with horror how, between "1979 and 1983, 35% of the workers who lost jobs because of plant closings in the United States were women." What they fail to point out, of course, is that this means that fully 65 percent of those who lost their jobs because of these same plant closings were men.[137] Moreover, if we look at the available evidence for issues like murder, suicide, homelessness, life expectancy, and mortality rates, we find that rather than a hegemonic gender-class, statistically men kill each other at a far greater rate than they do women, commit suicide at a rate almost three times that of women, constitute about 80 percent of the homeless in the United States, throughout virtually every community in the world live shorter lives than do women, and in the developed world suffer a mortality rate due to disease twice that for women.[138]

Crude characterizations of a hegemonic gender class thus display an anomalous capacity to ignore completely those facts that do not accord with ideological belief. And postmodern feminists have been most adroit at this, substituting the evidentiary requirements of systematic observation and reasoned argument for identity discourses that rely on "perceptions" and "feelings." In a recent survey conducted for the International Studies Association (ISA) by the Committee for Study on the Status of Women in International Relations, for example, Marie Henehan and Meredith Reid Sarkees frame their survey in such a way as to measure the subjective perceptions of respondents. "The respondents were asked whether they had perceived gender bias in the course of their career."[139] In an alternate survey conducted for the same ISA committee, Christine Sylvester notes that "many respondents report feeling isolated within their departments and from major networks in the field."[140] Aside from the obvious fact that perceptions of bias or feelings of isolation are not exclusive to women, questions of the methodological appropriateness of anecdotal evidence need also to be explored. That the reality of any situation can be gauged from personal narratives based exclusively upon perception makes for bad social science and leads, ultimately, to destructive debates that hurl about subjective accusations.[141] Witness, for example, the claims of matriarchal superiority when standpoint feminists insist that "women have a distinctive, superior view of the world, distinctive because shaped by those features of their experiences that distinguish them from men, superior on the . . . basis that the oppressed are capable of a higher form of awareness than the oppressor."[142] This is simply inverted patriarchy, premised on little more than fanciful whims about the innate characteristics of women vis-à-vis men. It replicates the privileging of one gender over another and discharges all hope of equality between genders on the basis of merit alone. Moreover, it invokes a crude and unsubstantiated argument derived through intuition, that women feel more deeply, are better knowers, and thus have better understandings of international politics. But how is this different from patriarchal-chauvinist claims that men are more rational, logical, strategic and women more emotional, less reasoned, and captive to their biological cycles? Both such arguments are equally as preposterous and need to be abandoned, not invoked as a means forward for understanding international relations. More obviously, such silly methods tend toward a perverse hierarchical index of who suffers the most, who bears the most burden, feels the most hurt. When Jacqui True notes that "states demand sacrifices of gendered citizens: mothers, for example, who are forced to devote "their lives to socializing these dutiful [male] citizens for the sovereign state as masculine deity," lest we should forget that male citizens have typically been the cannon fodder who have sacrificed their lives and limbs for the state.[143] If we wish to construct hierarchies of pain and suffering, none can be higher than the ultimate sacrifice, a sacrifice made throughout history overwhelmingly by male combatants.

The point of all of this, however, should not be to countenance against one type of suffering and in favor of others. Rather, the point is to take issue with those who view suffering, or at least disproportionate suffering, the preserve of one gender, women, and inflicted by another gender, men. More importantly, the point for International Relations must be to affirm as illegitimate all suffering and work actively to develop ways of understanding and prescriptions that might help in its eradication. The "gender variable" is not inappropriate in this regard, but only when used in inclusive ways.

Toward Some Conclusions: Postmodern Feminisms, Gender Bias, and International Relations

"One variable," notes Tom Kando, "does not make a theory." Gender, while important, on its own is only one element among many in international politics. Its contribution to International Relations might thus be assessed as only partial: part of a multitude of perspectives that attempt to contribute to our understanding of domination, exploitation, and inequality in the context of global politics.[144] Yet, this is not the way postmodern feminists position themselves in the discipline, admonishing all who stand opposed to making the "gender variable" the principal ontological vantage point from which to explain and understand international politics. Among radical feminists there is a deep-seated suspicion of International Relations, especially toward the discipline's traditional subjects of inquiry and modes of analysis. Not that this is unique to International Relations. The social sciences and humanities generally, and Western culture and Enlightenment thought in particular, are now viewed ominously. As Patricia Lança observes, for radical feminists the modernist-rational intellectual edifice is now "seen as a shelter from which malign entities (embodied in the bourgeoisie) especially since the Enlightenment, have sought to exercise power," while "the house of western culture" is depicted not as a "place of welcome where all mankind may find a place but of exclusion." Contributions to this edifice in whatever form are thus rendered complicitous in the "project of oppression," and the spread of Western culture as coterminous with imperialist exploitation and cultural genocide. Likewise, "meaning attributed to language by ordinary mortals" becomes a delusion, and true meaning the preserve of those who disassemble language itself. "Nothing is as it seems and the realists who believe otherwise are victims of logocentrism, or more radically, phallologocentrism where those who exercise control over the power system are essentially males who impose 'compulsory heterosexuality' on the unwilling masses of man and womankind."[145]

While Lança's comments are harsh, they probably explain the spate of nefarious and ideologically opinionated -isms that masquerade as theoretical formulations but which incite revolt, disturbance, and repudiation in favor of relativism and tribalism.[146] The irony in all of this, of course, is that such repudiationist formulations display a near panegyric celebration of the writings of white European men, Foucault, Derrida, and Nietzsche, for example, who never once wrote about the plight of women but are now lionized as the emissaries of their emancipation. This makes "male deconstructionists and their female epigones . . . the product of the narrowest Eurocentrism," while uniquely adept at rejecting all that is Western, European, modernist, rational, and scientific.[147] Indeed, the outright rejection of Enlightenment and Western values seems all the more peculiar considering how instrumental they have been in extending to women rights and freedoms that, elsewhere in the world, are only dreamt about. As Patricia Lança again observes, "If it were not tragic it would be hilarious that western female intellectuals, a privileged class indeed by global or even purely American standards, should demonize white, European, upperclass males and blame the power structures of western society for women's ills. For where has women's emancipation progressed further than in these very societies and, what is more, with the help, support and open initiative of many such males?"[148]

Similar sentiments might be extrapolated into International Relations where the discipline, its practitioners, and theories are castigated by postmodern and radical feminists for crimes of elitism, sexism, racism, and for marginalizing not just women but their ideas, perspectives, and approaches. The ISA Committee for the Study of the Status of Women in International Relations, for example, complained that "research by women is poorly integrated into the corpus of scholarship in this field" and that, overall, there is an "underrepresentation of women in an (sic) ISA journals."[149] Again, however, the facts would seem to make anomalous these accusations. As William Thompson and Brian Pollins, the editors of the ISA's *International Studies Quarterly* (*ISQ*), noted in responding to these allegations, while "women submitted fewer papers than one might expect," the probability of success was nonetheless what one would expect given the submission numbers.[150] In all, they added, the available data indicate "that the problem may lie more with what is submitted, where it is submitted, and how well it is crafted than it does with alleged bias on the part of specific journals."[151]

Cries of victimization and professional marginalization nonetheless persist, albeit issued from rather prestigious corners of the academy. Christine Sylvester, for example, issues hers via Cambridge University Press and the distinguished series, *Cambridge Studies in International Relations*; Cynthia Enloe via the University of California Press, Berkeley; and V. Spike Peterson via Westview Press.[152] Marginalization of this nature, not unnaturally, is the career goal of most junior faculty! Nor is there evidence of systemic discrimination in the academy in terms of hiring practices. As most junior faculty will be only to familiar with, affirmative action policies and an acute awareness of equity issues, regales throughout advertisements for faculty vacancies: the "University is an Equal Opportunity/Affirmative action employer; applications from women and minority candidates are specifically invited."[153] A commitment to diversity, an enhanced sensitivity to correcting historical disciplinary gender disparities, and an awareness of sexism have all made for a more even playing field in terms of academic recruitment practices. Sheilah Mann of the American Political Science Association (APSA), for example, reports that for graduating candidates in 1995–1996, the "placement success rates differ overall by gender and ethnicity," and that "more of the women graduates seeking jobs were successful (70%) than the men (62%)." Mann further notes that "among U.S. citizens, a higher percentage of each group of minority doctoral students got jobs than did all men and, to a lesser degree of difference, all women. Placement success rates were 77% for Latin Americans, 74% for Latinos, and 83% for Asian Americans."[154] Systemic discrimination, racism, bigotry, and gender bias are thus far from endemic, or even evident, across all the subfields of political science. This probably explains why allegations of such bias are typically only asserted and never substantiated with reference to fact or professional actualities.

But putting aside the ambit claims of postmodern feminists, the more important question for International Relations concerns the relevance of the strategies and theoretical approaches they recommend for the discipline. What might International Relations look like, do, research, and produce under the theoretical formula suggested by postmodern feminists? Are we to assume that observations derived through the experiences of Ruby the elephant a sufficient ontological starting point for the research agendas of the discipline? Will accusatory gender fingerpointing help in eradicating injustice, global poverty, and war? How do highbrow postmodern discourses or feminist ontologies help the truly needy, destitute, and impoverished? Can such insights be operationalized, used as tools to inform public policy, or utilized as formulae to help negotiate peaceful resolutions to ethnic conflict or territorial wars? Can we settle for a series of ongoing questions concerning "what it means to know, who may know, where knowers are located, and what the difference among them mean for the knowledges that result?"[155] Can the historiography of the Cold War really be understood by reference to the T-shirts worn by U.S. servicemen and the sex industry in the Philippines?[156] Should we prioritize the study of marriage and venereal disease, as Cynthia Enloe suggests, as equal to that of "studying military weaponry?"[157] Is theoretical endeavor really an attribute of journal entries from the travels of a U.S. academic living on a kibbutz in Israel, or the recollections of those who gather at ISA meetings and exchange narratives?[158] Does theoretical endeavor really extend to "how to make cups of tea, about washing clothes, about using the word processor, about driving a car, about collecting water, about joking," as Marysia Zalewski contends?[159]

Not all theory, of course, must conform to the strictures of utilitarian principles, able to be operationalized and used in an instrumental way to inform public and foreign policy. But some of it probably should, save the relevance of what we do might be lost on those at the coal face of international politics if not also many of its professional practitioners and academicians. Stimulating our theoretical imaginations, pushing the envelope, and exploring discursively the epistemological grounding of our collective knowledge is all good and well. But to suppose that this is all we should do, or even that it is the most important of our activities, would seem to marginalize the continuing dilemmas of international politics and those whose lives are made perilous because of them. Doubtless, feminist perspectives have made valuable contributions and enhanced our understanding of international politics, but such perspectives have yet to make a convincing case for the intellectual revolution and refocused research agendas they so earnestly propose.

Chapter Seven

In Defense of Theory
Reaffirming Reason, Rearticulating Relevance

> Of course, I do not wish to imply anything so absurd as that this study is value free. A study of this kind that did not derive from moral and political premises of some kind would be impossible, and, if it were possible, it would be sterile. What is important in an academic inquiry into politics is not to exclude value-laden premises, but to subject these premises to investigation and criticism . . .
>
> Hedley Bull

> Sometimes it seems as if international relations scholars have nothing better to do with their time than to argue about the proper way to study their subject.
>
> James N. Rosenau

With the outgrowth of reflectivist perspectives, poststructural theory, postmodern feminisms, and deconstructive agendas, theorists in International Relations could be forgiven for thinking that theoretical endeavor now constitutes a series of battles: "Battles over sovereignty within knowledge, and battles of different knowledges within the discourse on sovereignty."[1] Indeed, as an instrument of politics by other means, war seems to have found a home in the vocabulary of those who concern themselves with theory, where the penchant for conflict, animosity, and factionalism has made for different sovereign communities, each with different loyalties. To paraphrase Ashley, these are heroic battles fought in zealous defense of a sovereign authority, and with it the right to issue pronouncements about the world: about what is true and false, just and unjust, right and wrong. It is, in short, a battle for the right to adjudicate between legitimate and illegitimate knowledge, between what the research programs of International Relations should be as opposed to what in practice they are. As Steve Smith notes, the "stakes are high in such a debate," not because there is much to conquer but because to the victor goes the hearts and minds of the academy, the right to define the direction of scholarship and with it, the parameters, function, and purpose for which theory is pursued in the discipline.[2] Knowledge is power, postmodernists rightly insist, and the right to control and sanction it is a prize eagerly pursued.

Despite this, however, conversations on the current state of theory in International Relations tend invariably toward closure. As Ashley noted recently, there is an impasse in International Relations today, not in the sense that new theory is not being developed but in the sense that conversations between contending theoretical perspectives is not occurring.[3] On "the conversational battlefield of international relations," he writes, the attitude, style and orientation of participants is deafness, or what Colin Wight likens to apartheid for paradigms.[4] Discourse tends to be intraparadigmatic, not engagement with alternative epistemologies or opposed theoretical formulations. In fact, Kalevi Holsti might well have been proved correct. The dividing discipline has separated and we now have not one but two disciplines: an orthodox or traditional discipline operative within the modernist tradition, counterpoised against a hypercritical or perspectivist discipline operating within postmodern vistas.[5] The quest to subvert International Relations might thus be understood in this context: a battle between traditionalists and postmodernists, the latter adamant perhaps not of their own "sovereign authority," but certain that it no longer resides in modernist, scientific, realist theory. And realism, as Ashley so astutely notes, while perennially challenged is perennially reaffirmed, none less so than among the warring parties who theorize international politics: this is intellectual realpolitik.[6] In the late 1990s, theoretical debate is thus largely a phenomenon of discrete purviews, where neither discipline can get the other to adopt its ways, methods, or understandings and where neither shares a common purpose or language, let alone agreement about the facts and their interpretation. Studying international relations thus presents the student with abundant choices, not least of them which discipline to join and which calling to follow.

As Richard Rorty reminds us, however, "interesting philosophy is rarely an examination of the pros and cons of a thesis," but incredulous adulation for one perspective over another irrespective of the facts.[7] In International Relations too, theoretical creeds have themselves become icons for adulation, proxy political statements of faith, ethics, and belief about how the world should be viewed, how global justice is best achieved, what voices and histories should be analyzed, and on what configuration and structure future worlds should be built. Theory has always been part fervent desire, reflecting the biases and hopes of those who conceive it. But to suppose this the exclusive task of theoretical endeavor in International Relations returns us to the problem of epistemological duality so forcefully expressed by E. H. Carr and, more importantly, of the intrinsic dangers this enterprise harbors: "The inclination to ignore what was and what is in contemplation of what should be, and the inclination to deduce what should be from what was and what is."[8] "No Science," noted Carr, "deserves the name until it has acquired sufficient humility not to consider itself omnipotent, and to distinguish the analysis of what is from aspiration about what should be." Postmodernists perhaps forget this, positioning themselves in a way that ignores the actualities of global politics in favor of political advocacy and projects committed more to neoidealist sentiments about images of future societies than current world orders. On one level, the epistemological duality of theoretical debate in International Relations thus remains unchanged, reflecting the visceral division of our "dividing discipline" where the rubric of postmodern theory now accounts for its idealist other half. All, perhaps, is as it should be, the new neoidealists engaged in imaginative epistemological remappings in the hope of securing new worlds, while the more realist-inclined ontologists focus upon the structures, actors and processes of current orders and their consequences.

Victim to this latest round of idyllic sentiment, however, are the institutions of language and theory, appropriated for purely political ends and used by postmodernists as a podium to condemn an entrenched vocabulary deemed to have become a nuisance, while heralding "a half-formed new vocabulary which vaguely promises great things."[9] Postmodern theorists, for example, condemn modernist/positivist/realist theory for its constitutive role in the atrocities of the twentieth century, while promising not just new understandings but an emancipatory praxis culminating in changed realities and better worlds. Condemnation of the past and of those theories and theorists associated with it has thus conspired for a spate of cathartic expurgations: moral purges of the mind and discipline where the Third Great Debate has become both signifier of epochal change as we stand on the precipice of a new millennium and end of millennium stock-taking amid recriminations for the century we leave behind. And to those who profess expurgation from the past, a self-assured moral propriety has ensconced their (post)enlightened ways of thinking and doing international politics: an optimistic moral high ground untainted by the past and convinced that not again will its political blemishes be repeated under the new thinking. At the end of the millennium, one is either on the side of new perspectives and theory in pursuit of better worlds or on the side of reactionary conservatism complicitous in the maintenance of institutions which repress, exclude, and affront. Postmodern theory might thus be all the rage for reasons as laudable as they are timeless: hope for a better future. This probably explains its attractiveness among the young, idealist, historically aggrieved, and minority voices now vocal throughout the academy. Indeed, the passion and conviction with which these new approaches are held also explain the brawl over theory. Marysia Zalewski, for example, bemoans the fact that contemporary theoretical debates have the effect of bringing out the worst in people, conducted so often in "a spirit of 'jousting' verging on the hostile," where accusations and insults are hurled about so as to make "the sport of intellectual jousting and parodies of bar room brawling" appear functionally inevitable in the discipline.[10] Her point, however, is made amid recriminations that International Relations is "a paradigmatically masculinist discipline" whose theory "reifies and reflects the interests of the already powerful" and whose boundaries need to be disturbed.[11] Offense is in the eye of the beholder, and in International Relations almost everyone is offended. As Holsti warns, we are traveling down a road toward uncivil war, where the scenery is likely not very pretty and where scholarly discourse threatens to be nasty and brutish.[12]

Recriminations and Dejection: Ashley's Lament

If the pertinacity of participants in this ongoing theoretical "brawl" has foreclosed the possibility of theoretical commensurability, there is little reason to suppose that the return of Richard Ashley's voice to this conversational battlefield will change matters. Indeed, the very rationale for a conversation between these disciplines Ashley now sees as problematic:[13] "What possible reason is there to think that one more paltry recitation of these arguments on my part, just here, would somehow induce a readiness to hear among those who have repeatedly shown themselves so proficient at doing what it takes not to hear, not to take these strains seriously, not to follow their implications through?"[14]

Ashley's lament is clearly evident: indignity at not being listened to, bewilderment that many whom he so clearly understands to be wrong continue with their research projects. "Despite their rigour and despite their repetition," Ashley is piqued that discipline-wide capitulation to poststructural and postmodern perspectives has not ensued.[15] The accusations thus continue, the discipline again berated for its deafness and theorists for their feeblemindedness. Yet, while there is little new in Ashley's latest rendition of *The Achievements of Post-Structuralism*, there is a sense in which his most recent offering is revelatory, not of his own position so much as his near condemnation of those who practice a politics of subversion and who have attempted to assume the mantle of vanguard left in the wake of Ashley's silence.[16] It is as much to those who have attempted to continue his project that his most recent writings speak.

Much like his previous efforts, Ashley begins his latest treatise by rehearsing a "critical posture of estrangement" to demonstrate how these critical activities expose the manufacture of sovereign meaning, ascribe names and labels, and make real a socially constructed interpretation of reality by "fixing it" in time in order to present it as a transhistorical truth.[17] Critical strategies, by comparison, seek to show "that however inescapable may be one's recurrence to this model whenever one purports to offer a unique, monological representation of life making and its possibilities, one cannot assume . . . that the reality of human struggles to make life go on will finally and necessarily give proof to any rendition of this model, [or] any series of such renditions." After all is said and done, there is for Ashley "only the reality of actions working upon actions across all those varied localities where people struggle amidst difficulties, dangers and ambiguities to somehow make life go on."[18] Knowing and knowledge can only ever be transient, specific, local, and often indeterminate. To stand "heroically" and speak with authority as if from a sovereign terrain and issue forth foundational proclamations, definitive interpretations, and absolute knowledge displays only a kind of colonial mind, a "will to territorialise, to make some sort of sovereign territorialisation of life work[,] . . . a disposition somehow to discipline and constitute a bounded place" in order that we may lay claim to own and represent it.[19] Each of us, it seems, is yet again involved in a conspiracy of sorts, where, as theorists of international relations, we portend to "an idea of inhabiting a securely bounded territory of truth and transparent meaning beyond doubt, a place given as if by some author beyond time, a place where it is possible to appeal to the world in order to decide what things mean and to justify one's self and one's conduct beyond doubt."[20] Deluded by our own fictions and things not real but nonetheless labeled facts, we are also malicious, monsters in charge of "a place where the unruly can be reliably named and tamed and the person of unquestioning faith in the word can be secure."[21] We are, in short, unthinking, self-serving, and imperious automatons who dare to presume to know. This is Ashley's rendition of international relations theory today: impoverished, self-deluded, pernicious, and, apparently, morally bankrupt.

Again, however, this latest rendition begs the same questions as before: where does Ashley stand to make such dismissive and absolute pronouncements? What sovereign terrain does he inhabit that allows for such wisdom and disparagement? But more importantly, what does this say to those who stand opposed to International Relations and who practice subversive deconstruction? What does it say to his would-be followers? How can they justify their own sovereign territories from which they fight their battles, form their knowledges and truths, and which allow them to offer different, and from their perspective better, versions of history, meaning, understanding, and insight into international politics? In Ashley's panoply all are incriminated as purveyors of "imposed meaning," none can escape except perhaps the relativists and nihilists.[22] Standing upon the precipice of relativistic nihilism, Ashley is forced to condemn all who would suppose to know, all who appeal to foundationalist knowledge, and all who portend to a politics of subversion and an end to International Relations. Stranded in a hermeneutic circle, Ashley is entrapped by his own logic and unable to justify the merits of a "posture of estrangement" or a strategy of subversion without recourse to those epistemological and ontological standards for which he condemns others. Postmodern discourse thus snares would-be subversives in the same crimes they allege of others, rendering problematic the subversive-deconstructive project that so many have attempted to follow. Ashley is acutely aware of this and his withdrawal from ongoing conversations and poststructural renditions is perhaps a sign of his deep resignation. Never before have would-be followers been so assaulted by their mentor's dejection. In the end, save for repeating this oft-told parable that one cannot stand on secure epistemological footing, that such is only an illusion, Ashley has little else to say and little more to contribute. He thus proves to be no vanguard for postmodern feminists, proponents of identity politics, or postmodern protagonists of the discipline. Instead, his latest contribution stands as an irritant that makes insecure both his own position and those of other self proclaimed dissidents. More than any critique to have emanated from the discipline, it has been Ashley who has managed to subvert the subversives or at least estrange them from his own "critical posture of estrangement."

Convergent Diversity

Despite being reproached by their mentor's insights, however, the project(s) of subversive postmodernists continue to multiply. Identity politics, feminist postmodernism, or any number of alternative poststructural and postmodern approaches and issues all vie for space in their haste to "dismantle" and "undo" International Relations. To most observers, International Relations appears to be populated by a multiplicity of different posts and -isms, all celebrating perspectivism and vicissitude: all different in their desires, methodological aims, and political programs. This is not an unreasonable assumption upon first observation. After all, as I endeavored to demonstrate in chapter 3, there are many varieties or thematic motifs evident in the literatures of postmodern writings. Specifically, I identified three such motifs: technological or productionist postmodernism, critical or epistemological postmodernism, and what I termed subversive-deconstructive postmodernism. While these categories are by no means discrete, they illustrate how divergent are postmodern writings that address issues as disparate as textual deconstruction, art, aesthetics, culture, architecture, philosophy, political-economy, linguistics, and technological innovation among others. Defining postmodernism, as chapter 3 also demonstrated, is therefore problematic if only because postmodern writings are no more united in aim, objective, or focus than are the doctrines of conservatism, liberalism, leninism, or socialism that postmodernists conflate under the modernist rubric.

It must seem peculiar to those in International Relations, then, that for the most part we have only been treated to one of these thematic motifs, subversive-deconstructive postmodernism. The very diversity that otherwise defines postmodern scholarship elsewhere in the social sciences is noticeably absent in International Relations. Having to admit to what Chris Brown terms the radical unpredictability and diversity of postmodern writings, while certainly true of such authors as Michel Foucault, Jacques Derrida, Fredric Jameson, Charles Jencks, Jean Baudrillard, or Edward Soja, for example, it is far from accurate of their would-be emissaries in International Relations.[23] Inside our discipline the thematic singularity of postmodernists to challenge, invert, disturb, and dismantle orthodox theory and the epistemological constructs upon which it is built has become their sine qua non, rehearsed so often as to be trite and disingenuous. When transposed and imported into International Relations and distilled through the conduit of Ashley's penmanship, for example, all of us are only too well aware of how predictable postmodern ruminations have become. Richard Ashley, Robert Walker, David Campbell, Michael Shapiro, James Der Derian, Jim George, Christine Sylvester, Marysia Zalewski, or V. Spike Peterson, to name a few, all write in a similar tongue, united in their "different" projects against International Relations. Indeed, what strikes the reader about these authorial renditions are not their differences but their similarities, a singular unity or common project, a radical predictability which, with habitual monotony, rehearses time and again the deconstructive ethic endemic to dissidence. This, though, is a strange conundrum: unity where none should exist, similarity in the face of difference, purpose amid professed antifoundationalism and perspectivism, and all of this in a postmodern world marked, supposedly, by randomness and disjuncture. The postmodern montage that celebrates diversity, deviation, and irregularity have all been conflated, it seems, into a kind of conformist straightjacket in order that postmodernists can stand united against a discipline itself accused of rampant conformity and monotonal essentialism. And while, of course, there are subtle differences, contests for the right to claim a higher degree of victimhood, or minor disputes over esoteric nuances that inevitably infect each writer, postmodernists in International Relations display a cohesiveness realists would surely envy.

How then in International Relations are we to account for the similarity of those who profess difference? Why has International Relations evolved only one dominant postmodern motif to the detriment, if not invisibility, of other motifs? And why are postmodernists in International Relations singularly preoccupied with deconstruction as opposed to technological postmodernism or, say, issues of postfordism and structural changes in the global political-economy and geostrategic transformations?

By their very nature, questions of this type are extremely difficult to answer and I do not pretend to be able to offer a definitive reply. Instead, let me offer a few observations which might account for this state of affairs. There are two interrelated explanations that together give some insight as to why subversive-deconstructive postmodern theory has tended to dominate postmodern discourse in the discipline. The first stems from the unparalleled dominance positivism has enjoyed in International Relations until very recently. This alone probably explains the attraction subversive-deconstructive postmodernism holds for those who wish an end to positivism and that variety of theory, scholarship, and research program which has been routine in International Relations—particularly in North America. Deconstruction has proved an extremely serviceable tool for problematizing conventional research methods informed by positivist frameworks of inquiry and the language of science. Such research methodologies have been dethroned from the heights they once enjoyed in the discipline and shown to be no more or less valuable than other methodological approaches. As a tool for attacking what was once the inner sanctum of the scientific method, positivism, subversive-deconstructive postmodern theory has thus been the weapon of choice, enabling those opposed to this approach to go to the very heart of positivism's ontological and epistemological foundations and challenge them systematically through suggesting their complicity in a less than scientific project. If only for the damage subversive-deconstructive postmodernism promises to inflict upon positivist methodological approaches, it has thus tended to hold an innate attractiveness for those whose mission in life has been the destruction of politics as science. Similarly, the relative dominance of realist theory in International Relations and, in the 1980s and 1990s, the dominance of structural realist and neoinstitutionalist approaches, respectively, also made subversive postmodernism an attractive tool, particularly its ability to critique the structuralist and economistic logic indicative of structural realism and its positivist epistemology.[24] Subversive-deconstructive postmodernism has therefore provided detractors of realist and positivist approaches alike with a theoretical tool that not merely quibbles with peripheral elements of realist/positivist theory, but challenges the entire substructural basis on which such theory is founded.

The second explanation is more obvious but no less important and concerns the way in which postmodern theory was introduced into International Relations. For reasons that have traditionally isolated International Relations from the broader philosophical debates in the social sciences, namely the discipline's perceived status as a distinctive atheoretical domain, practitioners and theorists alike have largely conducted their research programs, if not unaware of the new philosophical/theoretical trends sweeping the academy, then certainly unconcerned about them. Before Ashley's writings, for example, postmodern theory was virtually unknown in the discipline. Consequently, those competent to engage with postmodern discourse and assess it critically were few. This provided postmodernists, or at least those masquerading as proponents of postmodernism, with a relatively benign intellectual sphere in which to propagate their views free of critical obstacles. And this, arguably, was precisely what happened: a series of intellectual importations of continental philosophy that, without critical appraisal or appropriate reflection, were allowed to colonize and spread. Ashley, for example, was the first to explore the writings of Michel Foucault and Jean Baudrillard among others, and import into International Relations, albeit with substantial and perhaps even gratuitous modifications, the motifs of these postmodern thinkers.[25] As I attempted to demonstrate in chapters 4 and 5, Ashley was the conduit through which those of us in International Relations came to know of postmodern theory. This probably explains its subsequent course of development in the discipline. First, those who were attracted to this variety of political program merely replicated it, rehearsing the ethic of deconstruction unproblematically and widening its scope to challenge yet more theories and destabilize the discipline still further—witness, for example, the unproblematic acceptance of the subversive-deconstructive agenda extended to the issue of gender by postmodern feminists. In other words, deconstruction itself became an unreflective "research project" whose aim was to undermine the disciplinary mainstays of positivism and realism. The project of incorporating the "other," whether in terms of gender, issues of race, culture or identity, merely went hand in hand with this project becoming a means of securing intellectual space and legitimacy for issues not traditionally the purview of International Relations. It was, perhaps, a simple confluence of interests and political agendas, helped by the theoretical deracination typical of postmodern -isms where the ethos of difference and discursiveness provided the intellectual wherewithal for importing any series of hitherto unstudied topics and political agendas. Second, amid this unreflective onslaught most orthodox practitioners found themselves ill equipped to meet this challenge, often unaware or simply perplexed by the epistemological motifs of this subversive-deconstructive program. Ashley's politically charged rendering of postmodern theory was therefore beyond critical appraisal, affording him an intellectual freedom unconstrained by questions about the authenticity of his interpretation of postmodern thinkers and his representation of the imperative for deconstruction. Nor should we underestimate the role political correctness played, and continues to play, in constraining scholars from critical analyses of postmodern perspectives. Few have been game to engage critically those who profess "victimization" or who have brought to the discipline "silenced" perspectives for fear of epithets alleging racism, bigotry, or sexism. In the reified atmosphere of political correctness, moral property has been the preserve of those seen to champion the oppressed and historically marginalized. To resist the tide of postmodern theory has thus been to perpetuate discrimination. Insulated in such a manner, subversive postmodernists have presented themselves not only as the champion of progressivist politics, but their program as the legitimate and authoritative expression of postmodern theory. Absent any critical inquiry of the underlying motifs or authenticity of this approach, the discipline thus fell victim to a false dichotomy: postmodern theory of the subversive/deconstructive variety as preached by Ashley, or modernist theory in its various positivist/rationalist manifestations. Subsequent adherents and like-minded "others" also fall victim to this false dichotomy, taking up the creed of subversion and deconstruction without reflection as to possible alternatives that might better serve their intellectual needs.

As I have attempted to demonstrate elsewhere in this study, however, it is not a question of whether postmodernism is or is not useful to the study of international relations, but of which particular versions are useful and which are not. Not all postmodern -isms were created equal: some are clearly more equal than others and thus better suited to the disciplinary concerns of International Relations. In this respect we have a choice, although this is not apparent in the writings of subversive postmodernists, who, if only because of their haste to colonize International Relations and propagate their political agendas, have tended to plead ignorant (and perhaps are) to the very real differences within postmodern thinking. Nowhere in Ashley's writings or those of postmodern feminists, for example, will one find even a suggestion that alternative motifs—motifs which render extremely problematic the salience of subversive-deconstruction—are available to those who wish them. Rather, there is an obvious inference in what is plainly a breach of Ashley's professed distaste for binary logic, that one is either for or against postmodernism and that one must take sides: a sort of divisive old-fashioned politics of left versus right. We need, then, look elsewhere for an understanding of postmodern theory in all its varieties and of their possible utility to the study of international relations. Ashley and subversive-deconstructive postmodernists have only distracted us from this task, co-opting postmodern theory in a project that has rendered impossible any meaningful debate, reflection, or theoretical progress.

Toward the Future: A Legacy for Postmodernism?

As a necessary prelude to thinking about and exploring the possible utilities of various forms of postmodern scholarship, this book has concentrated on debunking the fallacious debates and arguments offered by subversive-deconstructive postmodernists. Consequently, I have little explored those other varieties of postmodern scholarship identified in this study. So let me comment, albeit briefly, on future research directions that postmodern scholarship might pursue productively in the discipline. This is where the typology developed in chapter 3 proves useful by helping us disentangle and discriminate between different postmodernisms. It allows us to tease out the good from the bad, as it were, and make some preliminary observations about which type of postmodern theory might prove useful to International Relations, social scientific research, and the generation of theory knowledge from those which will not. There are, of course, limitations to such a typology dependent upon one's positional ontology vis-à-vis the question of modernity. From my perspective, I remain committed to modernist referents like rationality, progress, justice, emancipation, and indeed conceptions of good and bad. These, naturally, infer my particular disposition to the different types of postmodern theory identified in this study, as they will, obviously, to those who gravitate more to the antimodernist camp. My particular theoretical vista is thus colored by my commitment to the project of epistemology, a belief in some kind of minimal foundationalism, and my belief in the program of theory-knowledge as a means to truth and progress in the human condition. I am, in a word, a modernist, unconvinced by the proclamations of new ages, of the technobabble of tumultuous social/political change and new worlds, or of the merits of identity politics as a new means of political praxis and self-understanding. The typology developed in this study, is, then, above all else, a means for understanding the political as practiced by those who would subvert modernity in the name of new utopias. Applied in such a manner, the typologies of subversive, critical, and technological/productionist postmodernism allows us to draw a number of tentative conclusions about their relative merits.

First, the project of subversive-deconstructive postmodernism can be seen as contrary to the discipline of International Relations as a social science, designed not so much to generate knowledge as to disparage knowledge spawned through Enlightenment thinking and the precepts of rationality and science. At its most elemental, it is a project of disruption and an attack upon the "complacency" of knowledge generated in modernist quarters. Not that this is all bad. There is much good to come from a shakeup of the academy, from a reexamination of our ontological, epistemological, and axiological foundations and from the types of practices that ensue from certain modes of conceptualization and analysis. Pointing out silences and omissions from the dominant discourse is always fruitful and necessary, but, arguably, also accomplished under theories and paradigms and from critical quarters that are not necessarily postmodern and which do not seek to "undo" all knowledge simply on the basis of imperfection. Modernist discourse is not unreflective, can make autonomous corrections, engage in revisionist history, identify injustices, crimes of exclusion, and extend representation to groups that were otherwise not previously represented (think of liberalism or socialism for example!). This, after all, is why we understand modernity to be progressive and history a forward-moving narrative that is self-effusive. More importantly, given the self-defeating contradictions endemic to subversive-deconstructive postmodernism, especially its specious relativism, it requires no great mind to postulate that the use of modernist/rationalist/Enlightenment discourse will better make the case for a progressive politics of ever greater inclusion, representation, and justice for all than will sloganistic calls for us to "think otherwise." The simple and myopic assumption that social change can be engineered through linguistic policing of politically incorrect words, concepts and opinions, is surely one of the more politically lame (idealist) suggestions to come from armchair theorists in the last fifty years. By the same token, the suggestion that we engage in revisionism of the sort that would "undo" modernist knowledge so that we might start again free of silences, oppressions, and inequalities also smacks of an intelligentsia so idealist as to be unconnected to the world in which they live. The critical skills of subversive postmodernists, constrained perhaps by the success of the West, of Western capitalism, if not liberal democracy, as the legitimate form of representation, and having tried unsuccessfully through revolution and political uprising to dethrone it previously, have turned to the citadel of our communal identities and attacked not parliaments, nor forms of social-political-economic organization, but language, communication, and the basis of Enlightenment knowledge that otherwise enables us to live, work, and communicate as social beings. Clever though this is, it is not in the end compatible with the project of theory knowledge and takes us further away from an understanding of our world. Its greatest contribution is to celebrate the loss of certainty, where, argues John O'Neill, "men (sic) are no longer sure of their ruling knowledge and are unable to mobilize sufficient legitimation for the master-narratives of truth and justice." To suppose, however, that we should rejoice collectively at the prospects of a specious relativism and a multifarious perspectivism, and that absent any further constructive endeavor, the great questions and problems of our time will be answered or solved by this speaks of an intellectual poverty now famed perversely as the search for "thinking space."[26]

In the case of critical-epistemological postmodernism, the typology I developed helps elucidate its constitutive elements as an epistemological program in the tradition of Marxism or the critical social theory of the Frankfurt School. There is much to recommend this particular variety of postmodern theory, especially as a means of understanding the interstitial articulation of the economic, political and social, and of the systemic social relations this gives rise to in the context of historical change. It too has identified the nemesis of master narratives, of their tendency to exclusiveness and marginalization, but not in a way that rejects foundationalism or the emancipatory project of the Enlightenment. If anything, critical postmodernism is an attempt to refine this emancipatory project, extending its rationale beyond the legacy of its European origins and into the postcolonial era so as to encompass those who were either ignored by its Western origins or those who were the oppressed objects of its expansionist success. At base, it is the best of what is left of the left, socially progressivist and astutely aware of its role as critical theory. More importantly, it has proved the liferaft of Marxism, shedding Marxism of its teleological determinism, economism, essentialism, and crude structuralism in a way that makes it relevant and insightful to the contemporary workings of sociopolitical-economic relations. This is most evident, for example, in its elegant conceptualization of the heightened engagement between cultural and aesthetic sensibilities and their incorporation into commodity production—or what some might see as the articulation of a late-modern mode of production where image, style, culture, and aesthetics transform the consumption-production dialectic so that acts of consumption also become mediums of cultural/aesthetic production. This has important consequences for our understanding of the global economy, of how wealth generation has transformed itself from fordist/industrial production into a production matrix situated as much in the fashion (board) rooms of Milan, Giorgio Armani, Gianni Versace, Calvin Klein, Hollywood, or the computer-image manipulators of Microsoft, as in the industrial empires of Ford or General Motors. Again, ironically, it is probably those who are most opposed to capitalism, the critical postmodernists cum reborn Marxists, who are best equipped to explain its transformations, contradictions, the systemic properties of its ever-evolving modes of production, and the consequences of its social and political articulation. This makes critical postmodernism of continuing utility to the social sciences, if not for its technical insights, then certainly for its critical-analytical commentary on the condition of late capitalism and late modernity. International Relations has much to gain from this type of analysis, conjoining political-economy more fully into its traditional theoretical concerns with interstate relations that, historically, have tended to focus exclusively upon power.

Finally, the typology I identified as technological or productionist postmodern theory would seem to be of most pertinence to International Relations. This most closely approximates a traditional social scientific research agenda, providing a methodological guide for assessing critically systemic change and theorizing its objective effects upon our social-political institutions. Like critical postmodernism, technological postmodernism also reinvisions capitalism and its late-modern mode of articulation, situating this amid a radical indeterminacy as the logic of capital accumulation and circuits of capital are complexified and sped up by technological innovation. Technological postmodern theory shows that the early modern dialectics of capital and class, state and society, upon which much contemporary social, political, and economic theory has been based, are increasingly problematic. This has far-reaching implications for International Relations and the social sciences generally, challenging our traditional understanding of national borders, for example, or of the efficacy of governmental public policy in an era of transnational capitalism where capital mobility robs the nation-state of its economic sovereignty. Analytically, such perspectives might come to inform theorists in International Relations of the techno-capital regime of accumulation and the effect this has on the spatial location of power amid changing sites of production and the new consumptive taste cultures. Yet this is not a fatuous celebration of globalization, announcements of new worlds, or of the death of the nation-state, but a project cemented in understanding the manner in which technology, revolutions in communications, late capitalist modes of production, and the concomitant implications this harbors for the articulation of social, political, and economic space changes the systemic relationships of our social and political lives, of the relationship between state and society, and of state power and authority. Analytically, this might be translated into studies of political and economic territory, the relocation of sovereignty and the implications of this for state control over fiscal and monetary policy, or the power of the state in terms of its legitimacy and control over employment and wealth creation and the satisfaction of basic needs. This has important implications for state strength, of the relationship between domestic factors and international processes, and of the ability of the state to mediate between external and internal forces. Or, in terms of international political-economy, for example, we might envisage International Relations adopting perspectives that incorporate cultural aesthetics into theories of commodity production, and which analyze the production of global cultural goods/icons like Levi jeans, Coca Cola, the golden arches of MacDonald's, or the standardization of cultural consumption habits with universal signifiers like Chinese take-out, pizza, or American hamburgers. While perhaps innocuous in their own right, they symbolize a universalizing trend that affects values, ideas, and political sensibilities: attitudes toward war, for example, or of a spreading modernism and internationalism that moderates existing national animosities, signaling the possibility for regional formations to emerge, or of regional trading blocs and supranational political institutions. Nor should we forget the effect such universal cultural icons have on international production structures and distribution networks and how these impact domestic consumption habits that produce both increased national income and profit repatriation back to the cultural hegemon(s). More importantly, technological postmodernism is not bereft of understanding the articulation of power in such a setting, noting the seemingly contradictory trends of globalization at the same time as global wealth and power are often coalescing around increasingly few hegemonic centers. In this sense, technological postmodern theory displays an affinity for Gramscian method, seeing power in ways that are not simply tied to the production of guns and tanks, but located in the means of control over cultural goods, patents, and aesthetic commodities like film and television images. This, moreover, is linked to an understanding of postfordist economics that move away from mass production to niche and just-in-time production techniques, allowing for large production runs but in a way that accommodates taste variances on a mass scale. In other words, late modern production methods coupled with the diversification of late modern cultural habits feed off each other, providing the basis for more consumptive demand of dissimilar cultural products and in turn reproducing the late modern mode of production. Transnational economic production processes thus allow for the commercial manufacturing of multifarious tastes that create an atomized consumptive culture but otherwise similar because of its consumptive motif (the particularities of Japanese taste preferences, for example, vis-à-vis American taste preferences, but where both are based upon a culture of consumption which is itself becoming increasingly universalized). This is important for International Relations since it signifies the spread and growing acceptance of Westernized consumptive cultural icons, the spread of consumer culture, most notably in Asia but also in the Americas and now Eastern Europe, where economic convergence is making possible more complex regional trading blocs and fostering greater economic interdependence. In turn, we can observe related convergence in political and social institutions, where democratization and Western concepts of rights, freedoms, and liberties follow (but obviously not always) the free market ethos of capitalist relations, the latter in many instances serving as a platform for subsequent demands for greater participatory democracy. And while this process does not in itself displace nationalism as a powerful mediator of collective loyalties or signify the emergence of a global culture, it does create a crisscrossing of complexities and interdependencies that moderate realist images of anarchical spheres or the billiard ball model of antagonistic nation-states inevitably prone to war. Whatever, it spells a reconfiguration in the articulation of national political practices, of the manner in which political campaigns are conducted, for example, of the legitimacy of using military force or of unilateral aggression. Late modernity, in this respect, modifies relationships between nation-states but in a way that does not change the underlying systemic properties of global political relations—only their procedural particularities.

Thus, while technological postmodern theory does not suggest that the substantive nature of politics has changed, or that the logic of capital has been transformed, it does suggest that emergent dialectics present us with the need for innovative analytical tools if we are to understand and theorize late modernity. This, perhaps, is what makes technological postmodern theory so attractive to the project of the social sciences, acting like a barometer to the change that is taking place and of how this affects our state institutions and their operation. But rather than surrender us to the technobabble of prognostications that announce, for example, how the internet will yet cook our meals, modulate our household energy consumption, or displace nationalism through a new wired culture, technological postmodern theory reiterates the need to analyze the politics of power, who controls the new technologies, who benefits, who does not. Indeed, it reaffirms the importance of old questions, the who, why, and how type questions, where conflict and animosity can still emerge promoted by competition for the new technologies and of the material benefits they bestow. Innovations, change, and development still take place in the context of nation-states, national political systems, and national economic markets and social institutions, reminding us that issues of control, profit, power, and wealth still lie at the heart of social scientific analysis, and this still articulated globally as a phenomena of the interaction and relationships between national communities—nation-states. In this context, both technological and critical postmodernism have a role to play in International Relations, helping us understand the origins and mechanics of the global political economy of transnational relations, transformations in the sources of global power and hegemony, or the emergence of a transnational ethic situated in liberal democracy.[27]

Surprisingly, however, this particular motif is virtually absent in postmodern debates in International Relations. Instead, we need look toward departments of geography, anthropology, cultural studies, and sociology, for example, where an emphasis upon transnational and international political-economic relations has offered innovative theoretical approaches to address these developments.[28] In these disciplines the broad canvas of political economy provides a methodological backdrop conducive to the amalgamation of diverse issue areas which would seem of direct relevance to International Relations.[29] In geography, for instance, the political-economy approach tends to meld a focus upon the nation-state with that of capitalist markets, international trade, and regime formation and maintenance and combine this with insights derived through French regulation theory[30] to produce exceedingly keen insights into the interrelationship between nation-states and capitalism—an area all too often overlooked in International Relations.[31] Such methodological approaches have produced excellent commentaries on the relative power and autonomy of states to operate in the postfordist era, especially with regard issues of penetrated sovereignty and state strength and capacity.[32] So too, postmodern geographies that focus upon time, space, and place, particularly the reflexive interrelationships between new communications and transportations technologies and the mobility of capital and production sites, readily complement International Relations, offering interesting avenues to explore in terms of their effects upon the location of power and sovereignty over space and territory vis-à-vis the politics of power distribution and regime stability. In fact, there has been more scholarship conducted into the nature of place, space, and territory by postmodernist geographers than by theorists of international politics, a condition that could be remedied by exploring the motifs of technological-productionist postmodernism as they have developed outside International Relations. This is also true of the spatial revolution to have hit elsewhere in the social sciences, a concept that surely lends itself to International Relations, concerned as it is with spatial relationships across geographic space and time, but one that remains all but unknown to the discipline.[33]

A few such approaches are beginning to be explored tentatively in International Relations. Recent studies by authors like Barry Gills, Ronen Palan, and Craig Murphy among others, are welcome additions to expanding discourse in this direction.[34] In this respect, postmodern theory in its nonsubversive varieties doubtless will have a legacy in International Relations—one, hopefully, that will mark the closure of postmodernism's subversive phase in the discipline. Indeed, we can readily expect practitioners in the discipline to embrace these theoretical tools and perspectives, but only once the concept of postmodernism has been debunked of connotations that associate it with the practices of deconstruction and subversion and which, quite naturally, induce a deep aversion to its employment in International Relations for lack of its relevance and utility.

By Way of Conclusion:
Reaffirming Reason, Rearticulating Relevance

When reviewing four critical works on international relations theory recently, Mark Hoffman affirmed the call for what he termed the restructuring, reconstruction, reinscription, and rearticulation of international relations theory. The interpretive turn, he noted, would reanimate the study of international relations and the development of international theory. In fact, it was to be celebrated, signaling a movement away from neopositivism and "towards an interpretive view of theory as an endeavour at an ironic understanding and ambiguity, the uncertainty and the textuality of the world in which we live."[35]

Like many others, Hoffman seems to accept without reservation the idea that textuality, ambiguity, uncertainty, decentering, relativism, irregularity, and countless other instruments that detract from the Enlightenment enterprise are reasons for celebration, that they somehow represent intellectual breakthroughs and a form of theoretical progress, and that theory in International Relations needs to be restructured along lines proscribed by the humanities. Hoffman represents one of a growing number of scholars who is fervent in his desire to import and apply deconstructive postmodern theory to the sphere of international politics, both to unearth "hidden meanings" encrusted in the disciplines texts and to arrive at new meanings inferred from the discovery of "hidden practices." There is an almost blind faith that these new creeds hold answers which, under neopositivism, rationality, modernity, and the Enlightenment project have remained hidden from us. Like a great archeological excavation, treasures in the form of new wisdom, new prophecies, and a new politics await discovery for those willing to make the jump and convert to the postmodern cause. The 1990s have thus become a decade of rereadings and textual reinterpretations where the encrusted texts of realists have been reread and their "true" meaning exposed. Ashley reread Waltz and discovered his positivism, economism, and structuralism; Jim George reread realism and discovered its "silences" and "omissions"; Ann Tickner reread Hans Morgenthau and discovered his gender blindness; and Christine Sylvester reread the reinterpretations of rereadings undertaken by male dissidents and discovered their own misogyny and sexism.

For students of international politics who aspire to know, the answer(s) thus reside in textuality, in a life of rereading rereadings in order that hidden practices, silences, omissions, and new meaning can be discovered. The world, as such, can be safely ignored; writings about the world are what must occupy research, for in these writings are the constitutive essences that make up the "real" world. Nothing is given, there is "no there there," nothing is real until named. Women do not exist, Sylvester reminds us, much as for Ashley nation-states do not really exist until inscribed in writings and with names that give them ontological meaning. Meaning is thus in the text, the language, the word, not the thing or the object or the fact.

Let us for a moment, however, reflect on this "research program," on the importations of textual analysis and deconstructive theory, and what they might do to theoretical endeavor and the discipline of International Relations. Let us, for example, pose a few rudimentary questions that, despite their simplicity, go to the very essence of subversive postmodernism's relevance and utility to the study of international politics. What, for example, is "ambiguous" about war or "ironic" about peace? How does the admission of uncertainty change the face of theory, or how does textuality alter our experiences of the realities of international politics, of death squads, civil war, or autocratic rule? Why, suddenly, are irony, uncertainty, ambiguity, and textuality the prized attributes of theoretical endeavor? Are these to be our new epistemological motifs by which we judge the quality and usefulness of theory and research programs in International Relations? Are the problems of international politics and the answers to them hidden amid literary devices like paradox or the textual chicanery of double entendre? Will the practices of regional aggression displayed by Saddam Hussein, for example, be thwarted through textual rereadings of security texts, or the acrimonious diplomatic exchanges between the United States and Iraq? Can we change the course of political outcomes, avert the use of force, or persuade others to disavow aggression though textual reinterpretation?

If we believe Ashley, Hoffman, Walker, Sylvester, or James Der Derian, for example, then the answer is yes, in which case international theory must transpose itself into a form of literary criticism and employ the tools of textual deconstruction, parody, and the style of discontinuous narratives as a means of pondering the depths of interpretation. In doing so, however, we would approach the writings of Richard Ashley, who, utilizing such methods, can apprise students of international politics only of the fact that "there are neither right interpretations nor wrong," there are just "interpretations imposed upon interpretations."[36]

In what sense, however, can this approach be at all adequate for the subject of International Relations. What, for example, do the literary devices of irony and textuality say to Somalian refugees who flee from famine and warlords or to Ethiopian rebels who fight in the desert plains against a government in Addis Abbaba? How does the notion of textual deconstruction speak to Serbs, Croats, and Muslims who fight one another among the ruins of the former Yugoslavia? How do totalitarian narratives or logocentric binary logic feature in the deliberations of policy bureaucrats or in the negotiations over international trade or the formulations of international law? Should those concerned with human rights or those who take it upon themselves to study relationships between nation-states begin by contemplating epistemological fiats and ontological disputes? How does the reification of interpretivism and relativism assist such people in their understandings, problems, judgments, negotiations, and disputes? Is Ashley, for example, suggesting that we simply announce to those in the fray of international politics that there are neither right interpretations nor wrong, there are just interpretations imposed upon interpretations. Is this to be the epiphany of subversive postmodern international theory, its penultimate contribution to those who suffer on the margins for whom they professes great concern?

I am, of course, being flippant. Yet we do have a right to ask such questions of subversive postmodernists if only because they portend to a moral highground, to insights otherwise denied realists, modernists, positivists, and mainstream international relations scholars. We have every right to ask, for example, how subversive postmodern theory speaks to the practical problems endemic to international relations, to the actors and players who constitute the practices of world politics, or how literary devices and deconstructive readings help us better picture world society.

My point, of course, is much the same as Robin Brown's, that textual analysis and deconstruction does not, and cannot, speak to such problems other than to detect the limits of a particular "text by identifying origins, assumptions and silences." What it cannot do, however, "is deal with the practical problem of international relations."[37] Similarly, Hoffman too gives no answers to these questions save this justification for the turn to interpretivism. "This move," he writes, "connects international relations, both as a practice and a discipline, with similar developments within social and political theory and within the humanities."[38] But what justification or rationale is this? So we are now doing what literary theorists do: ruminating over international theory as if such were the verses of lyricists written for the pleasures of reading and consumed only for their wit and romance. But there is a difference between the concerns and interests of, say, English departments and those of departments of Political Science or International Relations. Where literary criticism delights in the ethereal play of words and has as its epistemic basis the belief that "one reads for pleasure," politics dabbles in the material, distributive, punitive play of power whose consequences effect much more than a sensibility committed to reading fiction.[39] Why should we assume that tools developed in English departments are useful to theorists of international relations? Why should we take heed of the writings of Jacques Derrida who never once addressed issues of international relations, but from whom postmodernists now claim a wisdom which they insist is reason enough to dispense with past theory and begin anew our theoretical and disciplinary enterprise?

But all this aside, let us contemplate for a moment how subversive-deconstructive postmodernism would constitute our disciplinary enterprise. Consider, for example, what Ashley would have us do, focus on, analyze, and concern ourselves with. Here Ashley is most emphatic: "Eschewing any claim to secure grounds, the appropriate posture would aspire to an overview of international history in the making, a view from afar, a view up high." The appropriate posture is disposed to a view very much like that of Michel Foucault's genealogical attitude: "a form of history which accounts for the constitution of knowledge, discourses, domains of knowledge, etc . . . ." And to emphasize what is important and what it is that we should focus on, Ashley notes, "From a distant genealogical standpoint, what catches the eye is motion, discontinuities, clashes, and the ceaseless play of plural forces and plural interpretations on the surface of the human experience. Nothing is finally stable. There are no constants, no fixed meanings, no secure grounds, no profound secrets, no final structures or limits of history. Seen from afar, there is only interpretation, and interpretation itself is comprehended as a practice of domination occurring on the surface of history. History itself is grasped as a series of interpretations imposed upon interpretations—none primary, all arbitrary."[40]

As scholars reconstituted under this "appropriate posture," or in later writings a "critical posture of estrangement," we would be condemned to read, to play with words, to interpret without purpose, and to sit amid a solipsistic intertext where words, meanings, referents, signifiers, authors, and subjects have no meaning or reality other than those we would construct individually.[41] With the knowledge that there is no true knowledge because of the absence of secure ground upon which to build knowledge, we would abandon the Enlightenment project and squander away our time in linguistic play as "floating signifiers" vied for our attention among the simulacra of images that each of us consumed. Knowing that we could not know, the task at hand would devolve into one of repudiating the entire stock of knowledge, understanding, and practices that constitute International Relations and developing instead an historical amnesia that favored "a view from afar, from up high."[42] Even interpretation, Ashley insists, a method permissible to most postmodernists, would eventually have to be abandoned along with theory.[43] Since "there is no there there" to be explained, and since interpretation would be but another method of affixing intrinsic meaning to a metaphysical nonreality, it too would have to be abandoned. In this newly constituted enterprise, nothing would await discovery, nothing would have intrinsic meaning, nothing would actually be present other than "absence," and hence nothing could be named. The state would not really exist, subjects would be transcendental fabrications who chase their empty identity throughout history, and history would be a mere interpretation, yet another "practice of domination."[44] Within this nihilistic chasm, subversive postmodernists would have us devolve our disciplinary enterprise into a form of philosophical mentalism, an attempt "to resist the metaphysical temptation in our culture, to assume that something so important must be namable and that the name must indicate a definite referent, an already differentiated identity and source of meaning that just awaits to be named."[45] Only minds situated amid their various contexts would exist and reality would be constituted not through the "realm of immediate sense experience" or "by direct observation of an independently existing world of 'facts,'" but through the thoughts of the mind.[46]

What, then, would we be left with and what could this newly constituted enterprise offer? As Ashley freely admits, it could offer little. It could not "claim to offer an alternative position or perspective" since there would be no secure ontological ground upon which these could be established.[47] Nor could it offer alternative interpretations save it would attempt to impose "interpretation upon interpretation" and capture history by imposing fixed meanings and understandings. Least of all could it offer theory, the very tyranny of modernist narratives that tends to "privilege" and "marginalize." Absent any theoretical legacy or factual knowledge, we would be forced into an endless intertextual discourse predicated on the consumption of words and the individual thoughts they evoke: a kind of purified anarchism albeit in a perpetual state of self-dispersal.[48] We would live in a world of relativistic knowledge claims, each "true" to those that think it, but its truthfulness unobtainable to those who would read it or wish to communicate it. Above all, we would be left without theory-knowledge as a basis for decision, judgment, prescription, and action, surrendering us to "a view from afar, from up high." But as Nicholas Onuf asks, "What does this leave for dealing with those close at hand?"[49]

In the end, however, the intellectual rift that separates these counterpoised disciplines is not so much a theoretical chasm as a political one. The attacks by Ashley and subversive postmodernists stem as much from a deep political suspicion not only toward the discipline, but the implicit project they think it harbors and the political-sectional elite interests they accuse it of representing. Robert Keohane's desire for theoretical synthesis of these contending approaches thus proves naïve, not least for the fact that subversive postmodernism is likely best appreciated as a neotheoretical tool for inflicting damage upon a discipline that subversive postmodernists would see done away with—a spanner in the works, as it were, which, much like sabotage threatens to clog the wheels of theoretical endeavor and reconstitute this machine in partisan terms defined by their respective political agendas.[50] Hence the need for vigilance, or more precisely, standards, in the evaluation of theory and of the various theoretical importations that are frequently attempted in International Relations. If only because of a liberal tolerance for intellectual dissonance, International Relations has been welcoming of all schools of thought and all perspectives. I, for one, support this, believing it to be the embodiment of intellectual discourse and progress. Yet this has to be reconciled amid a notion of discipline, one that demands some degree of conformity in terms of subject matter, aims, approach, and theory, save the very essence of our discipline dissipates into an intellectual free-for-all where anything goes, anything counts as theory, and where everything is assumed to fall within the purview of International Relations. This is not the case and is most definitely inappropriate. To be sure, intellectual innovations are nearly always controversial, the seeding of new ideas frequently derided as obtuse or unrelated, often requiring time to germinate and thereby to grow and mature. But never are intellectual innovations attempts at dismantling the basis of intellectuality by suggesting theoretical closure through deconstruction, or by initiating witch hunts that threaten to hunt down those implicated in the so-called modernist project. Such approaches fail the test of theory, falling short of the aims, ambitions, and purpose of a discipline that strives to understand, not to reproach.

Questions thus persist about Ashley's project and about those who have attempted to replicate his subversive agenda, about the elemental basis and usefulness of this exercise, its stock terms, phrases, and claims. The notion of postmodernity itself, for example, upon closer examination proves to be as hollow and empty as that of modernity. What precisely are these megahistorical divisions meant to imply or accomplish? As Fred Halliday notes, "Beyond the assertion of some large-scale, but pretty obvious changes in the world, it is dubious what empirical or ethical force can be attached to the concept 'post-modernity' at all."[51] Nor can these theorists refer to the real world for evidence of the correctness of their thesis. "Most of those who have used [the term *postmodernism*] . . . have precious little qualifications, or inclination, to talk about the real." In fact, postmodernists have become altogether too inebriated, Halliday suggests, with their own catchy phrases and run "the risk of becoming the new banality, a set of assertions as unlocated and useless as the vacuous generalities, be they balance of power or progressivist teleology, that they seek to displace."[52] "Witty incantations about alterity, dissolution and freeze-frames, and exaggerated claims about what has indeed changed in the world, are no substitute for a substantive engagement with history or a plausible conceptualisation of the alternatives for political and theoretical change."[53] As Michael Wallack observes of another self-declared dissident, Rob Walker: "However innocent of the complexities of the philosophical tradition . . . we may be, few of us expect the upward curve of deaths in war to be reversed by textual analysis and fewer still are apt to regard the untangling of puzzles in a very narrow band of international relations theory as a route to a better future."

Postmodernism in its subversive varieties thus turns out to be less an attempt to clarify the philosophical puzzles of our times or the issues of international relations than a rather pernicious attempt to change the subject itself.[54] And even where deconstructive postmodernists have attempted to grapple with epistemology puzzles, such has been the paucity of these attempts, so bland have been the generalities about the imminent closure and collapse of Western metaphysics, hermeneutics, and dialectics that they have "neither resolve[d] questions of [the] philosophy of science in general, nor contribute[d] to the theorization of IR [in particular]."[55] Certainly orthodox practitioners too have been far from successful in explaining and understanding international relations, in achieving peace, and avoiding war. Yet at least among those who disavow deconstructionism and postmodernist subversion, there is a desire for theory, a wish to better understand and explain international phenomena and, within this ambit, to manipulate and control certain aspects of international relations and thereby improve them. This is not control for its own sake, as postmodernists falsely accuse with Orwellian insinuations, but control and manipulation in order to improve, enhance, and better international relations such that world politics is not an anarchical realm populated by war-prone states. Our professional preoccupations were founded on such laudable objectives. More is the pity that these have now been turned against us as subversive postmodernists paint a grim and unfounded picture of modernist obsession with the technical manipulation of history for the sake of control.

Beyond this legacy it is hard to discern how subversive postmodernism might have any future relevance to International Relations other than as a footnote in historiographical essays of the evolution of the discipline. Beyond the very narrow concerns of subversive-deconstructive postmodernists, there exists a much richer, more vibrant, and informative tradition of scholarship that attempts to understand and explain international relations and perhaps even offers hope that in the future better pictures of world society and better understandings might yet lead to better and more peaceful worlds. That we get on with this project, refocus our attentions on these real issues, and return to the subject of international politics seems long overdue. Unlike Hoffman, then, it is time that we resist the urge to reinscribe, rearticulate, and restructure and begin again the process of reaffirming reason and rearticulating relevance in our theoretical pursuits.

Notes

Preface

1. C. Brown, 1994b, 142.
2. R. G. Gilpin, 1986, 303.
3. T. J. Biersteker, 1989, 266.
4. K. J. Holsti, 1985.
5. N. G. Onuf, 1989.
6. P. Darby and A. J. Paolini, 1994, 373.

Chapter One: Theory and Metatheory in International Relations

1. S. Hoffmann, 1989, 276.
2. At the very outset of this chapter, I want to dispel any notion of definitional precision in the lexicon of the Third Debate. Concepts such as postmodernism, poststructuralism, postpositivism, interpretivism, and reflectivism, for example, are used interchangeably and obviously have much overlap. Accordingly, I have chosen to follow this practice, employing these concepts in interchangeable fashion and somewhat loosely, leaving, as Roger Spegele suggests, the context in which they are used to firm up their meaning. Having said this, though, I tend to favor the term *postmodernism* simply because this is suitably nebulous enough and woefully imprecise as to apply to all those who count themselves as intellectual dissidents. See R. D. Spegele, 1992, 147.
3. C. T. Sjolander and W. S. Cox, 1994, 3.
4. P. Darby and A. J. Paolini, 1994, 374.
5. K. J. Holsti, 1989b, 34.
6. J. J. Weltman, 1982, 27.
7. R. L. Rothstein, 1991, xvii. See also K. J. Holsti, 1971, 172.
8. P. Darby and A. J. Paolini, 1994, 375.
9. A. Lijphart, 1974, 41.
10. S. Hoffmann, 1960, 6. See also F. Halliday, 1985, 407–12.
11. K. J. Holsti, 1993, 407.
12. C. T. Sjolander and W. S. Cox, 1994, 4.
13. T. J. Biersteker, 1989, 265.
14. C. T. Sjolander and W. S. Cox, 1994, 4.
15. R. Brown, 1993, 11; R. W. Cox, 1986, 207.

16. The question of cultural difference as it relates to international relations theory is addressed in N. J. Rengger, 1989, 237–50.
17. Y. Lapid, 1989b, 236–37.
18. T. J. Biersteker, 1989, 266.
19. S. Hoffmann, 1960, 5–6.
20. Ibid., 6.
21. Ibid.
22. Ibid.
23. Ibid., 8–9.
24. The words of Joseph Frankel are most instructive here. "The so-called 'facts,'" he notes, "are mere artificial constructions abstracted from complex and interwoven reality by means of arbitrary definitions and classifications. They are selected from the profusion of real life on the basis of implicit or explicit theories about what is important." What is important, therefore, are not facts, but "the ideas which determine our interpretation" of them. See J. Frankel, 1969, 17.
25. K. N. Waltz, 1986, 30. Similarly, Joseph Frankel observes, "The great advance in our knowledge of detail does not, however, add up to an understanding of the whole field; on the contrary, the detailed information available is sometimes excessive since it chocks the channels of communication and cannot be easily digested by individual scholars or even teams of them." See J. Frankel, 1969, 18.
26. K. N. Waltz, 1986, 33.
27. E. H. Carr, 1964, 3.
28. As quoted in ibid.
29. Ibid., 2 and 8.
30. Philip Windsor as quoted in N. Rengger and M. Hoffman, 1992, 127.
31. H. Morgenthau as quoted in S. Hoffmann, 1987, 71.
32. S. Hoffmann, 1960, 8.
33. E. H. Carr, 1964, 5. Hoffmann also recognizes these mutually exclusive strands within theory, labeling them 1. normative theory; 2. empirical theory; 3. policy science theory. Moreover, he also notes, like Carr, that "it is impossible to keep completely apart the three kinds of theory which we distinguished analytically from the viewpoint of purpose." See S. Hoffmann, 1960, 9. For a related discussion of this issue, see R. M. A. Crawford, 1996, 9–38; C. Brown, 1992, 1–2.
34. See, for example, the discussion in P. Shearman, 1993, 145.
35. F. S. Dunn, 1960, 14.
36. Ibid.
37. For a related discussion of the nature of theory, see the excellent article by R. Aron, 1967, 185–206. See also H. Bull, 1972b, 30–55.
38. N. G. Onuf, 1989, 11.
39. C. Brown, 1992, 1.
40. Not that this might be altogether bad. Ferguson and Mansbach, for example, albeit with tongue in cheek, think this might be a good thing since, were this not the case, these same practitioners "might decide that the emperor is indeed naked." See Y. H. Ferguson and R. W. Mansbach, 1988, 3.
41. F. Halliday, 1994, 7.
42. Ibid.

43. Although he does not use the term *social charter,* K. Holsti makes much the same argument, noting that "While some may argue that we have organized a field called international relations/politics because the phenomena are 'there,' the truth is that we study them because of a deeply held normative concern about the problem of war." As Holsti notes, "virtually every writer who has helped develop the filed has been animated by this concern, including Hobbes, Grotius, Erasmus, Vattel, Saint-Pierre, Rousseau, Kant and the moderns. Each has made some sort of implicit or explicit statement about the causes of war and, perhaps more prolifically, has proposed some sort of solution to the problem. . . ." K. J. Holsti, 1985, 8.

44. F. Halliday, 1994, 8.

45. In a similar way Bull viewed the ". . . house of International Relations as having many mansions and many different views of the world, each coherent, plausible and intellectually defensible." See the discussion in J. L. Richardson, 1990, 141. See also H. Bull, 1972a, 251–65; K. J. Holsti, 1989b, 27–40.

46. A more encompassing discussion of many of these themes can be found in S. Hoffmann, 1960, 1–12. See also the brief discussion in M. Neufeld, 1992, 83–97.

47. K. Hutchings, 1992, 51.

48. N. J. Rengger, 1990, 361.

49. C. Taylor, 1980, 139.

50. I. Bell, 1992, paper presented at the panel, "Critical International Theory and the New World Order," Thirty-third Annual Convention of the International Studies Association, Atlanta, Ga., March 31–April 4. The practical difficulties of studying international relations in terms of the structure/actor dialectic is addressed in J. G. Ruggie, 1989, 21–36.

51. One of the few people who have attempted such a synthesis is Wendt. See A. E. Wendt, 1987, 335–37; A. E. Wendt, 1992, 391–426.

52. R. Spegele, 1982, 584. For a further discussion see the forceful argument in P. F. Kress, 1979, 526–42.

53. See, for example, the discussion in T. J. Biersteker, 1989, 265.

54. D. Dessler, 1989, 445.

55. Ibid.

56. K. N. Waltz, 1979, 5.

57. Ibid., 8.

58. See, for example, the discussion in Y. H. Ferguson and R. W. Mansbach, 1988, 79–108.

59. See T. J. Biersteker, 1989.

60. W. P. Kreml and C. W. Kegley, Jr., 1990, 155.

61. Ibid., 169.

62. See, respectively, K. J. Holsti, 1985; M. Banks, 1985, 7–26.

63. R. Maghroori and B. Ramberg, 1982.

64. See Y. H. Ferguson and R. W. Mansbach, 1988; Y. H. Ferguson and R. W. Mansbach, 1986, 11–34. See also Y. H. Ferguson and R. W. Mansbach, 1991, 363–86.

65. See R. W. Cox, 1981, 126–51.

66. See C. T. Sjolander and W. S. Cox, 1994; S. Smith, K. Booth, and M. Zalewski, 1996. In the same genre, see also the chapters by J. George and D. Campbell in R. Higgott, ed., 1988.

67. Y. Lapid, 1989b, 235. See also Y. Lapid, 1989a, 77–88.

68. The issue of positivism and science as method in International Relations is also addressed in the recent article by J. George, 1996, 33–82.

69. See, for example, A. Linklater, 1990; 1992, 191–208.

70. I use the terms methodology, epistemology, and ontology in much the same manner as does H. Y. Alker, who notes, "epistemologies (philosophies of knowledge cumulation) are assumed to be grounded in ontologies (more or less metaphysical doctrines of 'being') and methodologies are thought of as applied epistemologies using particular techniques." See H. Y. Alker, Jr., 1992, 352, n.3.

71. Critical Theory is here capitalized following the distinction highlighted by Chris Brown who notes that Critical Theory concerns the classical variety of thought descended from the Frankfurt school while the noncapitalized term *critical theory* is often employed by those who identify themselves as postmodernists and poststructuralists. See, for example, the discussion in C. Brown, 1994c, 214.

72. C. Sylvester, 1994, 149.

73. C. Brown, 1994c, 216.

74. Ibid., 229.

75. Jacques Derrida as quoted in C. Brown, 1994a, 58.

76. See, for example, J. Baudrillard, 1983.

77. See the discussion in R. M. A. Crawford, 1999.

78. S. Whitworth, 1989, 266.

79. V. S. Peterson, 1992c, 8–11.

80. C. Sylvester, 1996a, 256–57.

81. Ibid., 254.

82. Cynthia Enloe as quoted in ibid., 263.

83. M. Zalewski, 1996, 346.

84. C. Sylvester, 1996a, 264.

85. M. Zalewski, 1996, 349.

86. Ibid. The reference to Godrej's work concerns F. Godrej, 1995, "Women and Post Cold War U.S. Foreign Policy: The Case of Filipina Prostitutes," a paper presented to the International Studies Association Conference, Chicago, February 21–25. How the slogan on a T-shirt, admittedly vulgar, or the experiences of Filipina prostitutes elucidates the nature or causes of the Cold War, I fail to appreciate. Certainly, I can see that these circumstances might represent a consequence of the Cold War in terms of a heightened U.S. military presence in Subic Bay in order to facilitate U.S. power projection into the Pacific region, but to suggest that this might be a starting point for understanding the Cold War, its origins, causes, or strategic basis seems obtuse in the extreme. Indeed, why the Cold War? Surely a more appropriate historical referent on which to narrate U.S. influence in the Philippines would begin with the Spanish-American war and the colonial policies of the U.S. in the Pacific around the turn of the century.

87. C. Sylvester, 1996a, 264.

88. See, for example, the contribution of K. Ferguson, 1996, 435–54.

89. As quoted in C. Sylvester, 1996a, 262.
90. N. J. Rengger, 1996, 218.
91. Critical theorists too have suggested the historically bounded nature of realist thinking. See, for example, R. W. Cox, 1986, 204–54.
92. N. J. Rengger and M. Hoffman, 1992, 131.
93. R. K. Ashley, 1991, 67.
94. As quoted in C. Brown, 1994c, 216.
95. S. Smith, 1995, 2–3.
96. J. George, 1996, 51.
97. R. K. Ashley, 1991, 43.
98. J. George, 1994, 11.
99. J. George, 1995, 217.
100. Ibid.
101. On nationalism and hegemony in international theory, see the collection of essays in R. M. A. Crawford and D. S. L. Jarvis, eds., 1999.
102. J. George, 1995, 215.
103. Ibid., 222.
104. Vaclav Havel as quoted by J. George, ibid., 221.
105. Ibid., 215.
106. W. Wallace, 1996, 301.
107. Ibid., 301–3. See also the discussion in A. L. George, 1993, 6–15.
108. M. McKinley, 1996, 8.
109. Ibid., 16.
110. Ibid., 17.
111. W. Wallace, 1996, 311.
112. K. J. Holsti, 1999.
113. M. Hoffman, 1987, 244–45.
114. Kalevi Holsti quoting the words of Jim George. K. J. Holsti, 1999.
115. W. Wallace, 1996, 306–7.
116. E. H. Carr, 1964, 11. See also the discussion in R. M. A. Crawford, 1996, 9–38.
117. S. Chan, 1994, 32–33.

Chapter Two: Contemplating the Crisis in the Crisis of Contemplation

1. R. W. Mansbach and Y. H. Ferguson, 1986, 11–34.
2. J. N. Rosenau, 1980b.
3. F. H. Hinsley, 1963, 6.
4. M. Wight, 1991, 1. H. J. Morgenthau arrived at a similar conclusion, noting, "That men throughout the ages have thought little of a theory of international politics is borne out by the fact that but rarely an explicit attempt to develop such a theory has been made; as rare instances of such attempts, Kautilya and Machiavelli come to mind." See H. J. Morgenthau, 1958, 48.
5. Ibid. In contradistinction to M. Wight's position, T. L. Knutsen has attempted recently to counter the "common assumption that the study of Inter-

national Relations has no theoretical tradition," and that, in fact, it displays a "chain of classic texts" as much as does political theory proper. See T. L. Knutsen, 1992, 1. In a similar genre see also the work of J. L. Holzgrefe, 1989, 11–26. See also A. Lijphart, 1974, 41–74. K. J. Holsti also argues for the existence of what he terms the classical tradition, albeit that the hegemony it enjoyed for so long has now ended. See K. J. Holsti, 1985, 1, 15–40.

6. N. G. Onuf, 1989, 36. An instance of the retroactive reconstruction of international theory is provided, for example, in the elegant writings of M. Wight, particularly his delineation of three paradigms of international theory: the realists or Machiavellians, the rationalists or Grotians and the revolutionists or Kantians. See M. Wight, 1991, 30–48. See also B. Porter, 1978, 64–74. More obvious examples of the reinscription of historical texts with theoretical propinquity to international relations would be the current approbation of Thucydides. Kenneth Waltz, for example, sees Thucydides as one of the first to recognize "the anarchic character of international politics"; Robert Gilpin, "Everything that the new realists find intriguing in the interaction of international economics and international politics can be found in *The History of the Peloponnesian War*"; and Robert Keohane, that Thucydides is an example of some of the fundamental assumptions of structural realism. See D. Garst, 1989, 3–27.

7. For fear of being labeled pedantic, let me be specific about my determination of international relations. In keeping with conventional wisdom, I too date the advent of the term *international relations* from around 1648 with the Peace of Westphalia. The argument—one which I think fairly standard—is that international relations/politics developed only after 1648 with the advent of the sovereign nation-state. By this definition, international relations are the product of a particular mode of European statist conduct that has now become universalized—albeit relatively recently. This, I hope, is not to be blinded by a Eurocentiric bias, but by historical fact that international relations were European in origin. Conversely, I am not attempting to suggest that external relations between epistemic communities, city states, or tribal communities did not exist prior to 1648 or outside of Europe. They most certainly did. To what extent such relationships can be counted as international or analyzed within the purview of a discipline which is itself a product of the universalization of the European state system is, however, problematic. If the history of international relations is to be told from a non-European perspective, from my standpoint this can only be done via a narrative of the consequences of the European age as they were forced upon non-European peoples along with alien forms of political-territorial organization. See, for example, the excellent study by T. Todorov, 1984. On the genealogy of the word *international* and its European origins and usage, see the fascinating history by H. Suganami, 1978, 226–32. See also the chapter by R. B. J. Walker, 1984, 182–216.

8. W. C. Olson and A. J. R. Groom, 1991, 9.

9. It need hardly be stated that Thucydides's observations of the Peloponnesian war constituted a historical and not a theoretical discourse. M. Wight, 1966, 32; H. Bull, 1991, xxi.

10. K. J. Holsti, 1985, 16.

11. M. Wight, 1966, 32–33. Wight's assertion that international politics is anomalous, constituting a sui generis, is refuted by Roy Jones who maintains that Wight

has incorrectly concerned himself "in detailed and elaborate ways with mythology." See R. E. Jones, 1988, 267–74. Similarly, Jones had earlier argued, albeit rather beratingly, for the closure of the English school, attacking Wight for a litany of apparent failings. See R. E. Jones, 1981, 1–13. An excellent rebuke to Jones's argument is provided by S. Grader, 1988, 29–44.

12. M. Wight, 1966, 24.
13. M. Donelan, 1978a, 77.
14. M. Wight, 1966, 21. See also the discussion by R. H. Jackson, 1990, 261–72; R. Epp, 1992. "The Multiple Identities of Martin Wight." Paper presented at the 33rd Annual Convention of the International Studies Association, Atlanta, Ga., March 31–April 4.
15. T. Hobbes, 1968, 189.
16. See the discussion in K. J. Holsti, 1985, 15–40.
17. T. Hobbes, 1968, 161.
18. Ibid.
19. H. Bull, 1991, xi. See also the excellent discussion in K. N. Waltz, 1965, 159–86. It is ironic to note, however, that Hobbes, while held in such high regard by international relations scholars, displayed remarkable brevity in addressing the subject of international politics. As C. Navari observed, "Since Hobbes wrote so little about relations between states, it is odd that there should be a 'Hobbesian tradition' of international relations." See C. Navari, 1982, 203.
20. T. M. Knox, 1967, 215. See also H. Williams, 1992, 92–104.
21. H. J. Morgenthau, 1958, 81. Earlier Morgenthau wrote, "Above the national societies there exists no international society so integrated as to be able to define for them the concrete meaning of justice or equality, as national societies do for their members." See H. J. Morgenthau, 1951, 34.
22. M. Wight, 1966, 21.
23. W. C. Olson and A. J. R. Groom, 1991, 22.
24. S. Hoffmann, 1965, 3–4.
25. See J. Bentham, 1974, 11–44; W. Wilson, 1923; Charles de Saint-Pierre, Abbe de Tiron, 1974, 1–61; I. Kant, 1957; S. Hoffmann, 1965, especially chapter 3, 54–87; S. Hoffmann and D. P. Fidler, 1991; J. J. Rousseau, 1974.
26. M. Wight, 1966, 20.
27. S. Hoffmann, 1977, 41.
28. The recalcitrance of the philosophes of the Enlightenment to engage in speculation on international matters, in fact their hostility to it as manifested in their antidiplomacy, is succinctly addressed in J. Der Derian, 1987, 160–67.
29. T. M. Knox, 1967, 214; T. L. Knutsen, 1992, 32.
30. As discussed in J. Der Derian, 1987, 102.
31. Ibid., 212.
32. H. J. Morgenthau, 1958, 48.
33. See, for example, the discussion in S. Hoffmann, 1965, 3–21. Useful overviews of the development of the discipline are provided in W. C. Olson, 1972, 3–29; H. Bull, 1972b, 30–55. Very useful discussions can also be found in K. Thompson, 1952, 433–67; W. T. Fox and A. B. Fox, 1961, 339–59; W. T. Fox, 1949, 67–79; F. S. Dunn, 1949, 80–95.

34. See, for example, the introductory comments in Y. H. Ferguson and R. W. Mansbach, 1988, 3–5.

35. Obviously I do not insist that theoretical incertitude is unique to international political theory. The social sciences generally have long suffered from a theoretical infancy that has become somewhat of a platitude amongst biographers of the field. My point, however, is that this is perhaps more evident in international political theory than in the more established and intellectually defined pursuits of, say, economics, history, or sociology, for example.

36. M. Wight, 1991, 40–41.

37. M. Donelan, 1978a, 75.

38. M. Wight, 1966, 20.

39. The first chair of International Relations was named after Woodrow Wilson and established at the University College of Wales, Aberystwyth, in 1919. It was first held by Sir Alfred Zimmern for two years who then resigned later to become the first Montague Burton professor of International Relations at Oxford in August 1930. See the discussion in W. C. Olson, 1972, 5, 12–13. See also D. J. Markwell, 1986, 279–92. On the founding of the first chair of International Relations at Aberystwyth, see the discussion by B. Porter, 1989, 27–36. A useful discussion of the development of the discipline is also provided in F. Halliday, 1990, 502–16.

40. As quoted in W. C. Olson and A. J. R. Groom, 1991, 90. See also the short introductory remarks by A. Zimmern, 1939, 6–13. The eclecticism which Zimmern thought entailed in the study of international relations is instructive of the disciplines' amorphous beginnings which, with hindsight, read as if a comic parody of our profession, especially given Zimmern's verbose and elegant style.

41. S. Hoffmann, 1965, 4.

42. S. Hoffmann, 1977, 42–43.

43. See E. H. Carr, 1964; H. J. Morgenthau, 1967.

44. S. Hoffmann, 1965, 4–5.

45. S. Hoffmann, 1977, 41, 59. On the intellectual hegemony of the American discipline, see the collection of essays in R. M. A. Crawford and D. S. L. Jarvis, eds., 1999.

46. Ibid., 47.

47. Ibid., 42. See also S. Hoffmann, 1965, 4–5.

48. H. J. Morgenthau, 1958, 47–48.

49. Ibid., 48.

50. P. Keal, 1991, 164.

51. J. N. Rosenau, 1980a, 32.

52. Sir Alfred Zimmern as quoted in D. J. Markwell, 1986, 289.

53. Sir Alfred Zimmern as quoted in ibid.; E. H. Carr, 1964, 39.

54. S. Hoffmann, 1977, 57.

55. See the retrospective assessment of science and International Relations by D. J. Puchala, 1990, 59–80.

56. The term *perspectivism* I borrow from K. J. Holsti to denote not only the tendency to theoretical pluralism in the discipline but also the propensity to construct theory in relation to identity politics whereby theory is developed through subjective

lenses dependent upon one's particular vantage point (i.e., class, gender, race, geographical locale, etc.). See the discussion in K. J. Holsti, 1989a, 255–61.

57. R. Higgott, 1991, 397.
58. J. N. Rosenau, 1980b, 11.
59. R. B. J. Walker and S. H. Mendlovitz, 1990, 7–8.
60. See H. Bull, 1977, 254.
61. J. A. Camilleri, 1990, 28, 33, 39. See also J. A. Camilleri and J. Falk, 1992.
62. See, for example, two recent edited volumes in this genre of literature which challenge the notion of physical (sovereign) and intellectual boundaries: M. J. Shapiro and H. R. Alker, 1996; J. MacMillan and A. Linklater, eds., 1995.
63. This is not to deny, of course, that disagreement, disunity, and disharmony have, to varying degrees, always been with us in International Relations. Ours is not an exact science, measurable, quantifiable, or predictable. The means to knowledge and understanding has not been based upon observation of the facts alone, but upon debate as to which facts are important, which not, and which medium of interpretation renders most apparent their meaning, context, and implications. Knowledge and understanding have thus been acquired not through ever larger data sets but discourse, dialogism, and thoughtful reflection. Thus, when K. J. Holsti refers to an intellectual consensus, he is, then, invoking the notion of a classical tradition which, until very recently, has defined the object(s) of our studies and its purpose—the "causes of war and the conditions of peace/security/order." Marxist, liberal, or realist, for example, positivist, critical theoretic, or classicist, regardless of one's ideological position or choice of epistemological tool, have all been motivated by a common problematic and shared goal, providing a sense of common purpose around which our discipline has coalesced. See K. J. Holsti, 1985, 1.
64. Ibid.
65. F. Halliday, 1985, 407.
66. M. Hoffman, 1987, 231.
67. See R. K. Ashley and R. B. J. Walker, 1990b, 259–68; J. George and D. Campbell, 1990, 269–94.
68. J. Der Derian, 1988, 189.
69. Y. Lapid, 1989b, 237.
70. Y. H. Ferguson and R. W. Mansbach, 1991, 363.
71. M. Hoffman, 1987, 231; Y. H. Ferguson and R. W. Mansbach, 1991, 363. There are, of course, some commentators who would argue that there is a core to the Third Debate. See, for example, the chapter by Richard Devetak, 1996, 179–209.
72. M. Hoffman, 1991, 169; J. George, 1989, 273.
73. J. George and D. Campbell, 1990, 289.
74. S. Burchill, 1996, 1.
75. Richard Bernstein as quoted in S. Burchill and A. Linklater, eds., 1996, 270.
76. Y. Lapid, 1989a, 77; M. Banks, 1985, 8.
77. J. L. Richardson, 1991, 19.

78. R. Higgott, 1991, 395.
79. M. Hoffman, 1991, 178.
80. T. J. Biersteker as quoted in Y. Lapid, 1989b, 238; M. Banks, 1985, 7.
81. G. A. Almond as quoted in Y. Lapid, 1989a, 81. See also R. Rorty, 1980, 165–209. This position is taken from Foucault, who engages in a "*reversement* of traditional views of the intellectual," noting that the intellectual is always "determined by specific events" and part of a knowledge-power system. See, for example, the discussion in E. T. Barnet, 1989.
82. W. Olson and N. G. Onuf, 1985, 11.
83. S. Smith, 1985, ix.
84. Ibid.
85. M. Hoffman, 1991, 177.
86. J. L. Richardson, 1991, 27.
87. N. J. Rengger, 1988, 81.
88. J. N. Rosenau, 1989, 2–3.
89. K. Marx and F. Engels, 1977, 37.
90. J. N. Rosenau, 1989, 5.
91. D. Harvey, 1991, 41.
92. J. N. Rosenau, 1989, 5.

Chapter Three: Sentinels of Dissidence

1. This chapter draws from an article which appeared in the journal *Politics and Society*. See D. S. L. Jarvis, 1998, 95–142.
2. J. Bowers, 1992, 111.
3. C. Newman, 1985, 31.
4. Ibid., 5.
5. D. Hebdige, 1988, 181.
6. Indeed, defining postmodernism is an improbable task as Devetak notes when he writes, "Unfortunately, a clear definition of postmodernism that will meet with general agreement is precisely what is not possible. Not only is the definition and meaning of postmodernism in dispute between proponents and critics, but also among proponents. Sometimes the different understandings of postmodernism amount to fairly minor differences of emphasis; sometimes they result in significantly divergent theoretical trajectories and conclusions. If there is anything clear about postmodernism it is that its meaning and definition is a source of great contention." In the end, Devetak's solution is to proceed to discuss postmodernism in the context of a "programmatic and nominalistic approach," a method I have otherwise adopted in this chapter. See the discussion in R. Devetak, 1996, 179–80.
7. J. Collins, 1992, 104. Indeed, postmodernism is probably best defined in the negative sense, that is, by what it stands against rather than what it stands for.
8. Hebdige as quoted in B. Reimer, 1989, 110–11. A useful introduction which provides some background to the modernist and postmodernist labels is found in B. Smart, 1990, 14–30.
9. In the case of geography, for example, Soja has gone as far to argue that the discipline has undergone a comprehensive "postmodernization," reconstitut-

ing its tapestry in ways that have disintegrated its traditional concerns and boundaries. See E. Soja, 1987, 289–94. See also M. Billinge et al., eds., 1984; P. Marden, 1990.

10. See the discussion, for example, in M. A. Rose, 1992a, 119–36.

11. D. Kuspit, 1990, 54.

12. A. Huyssen, 1984, 8.

13. See C. Norris, 1990; A. Callinicos, 1989.

14. Further to this, Silverman notes that "postmodernism has no place of origin—it can inscribe itself in different places, at various limit points." H. J. Silverman, 1990, 4. Jean-Francois Lyotard has gone even further, insisting that postmodernist knowledge treats its own development "as discontinuous, catastrophic and irrevocably flawed." As discussed in K. R. Scherpe, 1986–87, 102.

15. J. George, 1993, 216.

16. C. Norris as quoted in M. A. Rose, 1992b, 41.

17. Foster argues that despite its apparent discursivity, postmodernism "is singular in its repudiation of modernism." H. Foster, 1983a, xii.

18. K. Manzo, 1991, 8.

19. For discussions about the changed realities of world capitalism, relations of production, technologies, communications and thus in the political-economy of global relations, see B. Andrews, 1982, 135–63; P. F. Drucker, 1986, 768–91.

20. W. Brown, 1991, 63.

21. Arnold Toynbee as quoted in C. Coker, 1992, 189.

22. See F. Fukuyama, 1992.

23. See the following: F. Frobel et al., 1978, 123–42; N. Thrift, 1986, 12–67; J. A. Caporaso, 1981, 347–84; W. Andreff, 1984, 58–80; R. Peet, 1983, 105–11; R. D. Lipschutz, 1992. "Heteronomia: The Emergence of Global Civil Society." Mimeograph paper prepared for the International Studies Association Conference, Atlanta, Ga.: March 31–April 4; R. Leaver, 1988. "Restructuring in the Global Economy: From Pax Americana to Pax Nipponica?" Mimeograph, Peace Research Centre, Research School of Pacific Studies, Australian National University.

24. D. J. Elkins, 1995, 3–7.

25. Representative of this genre of literature is the recent study by J. MacMillan and A. Linklater, 1995. See also M. J. Shapiro and H. R. Alker, 1996; J. Camilleri and J. Falk, 1992. By contrast, the 1996 volume by Berger and Dore offers a superb analysis of the actual realities of the so-called new global economy, demonstrating how globalization is more imagined than real. See, in particular, the chapter by R. Wade, 1996, 60–88.

26. D. J. Elkins, 1995, 3.

27. Of these new theoretical forms the most obvious and successful has been the introduction of a spatial dialectic into social theory and political economy. See, for example, the writings of L. Jezierski, 1991, 177–84; D. U. Gregory, 1978, 38–46; 1989b, 185–214. The development by Giddens of structuration theory (the reflexive understanding of structure and agency in both spatial and historical contexts) has also radically transformed much social theory. See, for example, the excellent introductions: C. G. A. Bryant and D. Jary, eds., 1991; A. Giddens and J. Turner, 1987; A. Giddens, 1986.

28. See, for example, the volume by J. N. Rosenau and E. O. Czempiel, 1992.
29. A. Giddens, 1991, 3.
30. As quoted in P. Marden, 1992, 46.
31. See, for example, S. Huntington, 1989; S. Strange, 1987, 551–74; R. B. Duboff, 1989, 142–86.
32. R. K. Ashley, 1991, 48.
33. As quoted in D. Harvey, 1991, 39.
34. Jane Flax as quoted in J. George, 1993, 215–16.
35. P. Zagorin, 1990, 271.
36. In this genre, see, for example, M. Berman, 1988.
37. See the discussion in S. Best and D. Kellner, 1991, 29–31. See also W. E. Connolly, 1988.
38. R. Williams, 1977.
39. P. M. Rosenau, 1992, 15.
40. See H. Foster, ed., 1985, 121–37. See also H. Foster, 1984, 67–78; P. M. Rosenau, 1992; R. Rorty, 1980; M. Hoffman, 1991, 169–85.
41. Naturally, I do not insist that these categories constitute discrete boundaries. Rather, I use them as typologies or, in the Weberian sense, as ideal types for heuristic purposes in disentangling the assemblage of literature labeled postmodern. Moreover, I recognize that such typologies are liable to be confusing since many so-called postmodernists straddle the typologies presented, easily slipping into two or more of these categories simultaneously.
42. J. Baudrillard, 1988b, 128. See also J. Baudrillard, 1988a.
43. For background see Z. Tar, 1988. See also M. Horkheimer, 1972; D. Held, 1989a. See also the various essays in S. E. Bronner and D. M. Kellner, 1989. On the connections between critical theory and postmodernism, see the discussion in S. Best and D. Kellner, 1991, 215–55.
44. See, for example, R. A. Morrow, 1991, 27–69.
45. In a similar fashion to Derrida, Foster writes of the construction of a "culture of resistance." See H. Foster, ed., 1985, 157–79.
46. F. Jameson, 1992, ix. Jameson is referring here to the grand ethos of Western Enlightenment narratives that depict history as a process of humans against nature. Progress and development have thus been defined in terms of technological referents that attempt to build barriers and put a distance between humans and nature or tame nature. Thus the building of elaborate artificial environments that shut nature out as with modernist architecture or, more simply, the sense that nature was now under control regarding the West's domestication of agriculture and the ample provision of food, shelter, and clothing so that society was now free to pursue art and other aesthetic pastimes. This narrative is particularly evident in the context of the settlement of the New World with the taming of the American West as nature was brought under control via massive land clearing projects, farming settlement, and the extension of transportation links.
47. Ibid.
48. Ibid., 47–48.
49. Ibid., 412.
50. Ibid., 3.

51. Ibid., 5.

52. A similar thesis positing the deepening of consumer society and the reflexive effects of culture, technology, and economics is found in F. Jameson, 1983, 111–25.

53. S. Lash, 1990, 21, 23, 30, 37–52. On the rise of the cognitariat, see C. Jencks, 1986, 43. On the end of class and universalism, see the post-Marxist expositions of E. Laclau and C. Mouffe, 1985. Contra the post-Marxist thesis, see N. Geras, 1990.

54. C. Jencks, 1986, 43.

55. This new mode of production is variously depicted by Jameson as late capitalism. See F. Jameson, 1992. See also the conversation in A. Stephanson, 1988, 3–30.

56. F. Jameson, 1992, 4.

57. As quoted in D. Kellner, 1989, 61. See also his related discussion on the development of postmodernism in D. Kellner, 1988, 239–69.

58. This is not to suggest that Baudrillard is announcing the end of discrimination or exploitation, but rather that the traditional dialectics that were responsible for exploitation and discrimination under modernist-industrial modes of production have now changed. As Douglas Kellner notes: "Modernity for Baudrillard is . . . the era of production governed by the industrial bourgeoisie. The era of simulations by contrast is an era of information and signs governed by models, codes, and a system of general economy." The oppression of the masses, the exploitation of the workers, the class basis of extraction of a surplus, etc.—all these dialectics are now replaced by the postmodern system of general economy. See S. E. Bronner and D. M. Kellner, 1989, 60–92. See also J. Baudrillard, 1988b, passim.

59. D. Hebdige, 1988, 195.

60. Ibid.

61. J. F. Lyotard, 1993, 91. Lyotard, of course, is referring to the arrogance of Enlightenment thought which assumes rationality the only means to truth and understanding. For Lyotard, there are many roads to truth, and no one knowledge system is capable of proving itself more superior to any other. For postmodernists like Lyotard, then, truth is understood as a relativist-textual concept, since outside of the text there are no extratextual referents that can establish truth beyond reasonable doubt. Foundational knowledge and truth claims are thus seen as illusions generated by textual practices.

62. J. F. Lyotard, 1991, 36.

63. F. Nietzsche, 1968. On the resurgence of Nietzschean philosophy, especially as it relates to postmodernism, see P. Redding, 1990, 72–88.

64. A. Kroker and D. Cook, 1987, 8–9.

65. Ibid., vi–vii. On the crisis in Western culture, see E. Hobsbawm, 1992, 55–64. See also T. Eagleton, 1992, 29–41.

66. D. Hebdige, 1988, 201.

67. K. R. Scherpe, 1986–87, 95.

68. A. Kroker, 1992, 2–3.

69. J. F. Lyotard, 1991, 3.

70. See R. A. Morrow, 1991, 27.

71. A. Callinicos, 1989, 168.
72. Ibid.
73. Ibid., 170.
74. Ibid.
75. Ibid., 170–71.
76. From this definition my use of the term *critical postmodernism* should be apparent. Unlike subversive postmodernism, critical postmodernism is not adverse to truth claims, epistemology, or foundationalist propositions but, in fact, looks for such systemic properties in order to explain the configurations of social, political, and economic life. However, this is not to say that its understanding of truth is not subjectively situated—it is and very much tied to the emergence of identity politics as discussed later in this chapter.
77. For example, see the debates in E. Laclau and C. Mouffe, 1987, 79–106; N. Mouzelis, 1988, 107–23; E. B. Chilcote and R. H. Chilcote, 1992, 84–106; A. Szymanski, 1985, 315–31; A. Kumar, A. 1990, 149–55; J. Graham, 1991, 39–58; A. Callinicos, 1985, 85–101.
78. R. A. Morrow, 1991, 36. On the crisis in Marxism see J. Linday, 1981.
79. Perry Anderson as quoted in C. Norris, 1990, 1. M. Gonzales is even more scathing in his assessment of cultural theory and postmodernism, seeing critical theory the product of "frustrated radicals who have managed, over the last 20 years of chaotic growth and revolutionary restructuring of higher education, to translate their . . . [revolutionary rhetoric] . . . only into tenured academic positions." Critical theory, for Gonzales at least, is armchair theorizing, suitably deradicalized by now well-heeled and tenured academics. M. Gonzales, 1984–85, 206–10.
80. The developmental lineage of French philosophy, the impact of French radicalism and its culmination in the May 1968 uprisings and of their influence on poststructuralist and postmodernist philosophy is traced in L. Ferry and A. Renaut, 1990.
81. E. Laclau and C. Mouffe, 1985, 1.
82. The shift in critical theory from its more economistic moments to its current concerns with culture, aesthetics, art, and representation is addressed by P. Anderson, 1990, 85–138.
83. Z. Bauman, 1992, 187–88. See also Z. Bauman, 1988, 217–37.
84. Ibid.
85. Contrary to my position, Turner argues that the relationship of postmodern theory to radical politics is problematic depending on how one views the modernist project and its relationship to traditionalism. See B. S. Turner, 1990, 10.
86. This is not meant to suggest a similarity in approach as with Foucault or Derrida, for example. Fairly obviously, both these theorists attack modernity from radically different perspectives, the former with the use of psychoanalytics and the latter-via-textual deconstruction. Needless to say, these are very different methods. Rather, I am simply suggesting a similarity in the practical intent that each aims to achieve: a disruption in the project of modernity.
87. The term *organonist* I use derivatively from the Greek *Organon*, referring to the body of writings by Aristotle of the same title. Aristotle used the word to

refer to a process or series of steps leading toward knowledge, particularly the "problem of knowledge: what it is, how it is acquired, how it is guaranteed to be true, how expanded and systematized." Aristotle's organon, then, developed a system of reasoning or logic as an instrument of thought which became the basis of the Western intellectual tradition and valorized in reason and logic. See H. Tendennick and E. S. Forster, eds., 1938.

88. As quoted in A. Wellmer, 1985, 338.
89. Ibid.
90. M. Ryan, 1988, 559; P. Rabinow and W. M. Sullivan, 1979, 1.
91. As quoted in C. Brown, 1994c, 216.
92. R. J. Bernstein, 1988, 25; A. Wellmer, 1985, 341.
93. D. Harvey, 1991, 41. See also the article by R. J. Bernstein, 1986, 186–210. See also the excellent collection of essays in M. Hollis and S. Lukes, eds., 1982.
94. R. Rorty, 1980, 9–13. See also J. Margolis, 1986.
95. J. Trimbur and M. Holt, 1992, 73.
96. J. F. Lyotard, 1989, 314.
97. This is a central theme not only in the work of Lyotard but, more obviously, Foucault. See M. Foucault, 1984a, 32–75, 239–56.
98. A category, incidentally, that postmodernists often see the preserve of white males, exclusionary of ethnic, religious, linguistic minorities, and women, etc.
99. C. Brown, 1994c, 216.
100. Ibid., 229.
101. Stanley Aronowitz as quoted in W. Brown, 1991, 67.
102. Ibid.
103. Ibid.
104. Ibid., 70.
105. R. C. Holub, 1991, 143; A. Wellmer, 1985, 339.
106. S. Best and D. Kellner, 1991, 4. On the emergence of a spatial dialectic, see E. W. Soja, 1990.
107. M. Foucault, 1988, 104. Despite this statement, Foucault was at pains to point out later in his work that his project was not concerned with the phenomena of power, but rather, he wrote, "My objective, instead, has been to create a history of the different modes by which, in our culture, human beings are made subjects. My work has dealt with three modes of objectification which transform human beings into subjects." M. Foucault, 1984b, 417.
108. M. Foucault, 1984a, 51. See also M. Foucault, 1980.
109. S. Best and D. Kellner, 1991, 57.
110. W. Brown, 1991, 70.
111. D. Hebdige, 1988, 199.
112. M. Ryan, 1988, 560.
113. Ibid.
114. R. C. Holub, 1991, 135; D. Harvey, 1991, 52. See also J. Habermas, 1984.
115. As quoted in R. Rorty, 1991b, 151.

116. As quoted in M. Donougho, 1992, 71.
117. M. A. Rose, 1992b, 41.
118. D. Harvey, 1991, 49.
119. C. Norris, 1986, 63.
120. S. Best and D. Kellner, 1991, 4.
121. An excellent account of Rorty's position, particularly his mixture of poststructuralism and philosophic pragmatism, is found in Wolin's chapter entitled "Recontextualizing Neopragmatism: The Political Implications of Richard Rorty's Antifoundationalism." See R. Wolin, 1992, 149–69.
122. J. Trimbur and M. Holt, 1992, 80–83; R. Rorty, 1980, 158–59, 163. See also R. Rorty, 1982, 3–18. Notice that Rortyean postmodernism does not eschew rationality or logic but embraces them as a means of conversation and a yardstick by which participants in the conversation engage in ongoing inquiry, discourse, rebuttal, and the generation of new theory-knowledge. In fairness to Rorty, this position distinguishes him from the more virulent subversive postmodernists of the Continental school—a position that Rorty himself is keen to point out, calling his variety of postmodernism "postmodernist bourgeois liberalism." See R. Rorty, 1983, 583–89.
123. J. O'Neill, 1990, 78.
124. J. Trimbur and M. Holt, 1992, 81.
125. Logocentrism is interchangeably used with Western metaphysics, denoting the tendency in Western rationality to think in terms of dialectics and binary oppositions. Thus, the penchant to establish binary opposites as in hierarchy/anarchy, positive/negative, present/absent, etc. is representative of logocentric practices that, notes J. Culler, "assumes the priority of the first term and conceives the second in relation to it." More importantly, though, logocentric practices establish value patterns where the first term, the logos, as in hierarchy, for example, is seen as superior to its binary equivalent anarchy. See the discussion in J. Culler, 1982, 93. See also R. Rorty, 1991a, 107–18.
126. T. McCarthy, 1989–90, 153; M. Donougho, 1992, 71.
127. Derrida as quoted in T. McCarthy, 1989–90, 147.
128. P. M. Rosenau, 1992.
129. C. Norris, 1988, 147.
130. Of these themes, particularly the move toward inclusivity of marginal groups, B. Turner notes the corollary of postmodernism with liberalism: "The postmodern critique of hierarchy, grand narratives, unitary notions of authority, or the bureaucratic imposition of official values has a certain parallel with the principles of toleration of difference in the liberal tradition." Perhaps, then, we are dealing with a radicalized liberalism rather than a fundamentally new theoretical lexicon. See B. S. Turner, 1990, 11.
131. C. Norris, 1990, 147.
132. E. D. Hirsch, Jr., 1976, 13.
133. Ibid.
134. A. Callinicos, 1989, 2.
135. Ibid., 170.
136. E. D. Hirsch, Jr., 1976, 13.

137. A. Stephanson, 1988, 27.
138. J. O'Neill, 1990, 77–78.
139. Ibid., 78.
140. Outside of International Relations, such work is beginning to emerge. See, for example, the recent work of S. Lash and J. Urry, 1994.
141. V. S. Peterson, 1992b, 184.
142. R. K. Ashley and R. B. J. Walker, 1990a, 411.
143. A. Callinicos, 1989, 1.
144. The cult of political correctness, especially as it relates to the university, is told eloquently in two essays by A. Bloom entitled "The Crisis of Liberal Education" and "The Democratization of the University" in A. Bloom, 1990. See also the recent observations by M. Edmundson of the University of Virginia: M. Edmundson, 1997, 39–49.
145. A. Linklater, 1992, 77–100.

Chapter Four: Richard K. Ashley and the Subversion of International Political Theory

1. J. Der Derian and M. Shapiro, eds., 1989, ix.
2. While I affix the postmodernist label to the work of Ashley and Walker, it should be noted that, as far as my readings confirm, Ashley does not use the postmodernist title and identifies himself as a poststructuralist. Moreover, at various points he displays a liking for describing himself as a critical social theorist and at various other junctures refers to his critical technique as critical social theory. This, I presume, is intended to establish some affiliation between his work and the writings and practices of the Frankfurt school of critical social inquiry. If this is the case, however, it is confusing, since the Frankfurt school is surely more attuned to a modernist-rationalist understanding of social practices associated with the work of Lukacs, Horkheimer, and more recently Macuse, Habermas, and Offe. See, for example, the collection of edited works in P. Connerton, 1976. For bibliographic and background information on the intellectual works and careers of Ashley and Walker, see M. Griffiths, 1999.
3. Y. Lapid, 1989b, 235.
4. Ibid., 236.
5. R. O. Keohane, 1989, 249; 1988, 382.
6. Mario Bunge as quoted in Y. Lapid, 1989b, 235–36. See also J. Der Derian, 1988, 189.
7. R. K. Ashley, 1986, 282.
8. Ibid., 284.
9. In fact, these contributions can be counted on one hand. As far as I am aware, only four short articles have dealt directly with appraising critically Ashley's contributions. See, for example, the excellent, although brief, discussion in R. D. Spegele, 1992, 147–82; R. Roy, 1988, 77–83; W. E. Connolly, 1989, 323–42. See also a rather sympathetic critique, R. B. J. Walker, 1988, 84–88; R. G. Gilpin, 1986, 301–21. And although concerned with a general assessment of the utility of postmodernist approaches to international theory, Porter has also addressed

Ashley's contributions to international theory. See T. Porter, 1994, 105–27. A very brief discussion is also contained in J. George, 1994, 171–76.

10. D. U. Gregory, 1989a, xiii.

11. See R. Maghroori and B. Ramberg, 1982. See also Y. Lapid, 1989b, 235–54.

12. R. G. Gilpin, 1986, 303.

13. D. U. Gregory, 1989a, xiii.

14. J. Der Derian, 1992.

15. And where coauthored, with Ashley's primary intellectual collaborator, R. B. J. Walker. However, it should be noted that in doing so I am not implying a similarity in their respective approaches. Indeed, it is not my intention here to belittle the contributions of R. B. J. Walker or to leave the impression that he is Ashley's intellectual sidekick. Walker's solo-authored writings and contributions to the Third Debate tend to be of a very different nature, one I personally find more appealing than Ashley's contributions. Notwithstanding this, however, in dealing with Ashley's writings and his collaborative projects with Walker, I tend to treat them as one and the same. To what extent these collaborative projects represent more of Ashley's influence than Walker's, I cannot determine. Suffice it to say that there are very real differences between them but not, it would seem, in their collaborative endeavors.

16. In this early phase, 1980–85, I consider the following works in chronological order: R. K. Ashley, 1980; 1982, 204–36; 1983a, 495–535; 1983b, 463–96; 1984, 225–86. In the second phase, post-1985 to the present, I consider R. K. Ashley, 1987, 403–34; 1988a, 88–102; 1988b, 227–62; 1989, 259–321; R. K. Ashley and R. B. J. Walker, 1990a, 367–416; 1990b, 259–68; R. K. Ashley, 1991, 37–69. It should be noted that in Ashley's second, subversive phase, there is a considerable period of silence after 1991, punctuated only by his recent publication, R. K. Ashley, 1996. This most recent work and the tradition of scholarship which, I argue, it continues, is addressed in chapter 6.

17. Indeed, how one reads Ashley will largely determine how adequately one understands him. There are, I argue, two ways of reading Ashley. The first approaches his writings individually, assumes each work to be a self-contained and separate treatise and assesses the intellectual strengths and weaknesses of these works on the basis of this closed hermeneutic. On this reading, much of Ashley's writings appear confusing, thematically unrelated, and disparate. Witness, for example, the commentaries and critiques by R. Gilpin and F. Kratochwil in R. O. Keohane's *Neorealism and Its Critics,* 1986, where Ashley's article, "The Poverty of Neorealism," is treated in isolation from his preceding work. The second way of reading Ashley, however, is more rewarding. It approaches his work not as a series of discrete writings but constitutive of a larger project, a project as grand as any that Ashley would otherwise dismiss as metatheory or metanarrative. My point, simply, is that Ashley must be read in his entirety if he is to be understood properly, since his works are contributing chapters, so to speak, systemically related to an ideological commitment that is Ashley's modus operandi.

18. R. K. Ashley, 1980.

19. Ibid., ix.

20. Ibid.
21. Ibid., 210.
22. Ibid., 209.
23. The concepts of rationalism and behaviorism employed here are not to be confused as one and the same. Rather, rationalism refers to an epistemological knowledge system that appeals to reason as a means to truth validation. Behaviorism, on the other hand, can be thought of as the methodological application of this epistemology in applied settings.
24. J. L. Richardson, 1991, 31.
25. These concepts Ashley referred to as situational analysis.
26. This was the implicit project of the behaviorists in international political theory and of the behaviorist revolution in the social sciences generally. See J. L. Richardson, 1991, 32.
27. R. K. Ashley, 1980, 213.
28. Ibid.
29. Hans Morgenthau as quoted in ibid., 212.
30. Ibid.
31. Ibid., 213.
32. Ibid.
33. Or what Ashley would now call modernist discourse or positivism.
34. R. O. Keohane, 1988, 382–83, 388, 390–93.
35. It is somewhat amusing to note that after recommending such a savage overhaul of the reflectivist approach, Keohane then feels compelled to hope for the eventual synthesis of the rationalist and reflectivist approaches. One can only imagine what there might be left to synthesize! See R. O. Keohane, 1988, 393.
36. J. Der Derian, 1992, 8.
37. R. K. Ashley, 1980, 214.
38. Ibid., xv.
39. Ibid., 208, xv.
40. Ibid., 217.
41. On structuration theory see the work of A. Giddens, 1986.
42. R. K. Ashley, 1980, 216–17.
43. Ibid., 216.
44. Ibid.
45. Ibid., 208.
46. Ibid., 219.
47. Ibid., 214–15.
48. These works, in chronological order, are R. K. Ashley, 1981, 204–36; 1983a, 495–535; 1983b, 463–96; and 1986, 225–86.
49. See R. K. Ashley, 1986, 225–86; 1983b, 463–64.
50. R. K. Ashley, 1981, 204. See, for example, the writings of J. Habermas, 1991. See also the discussion in the edited volume by R. J. Bernstein, 1988.
51. R. K. Ashley, 1981, 204.
52. Ibid., 208.
53. Ibid.
54. Ibid., 207.

55. Karl Mannheim (1893–1947) postulated a theory of the sociology of knowledge that essentially understood knowledge as socially constituted in respect of membership to particular social groups, social classes, sects, and competition among these groups. In this way, Mannheim understood knowledge and truth as merely relativistic constructs embedded in beliefs that were themselves socially located and perfunctory of specific (material, ideological, competitive, cultural) interests. Consequently, Mannheim argued that all knowledge was relative, that there was no such thing as true beliefs, only accepted beliefs reflecting socially embedded tradition. There existed no socially independent criteria of truth since all knowledge-generating agents were socially constituted and biased. See, for example, K. Mannheim, 1986. Here Mannheim operationalized his theory with respect to the conservative classes and their beliefs. See also K. Mannheim, 1952.

56. R. W. Cox, 1986, 207. This rather trite observation reduces all knowledge to a power/materiality nexus, denying theory, or knowledge generation generally, any autonomy from the mode of production in which it operates. Power and materiality become determinist of theory, interpretation and understanding; theorists, we might also assume, become no more than automatons in the service of some mode of production. The position seems somewhat absurd, especially since Cox's dictum would also implicate his theoretical efforts in similar unvirtuous pursuits!

57. R. K. Ashley, 1981, 208, 215.

58. Ibid., 211.

59. Jurgen Habermas as quoted in ibid., 210.

60. Ibid., 212.

61. Ibid., 211–12.

62. Ibid., 212–13.

63. It is interesting and at times confusing to observe Ashley's love-hate relationship with Hans Morgenthau. At various points in Ashley's writings, for example, Morgenthau is upheld as the pillar of practical realism or classical realism, a form of realism that Ashley in his heroic phase implored his readers to return to. At other times, however, Ashley uses Morgenthau as an example of the nemesis of technical realism or scientific realism, tersely rejecting his work for its pretense to science and its use of positivist epistemology. Doubtless, readers will be confused justifiably as to which Morgenthau it is who is under consideration at any one moment in time, since Ashley fails to periodize Morgenthau's work or categorize his writings into discrete intellectual phases. Rather, the only explanation Ashley offers is to note that Morgenthau's "work . . . is exemplary . . . since both aspects ('practical' and 'technical' realism) appear in his work." One is left with the impression that Morgenthau is, at one and the same time, a technical, practical, scientific, positivist, and hermeneutic realist! See R. K. Ashley, 1981, 210.

64. Hans Morgenthau as quoted in ibid., 213. See also H. J. Morgenthau, 1958; 1967.

65. R. K. Ashley, 1981, 214.

66. Ibid., 222. A more thorough discussion of practical realism can be found in R. K. Ashley, 1984, 264–81.

67. Hans Morgenthau as quoted by R. K. Ashley, 1981, 214.
68. R. K. Ashley, 1983b, 480; R. K. Ashley, 1984, 279.
69. Hans Morgenthau as quoted in R. K. Ashley, 1984, 279.
70. Carr further notes, "Economics can be treated neither as a minor accessory of history, nor as an independent science in the light of which history can be interpreted." He continues, "Much confusion would be saved by a general return to the term 'political economy.'" See E. H. Carr, 1964, 114–20.
71. K. Polanyi, 1968, 57.
72. R. K. Ashley, 1981, 208.
73. See K. N. Waltz, 1979.
74. Kenneth N. Waltz as quoted in R. K. Ashley, 1981, 217.
75. R. K. Ashley, 1983a, 528.
76. R. K. Ashley, 1981, 235.
77. R. K. Ashley, 1984, 248.
78. Ibid., 250.
79. Ibid.
80. K. N. Waltz, 1986, 37.
81. See R. K. Ashley, 1984, 238–42; 1983b, 483.
82. R. K. Ashley, 1983b, 481.
83. R. K. Ashley, 1984, 239, 248. See also the discussion in E. F. Keyman, 1994, 153–81.
84. K. N. Waltz as quoted in R. K. Ashley, 1984, 256. The problem of generative structuralism and of Waltz's structuralist thesis is addressed by A. E. Wendt, 1987. See also R. Little, 1985; D. Dessler, 1989; and Wendt's recent ongoing contribution to this debate: A. E. Wendt, 1992.
85. R. K. Ashley, 1984, 258.
86. Ibid., 260.
87. Ibid., 260–61.
88. Ibid.
89. Ibid., 261.
90. See, for example, R. K. Ashley and R. B. J. Walker, 1990a, 396–402. See also R. K. Ashley, 1987, 403–34.
91. See the comments in R. K. Ashley and R. B. J. Walker, 1990a, 396–97.
92. R. K. Ashley, 1980, 226n., 251n., 317n.
93. Ibid., 226.
94. R. K. Ashley, 1981, 209.
95. Ibid., 208; 1980, xv.
96. Arguably, he also embraced many of the concepts termed post-Marxist. See, for example, E. Laclau and C. Mouffe, 1985.
97. See R. D. Spegele, 1992, 166n. The final transformation of Ashley from his "heroic" to subversive phase occurs with his 1987 publication: R. K. Ashley, 1987, 403–34. However, even by 1984 with the publication of "Poverty of Neorealism," we observe a subtle but encroaching commitment to the influence of Michel Foucault vis-à-vis Habermas.
98. Hoffman has also offered a useful, albeit restrictive, means of conceptualizing these contending traditions in critical scholarship. For Hoffman, critical

scholarship can be divided into two traditions. The first, critical interpretivism, is "characterised by a 'minimal foundationalism' which accepts that a contingent universalism is possible and may be necessary in both ethical and explicatory fields." The second, radical interpretivism, disparages "even the possibility or desirability of a minimal or contingent foundationalism" and adopts a deconstructionist position, seeing world politics in terms of textual narratives and intertexts. This classification, then, would characterize Ashley's "heroic" phase as critical interpretivism, where a contingent or limited foundationalism is evident amid his universal aspirations to global transformation, revolution, and emancipation, but in a critical rubric broadly conceived as postmodernist. See M. Hoffman, 1991, 169–85.

99. W. E. Connolly, 1989, 326–27.
100. R. K. Ashley, 1981, 207.
101. Ibid., 231.
102. R. K. Ashley and R. B. J. Walker, 1990b, 264–65; R. K. Ashley, 1987, 428.
103. R. K. Ashley, 1981, 234.
104. R. K. Ashley and R. B. J. Walker, 1990a, 397.
105. See T. Hobbes, 1968, 161. See also J. J. Rousseau, 1947.
106. R. K. Ashley, 1980, ix. Ashley's hostility toward the state as an instrument of control and a realm of power is more fully addressed in Ashley, 1988b, 227–62.
107. R. K. Ashley, 1987, 428–29.
108. R. K. Ashley and R. B. J. Walker, 1990a, 411.
109. R. K. Ashley, 1984, 240.
110. A. Bloom, 1987, 218.
111. See K. Marx and F. Engels, 1977.
112. R. K. Ashley, 1984, 275, 281.
113. R. K. Ashley, 1981, 234.
114. R. K. Ashley and R. B. J. Walker, 1990a, 397.
115. R. K. Ashley, 1984, 286.
116. Fred Halliday has gone further, suggesting that international theory has exhibited a "general shyness about the concept of capitalism" and a reticence to theorize its interrelationship with the rise of nation-states in order to offer a more thorough account of the development of the state system and its dynamics. See F. Halliday, 1993, 22–24.
117. T. Porter, 1994, 118–19.
118. See, for example, the excellent discussions in H. R. Alker, Jr., 1992; C. W. Kegley, Jr., 1993. See also F. W. Riggs, 1994.
119. I am thinking here of many of the cruder neo-Marxist theories that emerged during the 1960s and early 1970s. For example A. G. Frank's dependency theory, I. Wallerstein's world system theory, Emmanuel's theory of unequal exchange, and theories of economic imperialism. See, for example, A. Emmanuel, 1972; A. G. Frank, 1969; I. M. Wallerstein, 1976; S. Amin, 1976; H. Magdoff, 1969.
120. R. D. Spegele, 1992, 156.

121. R. K. Ashley, 1983a, 501.
122. T. Porter, 1994, 121.
123. See, for example, the discussion in R. Higgott, 1991, 394–426.

Chapter Five: Continental Drift

1. J. McGowan, 1991, 13.
2. Michel Foucault as quoted in S. Best and D. Kellner, 1991, 46–49.
3. Ibid., 50–51. The aesthetic dimension of power is evident in Ashley's dictum that "works of power . . . are also works of art." See R. K. Ashley, 1991, 61.
4. S. Best and D. Kellner, 1991, 50. A frequently cited example of this is the Bolshevik Revolution of 1917. While enacted under the auspices of reason and the Enlightenment principles of equality and liberation, it ended up creating new repressive rationalities in the name of the Soviet State and socialism.
5. Ibid., 57–58.
6. R. K. Ashley, 1988b, 254.
7. Ibid. Elsewhere, Ashley notes, "Put more simply, modern discourse presupposes an unexamined metaphysical faith in its capacity to speak a sovereign voice of suprahistorical truth." R. K. Ashley, 1989, 264.
8. R. K. Ashley, 1988b, 228–29.
9. Ibid.
10. R. K. Ashley, 1987, 411.
11. J. McGowan, 1991, 14; H. J. Silverman, 1990, 1; R. D. Spegele, 1992, 148.
12. R. K. Ashley and R. B. J. Walker, 1990a, 368; 1990b, 264; R. K. Ashley, 1988b, 228. See also R. K. Ashley, 1989, 271–72.
13. R. K. Ashley, 1988b, 253–54. See also R. K. Ashley, 1991, 56–63.
14. R. K. Ashley, 1988b, 250–51. See also R. K. Ashley, 1989, particularly pages 272–84, where Ashley rejects monological interpretation for radical poststructuralism.
15. R. K. Ashley, 1987, 408.
16. Ibid., 408–9.
17. Ibid., 409, 411.
18. Ibid., 419.
19. Ibid.
20. Ibid., 421.
21. R. K. Ashley, 1991, 67–68.
22. Ibid., 67.
23. R. D. Spegele, 1992, 148–49.
24. R. K. Ashley, 1987, 428.
25. R. K. Ashley and R. B. J. Walker, 1990b, 264.
26. R. K. Ashley and R. B. J. Walker, 1990a, 411, 413.
27. Ibid., 410–11.
28. In particular, *International Studies Quarterly, International Organization*, and *Millennium: Journal of International Studies*.
29. R. K. Ashley and R. B. J. Walker, 1990a, 411.

30. "Special Issue," 1990.
31. See M. Walzer, 1986; R. K. Ashley and R. B. J. Walker, 1990a, 390.
32. R. G. Gilpin, 1986, 301.
33. Ibid., 313.
34. C. Brown, 1992, 226–27.
35. T. Porter, 1994, 115–16.
36. R. G. Gilpin, 1986, 301.
37. J. N. Rosenau, 1980a, 28.
38. K. J. Holsti, 1993, 407.
39. T. Porter, 1994, 115.
40. See A. Giddens, 1986. See also A. E. Wendt, 1987, 335–71; 1992, 391–426.
41. T. Porter, 1994, 115.
42. C. Brown, 1992, 237.
43. W. E. Connolly, 1989, 339.
44. R. K. Ashley, 1987, 408.
45. R. Spegele, 1992, 165.
46. C. Brown, 1992, 216.
47. Ibid., 213, 216–17.
48. Ibid., 236.
49. Cited in ibid., 219.
50. R. K. Ashley, 1987, 428.
51. S. Best and D. Kellner, 1991, 53.
52. Michel Foucault as quoted in ibid.
53. See M. Wallack 1994, 203–4.
54. R. D. Spegele, 1992, 176.
55. Ibid., 174, 177.
56. Ibid., 158–59.
57. Ibid.
58. A. Bloom, 1987, 222.
59. Ibid., 217.
60. Ibid., 220.
61. If we follow Bloom's reasoning, we might also characterize them as pragmatic Marxists armed with the ruthlessness of Nietzschean weaponry.
62. A. Bloom, 1987, 220.
63. J. Bowers, 1992, 111.
64. R. K. Ashley, 1984, 281.
65. Indeed, I would go further and argue that critiques emanating from outside the postmodernist school in international relations theory are generally either little considered, judged incommensurate, or become inaudible to postmodernists since many fail to share their ideological commitments or employ the specialized nomenclature required to gain entry to that discourse.
66. W. E. Connolly, 1989, 337.
67. Richard Ashley as quoted in ibid., 335–36.
68. Ibid., 336

Chapter Six: Feminist Revisions of International Relations

1. C. Sylvester, 1993, 77. See also M. Zalewski, 1994a, 225.
2. C. Wight, 1996, 293.
3. J. B. Elshtain, 1987, 90–91.
4. Mary O'Brien as quoted in M. Zalewski, 1993, 17.
5. J. B. Elshtain, 1987, 91.
6. S. J. Ship, 1994, 131–33.
7. Sylvester's sense of exclusion is related to us when she notes that exclusion "is especially evident in the special issue of *International Studies Quarterly* (vol. 34, no. 3, 1990), entitled Speaking the Language of Exile: Dissidence in International Studies, where women are mentioned but our dilemmas of gender are not considered important enough to warrant article-length treatment." C. Sylvester, 1993, 87.
8. Marysia Zalewski discussing the work of Christine Sylvester in M. Zalewski, 1994b, 421, 417.
9. C. Sylvester, 1994, 8–9.
10. C. Sylvester, 1993, 87.
11. A. Linklater, 1992.
12. C. Sylvester, 1994, 210–11.
13. C. Wight, 1996, 293.
14. V. S. Peterson, 1992b, 191.
15. V. S. Peterson, 1997, 185–206.
16. C. Sylvester, 1994, 4, 211.
17. Ibid., 9. Similar sentiments are expressed by Halliday when he advances what he terms the invisibilization thesis. See F. Halliday, 1988, 420.
18. R. B. J. Walker, 1992, 179. Despite Walker's assertion, Marcus insists that, in the humanities at least, it is philosophy and musicology and in the sciences, mathematics that have "been the fields most zealously guarded" and gender-blind disciplines. In comparison to these, the case could be made that International Relations is a little more progressive than Walker's glib remark would otherwise suggest. See J. Marcus, 1982, 218.
19. H. Caldicott, 1984, 296. See also the discussion in C. A. MacKinnon, 1982, 1–30.
20. H. Caldicott, 1984, 296.
21. Ibid., 294.
22. Ibid., 306
23. Of course, not all feminists subscribe to such pseudobiological arguments. Enloe makes an excellent point when she argues that if men were naturally aggressive there would not need to be so much emphasis placed on inculcating aggressive/violent behavior in military training. That there is suggests that violence and aggression are socially inscribed. See C. Enloe, 1987, 526–47. See also the discussion in J. J. Pettman, 1996, 92–97.
24. The shape of missiles, of course, is widely reputed to be connected to aerodynamic laws! H. Caldicott, 1984, 296.

25. V. S. Peterson, 1997, 185–206.
26. J. Krause, 1996, 106–7.
27. J. J. Pettman, 1999.
28. Henry Nau as quoted in J. A. Tickner, 1996, 147.
29. C. Enloe, 1989.
30. C. Sylvester, 1994, 4, 211.
31. M. Zalewski, 1994b, 408.

32. These terms have been coined by Jones and Zalewski. See A. Jones, 1996, 405–29; M. Zalewski, 1994b, 407–23. See also the discussion in A. Assiter, 1996. Perhaps the most well-known and now widely invoked categorization of various feminist approaches is Harding's, who delineated four types of feminism: feminist epistemologies, feminist empiricism, feminist standpoint, and feminist postmodernism. See S. Harding, 1986.

33. A. Jones, 1996, 409.

34. C. Sylvester quoting C. Jencks and R. B. J. Walker; C. Sylvester, 1994, 12. The denaturalization of femininity and masculinity and their reinscription as socially constructed categories is explained succinctly by MacKinnon, who writes: "Implicit in feminist theory is a parallel argument: the molding, direction and expression of sexuality organizes society into two sexes—women and men—which division underlies the totality of social relations. Sexuality is that social process which creates, organizes, expresses and directs desire, creating the social beings we know as women and men, as their relations create society. As work is to Marxism, sexuality to feminism is socially constructed yet constructing, universal as activity yet historically specific, jointly comprised of matter and mind. As the organized expropriation of the work of some for the benefit of others defines a class—workers—the organized expropriation of the sexuality of some for the use of others defines the sex, women." See the discussion in C. A. MacKinnon, 1982, 2.

35. C. Sylvester, 1994, 52. The deconstruction of women is further addressed in S. Bordo, 1994, 458–82.

36. Elsewhere, Sylvester's categories of various feminisms also include feminist empiricism. See C. Sylvester, 1990, 230–53.

37. C. Sylvester, 1994, 13.
38. C. Sylvester, 1996a, 257.
39. C. Sylvester, 1994, 1–2.
40. Ibid., 213, 216.
41. C. Sylvester, 1993, 92.
42. C. Sylvester, 1994, 216.
43. Ibid., 215–16.
44. Ibid., 218–19.
45. Ibid., 211.
46. Ibid., 212.
47. Ibid., 212–13.
48. C. Sylvester, 1993, 92.
49. C. Sylvester, 1994, 216.
50. Ibid., 187.
51. G. Kirk as quoted in ibid., 187–88.

52. C. Sylvester, 1994, 196
53. Ibid., 198.
54. J. J. Pettman, 1996, 105.
55. J. True, 1996, 215.
56. M. Zalewski, 1994b, 421.
57. Ibid., 420.
58. Ibid., 418.
59. C. Enloe, 1989, 3.
60. Ibid., 11.
61. M. Zalewski, 1993, 17.
62. C. Sylvester, 1993, 86.
63. Ibid., 80.
64. M. Zalewski, 1993, 15.

65. Ibid., 16. Representative of the standpoint feminist position in International Relations is J. A. Tickner, 1991, 27–40.

66. M. Zalewski, 1993, 18.
67. R. Grant and K. Newland, 1991, 4.

68. C. Sylvester, 1993, 89. Interestingly, Sylvester does not problematize the category of women here by enveloping the word in inverted commas. This might be explained by the fact that she is discussing the relative merits of standpoint feminism and, in this context, talks of women as do standpoint feminists.

69. C. Enloe, 1989, 197.
70. J. True, 1996, 215.

71. Jean Bethke Elshtain discussing the work of Carol Gilligan. J. B. Elshtain, 1982, 144–45.

72. C. H. Sommers, 1994, 74. To be fair, not all standpoint feminists justify the ontological centrality of women-centered research on the basis of women's innate intellectual or moral characteristics. Sylvester is less convinced that women are better knowers because of their sex so much as the social positions they occupy by virtue of their marginalization. Commenting on standpoint feminism, Sylvester writes: the "overreaching analogy is men-women with master-slave, where the slave is a structural extension of the master's will, yet the master thinks the relationship is really co-determining, with slaves creating masters and masters simultaneously creating slaves. In Dyads like this, however well intentioned one may be, the real relations of humans with each other and with the natural world are not visible. To see them, one must look from the perspective of the subordinate, not the master." See the discussion in C. Sylvester, 1990, 241–45.

73. M. Zalewski, 1993, 15.
74. V. S. Peterson, 1992b, 197.
75. C. Sylvester quoting David Harvey: C. Sylvester, 1994, 61.
76. V. S. Peterson and A. S. Runyan, 1993.
77. Ibid., 15.
78. C. Enloe, 1989, 195. See S. M. Okin, 1989.
79. J. J. Pettman, 1996, 5–6.
80. C. Enloe, 1989, 195. See also the discussion in R. Grant, 1991, 8–26.
81. C. Enloe, 1989, 195.

82. V. S. Peterson, 1992a, 46.
83. Ibid.
84. Ibid.; V. S. Peterson and A. S. Runyan, 1993, 149.
85. V. S. Peterson quoting Lori Heise: V. S. Peterson, 1992a, 46.
86. C. Enloe, 1989, 123.
87. J. True, 1996, 234–35.
88. V. S. Peterson quoting Lori Heise. V. S. Peterson, ed., 1992c, 12–13. See also the discussion in V. S. Peterson and A. S. Runyan, 1993, 42–44.
89. C. Sylvester, 1990, 239–40.
90. Catherine MacKinnon as quoted in C. H. Sommers, 1994, 231.
91. Ibid., 275.
92. A. Jones, 1996, 429.
93. C. Sylvester, 1994, 211, 226.
94. J. True, 1996, 218.
95. See, for example, the recent edited collection by Y. Lapid and F. Kratochwil, 1996.
96. J. J. Pettman, 1996, xi.
97. C. Sylvester, 1994, 17–19.
98. Christine Sylvester quoting Joan Scott in C. Sylvester, 1996a, 262.
99. Ibid., 271.
100. M. Zalewski and C. Enloe, 1995, 282.
101. V. S. Peterson, 1993, 4.
102. Richard H. Brown, as quoted in ibid., 3.
103. Feminists, of course, insist that they do not ontologically privilege gender but use gender as a variable for understanding the configuration of power relations. As G. Pollock puts it, "It is a common misunderstanding that feminism is a perspective or approach which prioritizes gender over all other structures of oppression. I would argue that by focusing on issues not only of sex and gender but of sexual difference, feminism explores the complex configurations of power and difference which do indeed specify the question of sexual difference, but not exclusively." My objection stands, however. This position seems somewhat nonsensical, suggesting that while gender is not essentialized it is essential to understanding such relationships! To make the point further, Pollock employs the standard variety of postmodern speak, suggesting "feminism signifies a set of positions, not an essence; a critical practice, not a doxa; a dynamic and self-critical response and intervention, not a platform." I remain unconvinced that this in fact clarifies anything at all other than make Pollock's position yet more opaque. See G. Pollock, 1993, 98, 100.
104. M. Zalewski and C. Enloe, 1995, 283.
105. J. R. Martin, 1994, 647. We might also ask why amid the discourse of ever-emergent identities the issue of nationalism and national identity is so absent from feminist postmodern discourses? Indeed, why is nationalism and national identity rejected as unimportant when, for example, John Hutchinson and Anthony Smith note that in nationalism there is "power, of national loyalties and identities over those of even class, gender and race." See the discussion in J. Hutchison and A. D. Smith, eds., 1994.

106. Marysia Zalewski and Cynthia Enloe discussing the work of Ann Tickner. See M. Zalewski and C. Enloe, 1995, 284. See also J. A. Tickner, 1992.

107. J. R. Martin, 1994, 631.

108. Ibid., 650.

109. Ibid., 631.

110. Ibid., 654.

111. N. Soguk, 1996, 285.

112. D. Stienstra, 1994, 3.

113. Ibid., 3.

114. On the reification of difference, Patricia Lança makes the poignant, if stinging, observation that "The worst sin of both types of cultivators of these particular poisoned fruits of post-modernism is that they are attacking the essential unity of the human race. It is, after all, our capacity for rationality which goes hand in hand with the development of language, that brings people together." For Lança, all said and done, all of us are united by our basic capacity to reason, to think and communicate. Difference is thus really only a substructural set of variances on our essential commonalties whose importance is secondary and not constitutive of our human natures. See the discussion in P. Lança, 1996, 43.

115. B. Weiss, 1997 (March 18–22). "Reconstructing International/Intercultural Relations: Beyond Feminist Disturbances and Postmodern Deconstruction." Paper presented at the panel "Feminist Transformations of International Theory." 38th Annual Convention of the International Studies Association, Toronto, 8.

116. Ibid., 13.

117. M. Zalewski, 1997 (March 18–22). "Posthuman Bodies? Invasion, Erasure, Alienation." Paper presented to the International Studies Association Conference, Toronto, 20.

118. C. Enloe, 1989, 65.

119. Ibid., 68–71, 74.

120. M. Griffiths and T. O'Callaghan, 1999.

121. T. O'Callaghan, 1996. "The Real World of Normative Theory in International Relations." Mimeograph. Department of Politics, University of Adelaide, South Australia, 14.

122. See the discussion in A. Jones, 1996, 405–29.

123. Ibid., 423.

124. See, for example, U.S. Department of Justice, Bureau of Justice Statistics, Victimization Characteristics, http://www.ojusdoj.gov/bjs/cvict_v.htm.

125. This figure is somewhat higher than the FBI's Uniform Crime Report for 1990, which indicated that 102,560 women had been the victims of rape or attempted rape. See the discussion in C. H. Sommers, 1994, 209, 225. See also, for example, S. Donaldson, 1993.

126. C. Ringel, 1997, 2.

127. As quoted in L. Radford, 1996, 235. See also L. Schmittroth, 1991.

128. V. S. Peterson quoting Lori Heise. V. S. Peterson, 1992a, 46.

129. V. S. Peterson and A. S. Runyan, 1993, 158.

130. See, for example, D. Forrest, 1996. See also Amnesty International, 1993.

The findings by Jones are also instructive. Using a diverse collection of empirical evidence, he notes that during the era of the dirty war in Argentina, 70 percent of the victims who disappeared were male. Or, in the case of Nicaragua after the 1979 revolution, 93.4 percent of those killed in the insurrection were male. See A. Jones, 1996, 426–27.

131. See C. Enloe, 1993, 238–44.
132. A. Jones, 1996, 423–24.
133. Ibid., 423.
134. Christine Sylvester as quoted in ibid.
135. Ibid., 422.
136. V. S. Peterson and A. S. Runyan, 1993, 101.
137. Ibid.; A. Jones, 1996, 426–27n.
138. The mortality rate for men per one thousand of the population in developed countries is 3.37 compared to 1.50 for women, a female-to-male ratio of 0.45. See United Nations, 1995, 72 and also A. Jones, 1996, 423.
139. M. Henehan and M. Reid, 1997, 8.
140. C. Sylvester, 1996b, 12.
141. I am reminded at this juncture of a speech delivered to the Melbourne Writer's Festival by Germaine Greer, who, as Catharine Lumby reports, proclaimed the "revival of punk fashion featuring models with dark eye shadow and lipstick" as "evidence that girls' magazines encourage male violence." C. Lumby, 1997: 21.
142. C. Brown, 1997, 241.
143. J. True, 1996, 234–35.
144. T. Kando, 1996, 26–27.
145. P. Lança, 1996, 41.
146. T. G. Walsh, 1996, 36.
147. P. Lança, 1996, 42.
148. Ibid., 43.
149. M. A. Tetreault, 1997, 2–3.
150. The editors of the ISQ further note that "this information was communicated to the Committee and it is unfortunate that it evidently was not taken into consideration." See W. R. Thompson and B. Pollins, 1997, 4.
151. To these comments the editors of ISQ further note that "it is the current policy of ISQ to employ reviewers who share or, at least, do not reject out of hand the epistemological assumptions of submitted manuscripts. If submitted manuscripts are rejected at ISQ, it is usually because reviewers with similar orientations encountered serious problems with the manuscript and recommended against publication—and not because of glass ceiling gender bias or epistemological hostility." Ibid., 4.
152. See C. Sylvester, 1994; C. Enloe, 1989; V. S. Peterson and A. S. Runyan, 1993. Similarly, Zalewski, Enloe, and Sylvester have also been published in an edited volume for Cambridge University Press. See their chapters in S. Smith et al., 1996.
153. This example is taken from the American Political Science Association Personnel Service Newsletter, January 1997, vol. 4, no. 5: 9, for a faculty position at

Colgate University in International Relations. Examples of such wording are, of course, numerous.

154. "This overall positive placement record for 1995–1996 American minority doctoral students is consistent with the placement experience of their cohorts in the last several years." S. Mann, 1997, 604–5.

155. C. Sylvester, 1996a, 256–57.

156. M. Zalewski, 1996, 349.

157. C. Enloe, 1993, 195.

158. See, for example, the contribution of K. Ferguson, 1996, 435–54.

159. M. Zalewski, 1996, 346

Chapter Seven: In Defense of Theory

1. See J. Bartelson, 1995, 83–84.

2. S. Smith, 1996, 12.

3. R. K. Ashley, 1996, 244–47; K. Booth and M. Zalewski, 1996, 244–47.

4. Ibid., 250. See also C. Wight, 1996, 292.

5. K. J. Holsti, 1985. One has only to look at the very different traditions and types of scholarship to emerge from, for example, the United Kingdom (particularly the London School of Economics and Political Science, but also the University of Wales at Aberystwyth), compared to mainstream theoretical approaches indicative of North American perspectives—what Long recently referred to as the Harvard School and neoliberal institutionalism. See D. Long, 1995, 489–505.

6. See the discussion in R. K. Ashley, 1991, 37–69.

7. R. Rorty as quoted in J. Saurin, 1995, 244.

8. E. H. Carr, 1964, 11. See also the discussion in R. M. A. Crawford, 1996, 9–38.

9. Richard Rorty as quoted in J. Saurin, 1995, 244.

10. M. Zalewski, 1996, 351–52.

11. Ibid., 352.

12. K. J. Holsti, 1999.

13. There is a five-year gap between Ashley's publications: 1991, "The State of the Discipline," 37–69, and 1996, "The Achievements of Poststructuralism." For some, this represents a period of silence, one often seen as deleterious to the evolution of postmodern perspectives in as much as these theorists were deprived of a vanguard just as critical debates were gaining momentum in International Relations.

14. R. K. Ashley, 1996, 248.

15. Ibid.

16. The notion of Ashley's silence was related to me by Professor Nicholas Onuf of the Florida International University, Miami, who suggested, in private correspondence, that "Ashley's silence is heroic in its way—silence is the ultimate consequence of Ashley's program." The fact, however, that he has now written again, supposes either that this silence was inconsequential to his intellectual program or unrelated to it.

17. R. K. Ashley, 1996, 240–44.
18. Ibid., 244.
19. Ibid., 251–52.
20. Ibid., 252–53.
21. Ibid., 253.
22. Although, of course, relativism too is a foundational concept. To pronounce all knowledge to be relativist—that there is no absolute truth—presupposes that one has found that one true intellectual space which allows one to make such pronouncements.
23. A useful overview of the numerous strands in postmodernist thinking can be found in the edited volume by C. Jencks, 1992.
24. See, for example, the discussion in R. K. Ashley, 1983b, 463–96.
25. See, for example, J. Baudrillard, 1988b. See also M. Foucault, 1984a.; 1980; 1988.
26. J. O'Neill, 1990, 78.
27. Works of this genre are, for example, F. Fukuyama, 1992; P. F. Drucker, 1993; M. Carnoy et al., 1993; P. F. Drucker, 1989; S. Lash and J. Urry, 1994; N. G. Onuf, 1989; A. C. Robles, 1994; E. W. Soja, 1990.
28. This is not meant to discount the very considerable amount of work undertaken in International Relations under the rubric of international political economy (IPE) but only to suggest that this body of work has not evolved research agendas whose concerns address issues such as the reflexive effects of spatial dialectics and political economy upon sovereignty or conceptions of territoriality; or of the spatial-territorial features of particular modes of production in terms of their influence upon the forces of imperialism-colonialism, state expansionism, and war. See, for example, the discussion in R. Tooze, 1991, 198, where he identifies the major intellectual strands in current IPE research. On the application of technological postmodern perspectives in the social sciences, see, for example, B. S. Turner, 1994; S. Lash, ed., 1991; V. B. Leitch, 1996; V. Hubinger, 1996.
29. See, for example, R. Peet and N. Thrift, eds., 1989.
30. See M. Aglietta, 1979; A. Lipietz, 1987. See also A. C. Robles, 1994; D. F. Ruccio, 1989, 33–53.
31. See, for example, A. Giddens, 1985. See also D. Held, 1989b.
32. See, for example, A. Lipietz, 1992; H. M. Schwartz, 1994; T. Porter, 1993; S. Corbridge et al., 1994. See also D. Harvey, 1991; F. Jameson, 1992.
33. See, for example, the excellent studies by M. Billinge et al., 1984; D. U. Gregory, 1994; J. Pickles, 1985; R. Peet and N. Thrift, eds., 1989; J. Jenson et al., 1993.
34. See R. Palan and B. Gills, eds., 1994; C. N. Murphy and R. Tooze, eds., 1991.
35. M. Hoffman, 1991, 169–70, 184.
36. See R. K. Ashley, 1991, 65; 1987, 408–9.
37. R. Brown, 1993, 13.
38. M. Hoffman, 1991, 170.

39. N. G. Onuf, 1989, 12. See also F. Halliday, 1994, 41.
40. R. K. Ashley, 1987, 408–9.
41. R. K. Ashley, 1996, 240–54.
42. Ibid., 408.
43. N. G. Onuf, 1989, 12. As Ashley notes, poststructuralism "is not especially interested in—it in fact distrusts—'interpretation,' if by interpretation one means the attempt to recover and fix a meaning intrinsic to a particular text or set of practices." See R. K. Ashley, 1989, 278.
44. R. K. Ashley, 1987, 408.
45. R. K. Ashley, 1991, 65.
46. J. George, 1988, 78–81.
47. R. K. Ashley, 1989, 278.
48. N. G. Onuf, 1989, 284.
49. Ibid., 12.
50. See the discussion in R. O. Keohane, 1988, 382–93.
51. F. Halliday, 1994, 44.
52. Ibid.
53. Ibid.
54. M. Wallack, 1994, 204.
55. F. Halliday, 1994, 40.

Bibliography

Aglietta, M. 1979. *A Theory of Capitalist Regulation: The U.S. Experience*. Translated by D. Fernbach. London: New Left Books.
Alker, Jr., H. R. 1992. "The Humanist Movement in International Studies: Reflections on Machiavelli and Las Casas." *International Studies Quarterly* 36 (December): 347–72.
Althusser, L. 1977. *For Marx*. Translated by B. Brewster. London: New Left Books.
Amin, A. 1976. *Unequal Development*. Translated by B. Pearce. Sussex: The Harvester Press.
Amnesty International. 1993. *Getting Away with Murder: Political Killings and "Disappearances" in the 1990s*. London: Amnesty International Publications.
Anderson, P. 1990. "A Culture in Counterflow—II." *New Left Review* (July–August): 85–138.
Andreff, W. 1984. "The International Centralization of Capital and the Re-ordering of World Capitalism." *Capital & Class* 22 (Spring): 58–80.
Andrews, B. 1982. "The Political Economy of World Capitalism: Theory and Practice." *International Organization* 36 (Winter):135–63.
Aron, R. 1967. "What Is a Theory of International Relations?" *Journal of International Affairs* 21, no. 2: 185–206.
Ashley, R. K. 1980. *The Political Economy of War and Peace*. London: Pinter.
———. 1981. "Political Realism and Human Interests." *International Studies Quarterly* 25 (June): 204–36.
———. 1983a. "The Eye of Power: The Politics of World Modelling." *International Organization* 37 (Summer): 495–535.
———. 1983b. "Three Modes of Economism." *International Studies Quarterly* 27 (December): 463–96.
———. 1984. "The Poverty of Neorealism." *International Organization* 38 (Spring): 225–86.
———. 1986. "The Poverty of Neorealism." In Keohane, R. O., ed. *Neorealism and Its Critics*. New York: Columbia University Press, 225–86.
———. 1987. "The Geopolitics of Geopolitical Space: Toward a Critical Social Theory of International Politics." *Alternatives* 12, no. 4: 403–34.
———. 1988a. "Geopolitics, Supplementary, Criticism: A Reply to Professors Roy and Walker." *Alternatives* 13 (January): 88–102.
———. 1988b. "Untying the Sovereign State: A Double Reading of the Anarchy

Problematique." *Millennium: Journal of International Studies* 17 (Summer): 227–62.
———. 1989. "Living on Border Lines: Man, Poststructuralism, and War." In Der Derian, J., and Shapiro, M. J., eds. *International/Intertextual Relations: Postmodern Readings of World Politics.* New York: Lexington Books, 259–321.
———. 1991. "The State of the Discipline: Realism under Challenge." In Higgott, R., and Richardson, J. L., eds. *International Relations: Global and Australian Perspectives on an Evolving Discipline.* Canberra: Department of International Relations, Research School of Pacific Studies, Australian National University, 37–69.
———. 1996. "The Achievements of Poststructuralism." In Smith, S., Booth, K., and Zalewski, M., eds. *International Theory: Positivism and Beyond.* Cambridge: Cambridge University Press, 240–54.
Ashley, R. K., and R. B. J. Walker. 1990a. "Reading Dissidence/Writing the Discipline: Crisis and the Question of Sovereignty in International Studies." *International Studies Quarterly* 34 (September): 367–416.
———. 1990b. "Speaking the Language of Exile: Dissident Thought in International Studies." *International Studies Quarterly* 34 (September): 259–68.
Assiter, A. 1996. *Enlightened Women: Modernist Feminism in a Postmodern World.* London: Routledge.
Banks, M. 1985. "The Inter-Paradigm Debate." In Light, M., and Groom, A. J. R., eds. *International Relations: A Hand Book of Current Theory.* London: Pinter, 7–26.
Barnet, E. T. 1989. *Structuralism and the Logic of Dissent: Barthes, Derrida, Foucault, Lacan.* Hong Kong: University of Illinois Press.
Bartelson, J. 1995. *A Genealogy of Sovereignty.* New York: Cambridge University Press.
Baudrillard, J. 1983. *Simulations.* Translated by P. Foss. New York: Semiotext(e).
———. 1988a. *The Ecstasy of Communication.* Translated by B. and C. Schutze, edited by S. Lotringer (Foreign Agents Series). Brooklyn, N.Y.: Autonomedia.
———. 1988b. *Jean Baudrillard: Selected Writings.* Translated and edited by M. Poster. Stanford, Calif.: Stanford University Press.
Bauman, Z. 1988. "Is There a Postmodern Sociology?" *Theory, Culture and Society* 5 (June): 217–37.
———. 1992. *Intimations of Postmodernity.* London: Routledge.
Bentham, J. 1974. "Plan for Universal and Perpetual Peace." In Jacob, M. C., ed. *Peace Projects of the Eighteenth Century.* New York: Garland, 11–44.
Berger, S., and Dore, R., eds. 1996. *National Diversity and Global Capitalism.* Ithaca, N.Y.: Cornell University Press.
Berman, M. 1988. *All That Is Solid Melts into Air: The Experience of Modernity.* New York: Viking Penguin.
Bernstein, R. J. 1986. "The Rage against Reason." *Philosophy and Literature* 10 (October): 186–210.
———, ed. 1988. *Habermas and Modernity.* Cambridge, Mass.: MIT Press.
Best, S., and Kellner, D. 1991. *Postmodern Theory: Critical Interrogations.* New York: Guilford Press.

Biersteker, T. J. 1989. "Critical Reflections on Post-Positivism in International Relations." *International Studies Quarterly* 33 (September): 263–67.
Billinge, M., Gregory, D., and Martin, R., eds. 1984. *Recollections of a Revolution: Geography as a Spatial Science.* London: Macmillan.
Bloom, A. 1987. *The Closing of the American Mind.* New York: Penguin Books.
———. 1990. *Giants and Dwarfs: Essays 1960–1990.* New York: Simon and Schuster.
Booth, K. 1991. "Security in Anarchy: Utopian Realism in Theory and Practice." *International Affairs* 67 (July): 527–45.
Bordo, S. 1994. "Feminism, Postmodernism, and Gender Skepticism." In Herrmann, A. C., and Stewart, A. J., eds. *Theorizing Feminism: Parallel Trends in the Humanities and Social Sciences.* Boulder, Colo.: Westview Press, 458–82.
Bowers, J. 1992. "Postmodernity and the Globalisation of Technoscience: The Computer, Cognitive Science and War." In Doherty, J., Graham, E., and Malek, M., eds. *Postmodernism and the Social Sciences.* London: Macmillan, 111–26.
Bronner, S. E., and Kellner, D. M., eds. 1989. *Critical Theory and Society.* London: Routledge.
Brown, C. 1992. *International Relations Theory: New Normative Approaches.* Hertfordshire, England: Harvester Wheatsheaf.
———. 1994a. "Critical Theory and Postmodernism in International Relations." In Groom, A. J. R., and Light, M., eds. *Contemporary International Relations: A Guide to Theory.* London: Pinter, 56–68.
———. 1994b. Review of Campbell, D., and Dillon, M., eds. *The Political Subject of Violence* and Sjolander, C. T., and Cox, W. S., eds. *Beyond Positivism: Critical Reflections on International Relations. Millennium: Journal of International Studies* 23 (Spring): 142–44.
———. 1994c. "'Turtles All the Way Down': Anti-Foundationalism, Critical Theory and International Relations." *Millennium: Journal of International Studies* 23 (Summer): 213–36.
———. 1997. *Understanding International Relations.* London: Macmillan.
Brown, R. 1993. "Introduction: Towards a New Synthesis of International Relations." In Bowker, M., and Brown, R., eds. *From Cold War to Collapse: Theory and World Politics in the 1980s.* Cambridge, England: Cambridge University Press, 1–20.
Brown, W. 1991. "Feminist Hesitations, Postmodern Exposures." *Differences: A Journal of Feminist Cultural Studies* 4, no. 1: 63–84.
Bryant, C. G. A., and Jary, D., eds. 1991. *Giddens Theory of Structuration: A Critical Appreciation.* London: Routledge.
Bull, H. 1972a. "International Relations as an Academic Pursuit." *Australian Outlook* 26 (December): 251–65.
———. 1972b. "The Theory of International Politics, 1919–1969." In Porter, B., ed. *The Aberystwyth Papers: International Politics 1919–1969.* London: Oxford University Press, 30–55.
———. 1977. *The Anarchical Society: A Study of Order in World Politics.* London: Macmillan.

———. 1991. "Martin Wight and the Theory of International Relations." In Wight, M., *International Theory: The Three Traditions*. Edited by C. Wight and B. Porter. Leicester: Leicester University Press for the Royal Institute of International Affairs, ix–xxiii.
Burchill, S. 1996. "Introduction." In Burchill, S., and Linklater, A., eds. *Theories of International Relations*. New York: St. Martin's Press, 1–27.
Burchill, S., and Linklater, A., eds. 1996. *Theories of International Relations*. New York: St. Martin's Press.
Caldicott, H. 1984. *Missile Envy: The Arms Race and Nuclear War*. New York: William Morrow.
Callinicos, A. 1985. "Postmodernism, Post-Structuralism, Post-Marxism?" *Theory, Culture & Society* 2, no. 3: 85–101.
———. 1989. *Against Postmodernism: A Marxist Critique*. Cambridge: Polity Press.
Camilleri, J. A. 1990. "Rethinking Sovereignty in a Shrinking, Fragmented World." In Walker, R. B. J., and Mendlovitz, S. H., eds. *Contending Sovereignties: Redefining Political Community*. Boulder, Colo.: Lynne Rienner, 13–44.
Camilleri, J. A., and Falk, J. 1992. *End of Sovereignty?: The Politics of a Shrinking and Fragmenting World*. Brookfield, Vt.: Elgar.
Campbell, D. 1994. "The Deterritorialization of Responsibility: Levinas, Derrida, and Ethics after the End of Philosophy." *Alternatives* 19 (Fall): 455–84.
Caporaso, J. A. 1981. "Industrialization in the Periphery: The Evolving Global Division of Labour." *International Studies Quarterly* 25 (September): 347–84.
Carnoy, M. et al. 1993. *The New Global Economy in the Information Age: Reflections on Our Changing World*. University Park: Pennsylvania State University Press.
Carr, E. H. 1964. *The Twenty Years' Crisis, 1919–1939*. New York: Harper and Row.
Chan, S. 1994. "Critical Theory, Praxis and Postmodernism." In Girard, M., Eberwein, W. D., and Webb, K., eds. *Theory and Practice in Foreign Policy Making: National Perspectives on Academics and Professionals in International Relations*. London: Pinter, 26–33.
Chilcote, E. B., and Chilcote, R. H. 1992. "The Crisis of Marxism: An Appraisal of New Directions." *Rethinking Marxism* 5 (Summer): 84–106.
Coker, C. 1992. "Post-Modernity and the End of the Cold War: Has War Been Disinvented?" *Review of International Studies* 18 (Summer): 189–98.
Collins, J. 1992. "Post-Modernism as Culmination: The Aesthetic Politics of Decentred Cultures." In Jencks, C., ed. *The Post-Modern Reader*. London: Academy Editions, 94–118.
Connerton, P. 1976. *Critical Sociology*. Penguin.
Connolly, W. E. 1988. *Political Theory and Modernity*. Oxford: Basil Blackwell.
———. 1989. "Identity and Difference in Global Politics." In Der Derian, J., and Shapiro, M. J., eds. *International/Intertextual Relations: Postmodern Readings of World Politics*. New York: Lexington Books, 323–42.
Corbridge, S., Martin, R., and Thrift, N., eds. 1994. *Money, Power and Space*. Oxford: Blackwell.

Cox, R. W. 1981. "Social Forces, States and World Order: Beyond International Relations Theory." *Millennium: Journal of International Studies* 10 (Summer): 126–55.

———. 1986. "Social Forces, States and World Order: Beyond International Relations Theory." In Keohane, R. O., ed. *Neorealism and Its Critics.* New York: Columbia University Press, 204–54.

Cox, W. S., and Sjolander, C. T. 1994. "Critical Reflection on International Relations." In Cox, W. S., and Sjolander, C. T., eds. *Beyond Positivism: Critical Reflections on International Relations.* Boulder, Colo.: Lynne Rienner, 1–10.

Crawford, R. M. A. 1996. *Regime Theory in the Post Cold War World: Rethinking Neo-Liberal Approaches to International Relations.* Aldershot, U.K: Dartmouth.

———. 1999. *Realism and Idealism in International Relations: Toward Discipline.* London: Routledge.

Crawford, R. M. A., and Jarvis, D. S. L., eds. 1999. *International Relations: Still an American Social Science? Toward Diversity in International Thought.* Albany: State University of New York Press.

Culler, J. 1982. *On Deconstructionism.* Ithica, N.Y.: Cornell University Press.

Cutrofello, A. 1993. "Must We Say What 'We' Means: The Politics of Postmodernism." *Social Theory and Practice* 19 (Spring): 93–109.

Czempiel, E. O., and Rosenau, J. N., eds. 1989. *Global Changes and Theoretical Challenges: Approaches to World Politics for the 1990s.* Lexington, Mass: Lexington Books.

Darby, P., and Paolini, A. J. 1994. "Bridging International Relations and Postcolonialism." *Alternatives* 19 (Summer): 371–97.

Der Derian, J. 1987. *On Diplomacy: A Genealogy of Estrangement.* Oxford: Basil Blackwell.

———. 1988. "Introducing Philosophical Traditions in International Relations." *Millennium: Journal of International Studies* 17 (Summer): 189–93.

———. 1992. *Antidiplomacy: Spies, Terror, Speed, and War.* Oxford: Blackwell.

Der Derian, J., and Shapiro, M. J., eds. 1989. *International/Intertextual Relations: Postmodern Readings of World Politics.* New York: Lexington Books.

Dessler, D. 1989. "What's at Stake in the Agent-Structure Debate?" *International Organization* 43 (Summer): 441–74.

Devetak, R. 1996. "Postmodernism." In Burchill, S., and Linklater, A., eds. *Theories of International Relations.* New York: St. Martin's Press, 179–209.

Donaldson, S. 1993. "The Rape Crisis behind Bars." *New York Times* (29 December).

Donelan, M. 1978a. "The Political Theorists and International Theory." In Donelan, M., ed. *The Reason of States: A Study of International Political Theory.* London: George Allen and Unwin, 75–91.

———, ed.1978b. *The Reason of States: A Study of International Political Theory.* London: George Allen and Unwin.

Donougho, M. 1992. "The Derridean Turn." In Sills, C., and Jensen, G. H., eds. *The Philosophy of Discourse: The Rhetorical Turn in Twentieth-Century Thought.* Vol. 2. Portsmouth, N.H.: Heinemann, 66–101.

Drucker, P. F. 1986. "The Changed World Economy." *Foreign Affairs* 64 (Spring): 768–91.
———. 1989. *The New Realities*. New York: Harper and Row.
———. 1993. *Post-Capitalist Society*. New York: HarperCollins.
Duboff, R. B. 1989. *Accumulation and Power: An Economic History of the United States*. New York: M. E. Sharpe.
Dunn, F. S. 1949. "The Present Course in International Relations Research." *World Politics* 2 (October): 80–95.
———. 1960. "The Scope of International Relations." In Hoffmann, S., ed. *Contemporary Theory in International Relations*. Englewood Cliffs, N.J: Prentice-Hall, 13–16.
Eagleton, T. 1992. "The Crisis of Contemporary Culture." *New Left Review* (November–December): 29–41.
Edmundson, M. 1997. "On the Uses of a Liberal Education: As Lite Entertainment for Bored College Students." *Harpers Magazine* 295 (September): 39–49.
Elkins, D. J. 1995. *Beyond Sovereignty: Territory and Political Economy in the Twenty-First Century*. Toronto: University of Toronto Press.
Elshtain, J. B. 1982. "Feminist Discourse and Its Discontents: Language, Power, and Meaning." In Keohane, N. O., Rosaldo, M. Z., and Gelpi, B. C., eds. *Feminist Theory: A Critique of Ideology*. Chicago: University of Chicago Press, 127–45.
———. 1987. *Women and War*. New York: Basic Books.
Emmanuel, A. 1972. *Unequal Exchange: A Study of the Imperialism of Trade*. Translated by B. Pearce. London: New Left Books.
Enloe, C. 1987. "Feminist Thinking about War, Militarism and Peace." In Hess, B. B., and Ferree, M. M., eds. *Analyzing Gender*. Newbury Park: Sage Publications, 526–47.
———. 1989. *Bananas, Beaches and Bases: Making Feminist Sense of International Politics*. Berkeley: University of California Press.
———. 1993. *The Morning After: Sexual Politics at the End of the Cold War*. Berkeley: University of California Press.
Ferguson, K. 1996. "From a Kubbutz Journal: Reflections on Gender, Race, and Militarism in Israel." In Shapiro, M. J., and Alker, H. R., eds. *Challenging Boundaries: Global Flows, Territorial Identities*. Borderlines, vol. 2. Minneapolis: University of Minnesota Press, 435–54.
Ferguson, Y. H., and Mansbach, R. W. 1986. "Values and Paradigm Change: The Elusive Quest for International Relations Theory." In Karns, M. P., ed. *Persistent Patterns and Emergent Structures in a Waning Century*. New York: Praeger, 11–34.
———. 1988. *The Elusive Quest: Theory and International Politics*. Columbia: University of South Carolina Press.
———. 1991. "Between Celebration and Despair: Constructive Suggestions for Future International Theory." *International Studies Quarterly* 35 (December): 363–86.
Ferry, L., and Renaut, A. 1990. *French Philosophy of the Sixties: An Essay on Antihumanism*. Translated by M. S. Cattani. Amherst: University of Massachusetts Press.

Forrest, D. 1996. *A Glimpse of Hell: Reports on Torture Worldwide.* Amnesty International/Cassell: London.
Foster, H. 1983. "Postmodernism: A Preface." In Foster, H., ed. *The Anti-Aesthetic: Essays on Postmodern Culture.* Port Townsend, Wash.: Bay Press, ix–xvi.
———. 1984. "(Post)Modern Polemics." *New German Critique* 33 (Fall): 67–78.
———, ed. 1985. *Recordings: Art, Spectacle, Cultural Politics.* Port Townsend, Wash.: Bay Press.
Foucault, M. 1980. *Power/Knowledge: Selected Interviews and Other Writings, 1972–1977.* Translated and edited by C. Gordon et al. Brighton, England: Harvester Press.
———. 1984a. *The Foucault Reader.* Edited by P. Rabinow. New York: Pantheon.
———. 1984b. "The Subject and Power." In Wallis, B., ed. *Art after Modernism: Rethinking Representation.* New York: New Museum of Contemporary Art and David R. Godine, 417–32.
———. 1988. *Politics, Philosophy, Culture: Interviews and Other Writings, 1977–1984.* Translated and edited by L. D. Kritzman. New York: Routledge.
Fox, W. T. 1949. "Interwar International Relations Research: The American Experience." *World Politics* 2 (October): 67–79.
Fox, W. T., and Fox, A. B. 1961. "The Teaching of International Relations in the United States." *World Politics* 13 (April): 339–59.
Frank, A. G. 1969. *Latin America, Underdevelopment or Revolution: Essays on the Development of Underdevelopment and the Immediate Enemy.* New York: Monthly Review Press.
Frankel, J. 1969. *International Politics: Conflict and Harmony.* London: Penguin Press.
Frobel, F., Heinrichs, J., and Kreye, O. 1978. "The New International Division of Labour." *Social Science Information* 17, no. 1: 123–42.
Fukuyama, F. 1992. *The End of History and the Last Man.* New York: The Free Press.
Gallie, W. B. 1956. "Essentially Contested Concepts." *Proceedings of the Aristotelian Society* 56: 167–98.
Garst, D. 1989. "Thucydides and Neorealism." *International Studies Quarterly* 33 (March): 3–27.
George, A. L. 1993. *Bridging the Gap: Theory and Practice in Foreign Policy.* Washington, D.C: United States Institute of Peace Press.
George, J. 1988. "The Study of International Relations and the Positivist/Empiricist Theory of Knowledge: Implications for the Australian Discipline." In Higgott, R., ed. *New Directions in International Relations?: Australian Perspectives.* Canberra: Department of International Relations, Australian National University, 78–81.
———. 1989. "International Relations and the Search for Thinking Space: Another View of the Third Debate." *International Studies Quarterly* 33 (September): 269–79.

———. 1993. "Of Incarceration and Closure: Neo-Realism and the New/Old World Orders." *Millennium: Journal of International Studies* 22 (Summer): 197–234.

———. 1994. *Discourses of Global Politics: A Critical (Re)Introduction to International Relations.* Boulder, Colo.: Lynne Rienner.

———. 1995. "Realist 'Ethics,' International Relations, and Post-Modernism: Thinking beyond the Egoism-Anarchy Thematic." *Millennium: Journal of International Studies* 24 (Summer): 195–223.

———. 1996. "Understanding International Relations after the Cold War: Probobing beyond the Realist Legacy." In Shapiro, M. J., and Alker, H. R., eds. *Challenging Boundaries: Global Flows, Territorial Identities.* Borderlines, vol. 2. Minneapolis: University of Minnesota Press, 33–82.

George, J., and Campbell, D. 1990. "Patterns of Dissent and the Celebration of Difference: Critical Social Theory and International Relations." *International Studies Quarterly* 34 (September): 269–94.

Geras, N. 1990. *Discourses of Extremity: Radical Ethics and Post-Marxist Extravagances.* New York: Verso.

Giddens, A. 1985. *Nation-State and Violence.* Berkeley: University of California Press.

———. 1986. *The Constitution of Society: Outline of the Theory of Structuration.* Berkeley: University of California Press.

———. 1991. *The Consequences of Modernity.* Stanford, Calif.: Stanford University Press.

Gill, S., and Mittleman, J. H., eds. 1997. *Innovation and Transformation in International Relations Theory.* Cambridge: Cambridge University Press.

Gilpin, R. G. 1986. "The Richness of the Tradition of Political Realism." In Keohane, R. O., ed. *Neorealism and Its Critics.* New York: Columbia University Press, 301–21.

Gonzales, M. 1984–85. "Kellner's Critical Theory: A Reassessment." *Telos* 62, 206–10.

Grader, S. 1988. "The English School of International Relations: Evidence and Evaluation." *Review of International Studies* 14 (January): 29–44.

Graham, J. 1991. "Fordism/Post-Fordism, Marxism/Post-Marxism: The Second Cultural Divide?" *Rethinking Marxism* 4 (Spring): 39–58.

Grant, R. 1991. "The Sources of Gender Bias in International Relations Theory." In Grant, R. and Newland, K., eds. *Gender and International Relations.* Milton Keynes: Open University Press: 8–26.

Grant, R., and Newland, K., eds. 1991. *Gender and International Relations.* Milton Keynes, England: Open University Press.

Gregory, D. U. 1978. "Social Change and Spatial Structures." In Carlstein, T., Parkes, D., and Thrift, N., eds. *Timing Space and Spacing Time.* New York: John Wiley, 38–46.

———. 1989a. "Foreword." In Der Derian, J., and Shapiro, M. J., eds. *International/Intertextual Relations: Postmodern Readings of World Politics.* New York: Lexington Books, xiii–xxi.

———. 1989b. "Presences and Absences: Time-Space Relations and Structuration Theory." In Held, D. and Thompson, J. B., eds. 1989. *Social Theory of Modern Societies.* Cambridge: Cambridge University Press, 185–214.

———. 1994. *Geographical Imaginations.* Cambridge, Mass.: Blackwell.

Griffiths, M. 1999. *Fifty Key Theorists in International Relations.* London: Routledge.

Griffiths, M., and O'Callaghan, T. 1999. "The End of International Relations?" In Crawford, R. M. A., and Jarvis, D. S. L., eds. *International Relations: Still an American Social Science? Toward Diversity in International Thought.* Albany: State University of New York Press.

Habermas, J. 1984. *The Theory of Communicative Action.* Translated by T. McCarthy. Boston: Beacon Press.

———. 1991. *The Philosophical Discourse of Modernity: Twelve Lectures.* Translated by F. G. Lawrence. Cambridge, Mass.: MIT Press.

Halliday, F. 1985. "A 'Crisis' of International Relations." *International Relations* 8 (November): 407–12.

———. 1988. "Hidden from International Relations: Women and the International Arena." *Millennium: Journal of International Studies* 17 (Winter): 419–28.

———. 1990. "The Pertinence of International Relations." *Political Studies* 38, 502–16.

———. 1991. "International Relations: Is There a New Agenda?" *Millennium: Journal of International Studies* 20 (Spring): 57–72.

———. 1993. "The Cold War and Its Conclusion: Consequences for International Relations Theory." In Leaver, R., and Richardson, J. L., eds. *Charting the Post–Cold War Order.* Boulder, Colo.: Westview Press, 11–38.

———. 1994. *Rethinking International Relations.* Vancouver, Canada: University of British Columbia Press.

Harding, S. 1986. *The Science Question in Feminism.* Ithaca, N.Y.: Cornell University Press.

Harvey, D. 1991. *The Condition of Postmodernity: An Enquiry into the Origins of Cultural Change.* Oxford: Basil Blackwell.

Hebdige, D. 1988. *Hiding in the Light: On Images and Things.* London: Routledge.

Held, D. 1989a. *Introduction to Critical Theory.* Berkeley: University of California Press.

———. 1989b. *Political Theory and the Modern State: Essays on State Power and Democracy.* Stanford, Calif.: Stanford University Press.

Held, D., and Thompson, J. B., eds. 1989. *Social Theory of Modern Societies.* Cambridge: Cambridge University Press.

Henehan, M., and Reid, M. 1997. "Gender Discrimination in the Academy? Yes, Survey Indicates." *International Studies Newsletter* 24, no. 1: 8.

Higgott, R. 1991. "International Relations in Australia: An Agenda for the 1990s." In Higgott, R., and Richardson, J. L., eds. 1991. *International Relations: Global and Australian Perspectives in an Evolving Discipline.* Canberra: Department of International Relations, Research School of Pacific Studies, Australian National University, 394–426.

———, ed. 1988. *New Directions In International Relations?: Australian Perspectives.* Canberra: Department of International Relations, Research School of Pacific Studies, Australian National University.

Higgott, R., and Richardson, J. L., eds. 1991. *International Relations: Global and Australian Perspectives in an Evolving Discipline.* Canberra: Department of International Relations, Research School of Pacific Studies, Australian National University.

Hiley, D. R., Bohman, J. F., and Shusterman, R., eds. 1991. *The Interpretive Turn: Philosophy, Science, Culture.* Ithaca, N.Y.: Cornell University Press.

Hinsley, F. H. 1963. *Power and the Pursuit of Peace.* Cambridge: Cambridge University Press.

Hirsch, Jr., E. D. 1976. *The Aims of Interpretation.* Chicago: University of Chicago Press.

Hobbes, T. 1968. *Leviathan.* Edited by C. B. Macpherson. Harmondsworth: Penguin.

Hobsbawm, E. 1992. "The Crisis of Today's Ideologies." *New Left Review* 192 (March–April): 55–64.

Hoffman, M. 1987. "Critical Theory and the Inter-Paradigm Debate." *Millennium: Journal of International Studies* 16 (Summer): 231–49.

———. 1991. "Restructuring, Reconstruction, Reinscription, Rearticulation: Four Voices in Critical International Theory." *Millennium: Journal of International Studies* 20 (Summer): 169–85.

Hoffmann, S. 1960. "International Relations as a Discipline." In Hoffmann, S., ed. *Contemporary Theory in International Relations.* Englewood Cliffs, N.J: Prentice-Hall, 1–12.

———. 1965. *The State of War: Essays on the Theory and Practice of International Politics.* New York: Frederick A. Praeger.

———. 1977. "An American Social Science: International Relations." *Daedalus* 106 (Summer): 41–60.

———. 1987. *Janus and Minerva: Essays in the Theory and Practice of International Politics.* Boulder, Colo.: Westview Press.

———. 1989. "A Retrospective." In Kruzel, J., and Rosenau, J. N., eds. *Journeys through World Politics: Autobiographical Reflections of Thirty-four Academic Travelers.* Lexington, Mass.: Lexington Books, 263–78.

Hoffmann, S., and Fidler, D. P., eds. 1991. *Rousseau on International Relations.* Oxford: Clarendon Press.

Hollis, M., and Lukes, S., eds. 1982. *Rationality and Relativism.* Oxford: Basil Blackwell.

Holsti, K. J. 1971. "Retreat from Utopia: International Relations Theory, 1945–1970." *Canadian Journal of Political Science* 4 (June): 165–77.

———. 1985. *The Dividing Discipline: Hegemony and Diversity in International Theory.* Boston: Unwin Hyman.

———. 1989a. "Mirror, Mirror on the Wall, Which Are the Fairest Theories of All?" *International Studies Quarterly* 33 (September): 255–61.

———. 1989b. "Rooms and Views: Perspectives on the Study of International Relations." In Kruzel, J., and Rosenau, J. N., eds. *Journeys through World Poli-*

tics: Autobiographical Reflections of Thirty-four Academic Travelers. Lexington, Mass.: Lexington Books, 27–40.

———. 1993. "International Relations at the End of the Millennium." *Review of International Studies* 19 (October): 401–8.

———. 1999. "Along the Road of International Theory in the Next Millennium: Three Travelogues." In Crawford, R. M. A, and Jarvis, D. S. L., eds. *International Relations: Still an American Social Science? Toward Diversity in International Thought*. New York: State University of New York Press.

Holub, R. C. 1991. *Jurgen Habermas: Critic in the Public Sphere*. London: Routledge.

Holzgrefe, J. L. 1989. "The Origins of Modern International Relations Theory." *Review of International Studies* 15 (January): 11–26.

Horkheimer, M. 1972. *Critical Theory: Selected Essays*. Translated by M. J. O'Connell. New York: Herder and Herder.

Hubinger, V. 1996. *Grasping the Changing World: Anthropological Concepts in the Postmodern Era*. New York: Routledge.

Huntington, S. 1988. "U.S.—Decline or Renewal." *Foreign Affairs* 67 (Winter): 76–97.

Hurwitz, R. 1989. "Strategic and Social Fictions in the Prisoner's Dilemma." In Der Derian, J., and Shapiro, M. J., eds. *International/Intertextual Relations: Postmodern Readings of World Politics*. New York: Lexington Books, 113–34.

Hutchings, K. 1992. "The Possibility of Judgement: Moralizing and Theorizing in International Relations." *Review of International Studies* 18 (January): 51–62.

Hutchison, J., and Smith, A. D., eds. 1994. *Nationalism*. Oxford: Oxford University Press.

Huyssen, A. 1984. "Mapping the Postmodern." *New German Critique* 33 (Fall): 5–52.

Jackson, R. H. 1990. "Martin Wight, International Theory and the Good Life." *Millennium: Journal of International Studies* 19 (Summer): 261–72.

Jacob, M. C. 1974, ed. *Peace Projects of the Eighteenth Century*. New York: Garland.

Jameson, F. 1983. "Postmodernism and Consumer Society." In Foster, H., ed. *The Anti-Aesthetic: Essays on Postmodern Culture*. Port Townsend, Wash.: Bay Press, 111–25.

———. 1984. "The Politics of Theory: Ideological Positions in the Postmodern Debate." *New German Critique* 33 (Fall): 53–65.

———. 1992. *Postmodernism: Or, the Cultural Logic of Late Capitalism*. Durham: Duke University Press.

Jarvis, D. S. L. 1998. "Postmodernism: A Critical Typology." *Politics and Society* 26 (March): 95–142.

Jencks, C. 1986. *What Is Postmodernism?* London: Academy Editions.

———, ed. 1992. *The Post-Modern Reader*. New York: St. Martin's Press.

Jenson, J., Mahon, R., and Bienefeld, M. 1993. *Production, Space, Identity: Political Economy Faces the Twenty-First Century*. Toronto: Canadian Scholars Press.

Jezierski, L. 1991. "The Politics of Space." *Socialist Review* 21: 177–84.

Jones, A. 1996. "Does Gender Make the World Go Round?" *Review of International Studies* 22 (October): 405–29.

Jones, R. E. 1981. "The English School of International Relations: A Case for Closure." *Review of International Studies* 7 (January): 1–13.

———. 1988. "The Myth of the Special Case in International Relations." *Review of International Studies* 14 (October): 267–74.

Kando, T. 1996. "Postmodernism: Old Wine in New Bottles?" *International Journal on World Peace* 13, no. 3: 3–48.

Kant, I. 1957. *Perpetual Peace*. Edited by L. W. Beck. New York: Liberal Arts Press.

Keal, P. 1991. "Ethical Issues and International Relations." In Higgott, R., and Richardson, J. L., eds. *International Relations: Global and Australian Perspectives in an Evolving Discipline*. Canberra: Department of International Relations, Research School of Pacific Studies, Australian National University, 163–90.

Kegley, Jr., C. W. 1993. "The Neoidealist Movement in International Studies? Realist Myths and the New International Realities." *International Studies Quarterly* 37 (June): 131–47.

Kellner, D. 1988. "Postmodernism as Social Theory: Some Challenges and Problems." *Theory, Culture and Society* 5 (June): 239–69.

———. 1989. *Jean Baudrillard: From Marxism to Postmodernism and Beyond*. Stanford, Calif.: Stanford University Press.

Keohane, N. O., Rosaldo, M. Z., and Gelpi, B. C., eds. 1982. *Feminist Theory: A Critique of Ideology*. Chicago: University of Chicago Press, 1–30.

Keohane, R. O. 1988. "International Institutions: Two Approaches." *International Studies Quarterly* 32 (December): 379–96.

———. 1989. "International Relations Theory: Contributions of a Feminist Standpoint." *Millennium: Journal of International Studies* 18 (Summer): 245–53.

———, ed. 1986. *Neorealism and Its Critics*. New York: Columbia University Press.

Keyman, E. F. 1994. "Problematizing the State in International Theory." In Sjolander, C. T., and Cox, W. S., eds. *Beyond Positivism: Critical Reflections on International Relations*. Boulder, Colo.: Lynne Rienner, 153–81.

Knox, T. M. 1967. *Hegel's Philosophy of Right*. Oxford: Clarendon Press.

Knutsen, T. L. 1992. *A History of International Relations Theory: An Introduction*. Manchester: Manchester University Press.

Kratochwil, F. 1986. "Errors Have Their Advantages." *International Organization* 38 (Spring): 305–20.

Krause, J. 1996. "Gendered Identities in International Relations." In Krause, J., and Renwick, N., eds. *Identities in International Relations*. New York: St. Martin's Press, 99–117.

Kreml, W. P., and Kegley, Jr., C. W. 1990. "Must the Quest Be Elusive? Restoring Ethics to Theory Building in International Relations." *Alternatives* 15 (Spring): 155–75.

Kress, P. F. 1979. "Against Epistemology: Apostate Musings." *Journal of Politics* 41 (May): 526–42.

Kroker, A. 1992. *The Possessed Individual: Technology and the French Postmodern.* Montreal: New World Perspectives.

Kroker, A., and Cook, D. 1987. *The Postmodern Scene.* Montreal: New World Perspectives.

Kumar, A. 1990. "Towards Postmodern Marxist Theory: Ideology, State, and the Politics of Critique." *Rethinking Marxism* 3 (Fall–Winter): 149–55.

Kuspit, D. 1990. "The Contradictory Character of Postmodernism." In Silverman, H. J., ed. *Postmodernism—Philosophy and the Arts.* New York: Routledge, 53–68.

Laclau, E., and Mouffe, C. 1985. *Hegemony and Socialist Strategy.* Translated by W. Moore and P. Cammack. London: Verso.

———. 1987. "Post-Marxism without Apologies." *New Left Review* 166 (November–December): 79–106.

Lança, P. 1996. "Comment on Postmodernism: Old Wine in New Bottles?" *International Journal on World Peace* 13, no. 3: 41–44.

Lapid, Y. 1989a. "*Quo Vadis* International Relations? Further Reflections on the 'Next Stage' of International Theory." *Millennium: Journal of International Studies* 18 (Spring): 77–88.

———. 1989b. "The Third Debate: On the Prospects of International Theory in a Post-Positivist Era." *International Studies Quarterly* 33 (September): 235–54.

Lapid, Y., and Kratochwil, F. 1996. *The Return of Culture and Identity in IR Theory.* Boulder, Colo.: Lynne Rienner.

Lash, S. 1990. *Sociology of Postmodernism.* London: Routledge.

———, ed. 1991. *Post-Structuralist and Post-Modernist Sociology.* Aldershot, U.K.: Edward Elgar.

Lash, S., and Urry, J. 1994. *Economies of Signs and Space.* London and Thousand Oaks, Calif.: Sage Publications.

Leaver, R., and Richardson, J. L., eds. 1993. *Charting the Post–Cold War Order.* Boulder, Colo.: Westview Press.

Lee, R. L. M. 1994. "Modernization, Postmodernism and the Third World." *Current Sociology* 42 (Summer): 1–63.

Leitch, V. B. 1996. *Post-Modernism: Local Effects, Global Flows.* Albany: State University of New York Press.

Light, M., and Groom, A. J. R., eds. 1985. *International Relations: A Handbook of Current Theory.* London: Pinter.

Lijphart, A. 1974. "The Structure of Theoretical Revolution in International Relations." *International Studies Quarterly* 18 (March): 41–74.

Linday, J. 1981. *The Crisis in Marxism.* Bradford-on-Avon, Wiltshire: Moonraker Press.

Linklater, A. 1990. *Beyond Realism and Marxism: Critical Theory and International Relations.* Houndmills, Basingstoke: Macmillan.

———. 1992. "The Question of the Next Stage in International Relations Theory: A Critical-Theoretical Point of View." *Millennium: Journal of International Studies* 21 (Spring): 77–100.

———. 1996. The Achievements of Critical Theory." In Smith, S., Booth, K., and Zalewski, M., eds. *International Theory: Positivism and Beyond.* Cambridge: Cambridge University Press, 279–98.

Lipietz, A. 1987. "The Globalization of the General Crisis of Fordism." In Holmes, J., and Leys, C., eds. *Frontyard Backyard: The Americas in the Global Crisis*. Toronto: Between the Lines Press.

———. 1992. *Toward a New Economic Order: Postfordism, Ecology and Democracy*. Translated by M. Slater. Oxford: Polity Press.

Little, R. 1985. "Structuralism and Neorealism." In Light, M., and Groom, A. J. R., eds. *International Relations: A Handbook of Current Theory*. London: Pinter, 74–89.

Long, D. 1995. "The Harvard School of Liberal International Theory: A Case for Closure." *Millennium: Journal of International Studies* 24 (Winter): 489–505.

Lumby, C. 1997. "For Her Peers, No Milk of Kindness." *Sydney Morning Herald*. Friday, October 24: 21.

Lyotard, J. F. 1989. *The Lyotard Reader*. Edited by A. Benjamin. Oxford: Basil Blackwell.

———. 1991. *The Postmodern Condition: A Report on Knowledge*. Translated by G. Bennington and B. Massumi. Minneapolis: University of Minnesota Press.

———. 1992. *The Postmodern Explained*. Translated by J. Pefanis and M. Thomas. Minneapolis: University of Minnesota Press.

———. 1993. *Toward the Postmodern*. Roberts, R. H. and M. S. Roberts, eds. London: Humanities Press.

MacKinnon, C. A. 1982. "Feminism, Marxism, Method, and the State: An Agenda for Theory." In Keohane, N. O., Rosaldo, M. Z., and Gelpi, B. C., eds. *Feminist Theory: A Critique of Ideology*. Chicago: University of Chicago Press, 1–30.

MacMillan, J., and Linklater, A., eds. 1995. *Boundaries in Question: New Directions in International Relations*. New York: St. Martin's Press.

Magdoff, H. 1969. *The Age of Imperialism: The Economics of U.S. Foreign Policy*. New York: Monthly Review Press.

Maghroori, R., and Ramberg, B. 1982. *Globalism versus Realism: International Relations Third Debate*. Boulder, Colo.: Westview Press.

Mann, S. 1997. "Placement of Political Science Doctoral Students in 1996: Degrees Matter." *Political Science and Politics* 30 (September): 602–10.

Mannheim, K. 1952. *Essays on the Sociology of Knowledge*. Edited by P. Kecskemeti. New York: Oxford University Press.

———. 1986. *Conservatism: A Contribution to the Sociology of Knowledge*. Translated and edited by D. Kettler, V. Meja, and N. Stehr. London: Routledge and Kegan Paul.

Manzo, K. 1991. "Modernist Discourse and the Crisis of Development Theory." *Studies in Comparative International Development* 26 (Summer): 3–36.

Marcus, J. 1982. "Storming the Toolshed." In Keohane, N. O., Rosaldo, M. Z., and Gelpi, B. C., eds. *Feminist Theory: A Critique of Ideology*. Chicago: University of Chicago Press, 217–35.

Marden, P. 1990. "Deconstruction and Interpretivism: A Critical Appraisal of the Post-Structuralist Tendencies of Postmodern Geographies." Working paper no. 32, Department of Geography and Environmental Science, Monash University, Australia.

———. 1992. "The Deconstructionist Tendencies of Postmodern Geographies: A Compelling Logic?" *Progress in Human Geography* 16, no. 1: 41–57.
Margolis, J. 1986. *Pragmaticism without Foundations: Reconciling Realism and Relativism.* Oxford: Basil Blackwell.
Markwell, D. J. 1986. "Sir Alfred Zimmern Revisited: Fifty Years On." *Review of International Studies* 12 (October): 279–92.
Martin, J. R. 1994. "Methodological Essentialism, False Difference, and Other Dangerous Traps." *Signs: Journal of Women and Culture in Society* 19, no. 3: 630–57.
Marx, K., and Engels, F. 1977. *Manifesto of the Communist Party.* Peking: Foreign Languages Press.
McCarthy, T. 1989–90. "The Politics of the Ineffable: Derrida's Deconstructionism." *The Philosophical Forum* 21 (Fall–Winter): 146–68.
McGowan, J. 1991. *Postmodernism and Its Critics.* Ithica, N.Y.: Cornell University Press.
McKinley, M. 1996. "Discovering the 'Idiot Centre' of Ourselves: Footnotes to an Academic and Intellectual Culture of the Australian Security Policy Discourse." *AntePodium: An Electronic Journal of World Affairs* 8: http://www.vuw.ac.nz/atp.
Morgenthau, H. J. 1951. *In Defense of the National Interest.* New York: Alfred A. Knopf.
———. 1958. *Dilemmas of Politics.* Chicago: University of Chicago Press.
———. 1967. *Politics among Nations: The Struggle for Power and Peace.* New York: Alfred A. Knopf.
Morrow, R. A. 1991. "Critical Theory, Gramsci and Cultural Studies: From Structuralism to Poststructuralism." In Wexler, P., ed. *Critical Theory Now.* London: Falmer Press, 27–69.
Mouzelis, N. 1988. "Marxism or Post-Marxism?" *New Left Review* 167 (January–February): 107–23.
Murphy, C. N., and Tooze, R., eds. 1991. *The New International Political Economy.* Boulder, Colo.: Lynne Rienner.
Navari, C. 1982. "Hobbes and the 'Hobbesian Tradition' in International Thought." *Millennium: Journal of International Studies* 11 (Winter): 203–22.
Neufeld, M. 1992. "The Pedagogical Is Political: The 'Why,' the 'What' and the 'How' in the Teaching of World Politics." In Gonick, L. S., and Weisband, E., eds. *Teaching World Politics: Contending Pedagogies for a New World Order.* Boulder, Colo.: Westview Press, 83–97.
Newman, C. 1985. *The Post-Modern Aura: The Act of Fiction in an Age of Inflation.* Evanston, Ill.: Northwestern University Press.
Nietzsche, F. 1968. *The Will to Power.* New York: Random House.
Norris, C. 1986. "Deconstruction against Itself: Derrida and Nietzsche." *Diacritics* 16 (Winter): 61–69.
———. 1988. *Deconstruction and the Interests of Theory.* London: Pinter.
———. 1990. *What's Wrong with Postmodernism: Critical Theory and the Ends of Philosophy.* Baltimore: Johns Hopkins University Press.

Okin, S. M. 1989. *Gender, the Public and the Private*. Ontario: University of Toronto Press.
Olson, W. C. 1972. "The Growth of a Discipline." In Porter, B., ed. *The Aberystwyth Papers: International Politics 1919–1969*. London: Oxford University Press, 3–29.
Olson, W. C., and Groom, A. J. R. 1991. *International Relations Then and Now: Origins and Trends in Interpretation*. London: HarperCollins.
Olson, W. C., and Onuf, N. G. 1985. "The Growth of a Discipline: Reviewed." In Smith, S., ed. *International Relations: British and American Perspectives*. Oxford: Basil Blackwell, 1–28.
O'Neill, J. 1990. "Postmodernism and (Post)Marxism." In Silverman, H. J., ed. *Postmodernism—Philosophy and the Arts*. New York: Routledge, 69–79.
Onuf, N. G. 1989. *World of Our Making: Rules and Rule in Social Theory and International Relations*. Columbia: University of South Carolina Press.
Palan, R., and Gills, B., eds. 1994. *Transcending the State-Global Divide: A Neostructuralist Agenda in International Relations*. Boulder, Colo.: Lynne Rienner.
Peet, R. 1983. "Introduction: The Global Geography of Contemporary Capitalism." *Economic Geography* 59 (April): 105–11.
Peet, R., and Thrift, N., eds. 1989. *New Models in Geography: The Political Economy Perspective*. London: Unwin Hyman.
Peterson, V. S. 1992a. "Security and Sovereign States: What Is at Stake in Taking Feminism Seriously?" In Peterson, V. S., ed. *Gendered States: Feminist (Re)Visions of International Relations Theory*. Boulder, Colo.: Lynne Rienner, 31–64.
———. 1992b. "Transgressing Boundaries: Theories of Knowledge, Gender and International Relations." *Millennium: Journal of International Studies* 21 (Summer): 183–206.
———. 1993. "The Politics of Identity in International Relations." *The Fletcher Forum of World Affairs* 17 (August): 1–12.
———. 1997. "Whose Crisis? Early and Postmodern Masculinism." In Gill, S., and Mittleman, J. H., eds. *Innovation and Transformation in International Relations Theory*. Cambridge: Cambridge University Press, 185–206.
———, ed. 1992c. *Gendered States: Feminist (Re)Visions of International Relations Theory*. Boulder, Colo.: Lynne Rienner.
Peterson, V. S., and Runyan, A. S. 1993. *Global Gender Issues*. Boulder, Colo.: Westview Press.
Pettman, J. J. 1996. *Worlding Women: A Feminist International Politics*. London: Routledge.
———. 1999. "Transcending National Identity: The Global Political Economy of Gender and Class." In Crawford, R. M. A. and Jarvis, D. S. L., eds. *International Relations: Still an American Social Science? Toward Diversity in International Thought*. Albany: State University of New York Press.
Pickles, J. 1985. *Phenomenology, Science and Geography: Spatiality and the Human Sciences*. Cambridge: Cambridge University Press.
Plato. 1974. *The Republic*. 2nd ed. Introduction and translation by D. Lee. Penguin.

Polanyi, K. 1968. *The Great Transformation: The Political and Economic Origins of Our Time.* Boston: Beacon Press.

Pollock, G. 1993. "The Politics of Theory: Generations and Geographies, Feminist Theory and the Histories of Arts Histories." *Genders* 17 (Fall): 97–120.

Porter, B. 1978. "Patterns of Thought and Practice: Martin Wight's International Theory." In Donelan, M., ed. *The Reason of States: A Study of International Political Theory.* London: George Allen and Unwin, 64–74.

———. 1989. "David Davies: A Hunter after Peace." *Review of International Studies* 15 (January): 27–36.

———, ed. 1972. *The Aberystwyth Papers: International Politics 1919–1969.* London: Oxford University Press.

Porter, T. 1993. *States, Markets and Regimes in Global Finance.* Houndmills, England: Macmillan.

———. 1994. "Postmodern Political Realism and the Third Debate." In Sjolander, C. T., and Cox, W. S., eds. *Beyond Positivism: Critical Reflections on International Relations.* Boulder, Colo.: Lynne Rienner, 105–27.

Puchala, D. J. 1990. "Woe to the Orphans of the Scientific Revolution." *Journal of International Affairs* 44 (Spring–Summer): 59–80.

Rabinow, P., and Sullivan, W. M. 1979. *Interpretive Social Science: A Reader.* Berkeley: University of California Press.

Radford, L. 1996. "Women, Crime and Violence." In Madoc-Jones, B., and Coates, J., eds. *An Introduction to Women's Studies.* Oxford: Basil Blackwell, 228–49.

Redding, P. 1990. "Nietzschean Perspectivism and the Logic of Practical Reason." *The Philosophical Forum* 22 (Fall): 72–88.

Reimer, B. 1989. "Postmodern Structure of Feeling: Values and Lifestyle in the Postmodern Age." In Gibbins, J. R., ed. *Contemporary Political Culture: Politics in a Postmodern Age.* London: Sage Publications, 110–26.

Rengger, N. J. 1988. "Going Critical: A Response to Hoffman." *Millennium: Journal of International Studies* 17 (Spring): 81–89.

———. 1989. "Incommensurability, International Theory and the Fragmentation of Western Political Culture." In Gribbins, J. R., ed. *Contemporary Political Culture: Politics in a Postmodern Age.* Sage Modern Politics, vol. 23. London: Sage Publications, 237–50.

———. 1990. "The Fearful Sphere of International Relations." *Review of International Studies* 16 (October): 361–68.

———. 1996. "Clio's Cave: Historical Materialism and the Claims of 'Substantive' Social Theory in World Politics." *Review of International Studies* 22 (April): 213–31.

Rengger, N. J., and Hoffman, M. 1992. "Modernity, Postmodernism and International Relations." In Doherty, J., Graham, E., and Malek, M, eds. *Postmodernism and the Social Sciences.* Hong Kong: Macmillan, 127–47.

Richardson, J. L. 1990. "The Academic Study of International Relations." In Miller, J. D. B., and Vincent, R. J., eds. *Order and Violence: Hedley Bull and International Relations.* Oxford: Clarendon Press, 140–85.

———. 1991. "The State of the Discipline: A Critical Practitioner's View." In Higgott, R., and Richardson, J. L., eds. *International Relations: Global and Australian Perspectives in an Evolving Discipline*. Canberra: Department of International Relations, Research School of Pacific Studies, Australian National University, 19–36.

Riggs, F. W. 1994. "Thoughts about Neoidealism vs. Realism: Reflections on Charles Kegley's ISA Presidential Address, March 25, 1993." *International Studies Notes* 19 (Winter): 1–6

Ringel, C. 1997. "Sex Differences in Violent Victimization, 1994." *Bureau of Justice Statistics Special Report*. U.S. Office of Justice Programs (September): NCJ-164508.

Roberts, A. 1991. "A New Age in International Relations?" *International Affairs* 67 (July): 509–25.

Robles, A. C. 1994. *French Theories of Regulation and Conceptions of the International Division of Labour*. Basingstoke, England: Macmillan.

Rorty, R. 1980. *Philosophy and the Mirror of Nature*. Princeton, N.J.: Princeton University Press.

———. 1982. *Consequences of Pragmatism: Essays 1972–1980*. Minneapolis: University of Minnesota Press.

———. 1983. "Postmodern Bourgeois Liberalism." *Journal of Philosophy* 80 (October): 583–89.

———. 1991a. *Essays on Heidegger and Others: Philosophical Papers*. Vol. 2. Cambridge: Cambridge University Press.

———. 1991b. *Objectivity, Relativism, and Truth: Philosophical Papers*. Vol. 1. New York: Cambridge University Press.

Rose, M. A. 1992a. "Defining the Post-Modern." In Jencks, C., ed. *The Post-Modern Reader*. London: Academy Editions, 119–36.

———. 1992b. *The Post-Modern and the Post-Industrial: A Critical Analysis*. Cambridge: Cambridge University Press.

Rosenau, J. N. 1980a. *The Scientific Study of Foreign Policy*. London: Pinter.

———. 1980b. *The Study of Global Interdependence: Essays on the Transnationalization of World Affairs*. New York: Pinter.

———. 1989. "Global Changes and Theoretical Challenges: Toward a Postinternational Politics for the 1990s." In Czempiel, E. O., and Rosenau, J. N., eds. *Global Changes and Theoretical Challenges: Approaches to World Politics for the 1990s*. Lexington, Mass: Lexington Books, 1–20.

———. 1996. "Probing Puzzles Persistently: A Desirable but Improbable Future for IR Theory." In Smith, S., Booth, K., and Zalewski, M., eds. *International Theory: Positivism and Beyond*. Cambridge: Cambridge University Press, 309–17.

———, ed. 1993. *Global Voices: Dialogues in International Relations*. Boulder, Colo.: Westview Press.

Rosenau, J. N., and Czempiel, E. O., eds. 1992. *Governance without Government: Order and Change in World Politics*. Cambridge: Cambridge University Press.

Rosenau, P. M. 1992. *Post-Modernism and the Social Sciences*. New Jersey: Princeton University Press.

Rothstein, R. L. 1991. *The Evolution of Theory in International Relations: Essays in Honor of William T. R. Fox.* Columbia: University of South Carolina Press.
Rousseau, J. J. 1947. *Social Contract.* New York: Hafner.
——— 1974. "A Project for Perpetual Peace." In Jacob, M. C., ed. *Peace Projects of the Eighteenth Century.* New York: Garland.
Roy, R. 1988. "Limits of Genealogical Approach to International Politics." *Alternatives* 13 (January): 77–83.
Ruccio, D. F. 1989. "Fordism on a World Scale: International Dimensions of Regulations." *Review of Radical Political Economics* 21, no. 4: 33–53.
Ruggie, J. G. 1989. "International Structure and International Transformation: Space, Time and Method." In Czempiel, E. O., and Rosenau, J. N., eds. *Global Changes and Theoretical Challenges: Approaches to World Politics for the 1990s.* Lexington, Mass.: Lexington Books, 21–36.
Ryan, M. 1988. "Postmodern Politics." *Theory, Culture and Society* 5 (June): 559–76.
Saint-Pierre, Charles de, Abbe de Tiron. 1974. "A Shorter Project for Perpetual Peace." In Jacob, M. C., ed. *Peace Projects of the Eighteenth Century.* New York: Garland, 1–61.
Saurin, J. 1995. "The End of International Relations? The State of International Theory in the Age of Globalization." In Macmillan, J., and Linklater, A., eds. *Boundaries in Question: New Directions in International Relations.* London: Pinter, 244–61.
Scherpe, K. R. 1986–87. "Dramatization and De-Dramatization of 'The End.' The Apocalyptic Consciousness of Modernity and Post-Modernity." *Cultural Critique* 5 (Winter): 95–129.
Schmittroth, L. 1991. *Statistical Record of Women Worldwide.* Detroit, Mich.: Gale Research.
Schwartz, H. M. 1994. *States versus Markets: History, Geography and the Development of the International Political Economy.* New York: St. Martin's Press.
Shalom, A. 1990. "The Metaphilosophy of Meaning." *Dialectics and Humanism* 17 (Summer): 33–41.
Shapiro, M. J., and Alker, H. R. 1996. *Challenging Boundaries: Global Flows, Territorial Identities.* Borderlines, vol. 2. Minneapolis: University of Minnesota Press.
Shearman, P. 1993. "New Political Thinking Reassessed." *Review of International Studies* 19 (April): 139–58.
Ship, S. J. 1994. "And What about Gender? Feminism and International Relations Third Debate." In Sjolander, C. T., and Cox, W. S., eds. *Beyond Positivism: Critical Reflections on International Relations.* Boulder, Colo.: Lynne Rienner, 129–51.
Silverman, H. J. 1990. "Introduction: The Philosophy of Postmodernism." In Silverman, H. J., ed. *Postmodernism—Philosophy and the Arts.* New York: Routledge, 1–9.
Sjolander, C. T., and Cox, W. S., eds. 1994. *Beyond Positivism: Critical Reflections on International Relations.* Boulder, Colo.: Lynne Rienner.
Smart, B. 1990. "Modernity, Postmodernity and the Present." In Turner, B. S., ed. *Theories of Modernity and Postmodernity.* London: Sage Publications, 14–30.

Smith, S. 1995. "The Self Images of a Discipline: A Genealogy of International Relations Theory." In Booth, K., Smith, S., eds. *International Relations Theory Today*. University Park: Pennsylvania State University Press, 1–37.

———. 1996. "Positivism and Beyond." In Smith, S., Booth, K., and Zalewski, M., eds. *International Theory: Positivism and Beyond*. Cambridge: Cambridge University Press, 11–46.

Smith, S., ed. 1985. *International Relations: British and American Perspectives*. Oxford: Basil Blackwell.

Smith, S., Booth, K., and Zalewski, M., eds. 1996. *International Theory: Positivism and Beyond*. Cambridge: Cambridge University Press.

Soguk, N. 1996. "Transnational/Transborder Bodies: Reexistence, Accommodation, and Exile in Refugee and Migration Movements on the U.S.-Mexican Border." In Shaprio, M. J., and Alker, H. R., eds. *Challenging Boundaries: Global Flows, Territorial Identities*. Minneapolis: University of Minnesota Press, 285–325.

Soja, E. W. 1987. "The Postmodernization of Geography: A Review." *Annals of the Association of American Geographers* 77, no. 2: 289–94.

———. 1990. *Postmodern Geographies: The Reassertion of Space in Critical Social Theory*. London: Verso.

Sommers, C. H. 1994. *Who Stole Feminism?: How Women Have Betrayed Women*. New York: Simon and Schuster.

"Special Issue: Speaking the Language of Exile. Dissidents in International Studies." *International Studies Quarterly* 34 (September): 1990.

Spegele, R. D. 1982. "From the Incoherence of Systems Theory to a Philosophy of International Relations." *Review of Politics* 44 (October): 559–89.

———. 1992. "Richard Ashley's Discourse for International Relations." *Millennium: Journal of International Studies* 21 (Summer): 147–82.

Stephanson, A. 1988. "Regarding Postmodernism—A Conversation with Fredric Jameson." In Ross, A., ed. *Universal Abandon?: The Politics of Postmodernism*. Minneapolis: University of Minnesota Press, 3–30.

Stienstra, D. 1994. *Women's Movements and International Organizations*. New York: St. Martin's Press.

Strange, S. 1987. "The Persistent Myth of Lost American Hegemony." *International Organization* 41 (Autumn): 551–74.

———. 1988. *States and Markets*. London: Pinter.

———. 1989. "I Never Meant to Be an Academic." In Kruzel, J., and Rosenau, J. N., eds. *Journeys through World Politics: Autobiographical Reflections of Thirty-four Academic Travelers*. Lexington, Mass.: Lexington Books, 429–36.

Suganami, H. 1978. "A Note on the Origins of the Word 'International.'" *British Journal of International Studies* 4 (October): 226–32.

Sylvester, C. 1990. "The Emperors' Theories and Transformations: Looking at the Field through Feminist Lenses." In Pirages, D., and Sylvester, C., eds. *Transformations in the Global Political Economy*. London: Macmillan, 230–53.

———. 1993. "Homeless in International Relations? 'Women's' Place in Canonical Texts and Feminist Reimaginings." In Ringrose, M., and Lerner, A. J., eds. *Reimagining the Nation*. Buckingham, U.K.: Open University Press, 77–97.

———. 1994. *Feminist Theory and International Relations in a Postmodern Era*. Cambridge: Cambridge University Press.

———. 1996a. "The Contributions of Feminist Theory to International Relations." In Smith, S., Booth, K., and Zalewski, M., eds. 1996. *International Theory: Positivism and Beyond*. Cambridge: Cambridge University Press, 254–78.

———. 1996b. "Oral Histories Reveal That Junior Female Scholars Expect More from the Academy Than Their Senior Counterparts." *International Studies Newsletter* 23, no. 8: 12.

Szymanski, A. 1985. "Crisis and Vitalization in Marxist Theory." *Science and Society* 49 (Fall): 315–31.

Tar, Z. 1988. *The Frankfurt School*. New York: Schocken Books.

Taylor, C. 1980. "Formal Theory in Social Science." *Inquiry* 23 (June): 139–44.

Tendennick, H., and Forster, E. S., eds. 1938. *Aristotle: Organon*. London: William Heinemann.

Tetreault, M. A. 1997. "Study Finds Underrepresentation of Women in an [*sic*] ISA Journals." *International Studies Newsletter* 24, no. 4: 1–3.

Thompson, K. 1952. "The Study of International Politics: A Survey of Trends and Developments." *The Review of Politics* 14 (October): 433–67.

Thompson, W. R., and Pollins, B. 1997. "ISQ Editors Respond to Recent Critiques of the Journal." *International Studies Newsletter* 24, no. 6: 3–4.

Thrift, N. 1986. "The Geography of International Economic Disorder." In Johnston, R. J., and Taylor, P. J., eds. *A World in Crisis?* Oxford: Basil Blackwell, 12–67.

Tickner, J. A. 1991. "Hans Morgenthau's Principles of Political Realism: A Feminist Reformulation." In Grant, R., and Newland, K., eds. *Gender and International Relations*. Milton Keynes, England: Open University Press, 27–40.

———. 1992. *Gender in International Relations: Feminist Perspectives on Achieving Global Security*. New York: Columbia University Press.

———. 1996. "Identity in International Relations Theory: Feminist Perspectives." In Lapid, Y., and Kratochwil, F., eds. *The Return of Culture and Identity in IR Theory*. Boulder, Colo.: Lynne Rienner, 132–47.

Todorov, T. 1984. *The Conquest of America: The Question of the Other*. Translated by R. Howard. New York: Harper and Row.

Tooze, R. 1991. "International Political Economy: An Interim Assessment." In Higgott, R., and Richardson, J. L., eds. *International Relations: Global and Australian Perspectives on an Evolving Discipline*. Canberra: Department of International Relations, Research School of Pacific Studies, Australian National University, 191–208.

Trimbur, J., and Holt, M. 1992. "Richard Rorty: Philosophy without Foundations." In Sills, C., and Jensen, G. H., eds. *The Philosophy of Discourse: The Rhetorical Turn in Twentieth-Century Thought*. Vol. 1. Portsmouth, N.H.: Heinemann Books, 70–94.

True, J. 1996. "Feminism." In Burchill, S., and Linklater, A., eds. *Theories of International Relations*. New York: St. Martin's Press, 210–51.

Turner, B. S., ed. 1990. *Theories of Modernity and Postmodernity*. London: Sage Publications.

———. 1994. *Orientalism, Postmodernism and Globalism*. New York: Routledge.
United Nations. 1995. *The World's Women 1995: Trend and Transformation*. New York: United Nations.
Wade, R. 1996. "Globalization and Its Limits: Reports of the Death of the National Economy Are Greatly Exaggerated." In Berger, S., and Dore, R., eds. *National Diversity and Global Capitalism*. Ithaca, N.Y.: Cornell University Press, 60–88.
Walker, R. B. J. 1984. "World Politics and Western Reason: Universalism, Pluralism, Hegemony." In Walker, R. B. J., ed. *Culture, Ideology and World Order*. Studies on a Just World Order, no. 5. Boulder, Colo.: Westview Press, 182–216.
———. 1988. "Genealogy, Geopolitics and Political Community: Richard K. Ashley and the Critical Social Theory of International Politics." *Alternatives* 13 (Spring): 84–88.
———. 1992. "Gender and Critique in the Theory of International Relations." In Peterson, V. S., ed. *Gendered States: Feminist (Re)Visions of International Relations Theory*. Boulder, Colo.: Lynne Rienner, 179–202.
Walker, R. B. J., and Mendlovitz, S. H. 1990. "Interrogating State Sovereignty." In Walker, R. B. J., and Mendlovitz, S. H., eds. *Contending Sovereignties: Redefining Political Community*. Boulder, Colo.: Lynne Rienner, 1–12.
Wallace, W. 1996. "Truth and Power, Monks and Technocrats: Theory and Practice in International Relations." *Review of International Studies* 22 (October): 301–21.
Wallack, M. 1994. Review of Walker, R. B. J. 1993. *Inside/Outside: International Relations as Political Theory*. *Canadian Journal of Political Science* 27 (March): 203–4.
Wallerstein, I. M. 1976. *Modern World System: Agriculture and the Origins of the Modern World-Economy in the Sixteenth Century*. New York: Academic Press.
Walsh, T. G. 1996. "Reflections on the Antecedents of Postmodernism." *International Journal on World Peace* 13, no. 3: 35–40.
Waltz, K. N. 1965. *Man, the State and War*. New York: Columbia University Press.
———. 1979. *Theory of International Politics*. New York: Random House.
———. 1986. "Laws and Theories." In Keohane, R. O., ed. *Neorealism and Its Critics*. New York: Columbia University Press, 27–46.
Walzer, M. 1986. "The Politics of Michel Foucault." In Hoy, D. C., ed. *Foucault: A Critical Reader*. Oxford: Basil Blackwell, 51–68.
Wellmer, A. 1985. "On the Dialectic of Modernism and Postmodernism." *Praxis International* 4 (January): 337–62.
Weltman, J. J. 1982. "On the Interpretation of International Thought." *The Review of Politics* 44 (January): 27–41.
Wendt, A. E. 1987. "The Agent-Structure Problem in International Relations Theory." *International Organization* 41 (Summer): 335–71.
———. 1992. "Anarchy Is What States Make of It: The Social Construction of Power Politics." *International Organization* 46 (Spring): 391–426.
Whitworth, S. 1989. "Gender and International Relations: Beyond the Inter-Par-

adigm Debate." *Millennium: Journal of International Studies* 18 (Summer): 265-72.
Wight, C. 1996. "Incommensurability and Cross-Paradigm Communication in International Relations Theory: 'What's the Frequency Kenneth?'" *Millennium: Journal of International Studies* 25 (Summer): 291-319.
Wight, M. 1966. "Why Is There No International Theory?" In Butterfield, H., and Wight, M., eds. *Diplomatic Investigations*. London: George Allen and Unwin, 17-34.
———. 1991. *International Theory: The Three Traditions*. Wight, C. and Porter, B., eds. Leicester: Leicester University Press for the Royal Institute of International Affairs.
Williams, H. 1992. *International Relations in Political Theory*. London: Open University Press.
Williams, R. 1977. *Marxism and Literature*. Oxford: Oxford University Press.
Wilson, W. 1923. *Woodrow Wilson's Case for the League of Nations*. New York: Kennikat Press.
Wolin, R. 1992. *The Terms of Cultural Criticism: The Frankfurt School, Existentialism, Poststructuralism*. New York: Columbia University Press.
Zagorin, P. 1990. "Historiography and Postmodernism: Reconsiderations." *History and Theory* 24, no. 3: 263-74.
Zalewski, M. 1993. "Feminist Standpoint Theory Meets International Relations Theory: A Feminist Version of David and Goliath?" *The Fletcher Forum of World Affairs* 17 (August): 13-32.
———. 1994a. "What's New? Feminist Observations on the New Europe." In Carlsnaes, W., and Smith, S., eds. *European Foreign Policy: The EC and the Changing Perspectives in Europe*. London: Sage Publications, 223-37.
———. 1994b. "The Women/'Women' Question in International Relations." *Millennium: Journal of International Studies* 23 (Summer): 407-23.
———. 1996. "All These Theories Yet the Bodies Keep Piling Up: Theory, Theorists, Theorising." In Smith, S., Booth, K., and Zalewski, M., eds. *International Theory: Positivism and Beyond*. Cambridge: Cambridge University Press, 340-53.
Zalewski, M., and Enloe, C. 1995. "Questions about Identity in International Relations." In Booth, K., and Smith., S., eds. *International Relations Theory Today*. University Park: Pennsylvania State University Press, 279-305.
Zimmern, A. 1939. *University Teaching of International Relations*. Paris: International Institute of Intellectual Co-operation, League of Nations.

Index

abolitionism, 125
absolutism, 59, 112
accumulation, 68, 114, 191, 192
aesthetics, 59, 62, 65–69 passim, 74, 191, 218n. 82
  and postmodernism, 72, 73, 108, 184
affirmative action policies, 155
age of reason, 88
agencies, 15, 96, 97, 102, 113, 116, 129. *See also* agents; political-agency; subjectivities
agendas. *See* deconstructive, hierarchical agendas, research
agents, 38, 97, 102, 105, 123. *See also* agencies; political agency; subjectivities
ahistoricism, 166. *See also* historicism
Alker, H. R., 208n. 70
Allison, Graham, 94
Almond, Gabriel, 47
altruism, 154
ambiguity, 120, 196, 197
American Political Science Association (APSA), 176
Americanization, 60
Amnesty International, 171
anarchy, 8, 16, 38, 46, 48, 120, 147, 152
  and Ashley, 104, 121, 133
Anderson, Perry, 74
androcentrism, 154, 155, 166
antifoundationalism, 130–33, 185
antilogocentrism, 57. *See also* logocentrism

architecture, 53, 184
Argentina, 172
Aristotle, 11, 14, 40, 218n. 87
arms race, 30, 146
Aronowitz, Stanley, 79
art(s), 81, 85, 86, 170, 184, 218n. 82
Ashley, Richard, 19, 26, 61, 181–83
  "critical posture of estrangement," of 182, 183, 199
  early works of, 92–106
  observations on, 106–9
  postmortem on, 109–17
  and feminist scholarship, 144
  and IR theory, 45, 179
  limitations to critique of, 138–41
  and positivism, 87, 167
  and postmodernism, 90, 133–36, 184, 186, 187, 188
  subversive, 197, 198, 199, 200, 201
  and poststructuralism, 87, 123–26
  relevance of theory of, 108, 127–30
  substance of theory of, 130–33
  "rationality proper" of, 96, 97, 110
  scholarship of, 136–37
  and Waltz, 196
Auschwitz, 30, 56

balance of power, 42, 47, 92
Banks, Michael, 47
Baudrillard, Jean, 69, 135, 184, 186
Bauman, Zygmunt, 75
behaviorism, 223nn. 23, 26
behaviorist revolution, 43

Bentham, Jeremy, 39
Berlin Wall, 18
Bernstein, Richard, 77
Biersteker, Thomas, 17, 4
bigotry, 176, 187
Bleiker, Roland, 170
Bloom, Allan, 136–37
Bolshevik Revolution of 1917, 227n. 4
Bonaparte, Napoleon, 39
Bosnian war, 172
boundaries
    intellectual, 45, 51, 62, 70, 81
    and postmodernism, 53, 78, 119, 170
Bowers, John, 52
Brandom, Robert, 82
British Home Office, 171
Brown, Chris, 11, 20, 10, 78, 131, 132, 133, 184, 208n. 71
Brown, Richard, 164
Brown, Robin, 198
Brown, Wendy, 58, 79
Bull, Hedley, 45, 207n. 45
Burchill, Scott, 46
bureaucracy, 31, 94

Caldicott, Helen, 146, 147
Callinicos, Alex, 55, 72–73, 74, 75, 84
Camilleri, Joseph, 45
Campaign for Nuclear Disarmament (CND), 146
Campbell, David, 45, 46, 184
capital, 69, 71, 191, 194, 195
capitalism, 19, 58, 59, 60, 67, 68, 69, 119, 190–95 passim, 215n. 19
    and critical postmodernism, 72, 73, 75, 79, 114, 159, 191
Carr, E. H., 7, 9, 33, 41, 103, 180
Chan, Stephen, 33
change(s) (epochal, historical), 63, 67, 160, 180, 185, 190, 194, 202
    and Ashley, 116, 134
    and postmodernism, 67, 153, 191
chauvinism, 157
China, People's Republic of, 92
Cicero, 39
civil society, 33, 58

class, 67, 68, 69, 79, 81, 113, 119, 191
    diplomatic, 157–58
    end of, 69, 217n. 53
    struggle, 74, 159
Cold War, 12, 18, 24, 177
colonialism, 62, 159
color, 29, 161. *See also* race
Committee for the Study on the Status of Women in International Relations, 173, 175
commodification, 68
communication(s) (technological revolution in), 53, 58–63 passim, 98, 132, 195, 215n. 19
    and identity politics, 167
    and subversive postmodernists, 81, 82, 84, 190
    and technological postmodernism, 192
Comte, Auguste, 26
conflict, 101, 178
    and Ashley, 92, 111, 141
    resolution of, 146
    studies of, 172
    and technical postmodernism, 194
Connolly, William, 131, 139, 140
conspiracy theory, 115
constructivism, 15
consumption, 53, 59, 60, 62, 63, 65, 69, 193
consumption-production dialectic, 191
Container 96—Art across Oceans, 169
contextualism, 20, 23, 77, 78, 80, 108, 112, 115
Continental school, The, 220n. 122
control, 99, 143, 154, 192, 194
    and Ashley, 104, 109, 112, 113, 123
    and males, 158, 175
    and subversive postmodernism, 202
    Waltz on, 103
    of women, 153
cosmopolitanism, 167
Cox, Robert, 18, 100
Cox, Wayne, 19

crime figures, 171
critical theorists, 4, 33, 73, 116, 208n. 91
  theory, 19, 22, 110, 134, 144, 208n. 71, 218n. 82
cross-culturalism, 60, 98. *See also* culture
cultural analysis, 136
cultural forms, 62
cultural practices, 79
culture, 59, 66–69, 77, 83, 157, 167, 191, 193, 218n. 82
  and Ashley, 108, 116
  changes in, 63, 65, 67
  crisis in, 123
  and the "other," 187
  and postmodernism, 72, 184
    critical, 73
    subjective, 200
    subversive, 79, 84
    technological, 71
  and poststructuralism, 149
  mass, 59, 76
  Western, 62, 174, 175

Dahrendorf, Ralf, 33
Dante Aligheiri, 40
Darwin, Charles, 40
debt crisis, 172
decision making, 11, 12, 69, 96
deconstruction, 30, 32, 47, 48, 53, 55, 56, 61, 90, 149, 178, 195
  and Ashley, 131–32, 133, 134–35, 136
  ethic of, 186, 187
  and Nietzsche, 137
  and postmodernism, 17, 25, 184, 185
    subversive, 66, 77, 78, 183, 197
  and research methods, 185
  and textual analysis, 197, 198
  and theory, 201
  and the Third Debate, 20
deconstructionists, 3, 5, 82, 175
democracy, 60, 190, 193, 194
Der Derian, James, 45–46, 91, 96, 184, 197

Derrida, Jacques, 57, 85, 119, 135, 136
  and Callinicos, 84
  diversity in thought of, 184
  and international relations, 198
  and Western logocentrism, 83
  and women's emancipation, 175
Dessler, David, 16
determinism, 97, 102, 105, 115, 116, 136, 191
development studies, 54
Devetak, Richard, 214n. 6
dialogism, 20, 52, 66, 78
difference(s), 119, 135, 145, 147, 164, 184, 185, 188, 205n. 16, 233n. 114
  and Ashley, 118, 125, 127
  and identity politics, 79, 165–68
  and postmodernism, 67, 76, 125, 187
  and similarity, 185
diplomacy, 16, 37, 41, 40, 42, 101, 115
diplomatic corps, 159
discourse(s), 17, 20, 25, 52, 57, 66, 81, 199
  and Ashley, 106, 121
  critical, 57
  feminist, 164
  human, 156
  identity, 164, 170, 173
  intellectual, 64, 88, 201
  intertextual, 200
  modernist, 55, 57, 77, 189
  on sovereignty within knowledge, 178
  ontological, 149
  political, 166
  positivist, 104
  and postmodernism, 25–33 passim, 51–55 passim, 70, 72, 183, 186
    subversive, 66, 77
  radical matriarchal, 170
  rationalist, 55, 76, 136
  theoretical, 163
discrimination, 147, 155, 176, 187, 217n. 58

dissidents, 196
  and Ashley, 106, 128, 135, 183
  intellectual, 20, 89, 115, 143–44, 185, 205n. 2
domestic violence, 157, 158
Dunn, Frederick, 9
Durkheim, Emile, 11, 40

Eastern Europe, 2
eclecticism, 55, 62, 66
ecological crises, 22
economics, 65, 79, 86, 93, 103, 136, 193
economism, 93, 99–106, 115, 191, 196
El Salvador, 172
elites, 122
elitism, 75, 129, 175
Elkins, David, 58
Elshtain, Jean Bethke, 143
emancipation, 28, 30, 56, 74, 77, 78, 119, 189
  and Ashley, 107, 108, 112–23 passim, 128
  and subversive postmodernists, 84
  and technological postmodernists, 71
  and women, 143, 175
emancipatory praxis, 98, 99
empiricism, 32, 43, 148
English departments, 198
English school, The, 210n. 11
Enlightenment, 55, 56, 63, 66, 125, 157, 190
  and Ashley, 109, 120, 135
  enterprise, 196
  knowledge, 190
  philosophy, 37
  project, 21, 44, 77, 88, 107, 196, 199
  theory, 57
  thinking, 19, 83, 100, 189
Enlightenment thought, 20–25 passim, 30, 32, 39, 44, 57, 70
  and Ashley, 127, 134
  and feminism, 174
  and gender politics, 159
  and postmodernism, 53
  and women, 158–59
Enloe, Cynthia, 23, 153–57 passim, 172, 176, 229n. 23
  and identity politics, 164, 165
  and IR, 169, 170, 177
environment, 44, 87, 98, 100, 101. *See also* global environmental politics
environmental crises, 22
environmental degradation, 2
epistemology, 4, 15, 19, 57, 66, 76, 77, 159, 161, 189
  and Ashley, 99, 104, 107, 108, 114, 135
  critical, 72–76, 114
  Marxist, 66, 107
  positivist, 104, 186
  rationalist, 99, 139
  of reflectivist approach, 95
  and Sylvester, 150
equality, 173, 211n. 21
Erasmus, 37, 207n. 43
essentialism, 29, 166, 167, 185, 191
ethical relativism, 125, 131, 132
ethics, 85, 86, 131, 169, 179
ethnic cleansing, 2, 22, 30, 128
ethnic conflict, 177
ethnicity, 81
eugenics, 169
Eurocentrism, 3, 115, 175
exclusion (political, professional, social), 28, 83, 125, 144, 151, 175, 189
  and Ashley, 123, 124, 132
  and Enloe, 153
  and feminist scholarship, 144
  and males, 161
  and subversive postmodernists, 78
  and women, 155
exploitation, 161, 174, 175, 217n. 58

fact(s) (analysis and understanding of), 6, 7, 13, 18, 26, 27, 76, 102, 182, 196
  and Ashley, 100
  feminist visions of, 170–74
  and international politics, 40

and IR, 47, 179
and postmodernism, 76, 200
theory, 104
famine, 2, 22, 60
fascism, 42, 156
femininity, 153, 154, 158, 230n. 34
feminism, 23, 143, 148, 149, 174–77, 178
  epistemological, 148, 148–53
  standpoint, 148, 153–59
feminists, 23, 145
  and IR, 146, 148, 154, 174, 175
  postmodern, 23, 166, 173, 177, 183, 187, 188
  radical, 174, 175
Ferguson, Yale, 11, 18, 10, 36, 46
feudalism, 37
Flax, Jane, 62
foreign policy, 11, 12, 41, 42, 44, 94, 177
  and Ashley, 101, 102
Foster, Hal, 64
Foucault, Michel, 33, 57, 85, 135, 136
  and Ashley, 107, 186
  and Callinicos, 84
  criticism of, 125
  diversity in thought of, 184
  and emancipation, 119
  genealogical attitude, 199
  on the intellectual, 214n. 81
  and international theory, 121
  and power, 80–81
  and rationality, 134
  and women's emancipation, 175
  Western episteme, 76
foundationalism, 2, 20, 135, 189, 190
  and Ashley, 108, 130, 136
  and postmodernism, 131, 135
Frankel, Joseph, 206nn. 24, 25
Frankfurt school, 19, 66, 68, 73, 107, 190, 221n. 2
Freudianism, 70
functionalism, 11

Gadamer, Hans-Georg, 4
Gardner, John, 52

gender, 20, 23, 29, 147–49, 154, 161, 173
  and IR, 147, 159–70, 174–77
  and Morgenthau, 196
  and postmodernism, 69, 74, 78, 187
  and power, 81, 156
  and Sylvester, 150, 152, 159
  and women, 144, 145, 155
genealogy, 48, 66, 80, 90
genocide, 30, 56, 87, 175
geography, 54, 194–95
George, Jim, 27, 29–30, 46, 56, 184, 196
Germany, 103
Giddens, Anthony, 59, 67, 215n. 27
Gills, Barry, 195
Gilpin, Robert, 91, 126, 128, 210n. 6
global environmental politics, 6. *See also* environment
globalization, 18, 19, 28, 61, 160, 192, 193, 215n. 25
Godrej, Farah, 24
Gonzales, M., 218n. 79
government, 31, 32, 42, 69
Gramsci, Antonio, 66
Gramscian method, 18, 193
Great Depression, 103
Greenham Common, women of, 146, 152, 162
Greer, Germaine, 234n. 141
Griffiths, Martin, 169
Grotius, Hugo 37, 206n. 43
Gulf War, 172
gynocentrism, 159

Haas, Ernst, 94
Habermas, Jurgen, 81, 100, 107, 136, 221n. 2
Halliday, Fred, 12, 14, 45, 201, 226n. 116, 229n. 17
Harding, S., 230n. 32
Harvard School, The, 235n. 5
Harvey, David, 60, 77, 82
Hassen, Ihab, 76
Hebdige, Dick, 52, 53, 70
Hegel, Georg, 38, 39

Heidegger, Martin, 77
Henehan, Marie, 173
Hertz, John, 110
Higgott, Richard, 47
Hinsley, F. H., 36
Hiroshima, 30, 56
Hirsch, Eric, 84, 85
historical materialist perspective, 19
historicism, 105, 166
history, 14, 29, 71, 202
  and Ashley, 96, 97, 102, 108, 112, 114, 116, 120, 122, 123, 132, 135
  and capitalism, 68, 69
  and identity politics, 161–62
  and IR, 32, 36, 39, 41, 45, 202
  and Marxism, 136, 137
  and postmodernism, 63, 70, 97, 199, 200
    subversive, 77–78, 79, 80, 97, 183
  revisionist, 20, 189
  Western, 58, 159
history of ideas, 36
Hobbes, Thomas, 38, 39, 206n. 43
Hobbesian tradition, 211n. 19
Hoffman, Mark, 32, 64, 198, 225n. 98
  and IR theory, 45, 47, 195–196
  and subversive postmodernism, 197, 203
Hoffmann, Stanley, 1, 2, 8, 9, 39, 94, and IR, 3, 5, 6, 7, 42
Holsti, Kalevi, 32, 33, 37, 45, 129, 179, 181
  and classical tradition, 209n. 5, 213n. 63
  and IR theory, 179, 206n. 43
homosexuality, 157
human nature, 40
human rights, 6, 171, 172, 197. *See also* rights
humanism, 77
humanities, 9, 58, 76, 82, 174, 196, 198
  and postmodernism, 51, 76, 78, 86, 87
Hume, David, 26, 39

Hussein, Saddam, 197
Hutchings, Kimberly, 14
Huyssen, Andreas, 55
hypercommunications, 65, 70
hyperconsumerism, 60. *See also* consumerism

idealism, 33, 14, 190, 111
ideas, 44, 59, 64, 67, 150, 192, 201
  feminist, 153, 175
  and identity politics, 167
  importation of, 133–36
identities, 119, 147, 153, 168
  gender, 148, 154
  multiple, 164, 165, 167
  and Sylvester, 150, 151
identity, 20, 22, 71, 147, 150, 187
  and Ashley, 90, 134
  disciplinary, 3, 21
  and feminists, 148, 232n. 105
  national, 121, 164, 232n. 105
  and subjective postmodernism, 200
  and subversive postmodernists, 78, 80
identity politics, 22, 23, 75, 79, 80, 145, 189, 212n. 56
  and Ashley, 183
  critical postmodernism, 218n. 76
  feminist, 167
  international, 160, 164, 165, 167, 168
  and IR, 159–70, 183
  and subversive postmodernists, 79–80
ideology, 42, 77, 113, 157, 169
image(s), 20, 29, 60, 69, 191, 199
  and identity politics, 167
  and men in IR, 150
  and subversive postmodernists, 78
imperialism, 61, 114
individualism, 75, 80
industrial revolution, 75
industrialism, 60, 160
industry, 70, 85
inequality, 22, 174, 190
information age, 70, 71

Index 269

innovation(s), 58, 59, 194
  aesthetic, 69
  and postmodernists, 85
  intellectual, 201
  scientific, 68
  technological, 184, 191
  theoretical, 74
institutionalism, 154, 235n. 5
institutions, international (organizations), 6, 11, 12, 33, 39, 42, 49, 115
international political economy, 11, 12, 92, 160, 169, 192, 194
international political theory, 19, 90. *See also* international relations theory
international politics, 3, 15, 16, 19, 21, 131
international relations, 4, 37, 39, 48, 103, 142, 210n. 7
  and Ashley, 115, 116, 129, 135, 140
  crisis of, 123–24
  and facts, 170
  and feminism, 143–47, 163
  gendering of, 148–59
  and identity politics, 164
  and postmodernism, 86, 163, 188, 191
  and poststructuralist theory, 128
  study of, 30–31, 41, 89, 93, 141, 179, 188
  and texts, 133
  and theory, 1–2, 3, 125
  See also international relations theory
International Relations (discipline of), 17–25, 42, 159
  definition of, 5–6, 7, 8
  discipline of, 2, 31, 33, 36, 40, 41, 46, 48
  diversity in, 184–88
  "end of," 30, 32, 183
  and feminism, 145, 152–56
  and gender, 147, 172, 174
  and identity politics, 159–70
  and IR theory, 9–17, 44
  and postmodernism, 52, 54, 88, 90, 91, 174–77, 188–95
    subversive 183, 195–203
  purpose, method and questions of, 3, 5–9, 43, 47, 156, 157
  and theory, 26, 29, 178–81
international relations theory, 5, 8, 9–17, 32, 36, 46–49, 90, 178–81, 185
  Ashley on, 106, 107, 109, 116–17, 121, 130, 182
  Bleiker on, 170
  and identity politics, 161
  and intellectual importations, 134
  and postmodern theory, 88, 138
  and poststructural challenge, 123
  and the relevance of subversive postmodern theory, 195–203
  realist doctrine in, 122
  See also international political theory
International Studies, 41, 44
International Studies Association (ISA), 23, 24, 173, 175, 176, 177
International Studies Quarterly, 124, 144, 176
interpretation(s), 57, 113, 114, 131, 179
  and Ashley, 101, 102, 104, 122, 132, 133, 141, 182
  and postmodernism, 77, 79, 146, 162, 197–98, 199, 200
interpretivism, 2, 32, 73, 131, 147, 198
  and Ashley, 100, 101, 108, 121, 127, 133, 137
  politics of, 123–26
  See also textual analysis, literary criticism
intertextualism, 20, 22, 32, 48, 53, 90. *See also* textual analysis; literary criticism
Iraq, 172, 197

Jameson, Fredric, 67–68, 69, 85, 184
Jencks, Charles, 69, 184
Jones, Adam, 160, 170, 172, 234n. 130
Jones, Roy, 210n. 11
justice, 6, 70, 76, 189, 189, 190, 211n. 21
  and Ashley, 107, 128

270   Index

global, 180
and groups, 78
and IR, 17
and subversive postmodernism, 84, 86

Kando, Tom, 174
Kant, Immanuel, 39, 40, 207n. 43
Keal, Paul, 43
Kegley, Charles, 17
Kellner, Douglas, 217n. 58
Keohane, Robert, 90, 94, 95, 96, 126, 127, 200, 210n. 6
Kindleberger, Charles, 127
Kirk, Gwyn, 152
knowledge, 3, 4, 23, 36, 52, 59, 163
and Ashley, 90, 95–97, 100–103, 110–13, 121, 131, 133, 182
and facts, 7, 213n. 63
and identity politics, 165, 166, 167, 170
and IR, 10, 17, 32
and language, 56, 77
and modernists, 54, 81, 83, 87
and postmodernism, 54, 55, 62, 70, 199
feminist, 148–59
subversive, 66, 77, 82, 86, 183, 189
echnological, 71
and power, 23, 27, 179
and rationalist tradition of inquiry, 93, 96, 139
sociology of, 4, 16
sovereignty over, 178, 179
and technical rationality, 93, 96, 112
theory of, 15, 128
and the Third Debate, 21, 28
knowledge-power system, 47, 214n. 81. *See also* knowledge, and power
knowledge systems, 47, 66, 84, 95, 131
Knutsen, T. L., 209n. 5
Krasner, Stephen, 127
Krause, Jill, 147
Kreml, William, 17
Kroker, Arthur, 71

Kuspit, Donald, 54
Kuwait, 172

labor, 69, 114, 158, 159, 160
Lança, Patricia, 174–75, 233n. 114
language
and Ashley, 132, 135
and Hirsch, 84
and IR theory, 45, 179
and knowledge, 56, 77
and postmodernism, 55, 70, 83, 87, 180, 196
subversive, 66, 79, 81–82, 84, 190
feminist, 148, 155, 159, 175
Lapid, Yosef, 20, 46, 90, 143, 144
Lash, Scott, 68
law, 33, 39, 96, 119, 157
and IR, 36, 41
international, 11, 42, 197
Levin, Harry, 52
liberalism, 70, 119, 189, 220n. 130
liberation, 71, 77, 78, 84, 107. *See also* emancipation
life expectancy, 173
Lijphart, Arend, 3
linguistics, 74, 184. *See also* language; literary criticism
Linklater, Andrew, 144
literacy, 60
literary criticism, 54, 197, 198
literature, 62, 73, 143, 145
Locke, John, 26, 39
logic, 55, 75, 87, 125
and Ashley, 90, 93, 97, 99, 102, 126, 129, 131, 133
binary, 188, 197
emancipatory, 98, 102
and modernists, 77, 85
and subversive postmodernism, 66, 77, 84, 197, 220n. 122
logocentrism, 48, 83, 175. *See also* antilogocentrism
Lyotard, Jean-Francois, 70, 71, 77, 81, 135, 215n. 14

Machiavelli, Niccolò, 39

Maghroori, Ray, 18
males, 21, 23, 146, 158, 161, 175
"malestream" theory, 143, 154, 155, 162
man, 22, 159
Mann, Sheilah, 176
Mannheim, Karl, 224n. 55
Mansbach, Nicholas, 46
Mansbach, Richard, 10, 11, 18, 36
Manzo, Kate, 57
marginalization, 78, 124, 125, 155, 160, 176, 190
markets, 44, 159, 194
marriage, 157–58, 177
Martin, David, 33
Martin, Jane, 164, 166–67
Marx, Karl, 11, 39, 114, 136
Marxism, 22, 70, 119, 136–37, 190, 191
masculinism, 145, 147, 148, 149, 150, 153
masculinity, 154, 157, 158, 230n. 34
McGowan, John, 118
McKinley, Michael, 31
meaning(s), 20, 22, 87, 120, 196
  and Ashley, 90, 121, 122, 131, 132, 182
  and subjective postmodernism, 199, 200
  and subversive postmodernists, 78, 79, 183, 196
  and Sylvester, 150
  and technological postmodernism, 71
  and men, 76, 105, 148, 163, 169
  and IR, 145
  and knowledge, 151, 154, 155
  and subversive postmodernism, 76
  vulnerability of, 170–74
  and women, 144, 145–46, 153
metanarratives, 20, 48, 75, 100
metaphysics, 4, 51, 83, 158, 202
metatheory, 2, 28, 51, 73, 74, 80, 90
method(s), 5–9, 45
methodology, 46, 208n. 70
military force, 147, 193

military studies, 146
minorities, 4, 23, 25, 76
misogyny, 144, 154, 161, 196
Modelski, George, 126, 127
modernist project, 201. *See also* Enlightenment; Enlightenment project
modernist theory, 4, 27, 55, 57, 77–81 passim, 135, 136, 179
  and Ashley, 123
  charges against, 84
  and IR, 187
  modernist-realist, 28
  and postmodernism, 138, 180
modernists, 26, 55, 87, 88, 126, 127
modernity, 19, 22, 28, 30, 49, 65, 67, 70, 118
  and Ashley, 120, 121, 127, 128, 134, 141
  late, 193, 194
  and postmodernism, 55, 56, 57, 60, 61, 131, 135, 157, 191, 196, 201
  subversive, 77, 86
  technological, 71
modernization, 61, 63, 67
morality, 39, 42, 86, 155
Morgenthau, Hans, 8, 38, 40, 41–42, 94, 102, 196, 209n. 4
  and Ashley, 101, 102, 103, 116
Morrow, Raymond, 72, 74
mortality rates (men and women), 173. *See also* life expectancy
multinational corporations. *See* transnational corporations
murder, 157, 173
Murphy, Craig, 195

Nagasaki, 30
narratives, 24–30 passim, 66, 77, 78, 154, 167, 216n. 46
  and Ashley, 111, 122, 132
  and IR, 177
  master, 56, 57, 70, 74, 190
  modernist, 54, 77, 126, 131, 132, 200

personal, 163, 173
realist, 45, 111, 122
and subversive postmodernism, 197
totalitarian, 115, 197
nation-state(s), 8, 16, 19, 27, 38, 192
  and Ashley, 111, 196
  and identity politics, 165
  and IR, 5–6, 11, 18, 36, 37, 39, 48, 49, 147
  and postmodernism, 18, 49, 60, 195, 193
    feminist, 157, 159
    subversive, 197
  as social fabrication, 129–30
  See also states
national identity, 121, 164, 232n. 105
national interest, 42, 47, 102
national socialism, 73
nationalism, 29, 33, 193, 232n. 105
nature, 38, 67, 71
Navari, C., 211n. 19
neorealism, 89, 104, 105
  and Ashley, 90, 92, 93, 99, 103, 106, 111–15
  See also structural realism
New Mediaevalism, 45
Newman, Charles, 52
Nicaragua, 172
Nietzsche, Friedrich, 32, 70, 71, 136–37, 175
nihilism, 22, 70–71, 125, 130–33, 140, 183
1968 generation, 72–73, 74
Norris, Christopher, 55, 83, 84
nuclear proliferation, 42
Nye, Joseph, 94

O'Callaghan, Terry, 169
O'Neill, John, 85, 86, 190
objectivity, 4, 48, 75, 85, 87, 100, 121, 158
Okin, Susan Moller, 156
ontologies, 4, 15, 16, 19, 57, 104, 160, 177
Onuf, Nicholas, 10, 47, 200, 235n. 16

oppression, 28, 80, 119, 161, 190
  and Ashley, 113, 129
  and identity politics, 166, 167
  and women, 153, 154, 155, 159
order, 12, 37, 45, 46, 75, 101
  and Ashley, 110, 111, 113, 114
  world, 59, 99, 110, 111, 113, 114
organonist knowledge systems, 57, 76
"other," the, 76, 79, 144, 161, 187

Palan, Ronen, 195
patriarchy, 25, 29, 125, 145–48, 171, 173
  crisis in, 123
  and critical postmodernism, 74
  history of, 159
  and identity politics, 162
peace, 12, 33, 37, 45, 96, 168, 197
  and IR, 17, 46, 202
Peace of Westphalia (1648), 37, 39
Peloponnesian War, 37
perspectives
  feminist, 142, 152, 154, 156, 159, 160, 175, 177
  and IR, 177, 178, 179, 201
  postmodern, 181, 187
  poststructural, 181
perspectivism 13, 21, 22, 43, 44, 48, 80, 185
  and Ashley, 132
  and postmodernists, 62, 85, 88, 190
Peterson, V. Spike, 164, 171, 172, 176
  and IR, 145, 147, 184
  and standpoint feminism, 156, 157, 158, 159
Pettman, Jan Jindy, 152, 162
Philippines, 24
philosophy, 28, 39, 54, 90, 108, 184, 229n. 18
  continental, 56
  and IR theory, 36, 40
  Western, 57, 76, 82
Plato, 11, 40
pluralism, 13, 55,
Polanyi, Karl, 103

Index   273

political correctness, 75, 84, 88, 126, 160, 187
political economy, 60, 69, 85, 185, 215n. 27
  and postmodernism, 62, 133, 184, 191
  See also international political economy
political movements, 137
political prisoners, 171–72
political science, 9, 176
political-agency, 113. *See also* agencies; agents
politics, 29, 43, 79, 80, 94, 101, 129
  and Ashley, 100, 103, 106, 110, 120, 132
  changes in, 65, 67
  domestic, 39, 44, 156
  emancipatory, 69, 110
  global/international/world, 11, 26, 27, 28, 40, 153, 174
  and Ashley, 95, 96, 102, 105, 113–21 passim, 130
  and gender, 147, 154, 157, 164, 174
  and history, 37, 122
  and identity politics, 160, 164, 165, 167, 168
  and IR, 38, 46, 48, 170, 202
  and postmodern feminism, 142, 153–56, 163, 173
  and subversive postmodernism, 183, 196, 197
  and theory, 36, 46, 95, 99, 104, 177, 179, 196
  left-wing, 74, 75
  of literary criticism, 198
  and postmodernism, 54, 86, 194
  power, 61, 112, 113
  progressive, 187, 189
  and science, 86, 186
  transformational, 108, 111
  and women, 152, 156
"politics of inclusion," 75, 76
Pollins, Brian, 176
Pollock, G., 232n. 103

Popper, Karl, 26
Porter, Tony, 114, 127, 131
positivism, 4, 28, 33, 43, 44, 66, 109, 127, 187
  and Ashley, 90, 99–110 passim, 113, 116, 120, 127, 128, 129, 140
  in IR, 17, 185
  of Waltz, 196
  and women, 157, 159
postfordism, 69, 185
"postmodern condition," 59
postmodernism, 2, 51, 138
  and Ashley, 108, 133–36, 137, 140
  critical, 66, 86, 184, 189, 194, 218n. 76
  critical-epistemological, 72–76, 108, 190–91
  and critical examination, 125
  critiques of, 124–25
  definition of, 51–53, 133, 184, 218n. 76
  destruction of, 131
  epistemological, 184
  feminist, 148, 149, 152–53, 162, 167
  and IR, 161, 163, 183
  in IR, 91, 186, 188
  research directions for, 188–95
  subversive, 76–85, 108, 137, 140, 195
  subversive-deconstructive, 66, 184–88, 189–90
  technological/productionist, 65, 67–71, 86, 184, 185, 189, 191–95
  and the Third Debate, 17–25
  toward an understanding of, 85–88
  See also Ashley, Richard; postmodern theory; Sylvester, Christine
postmodern theory, 17, 28, 52, 67, 87
  and complexification, 80
  critical, 73
  and critical analysis, 88
  and cultural goods, 72
  as epochal change, 57–63
  feminist, 162

274   Index

idealism of, 180, 181
ideology of, 138
in IR, 186–88
and Marxism, 137
motifs of, 66–67
poverty of, 125
and realism, 25–30
as resistance and disturbance, 54–57
subversive, 87, 183, 187, 188
and subversive postmodernists, 187
success of, 85
and texts, 132
and theoretical discourse, 16, 85, 138, 179, 185
typologies of, 64–65
See also postmodernism; theory
postmodernity, 201
poststructuralism, 4, 21, 77, 80, 139, 140, 149, 237n. 43
power, 4, 8, 16, 18, 42, 156, 193
  and Ashley, 90, 99, 100, 102, 113, 114, 129
  centrality of, 61
  Foucault on, 80–81, 119
  and gender, 147
  global, 61, 194
  Hobbes on, 38
  and IR, 40, 147, 154
  and knowledge, 23, 27, 47, 179, 214n. 81
  and males, 159, 175
  and national interest, 42
  political, 102, 114, 156, 194
  and postmodernism, 70, 75, 80, 192
  and radical feminists, 175
  and social scientific analysis, 194
  and states, 192, 195
  Thucydides on, 39
  will to, 137
  and women, 155
  and world economy, 6
pragmatism, 77, 137
prisoners' dilemmas, 152
problem-solving theory, 26, 94, 95, 96, 98, 129

production, 19, 59, 61–70 passim, 215n. 19
  and Ashley, 114, 115, 129
  global, 44, 48
  just-in-time, 193
  mode(s) of, 60, 66, 68, 69, 114, 115, 191, 193
  nature of, 53
  and postmodernism, 72, 192
progress, 3, 4, 28, 59, 102, 189, 201
  costs of, 62
  and technological postmodernists, 71
public policy, 31, 33, 177, 192
purpose, 4, 22, 71
  and Ashley, 131
  and IR, 5–9, 43, 179
  and Marxism, 136
  and postmodernism, 79, 185
  and poststructuralists, 131

race, 29, 81, 161, 187. *See also* color
racism, 125, 128, 175, 176, 187
Radford, Lorraine, 171
Ramberg, Bennett, 18
rape, 154, 157, 171, 172
rational choice, 93, 94
rationalism, 32, 44, 54, 55, 57, 83, 94, 223n. 23
rationality, 19, 20, 22, 28, 30, 76, 78, 189
  and Allison, 94
  and Ashley, 104, 109, 110, 116, 121, 134
  "death of," 48
  economic, 103
  and Foucault, 80
  and language, 81–82
  and postmodernism, 57, 53, 71, 76, 196
  and Rorty, 220n. 122
  technical, 92–106, 110, 111, 120, 127, 128
  and women, 157
  See also rationality, technical
"rationality proper." *See* Ashley, Richard

"relations international." *See* Sylvester, Christine
realism, 16, 18, 45, 61, 116, 132
  and Ashley, 99, 100, 101, 102, 111–16, 124–29 passim, 132
  deconstruction of, 187
  discourse of, 162
  George on, 196
  and IR, 13, 33, 154, 179
  and masculinist inscriptions, 142
  and Morgenthau, 101
  political, 99, 122
  and postmodernism, 25, 25–30
  practical, 100, 101, 102, 110, 112, 116
  and silence, 122
  and the state, 122–23
  structural, 113, 129, 132, 186, 210n. 6
  technical, 111, 112
realists, 15, 16, 27, 88, 112, 124, 126, 127
realist theory, 26, 27, 29, 30, 135
  in IR, 4, 13, 179, 186
  and postmodern theorists, 180
  and women, 157, 159
reality, 9, 20, 21, 27, 77, 95, 182
  and Ashley, 96, 97, 121
  and modernists, 83
  and postmodernism, 63, 66, 78, 81, 85, 200
  and poststructuralists, 131
  and practical realism, 102
  and theory, 15, 82
realpolitik, 27, 90, 165, 179
reason, 55, 70, 76, 87, 121
  and Ashley, 90, 102, 104, 120, 123, 130
  and Foucault, 80
  and masculinity, 158
  and modernists, 85
  O'Neill on, 85
  and postmodernism, 66, 77, 84, 119
  and power, 81, 119
  reaffirming of, 195–203
  and relativism, 77

reductionism, 74, 93, 99
reflexivity, 143
regimes, 6, 11, 129
rejectionism, 3, 25, 134
relativism, 2, 22, 87, 175, 183, 196, 236n. 22
  and Ashley, 130–33, 140
  and IR, 48, 198
  linguistic, 56
  and postmodernism, 80, 85, 189, 190
Renaissance, 45, 51
Rengger, Nicholas, 25, 14
representation(s), 2, 15, 53, 59, 76–77, 81, 83, 189, 190, 218n. 82
  and Ashley, 116, 119, 130
  crisis in, 121, 123
  and feminists, 148, 156
  of ideas, 133–36
  and postmodernism, 79, 81, 82, 87
Republic (Plato), 11
revolution, 72, 73, 93, 137
Richardson, James L., 48, 93
rights, 6, 157, 171, 172, 193, 197
Rorty, Richard, 47, 64, 77, 82, 179
Rosenau, James, 36, 43, 44, 49
Rosenau, Pauline, 64, 83
Rousseau, Jean Jacques, 39, 40, 207n. 43
Ryan, Michael, 81

Saint-Pierre, Charles de, Abbe de Tiron, 39, 207n. 43
Sarkees, Meredith Reid, 173
Schelling, Thomas, 94
scholarship, 33, 40, 84, 145, 179, 184
  and Ashley, 95, 108
  feminist, 142–47, 166
  in IR, 144, 185
  and postmodernism, 51, 55, 188–95
scholasticism, 31
science, 22, 30, 58, 76, 87, 180
  and Ashley, 90, 91, 103, 107, 112
  changes in, 65, 67
  and Foucault, 80

and IR, 43, 44, 170
and knowledge, 170, 189
and modernity, 60, 65, 70, 85, 158
and neorealist theory, 99, 104
and postmodernism, 25, 53, 56, 75, 76, 77, 86
and reason, 85, 86
subversive, 185, 186, 202
scientific method, 43
Scott, Joan, 24
security, 6, 9, 16, 37, 45, 47
and Ashley, 92, 94, 96
feminist perspectives on, 152, 157, 158
and IR, 11, 46, 48
studies, 152, 157
self-identification (identity groups), 160, 162, 164
sex. *See* gender
sexism, 144, 164, 175, 176, 187, 196
sexual harassment, 157
sexuality, 81, 148, 230n. 34
Shapiro, Michael, 184
sign(s), 20, 21, 53, 65, 69, 78
silence(s), 122, 166, 168, 189, 190, 196, 198
Ashley, 124, 182
and feminist perspectives, 144, 149
Silverman, H. J., 215n. 14
similarity, 167, 184, 185. *See also* difference
situational analysis, 223n. 25
Sjolander, Claire Turenne, 19
Smith, Adam, 11, 40
Smith, Anthony, 232n. 105
Smith, Steve, 19, 26, 145, 179
social charter (in IR), 12
social movements, 74, 75
social science(s), 9, 12, 14, 23, 30, 36, 58, 98, 195
and Ashley, 100
behaviorist revolution in, 223n. 26
disquiet in, 46
diversity in, 184
and emancipatory logic, 98
and feminism, 174

and international relations, 39
positivist, 124
and postmodernism, 51, 78, 86, 87, 191, 192, 194
and Rorty, 82
and schematic typologies, 64
and theory, 62, 211n. 35
socialism, 73, 74, 75, 189
society, 38, 68, 101
changes in, 63, 65, 67
and state, 121, 192
and technological postmodernism, 71, 79, 191
Soja, Edward, 184, 214n. 9
Sommers, Christina Hoff, 155
sovereignty, 8, 16, 47, 49, 195
diminishing, 19
economic, 192
and IPE, 236n. 28
and knowledge, 178
political, 119
state, 44–45, 61, 164
Soviet Russia/Union, 75, 92
space (intellectual), 69, 119, 122, 167
intellectual, 75, 161, 162
and postmodernism, 78, 80, 195
Spegele, Roger, 15, 132, 134, 135, 205n. 2
state(s), 39, 156, 157, 158
and Ashley, 90, 104, 111, 113, 114, 116, 122
and postmodernism, 71, 165, 191, 200
power of, 68, 192
and realism, 122–23
reason of, 40, 68
and society, 121, 192
sovereign, 37–38
and Sylvester, 159
and Waltz, 105
See also nation-states
state-as-actor, 11, 16, 47, 104, 105, 106
and Ashley, 111, 116, 127
statecraft, 16, 115
statesmanship, 101

statesmen, 115, 122
strategic studies, 11, 146, 147
structural realism, 16, 92. *See also* neorealism
structuralism, 74, 136, 191, 196
  and Ashley, 93, 99–106, 112, 116
"structure of feeling," change in, 62, 63
"structure of resistance," 66, 83
subjectivities, 102, 105, 113, 122, 130, 151
  agency of, 115
  and Enloe, 153
  gender, 155
  marginal, 162
  See also agencies; agents; political agency
subjectivity, 75, 158, 169
subversion, 25, 33, 76–85, 144, 182, 183, 195. *See also* postmodernism; postmodern theory; postmodernists
Sylvester, Christine, 20, 23, 24, 159, 184, 197
  and feminism, 148–53, 155
  and gender, 172
  and "homesteading" of IR, 150, 152, 160
  and identity politics, 162–63, 165
  and IR, 145, 159, 160–61, 173, 184
  and male dissidents, 196
  and marginalization, 176
  "relations international," 151, 152, 162
  and the Third Debate, 143–44
  and women, 149, 153, 163–64, 173, 196

technology, 44, 58, 60, 192, 195, 215n. 19
  changes in, 65, 67
  and modernists, 85
  and modernity, 65
  and postmodernism, 53, 71, 77
territorial disputes, 22

terror, 56, 68, 172
"terror of theory," 81, 88
terrorists, 49
texts, 82, 196, 197
  and Ashley, 101, 102, 131, 132
textual analysis, 196, 198, 202. *See also* interpretation(s); interpretivism; intertextualism; literary criticism
theory, 1, 3, 4, 6, 8, 11, 23–24, 36, 64, 65, 67, 68, 74, 87, 99, 101, 166, 174, 177 180
  and Ashley, 92, 93, 101, 103, 104, 108–10, 116–17, 120, 121, 123, 128, 131
  constructive, 5, 130
  critical, 115, 191, 218nn. 79, 82
  and critical postmodernists, 73
  critical social, 190, 221n. 2
  cultural, 218n. 79
  deconstructive postmodernism, 196
  deterrence, 102
  dissident, 135
  economic, 191
  elite, 115
  empirical, 4, 6, 42, 44, 95, 206n. 33
  feminist, 90, 144, 145, 160
  French post-structuralist, 56
  French regulation, 194
  game, 102
  integration, 11
  international political theory, 42, 47, 99, 139
  "islands of," 62, 139
  "malestream," 143, 154, 155, 162
  Marxist, 66, 68, 73, 74, 114
  modern social, 139
  modernist-realist, 28
  neofunctional integration, 102
  neoliberal, 159
  neorealist, 96, 99, 104–5, 106, 116
  normative, 14, 16, 206n. 33
  objective, 116
  of cultural forms, 74
  of language, 82
  orthodox, 143
  policy science, 206n. 33

political, 21, 28, 98, 191
positivist, 112, 135, 138, 148, 180
positivist-modernist, 27
postmodernist, 81, 136, 148
postpositivist, 148
poststructural, 56, 108, 124–33, 134, 136, 178
purpose of, 140, 141
rational choice, 103
and rationalist tradition of inquiry, 139
rationalistic, 95
realist/positivist, 186
and reality, 82
reflective, 95
role, functions and purpose of, 25–30, 60
and subversive postmodernism, 66, 83–84, 86
scientific, 135, 179
social, 21, 28, 55, 107, 191, 215n. 27
social construction of, 129
structuralist, 19, 97, 215n. 27
structuration, 130
technical, 26, 112
and technical rationality, 96, 129
terror of, 81, 88
and the Third Debate, 4, 21
universal, 48
Waltz on, 104
See also international relations theory; modernist theory; postmodern theory
theory-knowledge, 77, 81, 83, 189, 190, 200, 220n. 122
Third [Great] Debate, 2, 3–4, 5, 8, 28, 46, 180
arrival of, 17–25
and Ashley, 116, 128
and feminist scholarship, 143, 145
and gender, 151
limitations of, 91
Third World, 172
Thompson, William, 176

Thrasymachus, 39
Thucydides, 37, 39, 210n. 6
Tickner, J. Ann, 164–65, 170, 172, 196
torture, 170, 171, 172
totalitarianism, 33
Toynbee, Arnold, 58
trade, 6, 11, 44, 58, 96, 194, 197
trade regime, 60, 61
tradition(s), 21, 26, 40, 158
and Ashley, 101, 102, 107, 116
Cartesian-Kantian, 77, 82
classical, 38
critical, 115
Hellenic, 39
modernist, 179
realist, 38, 110, 111
Western intellectual, 66, 76
transformation(s), 68, 137, 185, 191
and Ashley, 113, 120, 128, 123, 133, 134
global, 112, 120, 128
political, 110, 113, 128
transnational corporations, 6, 48, 49, 160. *See also* multinational corporations
transnationalism, 2, 18, 28
Trimbur, J., 83
True, Jacqui, 155, 158, 174
truth(s), 20, 22, 48, 70, 189, 190
and Ashley, 90, 97, 107, 108, 114, 121, 130, 132, 140, 182
and critical theory, 75
and IR discourse, 143
and language, 56
and modernist theory, 81
and modernists, 83
and postmodernism, 57, 66, 86, 76, 77, 78, 84, 183, 218n. 76
and poststructuralists, 131
as relativist-textual concept, 217n. 61
Tucker, Robert W., 127
Turner, B. S., 218n. 85, 220n. 130

understanding, 9, 87, 99, 139
and Ashley, 96, 100, 141

and facts, 7, 213n. 63
and identity politics, 165, 166, 167, 170
of IR, 174, 177
and postmodernism, 86, 180, 183
United States, 29, 92, 115, 172, 173, 197
  domination of, 61, 68
  and international politics/relations, 42, 47, 98, 102
United States Department of Justice (USDJ), 171
universalism, 2, 20, 29, 76, 80, 119, 135, 136, 166
  and Ashley, 108, 112
  end of, 217n. 53
universities, 31, 87
utilitarianism, 99, 105, 106
utility theory, 93

value hierarchies, 76, 84
value systems, 91
values, 4, 57, 67, 76, 192
  and Ashley, 104
  and feminism, 148, 175
venereal disease, 157, 177
victimization, 55, 144, 171, 172, 176, 187
  and Ashley and Walker, 124, 126
Vietnam War, 171
violence, 112, 125, 157, 158, 168
  and Ashley, 92, 98, 114, 124, 128, 132
  and Left critical theory, 137
  and men and women, 170–74
  as socially inscribed, 229n. 23

Walker, R. B. J., 87, 128, 135, 144, 202
  and IR, 45, 145
  and postmodernism in IR, 90, 134, 184, 197
  and poststructuralist challenge, 123–25, 126

Wallace, William, 30–32, 33
Wallack, Michael, 202, 210n. 6
Waltz, Kenneth, 7, 16
  and Ashley, 103–5, 127, 133, 196
Walzer, Michael, 125
war, 9, 14, 22, 33, 38, 128, 146, 168, 177
  and Ashley, 111, 128
  avoidance of, 12
  banishment of, 39
  causes of, 16, 37, 43, 45, 207n. 43
  deaths in, 202
  and gender, 147, 159
  and history, 37
  and IR, 7, 40, 48, 172, 202
  and nation-states, 193
  and national interest, 42
  politicization of, 41
  possibility of, 152
  and realism, 13
  and science, 44
  and subversive postmodernism, 197
  and women, 154, 157, 171
Weber, Max, 11, 30
Weiss, Birigit, 168–69, 170
Weltman, John, 2
Western thought, 20, 21, 78, 158, 159
Wight, Colin, 179
Wight, Martin, 15, 23, 36, 37, 40, 210n. 6
Wilson, Woodrow, 39
Windsor, Philip, 8
Wittgenstein, Ludwig, 77
women, 29, 62, 76
  and domestic sphere, 156, 170
  and international politics, 155
  and IR, 143, 145
  and ISA journals, 176
  as "knowers," 155, 156, 173
  and men, 145–46, 154, 157, 159
  perspectives on, 23, 142, 144, 148, 158, 159, 160, 169
  Sylvester, 149, 163–64, 196
  and research, 156, 157, 177, 175

and theorists, 76, 87, 105, 144, 148, 153, 162
and violences, 157, 158, 170–71
and welfare policies, 157
workers, 160, 230n. 34
World War I, 12, 41
World War II, 12, 41, 103

writing(s), 62, 81, 90, 132, 196
feminist, 144, 170
and postmodernism, 54, 82, 84, 184

Zalewski, Marysia, 24, 153, 164, 169, 177, 184, 181, 234n. 152
Zimmern, Sir Alfred, 41, 43